W9-ABY-175

WITHDRAWN

Salem Academy and College
FRIENDS of the LIBRARY

Gift of

The Friends of
the Library

Gramley Library
Salem Academy and College
Winston-Salem, N.C. 27108

W. S. MERWIN

COLLECTED POEMS 1996–2011

J. D. McClatchy, *editor*

THE LIBRARY OF AMERICA

Gramley Library
Salem Academy and College
Winston-Salem, N.C. 27108

Volume compilation, notes, and chronology copyright © 2013 by
Literary Classics of the United States, Inc., New York, N.Y.
All rights reserved.
No part of the book may be reproduced commercially
by offset-lithographic or equivalent copying devices without
the permission of the publisher.

The Vixen copyright © 1996 by W. S. Merwin; *The Folding Cliffs*
copyright © 1998 by W. S. Merwin; *The River Sound* copyright © 1999
by W. S. Merwin; *The Pupil* copyright © 2001 by W. S. Merwin.
Published by arrangement with Alfred A. Knopf, an imprint of The
Knopf Doubleday Publishing Group, a division of Random House, Inc.
Reprinted by permission of W. S. Merwin.
Present Company copyright © 2005 by W. S. Merwin; *The Shadow of
Sirius* copyright © 2008 by W. S. Merwin. Published by arrangement
with Copper Canyon Press. Reprinted by permission of W. S. Merwin.
Uncollected poems copyright © W. S. Merwin;
reprinted by permission of W. S. Merwin.
For more information on specific texts see the Note on the Texts.

The paper used in this publication meets the
minimum requirements of the American National Standard for
Information Sciences—Permanence of Paper for Printed
Library Materials, ANSI Z39.48—1984.

Distributed to the trade in the United States
by Penguin Group (USA) Inc.
and in Canada by Penguin Books Canada Ltd.

Library of Congress Control Number: 2012945849
ISBN 978-1-59853-209-8

———

First Printing
The Library of America—241

Contents

just dead with no sign of how it had come to happen
    no blood the long fur warm in the dewy grass
nothing broken or lost or torn or unfinished
    I carried her home to bury her in the garden
in the morning of the clear autumn that she had left
    and to stand afterward in the turning daylight

    *   *   *

There are the yellow beads of the stonecrops and the twisted flags
    of dried irises knuckled into the hollows
of moss and rubbly limestone on the waves of the low wall
    the ivy has climbed along them where the weasel ran
the light has kindled to gold the late leaves of the cherry tree
    over the lane by the house chimney there is the roof
and the window looking out over the garden
    summer and winter there is the field below the house
there is the broad valley far below them all with the curves
    of the river a strand of sky threaded through it
and the notes of bells rising out of it faint as smoke
    and there beyond the valley above the rim of the wall
the line of mountains I recognize like a line of writing
    that has come back when I had thought it was forgotten

Oak Time

    Storms in absence like the ages before I was anywhere
        and out in the shred of forest through the seasons
a few oaks have fallen towering ancients elders
        the last of elders standing there while the wars drained away
they slow-danced with the ice when time had not discovered them
        in a scrap of what had been their seamless fabric these late ones
are lying shrouded already in eglantine and brambles
        bird-cherry nettles and the tangled ivy
that prophesies disappearance and had already
        crept into the shadows they made when they held up their lives
where the nightingales sang even in the daytime
        and cowbells echoed through the long twilight of summer
the ivy knew the way oh the knowing ivy
        that was never wrong how few now the birds seem to be
no animals are led out any longer from the barns
        after the milking to spend the night pastured here
they are all gone from the village Edouard is gone
        who walked out before them to the end of his days
keeping an eye on the walnuts still green along the road
        when the owl watched from these oaks and in the night
I would hear the fox that barked here bark and be gone

the taste needed for scythe blades sickles kitchen knives
        we preferred to use carriage springs to make them from
in the forge outside the barn there and his were sought after
        oh when he had sold all he took to the fair the others
could begin I still have the die for stamping the name
        of the village in the blade at the end so you could be sure

Walkers

Then I could walk for a whole day over the stony
        ridges along fallen walls and lanes matted with
sloe branches and on through oak woods and around springs
        low cliffs mouths of caves and out onto open
hillsides overlooking valleys adrift in the distance
        and after the last sheep in their crumbling pastures
fenced with cut brush there would be only the burr of a wren
        scolding from rocks or one warbler's phrase repeated
following through the calls of crows and the mossed hush
        of ruins palmed in the folds of the crumpled slopes
in deep shade with the secret places of badgers
        and no other sound it was the edge of a silence
about to become as though it had never been
        for a while before emerging again unbroken
once I looked up a bank straight into the small eyes
        of a boar watching me and we stared at each other
in that silence before he turned and went on with his
        walk and once when I had dried figs in my pocket
I met an old woman who laughed and said this was the way
        she had come all her life and between two fingers she
accepted a fig saying Oh you bring me dainties
        there was still the man always astray in the dark suit
and string tie who might emerge from a barn and gaze
        skyward saying Ah Ah something had happened to him
in the war they said but he never took anything
        and there was the gnarled woman from a remote hamlet
hurrying head down never looking at anyone
        to a house she owned that had stood empty for decades
there to dust the tables sweep out the rooms cut weeds
        in the garden set them smouldering and as quickly
bolt the windows lock the door and be on her way

Ill Wind

As long as the south wind keeps thrashing the green branches
    caught in themselves so that they twist trying to find somewhere
else to be left in peace while the wind-scorched leaves wither
    curl and are snatched away whipped in the hissing rush
over restless litter and cracked ground until the boughs
    groan crash finally snap striking back flailing
finding as they fall the vain gestures of feelings
    never to be known and thick trunks split and the tender
seedlings lie down and shrivel and we sleep lightly
    as dust to be wakened by wind wearing at us
from inside all through the gray dark and into
    the bleached morning attaching itself to us
dragging us keeping at us weighing upon us
    like rumors of dreaded news sapping us wherever
we turn until we suspect it of having a mind
    devious implacable malevolent that we
cannot but recognize while denying it we are sharing
    that apprehension with ancestors many as leaves
this was the scourge of harvests that devastated
    vineyards sent roofs sailing brought down the big trees
those who have watched over the lives of things have known it
    wherever they were and reminded themselves that always
it went as it came and the fragile green survived it

Net

We were sitting along the river as the daylight
    faded in high summer too slowly to be followed
a pink haze gathering beyond the tall poplars
    over on the island and late swallows snapping at gnats
from the glassy reaches above the shallows
    where feathers of a gray mist were appearing
trout leapt like the slapping of hands behind the low voices
    that went on talking of money with the sound of rapids
running through them the boots smelled of former water
    the piled nets smelled of the deaths of fish I will know now
how night comes with eyes of its own to a river
    and then it was dark and we were seeing by river light
as the oldest got up first taking a coil of rope
    down and disappeared into the sound then we
went after him one by one stepping into the cold pull
    of the current to feel the round stones slip farther
below us and we uncoiled the nets with the voices

scarcely reaching us over the starlit surface
until we stood each alone hearing only the river
        and held the net while the unseen fish brushed past us

Garden

When I still had to reach up for the door knob
        I was wondering why the Lord God whoever that was
who had made everything in heaven and the earth
        and knew it was good and that nobody could hurt it
had decided to plant a garden apart
        from everything and put some things inside it
leaving all the rest outside where we were
        so the garden would be somewhere we would never see
and we would know of it only that it could not be known
        a bulb waiting in pebbles in a glass of water
in sunlight at a window You will not be wanting
        the garden too the husband said as an afterthought
but I said yes I would which was all I knew of it
        even the word sounding strange to me for the seedy
tatter trailing out of its gray ravelled walls
        on the ridge where the plateau dropped away to the valley
old trees shaded the side toward the village
        lichens silvered the tangled plum branches hiding
the far end the scrape of the heavy door as it dragged
        across the stone sill had deepened its indelible
groove before I knew it and a patch of wilting
        stalks out in the heat shimmer stood above potatoes
someone had cultivated there among the stately nettles
        it was not time yet for me to glimpse the clay
itself dark in rain rusting in summer shallow
        over fissured limestone here and there almost
at the surface I had yet to be shown how the cold
        softened it what the moles made of it where the snake
smiled on it from the foot of the wall what the redstart
        watched in it what would prosper in it what it would become
I had yet to know how it would appear to me

Letters

You could not see the valley unrolled below me
        the rusted towers haunting one hill and the glint
of farms on a faded south slope across the suspended
        still afternoon unrepeatable as a cloud
that I watched while I wrote to you taking up at a point

              farther along it the edge of that loose fabric
already of some length but by then torn here and there
              frayed worn stained its pattern always complicated
but beginning to emerge perhaps as what we could
              recognize after all under the name of friendship
and from what gulfs and distances and how fitfully
              from there on it came to remind us of the time
when you had always made much of being my
              elder and then you confessed your amazement at finding
yourself past forty with all the early ambitions
              surfeited all that brilliance rewarded you were no longer
boasting but finding it empty wondering what
              else there might be where else to look and you raised
the subject of the fleet in the bay at Aulis
              on the way to Troy when the wind dropped we would return
to that through the years almost as often as you
              went over your classic animosities
dissolving marriage continuing restlessness
              yet in your words so little appeared in color
of the countenance of your life you wrote from England
              alluding to pastoral scenery as though it
belonged to you but you complained of the English evening
              always about to descend so that I thought I could see that
but even in your late desperate grasping
              at a youthfulness that had never been yours
in your confidences I could not see her there were only
              your spiralling explanations your insistence
your vertigo it was spring then and the stove burning low
              smelled of tar while honeysuckle swayed at the window
and along the rough wall quince petals were holding up
              the light that was theirs as it was passing through them
among the many things of which we would not have spoken

Commemoratives

This was the day when the guns fell silent one time
              on old calendars before I was born then the bells
clanged to say it was over forever again
              and again as they would every year when the same
hour had found the yellow light in the poplars
              tan leaves of sycamores drifting across the square
out of the world and those who remembered the day
              it was first over sat around tables holding
reflections in their hands thinking here we are
              while the speeches reverberated in their faces
here we are we lived these are our faces now we are singing
              these are ourselves standing out under the same trees

Gramley Library
Salem Academy and College
Winston-Salem, N.C. 27108

smoking talking of money we are the same we lived
    with our moustaches our broadening features our swellings
at the belt our eyes from our time and in that chill air
    of November with its taste of bronze I took the winding
road up the mountain until it hissed in the chestnut forest
    where once the hunters had followed the edge of the ice
I came to sounds of a stream crossing stones a hare moving like
    one of the shadows jays warning through bare branches
the afternoon was drawing toward winter the signposts
    at the crossroads even then were rusted over

White Morning

On nights toward the end of summer an age of mist
    has gathered in the oaks the box thickets the straggling
eglantines it has moved like a hand unable to believe
    the face it touches over the velvet of wild thyme
and the vetches sinking with the weight of dew it has found
    its way without sight into the hoofprints of cows
the dark nests long empty the bark hanging alone the narrow
    halls among stones and has held it all in a cloud
unseen the whole night as in a mind where I came
    when it was turning white and I was holding a thin
wet branch wrapped in lichens because all I had thought
    I knew had to be passed from branch to branch through the empty
sky and whatever I reached then and could recognize
    moved toward me out of the cloud and was still the sky
where I went on looking until I was standing on
    the wide wall along the lane to the hazel grove
where we went one day to cut handles that would last
    the crows were calling around me to white air
I could hear their wings dripping and hear small birds with lights
    breaking in their tongues the cold soaked through me I was able
after that morning to believe stories that once
    would have been closed to me I saw a carriage go under
the oaks there in full day and vanish I watched animals there
    I sat with friends in the shade they have all disappeared
most of the stories have to do with vanishing

Color Merchants

They had no color themselves nothing about them
    suggested the spectrum from which they were making
a living the one who had arrived with experience
    from the city to open a shop in the old square

wearing his glasses on his forehead vowing allegiance
       to rusticity understanding what anyone
wanted to the exact tone a head waiter of hues
       or the one who had gone away to be a painter
in Paris and had come back in the war no longer
       young wearing his beret with a difference
a hushed man translucent as paper who displayed
       artists' supplies in a town without artists and could
recall the day when he and a few old men
       and farm boys ambushed the column of Germans heading
north to the channel after the invasion
       and held them up for most of an hour and afterward
how he had sat with his easel day after day at one end
       of the low bridge where the guns had blackened that
summer afternoon and had listened to the rustle
       of the leaves of limes and plane trees and to the shallow
river whispering one syllable on the way
       to the island and he had tried to find the right shades
for the empty street and the glare on the running water

Entry

When it seems that the world is made of a single
       summer as it always has been and that the gray leaves
will hang that same way without moving above the empty
       road until the end while the wheat goes on standing
in its sleep with no dreams soundless and shining into
       the hovering day along the stopped film of the river
and when the doors facing south have turned to stone every one
       and the parched syllable of cicadas through the hush
of fields hangs still in the light and from shuttered
       windows voices sift like the settling of dust
all at once the blank sky will be half dark with the black
       cloud welling out of which a cold wind rolls and the first
thunder splits all around to build upon its own
       deafening echoes then suddenly the light will be only
the weight of rain cascading shot through with lightning
       at that time if you are away from home and can stumble
to any house they will let you in to a dark room
       that will close behind you at the heart of the roar
and you will see as through water an unknown face but you
       will hear no sound it makes and behind it others
will be looking up in silence from around a table
       knowing nothing about you except why you are there

Forgotten Streams

The names of unimportant streams have fallen
        into oblivion the syllables have washed away
but the streams that never went by name never raised the question
        whether what has been told and forgotten is in
another part of oblivion from what was never remembered
        no one any longer recalls the Vaurs and the Divat
the stream Siou Sujou Suzou and every speaker
        for whom those were the names they have all become
the stream of Lherm we do not speak the same language
        from one generation to another and we
can tell little of places where we ourselves have lived
        the whole of our lives and still less of neighborhoods
where our parents were young or the parents of our friends
        how can we say what the sound of voices was or what
a skin felt like or a mouth everything that the mouths did
        and the tongues the look of the eyes the animals the fur
the unimportant breath not far from here an unknown
        mason dug up a sword five hundred years old
the only thing that is certain about it now
        is that in the present it is devoured with rust
something keeps going on without looking back

Present

She informed me that she had a tree of mirabelles
        told me it was the only one anywhere around
she did not want everyone to realize she had it
        it might go for years and bear nothing at all
flowering with the other plums but then nothing
        and another year it would be covered with mirabelles
you know they are not so big as all the others
        but they are more delicate for those acquainted with them
she promised me mirabelles if it was the year for them
        she lived in a house so small she must have been able
to reach anything from where she was and her garden
        was scarcely larger she grew corn salad in winter
after Brussels sprouts well it was a cold garden
        facing north so it was slow in spring better for summer
one of the knotted gray trees leaning against the wall
        to the south was the mirabelle a snow of plum blossoms
swept across the valley in the morning sunlight
        of a day in March and moved up the slope hour by hour
she told me later she thought it would be a year
        of mirabelles unless it froze when she bent in her garden

she disappeared in the rows it took her a long time
 to stand up to turn around to let herself through
the gate to walk to do anything at my age
 I have all I need she said if I keep warm
late one day that summer she appeared at the wall
 carrying a brown paper bag wet at the bottom
the mirabelles she whispered but she would not come in
 we sat on the wall and opened the bag look she said
how you can see through them and each of us held up
 a small golden plum filled with the summer evening

Passing

The morning after the house almost burned down
 one night at the end of a season of old wood
of dust and tunnels in beams and of renewals and the tuning
 of hinges and putty soft around new panes in the clear
light of autumn and then the fire had led itself
 in the dark through the fragrance of doors and ceilings
the last flame was scarcely out in the cellar
 and we were still splashing soaked sooty red-eyed
in black puddles all the neighbors with vineyard sprayers
 hosing into cracks and the acrid steam persisting
in our breath when the message came from the village
 the telephone it was my father on his
impromptu journey asking me to be surprised
 not taking in a word about the fire but inquiring
about changing money about where I could meet him
 about trains for the Holy Land and when I drove him
from the station the long way round so he could see the country
 for the first time he seemed to be seeing nothing
and I did not know that it was the only time

The Bird

Might it be like this then to come back descending
 through the gray sheeted hour when it is said that dreams
are to be believed the moment when the ghosts go home
 with the last stars still on far below in a silence
that deepens like water a sinking softly toward them
 to find a once-familiar capital half dissolved
like a winter its faces piled in their own wreckage
 and over them unfinished towers of empty
mirrors risen framed in air then beside pewter rivers

under black nests in the naked poplars arriving
at the first hesitations of spring the thin leaves
        shivering and the lights in them and at cold April with trees
all in white its mullein wool opening on thawed banks
        cowslips and mustard in the morning russet cows on green slopes
running clouds behind hands of willows the song of the wren
        and both recognizing and being recognized with doubting
belief neither stranger nor true inhabitant
        neither knowing nor not knowing coming at last
to the door in sunlight and seeing as through glasses far
        away the old claims the longings to stay and to leave
the new heights of the trees the children grown tall and polite
        the animal absences and scarcely touching anything
holding it after all as uncertainly
        as the white blossoms were held that have been blown down
most of them in one night or this empty half
        of a bird's egg flung out of the bare flailing branches

Returning Season

When the spring sun finds the village now it is empty
        but from the beginning this was the afterlife
it was not so apparent a generation gone
        these were still roofs under which the names were born
that came home winter evenings before all the wars to sleep
        through freezing nights when the dogs curled low in the cow barns
and sheep nudged their rank clouds in the dark as one
        now only wagons sleep there and stalled plows
and machine skeletons rusting around stopped notes
        of far-off bells in a cold longer than winter's
they will not be wanted again nor wake into any life
        when the recesses from a better world begin
the year goes on turning and the barns remain without breath
        and now after sundown a city bulb keeps an eye on the village
until past midnight but the owls sweep by the low eaves
        and over black gardens in the light of finished stars

End of a Day

In the long evening of April through the cool light
        Baille's two sheep dogs sail down the lane like magpies
for the flock a moment before he appears near the oaks
        a stub of a man rolling as he approaches
smiling and smiling and his dogs are afraid of him

we stand among the radiant stones looking out across
green lucent wheat and earth combed red under bare walnut limbs
    bees hanging late in cowslips and lingering bird cherry
stumps and brush that had been the grove of hazel trees
    where the land turns above the draped slopes and the valley
with its one sunbeam and we exchange a few questions
    as though nothing were different but he has bulldozed the upland
pastures and shepherds' huts into piles of rubble
    and has his sheep fenced in everyone's meadows now
smell of box and damp leaves drifts from the woods where a blackbird
    is warning of nightfall and Baille has plans now to demolish
the ancient walls of the lane and level it wide
    so that trucks can go all the way down to where the lambs
with perhaps two weeks to live are waiting for him at the wire
    he hurried toward them as the sun sinks and the hour
turns chill as iron and in the oaks the first nightingales
    of the year kindle their unapproachable voices

Other Time

There was a life several turns before this one
    and it woke to these seasons these same flowers this rain
these branches and roots of feeling that divide and divide again
    reaching into ruins into the treasures
and palaces of ruin and I knew the way then
    to a hundred ruins I could walk to in an hour
each with its own country and prospect its own birds
    and silence and in every roof part of the sky
that was the day I had come to be standing in
    which no one who had been born there had lived to see
whatever they may have watched from those hollow windows
    and coveted on those stairs that led up at last into trees
clear light went on staring out of the stone basins
    recalling clouds and I was in a future no one from there
could have conceived of or believed when they were sure
    that they would be there in it just as they were then
and not as strangers too long ago to be anyone

François de Maynard 1582–1646

When I cannot see my angel I would rather
    have been born blind and miserable I wrote at one time
then the season of flowers I said appeared to be
    painted black and it was impossible through those days

to imagine how I could have tarried so long
        on the earth while the syllables of thirty Aprils
had dripped like ice in the mountains and I had listened
        to the water as a song I might know and now
the autumn is almost done and the days arrive each one
        expecting less how long it is since I left
the court I loved once the passions there the skins of morning
        the colors of vain May and my hopes always for something
else that would be the same but more and never failing
        more praise more laurels more loves more bounty until I
could believe I was Ronsard and I wrote that I would have
        a monument as for a demigod whatever
that might be when I will be lucky to be buried
        as the poor are buried without noise and the faces covered
and be gone as the year goes out and be honored as a blank wall
        in a cold chapel of the church where I shivered as a child
beside my father the judge in his complete black those years when
        soldiers clattered and clanged through the streets horsemen clashed
under the windows and the nights rang with the screams
        of the wounded outside the walls while the farms burned
into dawns red with smoke and blood came spreading
        through the canals at the foot of those towers on the hill
that I would see again and again after every absence
        fingers of a hand rising out of the gray valley
in the distance and coming closer to become here as before
        where my mother wanted me where I married
where the banquets glittered along the river to my songs
        where my daughter died and how cold the house turned all at once
I have seen the waves of war come back and break over us here
        I have smelled rosemary and juniper burning in the plague
I have gone away and away I have held a post in Rome
        I have caught my death there I have flattered evil men
and gained nothing by it I have sat beside my wife
        when she could move no longer I sat here beside her
I watched the gold leaves of the poplars floating on the stream
        long ago the gold current of the river Pactolus
was compared to eternity but the poplar leaves have gone
        in the years when I rode to Aurillac I used to stop
at a place where the mountains appeared to open before me
        and turning I could still see all the way back to here
and both ways were my life which now I have slept through to wake
        in a dark house talking to the shadows about love

Hölderlin at the River

The ice again in my sleep it was following someone
    it thought was me in the dark and I recognized its white tongue
it held me in its freezing radiance until I
    was the only tree there and I broke and carried
my limbs down through dark rocks calling to the summer
    where are you where will you be how could I have missed you
gold skin the still pond shining under the eglantines
    warm peach resting in my palm at noon among flowers
all the way I was looking for you and I had nothing to say who I was
    until the last day of the world then far below I could see
the great valley as night fell the one ray withdrawing
    like the note of a horn and afterwards black wind took
all I knew but here is the foreign morning with its clouds
    sailing on water beyond the black trembling poplars
the sky breathless around its blinding fire and the white flocks
    in water meadows on the far shore are flowing past their
silent shepherds and now only once I hear the hammer
    ring on the anvil and in some place that I have not seen
a bird of ice is singing of its own country
    if any of this remains it will not be me

In the Doorway

From the stones of the door frame cold to the palm
    that breath of the dark sometimes from the chiselled
surfaces and at others from the places between them
    that chill and air without season that acrid haunting
that skunk ghost welcoming without welcome faithful without
    promise echo without echo it was there again
in the stones of the gate now in a new place but its own
    a place of leaving and returning that breath of belonging
and being distant of rain in box thickets
    part of it and of sheep in winter and the green stem
of the bee orchis in May that smell of abiding
    and not staying of a night breeze remembered only
in passing of fox shadow moss in autumn the bitter
    ivy the smell of the knife blade and of finding again
knowing no more but listening the smell of touching and going
    of what is gone the smell of touching and not being there

One of the Lives

If I had not met the red-haired boy whose father
    had broken a leg parachuting into Provence
to join the resistance in the final stage of the war
    and so had been killed there as the Germans were moving north
out of Italy and if the friend who was with him
    as he was dying had not had an elder brother
who also died young quite differently in peacetime
    leaving two children one of them with bad health
who had been kept out of school for a whole year by an illness
    and if I had written anything else at the top
of the examination form where it said college
    of your choice or if the questions that day had been
put differently and if a young woman in Kittanning
    had not taught my father to drive at the age of twenty
so that he got the job with the pastor of the big church
    in Pittsburgh where my mother was working and if
my mother had not lost both parents when she was a child
    so that she had to go to her grandmother's in Pittsburgh
I would not have found myself on an iron cot
    with my head by the fireplace of a stone farmhouse
that had stood empty since some time before I was born
    I would not have travelled so far to lie shivering
with fever though I was wrapped in everything in the house
    nor have watched the unctuous doctor hold up his needle
at the window in the rain light of October
    I would not have seen through the cracked pane the darkening
valley with its river sliding past the amber mountains
    nor have wakened hearing plums fall in the small hour
thinking I knew where I was as I heard them fall

Night Singing

Long after Ovid's story of Philomela
    has gone out of fashion and after the testimonials
of Hafiz and Keats have been smothered in comment
    and droned dead in schools and after Eliot has gone home
from the Sacred Heart and Ransom has spat and consigned
    to human youth what he reduced to fairy numbers
after the name has become slightly embarrassing
    and dried skins have yielded their details and tapes have been
slowed and analyzed and there is nothing at all
    for me to say one nightingale is singing
nearby in the oaks where I can see nothing but darkness
    and can only listen and ride out on the long note's

invisible beam that wells up and bursts from its
    unknown star on on on never returning
never the same never caught while through the small leaves
    of May the starlight glitters from its own journeys
once in the ancestry of this song my mother visited here
    lightning struck the locomotive in the mountains
it had never happened before and there were so many
    things to tell that she had just seen and would never
have imagined now a field away I hear another
    voice beginning and on the slope there is a third
not echoing but varying after the lives
    after the goodbyes after the faces and the light
after the recognitions and the touching and tears
    those voices go on rising if I knew I would hear
in the last dark that singing I know how I would listen

Untouched

Even in dreams if I am there I keep trying
    to tell what is missing I have left friends in their days
I have left voices shimmering over the green field
    I have left the barns to the owls and the noon meadows
to the stealth of summer and again and again
    I have turned from it all and gone but it is not that
something was missing before that something was always
    not there I left the walls in their furs of snow
Esther calling the hens at dusk *petit petit*
    Viellescazes sucking the last joints of a story
Edouard bending into shadows to pick up walnuts
    before the leaves fell and I have left the weasel in the ivy
the lanes after midnight the clack of plates in the kitchen
    the feel of the door latch yielding it has hidden
in the presence of each of them whatever I missed
    I left the stream running under the mossy cliff

Romanesque

Inside the light there was a stone and he knew it
    inside the stone there was a light and all day he kept
finding it the world in the light was stone
    built of stone held up by stone and in a stone house
you began you stood on a stone floor the fire played
    in its stone place and the sky in the window passed
between stones and outside the door your feet followed

stones and when the fields were turned over in the light
they were made of stones the water came out of a stone
    some of the stones were faces with faces inside them
like every face and some of the stones were animals
    with animals inside them some of the stones were skies
with skies inside them and when he had worked long enough
    with stones touching them opening them looking inside
he saw that a day was a stone and the past was a stone
    with more darkness always inside it and the time to come
was a stone over a doorway and with his hand he formed
    the stone hand raised at the center and the stone face
under the stone sun and stone moon and he found the prophet
    who was stone prophesying stone he showed the stone limbs of childhood
and old age and the life between them holding up the whole
    stone of heaven and hell while the mother of us all
in her naked stone with the stone serpent circling
    her thigh went on smiling at something long after
he was forgotten she kept smiling at something he had known
    and at something he had never known at the time

Dry Ground

Summer deepens and a root reaches for receding
    water with a sense of waking long afterward
long after the main event whatever it was
    has faded out like the sounds of a procession
like April like the age of dew like the beginning
    now the dry grass dying keeps making the sounds of rain
to hollow air while the wheat whitens in the cracked fields
    and they keep taking the cows farther up into the woods
to dwindling pools under the oaks and even there
    the brown leaves are closing their thin hands and falling
and out on the naked barrens where the light shakes
    in a fever without a surface and the parched shriek
of the cicadas climbs with the sun the bats
    cling to themselves in crevices out of the light
and under stone roofs those who live watching the grapes
    like foxes stare out over the plowed white stones
and see in all the hueless blaze of the day nothing
    but rows of withered arms holding up the green grapes

Battues

Never more alien never born farther away
        never less acquiescent in all that on all sides
is taken for granted never hearing with such
        clarity the fatal intent of the voices
as when they ring the upland out of thickets
        along the edges of oak woods and beside hollows
still harboring sweet night and spring up from shadows
        in cleft rocks that gaze out over the naked
stony barrens those rough shouts suddenly struck from
        raw metals commanding the dogs whipping them on
echoing over the lit baying of the racing
        hounds those voices that have called to each other all
their lives growing up together with this pitch always
        in them they know it this fire shaking and beating
burning as one toward the careful cellars of badgers
        boars' coverts the tunnels of foxes the bursting owls
to the end of flight and the cornered eyes they go on
        I keep hearing them knowing them they are the cavalry
at Sand Creek they are Jackson's finest rooting out
        the infants of the Seminoles they are calling
names I know words we speak every day they are using
        language that we share which we say proves what we are

Snake

When it seemed to me that whatever was holding
        me there pretending to let me go but then bringing
me back each time as though I had never been gone
        and knowing me knowing me unseen among those rocks
when it seemed to me that whatever that might be
        had not changed for all my absence and still was not changing
once in the middle of the day late in that time
        I stood up from the writings unfinished on the table
in the echoless stone room looking over the valley
        I opened the door and on the stone doorsill
where every so often through the years I had come
        upon a snake lying out in the sunlight I found
the empty skin like smoke on the stone with the day
        still moving in it and when I touched it and lifted
all of it the whole thing seemed lighter than a single
        breath and then I was gone and that time had changed and when
I came again many years had passed and I saw

one day along the doorsill outside that same room
a green snake lying in the sunlight watching me
          even from the eyes the skin loosens leaving the colors
that have passed through it and the colors shine after it has gone

Vehicles

This is a place on the way after the distances
          can no longer be kept straight here in this dark corner
of the barn a mound of wheels has convened along
          ravelling courses to stop in a single moment
and lie down as still as the chariots of the Pharaohs
          some in pairs that rolled as one over the same roads
to the end and never touched each other until they
          arrived here some that broke by themselves and were left
until they could be repaired some that went only
          to occasions before my time and some that have spun
across other countries through uncounted summers
          now they go all the way back together the tall
cobweb-hung models of galaxies in their rings
          of rust leaning against the stone hail from René's
manure cart the year he wanted to store them here
          because there was nobody left who could make them like that
in case he should need them and there are the carriage wheels
          that Merot said would be worth a lot some day
and the rim of the spare from bald Bleret's green Samson
          that rose like Borobudur out of the high grass
behind the old house by the river where he stuffed
          mattresses in the morning sunlight and the hens
scavenged around his shoes in the days when the black
          top-hat sedan still towered outside Sandeau's cow barn
with velvet upholstery and sconces for flowers and room
          for two calves instead of the back seat when their time came

Late

The old walls half fallen sink away under brambles
          and ivy and trail off into the oak woods that have been
coming back for them through all the lives whose daylight
          has vanished into the mosses there was a life once
in which I lived here part of a life believing
          in it partly as though it were the whole story
and so not a story at all and partly knowing
          that I clung to it only in passing as in

the words of a story and that partly I was still
     where I had come from and when I come back now later
and find it still here it seems to be a story
     I know but no longer believe and that is my place in it

Season

This hour along the valley this light at the end
     of summer lengthening as it begins to go
this whisper in the tawny grass this feather floating
     in the air this house of half a life or so
this blue door open to the lingering sun this stillness
     echoing from the rooms like an unfinished sound
this fraying of voices at the edge of the village
     beyond the dusty gardens this breath of knowing
without knowing anything this old branch from which
     years and faces go on falling this presence already
far away this restless alien in the cherished place
     this motion with no measure this moment peopled
with absences with everything that I remember here
     eyes the wheeze of the gate greetings birdsongs in winter
the heart dividing dividing and everything
     that has slipped my mind as I consider the shadow
all this has occurred to somebody else who has gone
     as I am told and indeed it has happened again
and again and I go on trying to understand
     how that could ever be and all I know of them
is what they felt in the light here in this late summer

Emergence

From how many distances am I to arrive
     again and find I am standing on the bare outcrop
at the top of the ridge by the corner of the ancient wall
     with the sloe thickets the sheep tracks the gray ruins
oak woods abrupt hollows and the burials of the upland
     rolling away behind me farther than I can guess
and before me the path down through rocks and wild thyme
     into the village its tiled roofs washed out with sunlight
its trees glinting in the faded day and beyond them
     the valley blue and indelible as a vein
sometimes it is spring with the white blossoms opening
     their moments of light along the thin naked branches
sometimes snow has quilted the barns the houses the small fields

the waves of moss on the walls but always it is autumn
with the rest inside it like skies seen in water
        and the summer days folded into the stones and I have come
not to live there once more nor to stay nor to touch
        nor to understand arriving from farther and farther
from the time of alien cities from the breathing
        of traffic from sleepless continents from the eye of water
from flying at altitudes at which nothing
        can survive and from the darkness and from afterward

The Speed of Light

So gradual in those summers was the going
        of the age it seemed that the long days setting out
when the stars faded over the mountains were not
        leaving us even as the birds woke in full song and the dew
glittered in the webs it appeared then that the clear morning
        opening into the sky was something of ours
to have and to keep and that the brightness we could not touch
        and the air we could not hold had come to be there all the time
for us and would never be gone and that the axle
        we did not hear was not turning when the ancient car
coughed in the roofer's barn and rolled out echoing
        first thing into the lane and the only tractor
in the village rumbled and went into its rusty
        mutterings before heading out of its lean-to
into the cow pats and the shadow of the lime tree
        we did not see that the swallows flashing and the sparks
of their cries were fast in the spokes of the hollow
        wheel that was turning and turning us taking us
all away as one with the tires of the baker's van
        where the wheels of bread were stacked like days in calendars
coming and going all at once we did not hear
        the rim of the hour in whatever we were saying
or touching all day we thought it was there and would stay
        it was only as the afternoon lengthened on its
dial and the shadows reached out farther and farther
        from everything that we began to listen for what
might be escaping us and we heard high voices ringing
        the village at sundown calling their animals home
and then the bats after dark and the silence on its road

Old Question

Can anyone tell me what became of the voices
    that rang here in the lane every morning at the beginning
of autumn those mornings those autumns if there were more
    than one and that was the way the autumn morning
was to begin then with a sound somewhere between bird echoes
    and brook water over pebbles coming closer
a flight of high bells the small girls from farther along
    the ridge walking to school some of them still with their hair
down to their waists or whatever happened to the voice
    of the head mason scolding later in the sunlight
at the house below the long field he kept rasping No
    No over the rasp of the shovels mixing wet mortar
I tell you No and they all kept right on at what they
    were doing knowing that it was simply the way
he always talked and the wall rose into the day
    and its own silence where it seemed to have been before
anyone could remember or in what country now
    is the sound of the gate that never went away

One Time

When I was a child being taken home from the circus
    late at night in the rumble seat of the old car
in which I had never ridden and my head was afloat
    in the lap of a woman whom now I would think of
as young and who then was fragrant strange and as hard to believe
    as Christmas as she went on agreeing in a low voice
about how late it was and I kept watching her breath
    flying away into the cold night overhead
in which the naked stars were circling as we turned
    from the river and came up along the dark cliff
into our own echoes that wheeled us under the black
    leafless branches here it was already morning
and a figure whom I have known only bent with age
    was taking the cows out in his high youth onto
the untouched frost of the lanes and his burly son
    my neighbor was an infant and the woods furred the ridge
all the way down to the white fields with their pencilled walls
    the one cowbell rang cold and bright before him and crows
called across the blank pastures and early shadows

Peire Vidal

I saw the wolf in winter watching on the raw hill
     I stood at night on top of the black tower and sang
I saw my mouth in spring float away on the river
     I was a child in rooms where the furs were climbing
and each was alone and they had no eyes no faces
     nothing inside them any more but the stories
but they never breathed as they waved in their dreams of grass
     and I sang the best songs that were sung in the world
as long as a song lasts and they came to me by themselves
     and I loved blades and boasting and shouting as I rode
as though I was the bright day flashing from everything
     I loved being with women and their breath and their skin
and the thought of them that carried me like a wind
     I uttered terrible things about other men
in a time when tongues were cut out to pay for a kiss
     but I set my sail for the island of Venus
and a niece of the Emperor in Constantinople
     and I could have become the Emperor myself
I won and I won and all the women in the world
     were in love with me and they wanted what I wanted
so I thought and every one of them deceived me
     I was the greatest fool in the world I was the world's fool
I have been forgiven and have come home as I dreamed
     and seen them all dancing and singing as the ship came in
and I have watched friends die and have worn black and cut off
     the tails and ears of all my horses in mourning
and have shaved my head and the heads of my followers
     I have been a poor man living in a rich man's house
and I have gone back to the mountains and for one woman
     I have worn the fur of a wolf and the shepherds' dogs
have run me to earth and I have been left for dead
     and have come back hearing them laughing and the furs
were hanging in the same places and I have seen
     what is not there I have sung its song I have breathed
its day and it was nothing to you where were you

The View

No wonder there are those lights of suspicion moving
     endlessly over memory and its faces
over the way of memory itself the way
     of remembering which is the way of forgetting
the way of horizons the way beyond reach the way

of another which appears at times to be the only way
when not one thing not one moment with its heavenly
    bodies flying through unrepeated places not one
sound or shining is what it was the one time before
    it was remembered when I was in the midst of it
looking out thinking about something far from there
    bodies and death and taxes and what I did not want
and have forgotten while Lande was plowing the length
    of the field under the walnut trees in September
for the last time going on talking to the cows
    tapping lightly on their yoke with the slender stick
that he had cut in the hazel grove one year when he
    was young I watched the cows follow him out of the field
and the shadows filled it and the small lights appeared in the valley
    each of them coming from what was already gone

Old Walls

When the year has turned on its mountain as the summer
    stars begin to grow faint and the wren wakes into
singing I am waiting among the loosening stones
    of the enclosure beyond the lower door of the far barn
the green stitchwort shines in the new light as though it were
    still spring and no footprint leads through it any longer
the one apple tree has not grown much in its corner
    the ivy has taken over the east wall toward the oak woods
and crept into the bird cherry here I listened
    to the clack of the old man's hoe hilling the potatoes
in his dry field below the ash trees and here I looked up
    into the quince flowers opening above the wall
and I wanted to be far away like the surface
    of a river I knew and here I watched the autumn light
and thought this was where I might choose to be buried
    here I struggled in the web and went on weaving it
with every turn and here I went on yielding
    too much credit to an alien claim and here I came
to myself in a winter fog with ice on the stones
    and I went out through the gap in the wall and it was done
and here I thought I saw myself as I had once been
    and I was certain that I was free of an old chain

The Furrow

Did I think it would abide as it was forever
    all that time ago the turned earth in the old garden
where I stood in spring remembering spring in another place
    that had ceased to exist and the dug roots kept giving up
their black tokens their coins and bone buttons and shoe nails
    made by hands and bits of plates as the thin clouds
of that season slipped past gray branches on which the early
    white petals were catching their light and I thought I knew
something of age then my own age which had conveyed me
    to there and the ages of the trees and the walls and houses
from before my coming and the age of the new seeds as I
    set each one in the ground to begin to remember
what to become and the order in which to return
    and even the other age into which I was passing
all the time while I was thinking of something different

The Time Before

Out on the upland before I was there to see
    they were walking over the bare stone carrying
their shoes because it was going to be a long way
    their day was ringing the barrens in a loud wind
and they were taking their seasons with them as animals
    through the beating light urging on the sheep of autumn
the pigs of winter the lambs of spring the cows of summer
    all heading the same way along the rough walls of the lanes
so old that they had no beginnings and no memory
    their voices and the sounds of their feet flew up from them like
flocks of finches and blew away with all the names that they
    used for themselves and were continually saying
and all the words that were what they had then and were what they
    were saying to each other as they went along and as they
greeted each other when they met where the lanes came
    together and when they told where they were going

Portrait

    One ninth of March when for reasons that we can only
        suppose Monseigneur who bore the name of a saint
    gone into legend had wished to be rendered immortal
        in tapestry and he had for his agent in this
affair none other than the priest who was

precentor and canon at the cathedral named for
the same saint the said priest signing for him on the one hand
    and Adrian a merchant from Brabant on the other
having made certain pacts and agreements touching upon
    the design and depicting of the same Monseigneur
to be portrayed with his story in lengths of tapestry
    of certain form and style determined by those same
the said tapestry to be brought by said Adrian
    to the city of Bordeaux and left in the house
of honest Yzabeau Bertault widow for her
    to send it on to the said priest after making
payment of certain moneys and on this same day
    said delivery having been made and said payment
given before two further agents of Monseigneur
    because they themselves were not qualified to say
whether said tapestry made up of eight lengths six long
    two short was of the same worth and value that the same
Adrian claimed and was receiving namely two hundred
    forty livres ten sous two other merchants experts
of that city were present to bear witness to its worth
    there is no tapestry only the signatures

Possessions

Such vast estates such riches beyond estimation
    of course they all came out of the ground at some time
out of dark places before the records were awake
    they were held by hands that went out like a succession of flames
as the land itself was held until it named its
    possessors who described and enumerated it
in front of magistrates dividing the huge topography
    multiplying the name extending the chateau
house gardens fields woods pastures those facing
    the hill of Argentat with also the road leading
through them and the land called Murat and the fields and woods
    of the hill of Courtis and other designated
dependencies chapel stables dovecote additional
    lands south of the lane to which others were added by
marriage by death by purchase by reparation
    complicating the names of the legitimate offspring
lengthening the testaments that were meant to leave nothing out
    furnishings plates linens each mirror and its frame
the barrels and oxen and horses and sows and sheep
    the curtained beds the contents of the several kitchens
besides all such personal belongings as money
    and jewels listed apart which were considerable

by the time Madame la Vicomtesse who was heir to it all
       found it poor in variety and after her marriage
was often away visiting family and so on
       leaving the chateau in the keeping of her
father-in-law who was almost totally deaf
       so it happened that one night during a violent
thunderstorm the son of a laborer managed
       to climb through an upper window and into Madame's
bedroom where with the point of a plowshare he opened
       her jewel case and removed everything in it
and two nights later the gold crown studded with precious
       stones that was a gift of His Holiness Pius the Ninth
also was missing it was these absences
       that were commemorated at the next family wedding
at which the Vicomtesse wore at her neck and wrists
       pink ribbons in place of the jewels that had been hers
it was for the ribbons that she was remembered

Legacies

When he was beginning perhaps to feel his age
       Louis the carpenter one sunny day in spring
took me and his elder son who was then a thin
       young man to look at his walnut trees still without
leaves on their new branches that waved like wands above the clouds
       of sloe bushes in full flower along the hedges
up on the land plowed in the autumn on the windswept
       ridge those fields that had come to him from his grandmother
who had lived beside them once in the hamlet
       under the old lime trees where only the barns by the time
I saw it were inhabited it was just sheep now he told me
       we could hear them calling in the pastures beyond the roofs
and he said that when those walnut trees were planted
       a few years back when his son was a child they had dug
down to the limestone and had tipped into each hole
       half a cart load of wool waste left over from the carding machine
there were finches blowing across the blue sky behind
       the bare limbs as he talked and he touched the young trees
with their grafting scars still plain on the bark and their branches
       formed of wool that had grown through a single summer
and come back to winter barns carrying the day's weather

The Red

It was summer a bright day in summer and the path kept
    narrowing as it led in under the oaks
which grew larger than those I was used to in that country
    darker and mossed like keepers it seemed to me
of an age earlier than anything I could know
    underfoot the ground became damp and water appeared
in long scarves on the trail between overhanging
    ferns and bushes and reflected the sky through the leaves
the birds were silent at that hour and I went on
    through the cool air listening and came to a corner
of ruined wall where the way emerged into
    a bare place in the woods with paths coming together
the remains of walls going on under trees and the roofless
    shoulders of stone buildings standing hunched among heavy
boughs all in shade the mud tracks of animals led
    past a tall stone in the center darker than the stone
of that country and with polished faces and red
    lines across them which when I came close I saw
were names cut deep into the stone and beside each one
    a birth date with each letter and numeral painted
that fresh crimson I read without counting to the foot
    of one side and the date of death and the account
of how it had come to them one day in summer when they
    were brought out of those buildings where they had lived
old people most of them as the dates indicated
    men and women and with them children they had been
ordered in German to that spot where they were
    shot then the Germans set fire to the buildings
with the animals inside and when they had finished
    they went off down the lane and the fires burned on
and the smoke filled the summer twilight and then the warm night

Completion

Seen from afterward the time appears to have been
    all of a piece which of course it was but how seldom
it seemed that way when it was still happening and was
    the air through which I saw it as I went on thinking
of somewhere else in some other time whether gone
    or never to arrive and so it was divided
however long I was living it and I was where
    it kept coming together and where it kept moving apart
while home was a knowledge that did not suit every occasion
    but remained familiar and foreign as the untitled days

and what I knew better than to expect followed me
    into the garden and I would stand with friends among
the summer oaks and be a city in a different
    age and the dread news arrived on the morning when the plum trees
opened into silent flower and I could not let go
    of what I longed to be gone from and it would be that way
without end I thought unfinished and divided
    by nature and then a voice would call from the field
in the evening or the fox would bark in the cold night
    and that instant with each of its stars just where it was
in its unreturning course would appear even then
    entire and itself the way it all looks from afterward

Passing

One dark afternoon in the middle of the century
    I came over a low rise into the light rain
that was drifting in veils out over the exposed barrens
    long long after the oak forests had been forgotten
long after the wandering bands and the last lines
    of horsemen carrying the raised moments of kings
a few surviving sparrows flew up ahead of me
    from gray splinters of grass hidden under the bitter
thymes and across the stony plain a flurry of sheep
    was inching like a shadow they had the rain behind them
they were stopping to nose the scattered tufts while two silent
    dogs kept moving them on and two boys with blankets
on their shoulders would bend one at a time to pick up
    a stone and throw it to show the dogs where to close in
on the straggling flock the far side of it already
    swallowed up in the mist and I stood watching
as they went picking up stones and throwing them farther
    and the dogs racing to where the stones fell the sheep starting up
running a few steps and stopping again all of them
    flowing together like one cloud tearing and gathering
I stood there as they edged on and I wanted to call
    to them as they were going I stood still wanting
to call out something at least before they had disappeared

Substance

I could see that there was a kind of distance lighted
    behind the face of that time in its very days
as they appeared to me but I could not think of any

words that spoke of it truly nor point to anything
except what was there at the moment it was beginning
    to be gone and certainly it could not have been proven
nor held however I might reach toward it touching
    the warm lichens the features of the stones the skin
of the river and I could tell then that it was
    the animals themselves that were the weight and place
of the hour as it happened and that the mass of the cow's neck
    the flash of the swallow the trout's flutter were
where it was coming to pass they were bearing the sense of it
    without questions through the speechless cloud of light

The Shortest Night

All of us must have been asleep when it happened
    after the long day of summer and that steady
clarity without shadows that stayed on around us
    and appeared not to change or to fade when the sun
had gone and the red had drained from the sky and the single
    moment of chill had passed scarcely noticed across
the mown fields and the mauve valley where the colors were stopped
    and after the hush through which the ends of voices
made their way from their distances when the swallows
    had settled for the night and the notes of the cuckoo
echoed along the slope and the milking was finished
    and the calves and dogs were closed in the breath of the barns
and we had sat talking almost in whispers long past
    most bedtimes in the village and yet lights were not lit
we talked remembering how far each of us had come
    to be there as the trembling bats emerged from
the small veins in the wall above us and sailed out
    calling and we meant to stay up and see the night
at the moment when it turned with the calves all asleep
    by then and the dogs curled beside them and Edouard
and Esther both older than the century sleeping
    in another age and the children still sleeping
in the same bed and the hens down tight on their perches
    the stones sleeping in the garden walls and the leaves
sleeping in the sky where there was still light with the owls
    slipping by like shadows and the moles listening
the foxes listening the ears the feet some time there
    we must have forgotten what we had meant to stay
awake for and it all turned away when we were not
    looking I thought I had flown over the edge
of the world I could call to and that I was still flying
    and had to wake to learn whether the wings were real

A Taste

When the first summer there was ending more than half
        my life ago Mentières with his strawberry nose
and features to match and his eyes stitched down inside them
        in the shade of his black-vizored cap which proclaimed
to the world that he had taken his retirement
        not from the land but from the railroad Mentières with his
leer and his vest stretched over his large protuberance
        and his walk like a barrel neither full nor empty
he whom nobody trusted thereabouts laying their
        fingers beside their noses Mentières from elsewhere
the custodian of keys who had no land of his own
        so had been using the garden to grow his potatoes in
and had been picking up the plums from under the trees
        to make his own plum as he put it meaning of course
clear alcohol the water of life but it was
        too hard for him to bend any more in his striped
trousers to hoe the furrows and grope for the plums
        and he would not be doing it another year
so he brought back the big keys and with them a couple of
        old corked bottles from the year before and another
already opened for tasting the pure stuff the essence
        of plum to breathe it down your nose
and out like watching your breath on a winter day
        that was what kept them warm in the trenches he told me
a drop of that in your coffee he said holding up
        a thick finger and when his wife fell sick everyone
said they were sorry for her and when she died they said
        they were sorry for the daughter who never married
and looked after him he sat on the front step watching
        the road and waving to anyone but when he was gone
nobody seemed to notice the cork is beginning
        to crumble but the taste is the same as it was
the pure plum of the year before that has no color

Upland House

The door was not even locked and all through the day
        light came in between the boards as it had always done
through each of the lives there the one life of sunlight slipping
        so slowly that it would have appeared to be
not moving if anyone had been there to notice
        but they were all gone by then while it went on tracing the way
by heart over the cupped floorboards the foot of the dark bed
        in the corner the end of the table covered

with its crocheted cloth once white and the dishes yet on it
    candlestick bottles stain under one bulge in the black
ceiling the ranges of cobwebs roots of brambles
    fingering the fireplace the line continued across them
in silence not taking anything with it as
    it travelled through its own transparent element
I watched it move and everything I remembered
    had happened in a country with a different language
and when I remembered that house I would not be the same

Bodies of Water

In the long stone basin under the apple tree
    at the end of one spring in the garden I saw the faces
of all the masons who had built there on the edge
    of the rock overlooking the valley their reflections
smiled out from the still surface into the speechless
    daylight each of them for a moment the only one
with all the others lined up in them like stairs I could not
    see whether they led up or down then a wind rustled
across the garden waking it to the time it was then
    turning to summer in one of whose days I came
to the old trees off by themselves on the bleached hill
    cool darkness under them suddenly and the largest
stood at the end of a green where a fountain
    chattered on into a stone basin and on each side
among the shadow were stone walls and the shuttered ruins
    of a village with one stone arch leading into a courtyard
before a tall house and tower and a barn beyond them
    by the open house door an old man was sitting
who told me that it was the place where he had lived
    all his life and he said he would soon be ninety
now he slept up on the hill with his great-grandchildren
    who would sell whatever they could but he assured me
he would sell nothing in his lifetime this was where he came
    every day and sat by the door under the lime tree
and now look he said standing and walking slowly
    past the barn and pointing to five slender walnut trees
fifteen years from the seed he said and I grafted them
    last year myself and every one of them took
he said these give me something to look forward to

After Fires

In the time when witches were still burning and
　　the word of the king meant so little in the mountains
that tribunals were dispatched into the outlying
　　darkness with power to administer the law
on the spot a woman was brought in one day accused
　　of burning down two or three houses and perhaps more
for the courtiers were given to understand
　　that this was customary in the region when someone
had been displeased and when the snow was upon the mountain
　　then they set their fires but the setting was hard to prove
for the fires were plotted in secret and set at night
　　and when it was said that she had been seen leaving
her house after dark carrying fire and later
　　that night a house had burned she denied any part in it
and the witness was muddled and useless and although
　　it was plain that this was a woman of unsavory
conduct she having produced several children without
　　being married which she said was the men's doing
when she was condemned to the question a matter
　　in that place of nothing more than a violent
stretching she bore it with firmness and confessed nothing
　　saying only that the judge hoped for a reason
for hanging her and so at last she was branded
　　with the lily and banished to burn some said other houses
and beget other offspring I thought of her long after
　　she had gone like smoke and after those courts were dust
and after the time when everyone stopped in the middle
　　of the noon meal in a moment of autumn sunlight
and suddenly we were running up the white road
　　toward the column of dark smoke rising out of itself
swelling and unfurling into the blue sky over
　　the ridge we were halfway there before the first bells
rang behind us too late too late and when we came in sight
　　the neighbors had carried out the old woman and left her
on a mattress on the ground she was not even watching
　　the neighbors throwing their buckets of water and
her son dragging out one smoking thing after another
　　none of them what he wanted he had not been there
when it began and nobody knew how it started
　　so everyone informed everyone as the fire truck
finally got there and the hoses began unrolling
　　then the firemen and the son were sorting through the hissing
remnants and fallen stones trying to find a box
　　as everyone told everyone and the old woman
said yes there was the box they should look for the box
　　it was all in the box the papers and the money and they

peered under the rubble with the smoke still
    threading upward from the charred ends of rafters
she said the box was made of iron it was under the stairs
    which were no longer there they found it at last the iron
too hot to touch and they wet it down and took it
    to the old woman who nodded but then they were
some time getting it open since the key was lost and the hoses
    went on playing the rest of the tank of water
onto the ruins through the glass dome of the afternoon
    and the ring of the curious was hushed around the mattress
when the son pried the lid off letting us all see
    that there was nothing inside but a small drift of black snow

Thread

One morning a single bead turns up in the garden
    some kind of glass filled now with dark soil where the silk went
when they were all here together picking up the light
    it seemed that they had always been the age they were then
and that they would never be different even Viellescazes
    transparent as a doorway who sat through his late days
on the wall in the shade by the road where stories
    came back to him from so long before that they sounded
like a former life Esther who lulled her complaining knees
    hunched on the bench beside a few embers and mumbled
about dogs Edouard at eighty sickling the new grass
    under the plum trees in the cool summer mornings
one by one they dropped away and this winter Richard
    the mason with the long face white as a baker's
went and Berg who was stricken driving his tractor
    and survived to kneel for hours by his peonies
quiet people never divulging much and this spring
    Adrienne died in the home where she had taken
to going for the cold months she had not thought she would
    last so long after Jean her husband the cloud-voiced
roofer was buried but after a while she went on
    riding her bicycle slowly and smiling like a passing queen
and she was still in demand when they killed a pig anywhere
    famous as she had become for the way she made sausage
they say nobody ever managed to learn how she did it

The Cisterns

At intervals across the crumpled barrens
    where brambles and sloes are leading back the shy oaks
to touch the fallen roofs the leaves brush flat stones under which
    in single notes a covered music is staring
upward into darkness and listening for the rest of it
    after a long time lying in the deep stone without
moving and without breath and without forgetting
    in all that unmeasured silence the least of the sounds
remembered by water since the beginning
    whir of being carried in clouds sigh of falling
chatter of stream thunders crashes the rush of echoes
    and the ringing of drops falling from stones in the dark
moment by moment and the echoes of voices
    of cows calling and of the whispers of straw and of the cries
of each throat sounding over the one still continuo
    of the water and the echoes sinking in their turns
into the memory of the water the tones
    one here one there of an art no longer practised

Ancestral Voices

In the old dark the late dark the still deep shadow
    that had travelled silently along itself all night
while the small stars of spring were yet to be seen and the few
    lamps burned by themselves with no expectations
far down through the valley then suddenly the voice
    of the blackbird came believing in the habit
of the light until the torn shadows of the ridges
    that had gone out one behind the other into the darkness
began appearing again still asleep surfacing in their
    dream and the stars all at once were gone and instead the song
of the blackbird flashed through the unlit boughs and far
    out in the oaks a nightingale went on echoing
itself drawing out its own invisible starlight
    these voices were lifted here long before the first
of our kind had come to be able to listen
    and with the faint light in the dew of the infant
leaves goldfinches flew out from their nests in the brambles
    they had chosen their colors for the day and they sang
of themselves which was what they had wakened to remember

Old Sound

The walls of the house are old as I think of them
    they have always been old as long as I have known
their broken limestone the colors of dry grass patched
    with faded mortar containing the rusted earth
of the place itself from which the stones too had been
    taken up and set in the light of days that no one
has known anything about for generations
    many lives had begun and ended inside there
and had passed over the stone doorsill and looked from the windows
    to see faces arriving under trees that are not
there any more with the sky white behind them and doorways
    had been sealed up inside the squared stones of their frames
and fires that left the stones of one corner red
    and cracked had gone cold even in their legends
the house had come more than once to an end and had stood
    empty for half a lifetime and been abandoned
by the time I saw the roof half shrouded in brambles
    and picked my way to peer through the hole in the crumbling
wall at the rubble on the floor and ivy swaying
    in the small north window across the room now the house
is another age in my mind it is old to me
    in ways I thought I knew but they go on changing
now its age is made of almost no time a sound
    that you have to get far away from before you hear it

Green Fields

By this part of the century few are left who believe
    in the animals for they are not there in the carved parts
of them served on plates and the pleas from the slatted trucks
    are sounds of shadows that possess no future
there is still game for the pleasure of killing
    and there are pets for the children but the lives that followed
courses of their own other than ours and older
    have been migrating before us some are already
far on the way and yet Peter with his gaunt cheeks
    and point of white beard the face of an aged Lawrence
Peter who had lived on from another time and country
    and who had seen so many things set out and vanish
still believed in heaven and said he had never once
    doubted it since his childhood on the farm in the days
of the horses he had not doubted it in the worst
    times of the Great War and afterward and he had come
to what he took to be a kind of earthly

model of it as he wandered south in his sixties
by that time speaking the language well enough
       for them to make him out he took the smallest roads
into a world he thought was a thing of the past
       the wild flowers he scarcely remembered the neighbors
working together scything the morning meadows
       turning the hay before the noon meal bringing it in
by milking time husbandry and abundance
       all the virtues he admired and their reward bounteous
in the eyes of a foreigner and there he remained
       for the rest of his days seeing what he wanted to see
until the winter when he could no longer fork
       the earth in his garden and then he gave away
his house land everything and committed himself
       to a home to die in an old chateau where he lingered
for some time surrounded by those who had lost
       the use of body or mind and as he lay there he told me
that the wall by his bed opened almost every day
       and he saw what was really there and it was eternal life
as he recognized at once when he saw the gardens
       he had planted and the green field where he had been
a child and his mother was standing there then the wall would close
       and around him again were the last days of the world

Distant Morning

We were a time of our own the redstart reappeared
       on the handle of the fork left alone for that moment
upright in the damp earth the shriek of the black kite
       floated high over the river as the day warmed
the weasel slipped like a trick of light through the ivy
       there was one wryneck pretending to be a shadow
on the trunk of a dead plum tree while the far figures
       of daylight crossed the dark crystal of its eye
the tawny owl clenched itself in the oak hearing the paper
       trumpet and rapid knocking that told where the nuthatch
prospected and the gray adder gathered itself
       on its gray stone with the ringing of a cricket suspended
around it the nightwalkers slept curled in their houses
       the hedgehogs in the deep brush the badgers and foxes
in their home ground the bats high under the eaves
       none of it could be held or denied or summoned back
none of it would be given its meaning later

Vixen

Comet of stillness princess of what is over
    high note held without trembling without voice without sound
aura of complete darkness keeper of the kept secrets
    of the destroyed stories the escaped dreams the sentences
never caught in words warden of where the river went
    touch of its surface sibyl of the extinguished
window onto the hidden place and the other time
    at the foot of the wall by the road patient without waiting
in the full moonlight of autumn at the hour when I was born
    you no longer go out like a flame at the sight of me
you are still warmer than the moonlight gleaming on you
    even now you are unharmed even now perfect
as you have always been now when your light paws are running
    on the breathless night on the bridge with one end I remember you
when I have heard you the soles of my feet have made answer
    when I have seen you I have waked and slipped from the calendars
from the creeds of difference and the contradictions
    that were my life and all the crumbling fabrications
as long as it lasted until something that we were
    had ended when you are no longer anything
let me catch sight of you again going over the wall
    and before the garden is extinct and the woods are figures
guttering on a screen let my words find their own
    places in the silence after the animals

A Given Day

When I wake I find it is late in the autumn
    the hard rain has passed and the sunlight has not yet reached
the tips of the dark leaves that are their own shadows still
    and I am home it is coming back to me I am
remembering the gradual sweetness of morning
    the clear spring of being here as it rises one by one
in silence and without a pause and is the only one
    then one at a time I remember without understanding
some that have gone and arise only not to be here
    an afternoon walking on a bridge thinking of a friend
when she was still alive while a door from a building
    being demolished sailed down through the passing city
my mother half my age at a window long since removed
    friends in the same rooms and the words dreaming between us
the eyes of animals upon me they are all here
    in the clearness of the morning in the first light
that remembers its way now to the flowers of winter

THE FOLDING CLIFFS:
A NARRATIVE

(1998)

For Olivia Breitha

THE CENTRAL EVENTS of the story all happened and the principal characters existed but the evidence for both is fragmentary and most of it second or third hand, refracted and remote. This is a fiction but it was not my purpose to belie such facts as have come down to us. Some of them have been moving toward legend since they occurred.

For what I have learned of them I am profoundly indebted first to Frances Frazier, whose editing and translation of Pi'ilani's account told by Sheldon was my own introduction to this story. Agnes Conrad, whose grasp of the trove of the Hawaiian State Archives approaches magic, repeatedly conjured up startling treasures that had slumbered there for a hundred years. Frederick B. Wichman has been unfailingly open with his own long-accumulated erudition on the subjects of the legends and history and names of the island of Kauai. Carol Wilcox has given me other invaluable details of the history and people of the island. Pat Boland and Anwei Skinsness have both put at my disposal their extensive work on the history of Kalaupapa and of leprosy in Hawai'i.

The word "leper," of course, is offensive in any modern reference. I have used it throughout simply because it was the ordinary usage at the time of the story, part of the appalling cruelty of the history of what Hawaiians came to call "the separating sickness."

A note of any complexity about Hawaiian pronunciation would probably be ignored, and for those who are interested one can easily be found. But it might be useful here to say that if the vowels are accorded individual attention and sounds roughly resembling Spanish or Italian, and double vowels pronounced with a glottal stop between them (as in 'oh-oh') it will at least be a courteous if faltering step toward a rich, subtle, ancient and elegant language.

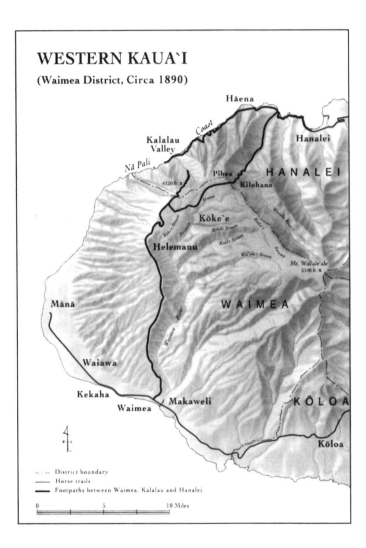

WESTERN KAUA`I

(Waimea District, Circa 1890)

Hāena

Coast

Kalalau
Valley

Nā Pali

Hanalei

Pihea

Kīlohana

HANALEI

4120 ft X

Kōke`e

Helemanu

Mt. Wai`ale`ale
5148 ft X

Mānā

WAIMEA

Waiawa

Kekaha

Makaweli

KŌLOA

Waimea

Kōloa

– · – District boundary
——— Horse trails
━━━ Footpaths between Waimea, Kalalau and Hanalei

0   5   10 Miles

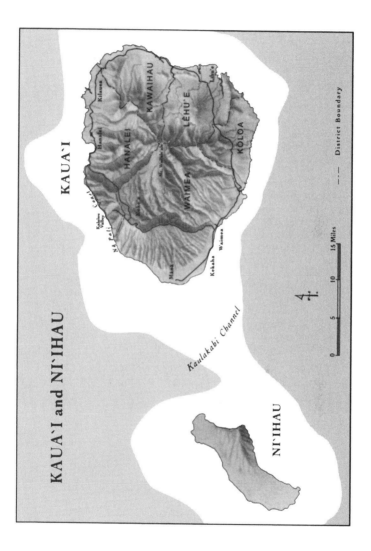

KAUAʻI and NIʻIHAU

KAUAʻI

NĀ Pali Coast

Hāʻena
Hanalei
Kīlauea

HANALEI

KAWAIHAU

Kalalau Valley

LĪHUʻE

Līhuʻe

WAIMEA

KŌLOA

Mānā
Kekaha
Waimea

Kaulakahi Channel

NIʻIHAU

- - - District Boundary

0   5   10   15 Miles

CLIMBING

1.

Climbing in the dark she felt the small stones turn
        along the spine of the path whose color kept rising in her mind
burned-in color moment of rust dried blood color other color
        gone color by day and she knew what color was there
when she could not see it and when one of the stars was the darkness
        before any breath of daylight and the way was in her feet again
the star of Kaoʻea rushed between clouds when the dawn wind
        came toward her down across the ridges of the mountain
carrying the scent of water from the peak of Waialeale
        At a high twist of the trail far down to the left behind her
over the naked roots of the slope and the widening hollow of Waiaka
        where the folds of the mountain were still touched by the moon
she saw the sea outside the curve of coast glinting
        past Waimea beyond the dark land and the hidden houses
in one of them her father was invisible in sleep
        and past there the sea outside Kekaha where she had been born
by the shore of Oʻomano all of it barely a shadow
        from which she had set out and nobody had heard her go
even the dogs in the moonlight never barked when she went past
        looked up and watched and never barked knowing who she was
and with the next step that whole horizon was gone behind the mountain
        the blackness beginning to the right of her was the chasm of Waimea
the air running from the edge of it rustled the finer leaves of the koas
        above her the voices of the plovers stitched the night

2.

She knew the way now as something of hers a sound of the name
        that had been hers from the beginning waiting for her
when she woke into the world on the coast at Kekaha
        her night name from before anyone had seen her and from
before that always hers but more of her had answered to it
        after she had tasted what she would not taste again
infancy when the belly turns up and the echo
        of the waves rocks it and then childhood the naked rapids
then the petal pleasure of everyone's eyes on her
        telling her how beautiful she had become how
beautiful she was and then her watching him differently
        whom she had known for as long as she could remember
since they had been children there running on that same sand
        and then the feeling of him watching her and the time he first

came to her and all their early age together
        the house they lived in after the wedding when she had heard
his full name as though she had never known it although
        everyone knew it and when she heard it that time
a cold finger touched her at the top of her forehead
        and ran down the front of her over her face and her breast
to her navel and below and she had shivered and heard
        nothing for a moment until the voice of Reverend Rowell
who had taught them both to read and write turned to her and said
        her name Pi'ilani and asked her the lifelong question

3.

When she had gone up that trail for the first time they had been together
        all of them on horses Ko'olau her husband
ahead of her in the dark and Kua his friend and elder
        riding ahead of him Kua Papiohuli
who had taught Ko'olau from the beginning always an eye on him
        throwing the fishnet holding the spear the paddle
taught him the currents on the surface and the ones below
        who they were where they came from what things they had done
what it was best to expect from them in what order
        as the hours turned in the sky and Kua taught him the touch
with horses so that even as a boy Ko'olau
        was famous for his way with horses and Kua taught him
the braiding of leather the life of a sinew the spring
        of a lariat and taught him to use the lariat
so that it seemed to rise out of his hand by itself
        and fly wherever he willed it to go and drop there
like a tern fishing Kua taught him the tracks on the ridges
        and the gun the handling of the gun and Ko'olau
they would say never misses he never misses

4.

She saw it as a leaf floating under calm water
        in the sunlight of its afternoon that was slowly ending
it was before her eyes but she could not hear it
        could not touch it a time not yet gone they had been
getting ready all day the ones who were going
        Ko'olau and their son Kaleimanu still a child
and sick and Kepola her mother and Ida
        the daughter of her mother's sister Kinoulu
they had kept deciding what they would be able to carry

when the time came and Kukui his mother kept giving them
things to eat she kept cooking making things that they
        would leave behind and Kinoulu kept telling Ida
what to remember and all afternoon one by one
        the family came and tried to help or sat saying nothing
while Koʻolau's grandmother Kawaluna from whose dream
        his name had come sat outside the door on the ground
facing the mountain humming and patting her knee
        when they had decided that they were going she was the one
Koʻolau had asked to say what night would be good for it
        and she had not answered for days and then had named
a night some time before the new year and the rising
        of the Pleiades and late that day he and Kua
brought the horses to the back of the house and saddled them
        and loaded the bags and what they were taking after all
and then they stopped and watched the sun go down past Niʻihau
        then Koʻolau's father Kaleimanu for whom their son
had been named stood up and all at once they were silent
        Kawaluna was humming and Koʻolau told their son
Kaleimanu to say good-bye to them each in turn
        and they all said good-bye crying as quietly as they could
to make little noise holding each other in their arms
        and Piʻilani's father Hoʻona said that they must pray
and he prayed like Reverend Rowell standing in church
        but Kawaluna kept on humming she was the only one
not crying and she looked up at each face in the gray light
        and did not speak but stood up and put her arms around them
one after the other and kissed them before they mounted
        and Kua turned his horse toward the mountain and they followed
now as she walked they rode through her and kept appearing ahead
        and she was riding among them a ghost among the ghosts

5.

She had been climbing for a long time and the moon had set
        she had passed the place where the ghost smelling of dried fish
waited by the side of the trail and she had walked on
        the night kept growing colder as the trail wound upward through trees
she stopped and bent to pull the black shawl from the bag
        she looked up through the branches to see where the stars were
she watched for them through the leaves and clouds but there was only
        darkness over her and she sat in the ferns by a trunk
not wanting to stay long and get up chilled and stiff
        she lay staring at the night above the mountain
her feet went on without moving like the sound in a shell
        she was at home in the night on the mountain and she felt

the mountain at her back the black underneath of it behind her
 going down to its dark root under the sea and the black stone
above the heart of the fire that kept turning without light
 the spring of night from which the night was coming
her head was toward the top of the mountain and she was sure
 that she was on the other side of the mountain hearing
the sound of one of the streams there and water falling
 from higher in the valley and the night rain beginning
but it was a sound the trees made and the branches
 were dripping around her and then onto her feet and her face
and she stood up listening and then she turned and went on

6.

The first shadow was beginning to surface in the darkness
 through a net of trees when she came to the swollen stream
of Halemanu the house of birds where in earlier dawns
 the birds had the forest to themselves waking there
into plumage and colors never seen anywhere
 crests and feathers heads and motions never before
entered upon voices never heard before singing out of
 a source in the yolk of their unmeasured morning
inexhaustibly beginning and beginning
 as the undisturbed trees and flowers kept beginning around them
finding in each place the morning as it was then
 in an age without numbers changing too slowly
for a single life to see it moving unperceived
 like the voyage of the mountain itself into the northwest
the eon of the birds seemed perpetual like the mountain
 long before another side of the night gave birth to humans
and for an age after that there was no sign of them
 growing closer around the unbroken horizon
the streams went on overflowing seaward taking with them
 the mountain a grain at a time and small fish and crayfish
brought their salt in from the sea and swam up the falling water
 to live in the falling before time until the first canoe
appeared in the west and only the birds saw it

7.

A light rain reached down to her face the fringe of a mist
 there was no color yet in the ghost dawn but around her
through the full consonance of the stream came here and there
 clear voices opening as she passed close to them

trills telling of water questions not continued
  some of the voices were lights flying beside her
the amakihi a yellow brilliance the olokele
  a flicker of scarlet but the light was the complete gray
before daybreak with the black bands of the trees floating
  through it then before a condensation of green seeped
into the tall reaches of the valley opening ahead of her
  the house appeared Halemanu at the end of a long rise
with the lifted shell of high trees raised above it
  the mountain palm towering behind and as her feet
brushed the wet grass she saw the four pale long uprights
  of the verandah the new wide steps leading up to it
and the dark arms of the house reaching forward toward her
  someone was there the smell of woodsmoke floated in the mist
and as she stepped forward a small light passed at a window
  she stopped and watched and a woman came out with no light
and stood at the top of the steps a tall figure in a long gown
  the hair built high on her head the same color as the hour

8.

They both stood listening and they heard the small stream nearest
  to the house the Brook of Tears Nawaimaka high
with the rains at that time of year the tall woman
  outside the door was looking into the trees and had not seen
Pi'ilani she came down the steps slowly watching
  the trees and Pi'ilani walked toward her up the slope
and without raising her voice said—Makuahine—
  and the woman turned not sure whether she had heard anything
Pi'ilani went closer and said again—Makuahine—
  and the woman said—Who is it—and then saw her but could not
make out who it was and Pi'ilani pronounced her own name
  in a voice so low she hardly heard it herself
—Can it be you Pi'ilani—and Pi'ilani stepped
  toward her and for the third time called the white woman mother
—Makuahine—and the woman said—Pi'ilani—
  and came to embrace her but Pi'ilani said
—I will make you wet—and the woman laughed and embraced her
  and then said—You are completely soaked Who is with you—
—Nobody else—Pi'ilani said and the woman said—Come in
  Come in at once there is a fire are you really
up here alone—and as they turned the rain began again

9.

As they went up the steps the white woman called—Makaʻe
        Makaʻe—calling again at the door and to Piʻilani
she said—Come in come in—drawing her by the arm toward the fire
        as a Hawaiian woman appeared in the far doorway
—Makaʻe I know you remember our friend Piʻilani
        We have been out in the rain and are cold and hungry this morning—
Makaʻe ran to Piʻilani and embraced her
        —How are you—she asked—Well——Who is with you——Nobody—
Makaʻe shook her head and without a word unwound
        the sodden shawl and hung it over by the fire
and the other woman picked up a blanket from a chair
        and put it around Piʻilani and brought her to sit
in the glow of the fire while Makaʻe piled on more logs
        and then was gone—I did not know you were here—Piʻilani said
The woman nodded—We almost never come up here
        in the winter any more it is so long since I was here
at this time of the year in the rain with the streams roaring
        hard for the horses to cross how did you ever cross—
Piʻilani said—Yes the water is high now—and she held out
        her dripping skirt in front of the fire—The first time I came—
she said—it was this time of year it was the same night
        and there was nobody here then and the children were half asleep
we tied the horses out of the rain and we ate something
        out there on the steps and rested there for a while—
—If we had been here—the older woman said—we could
        have given you something to eat that time——Maybe—
Piʻilani said—But that time was different—

10.

At that moment the rain began to thunder down on the roof
        with the deep pounding of a waterfall and the planked room
became a sounding box with the shadows cast by the fire
        playing around it as reflections play beside water
if they had shouted they would not have heard each other
        The older woman whose name was Anne looked up at the ceiling
Anne Sinclair Knudsen born in Scotland in Stirling
        more than sixty years earlier her father a captain
in the British Navy The ceiling was a deep hollow and she felt
        the house shudder Piʻilani looked up from the fire
to the salt-frosted boards of the walls the flowers
        trembling in a jug and she saw the silver rain
sheeting down outside the house and the shadowy trees
        waving through it she looked up into the dark rafters

two women who had lost their husbands recently
    raised their faces toward the roaring and stared upward
and the days after the deaths dissolved behind them and Anne
    saw the beams of the ceiling thirty years before
and her husband Valdemar talking of how the timbers
    were all from New Zealand she saw the men heaving them
onto oxcarts then onto mules then carrying them
    when she left the babies with the nurse and rode up with Valdemar
to the grass mountain hut before Eric was born
    she had come there with Valdemar after they were engaged
the grass hut had been here where she was sitting now
    they had built this in its place and she had cherished the thought
that the boards had come from New Zealand the first world
    that she remembered to which her parents had taken her
when she was a small child and they had built the house there
    room by room around her looking down to the bay from which
one day the news came that her father and brother were lost at sea
    and the grieving cries of the Maoris still pressed upon her
though she could not hear a sound out of all that time

II.

Looking up into the same deafening recesses
    above them at the same time Pi'ilani saw
faces in the wood and eyes and deep shadows stretching
    back into themselves through the roar and then those became
a stone overhang in a steep valley where she was lying
    looking up waiting feeling the rock tremble under her
hearing the rolling explosions echoing circling
    around the valley and the hollow crack of the cannon
starting the echoes rolling again wave after wave
    just as they began falling away and she could tell
down her back when a shell from the cannon struck the cliff face
    sending huge stones leaping and smashing down through the trees
and behind that there were the other cave roofs in the valley
    that she had stared up into and seen only darkness
as she lay awake hearing the sound of the valley
    on and on and how she had prayed up into the stone
in the first days starting with the prayers in white English
    that Reverend Rowell had taught them in Sunday School
and then the others that Kawaluna had said
    were secret the ones that Keiwi kept warning her
had to be spoken perfectly names to be said only
    from the soles of the feet words to the sleep of no return
those prayers many times under her breath with her eyes open
    then hearing the roar of the night with no sound no answer

12.

They did not hear Maka'e come in with a tray
    and set it on the table and then she was standing
in front of Anne with her hands spread out declaring
    helplessness looking up in her turn at the ceiling
to see whether there was a leak somewhere and all at once
    the rain began to let up and they listened as it
moved away through the trees dragging its sounds after it
    leaving the raised rushing voice of the Brook of Tears
in its place and Maka'e when she could be heard
    asked Anne whether she would have breakfast at the table
or by the fire and Anne said they should stay by the fire
    Maka'e set a low table in front of them
—It is an everything breakfast—she said and laughed—It is what
    was left out there I made your porridge and your tea
but all the rest is cold—Maka'e said looking
    at Anne and then at Pi'ilani whose eyes were reflecting
the fire—That will be perfect Maka'e thank you—Anne said
    and Maka'e left looking back at them sitting there
with the tea things and porridge on the tray and the cold
    bannocks a pot of jam cold purple sweet potatoes
cold taro cold pigeon dried mountain apples—Well do you drink tea—
    Anne asked Pi'ilani—If you please—Pi'ilani said
—Will you have porridge—Anne asked—If you please—and the rain
    stopped and they heard the tea being poured and the notes
of spoons on china and the fire and the stream rushing

13.

Anne said—We were together this month at Makaweli
    with Eric and Jane and Helen and the others
over from Ni'ihau and when some of them were going home
    I wanted to come up here for no reason as I thought
to begin with but then reasons came flocking to me
    we were here this last summer of course and that was the first
return after Valdemar died but this was something to do
    with wanting to be here as the century is ending
bringing all those whom I have known and have lost
    up here along with me once more in the rain and mist
often lately my cousin Isabella is in my mind
    she knew so much and was so learned and made the studies
and paintings of flowers and she worked on her book here
    we were here together years ago in the winter
she wanted to study the birds then and everything growing
    in the rainy season well I came this time with Eric
and the boys from Ni'ihau and a few to help us

and when the others left I wanted to stay on alone
for a while I have begun to note things that I may
    not do again such as coming up here in the winter
and I am glad I came this time but before long now
    we must be going back I had thought it might be
tomorrow but we could go today if you would rather
    come down with us some time during the afternoon—
After a moment Pi'ilani said—Thank you—and shook her head

14.

She looked into the fire until Anne was wondering whether
    she had forgotten where she was but then at last she said
—They are telling me again three times now someone has said to me
    that he has been found that the grave has been discovered
and they have dug him up and have taken his bones and his gun—
    —Who told you that—Anne asked—Kekaha people—Pi'ilani said
—One of them whispered to my mother but said not to tell me—
    —Where did they hear it—Anne asked—One said he heard it
in town from somebody he had not seen there for
    a long time——What kind of person——He told me it was
nobody from here but they know all about how to
    sell things like that and who will give money for them—
—Did he tell you any names—Anne asked—No names—Pi'ilani said
    —Nobody's names ever but they talked about his gun
how his gun had been found somebody had dug it up
    and his bones——Did you talk about this with anyone else—
—No—Pi'ilani said—I never said anything
    only that nobody knows the place where I left them—

15.

Anne watched Pi'ilani looking into the flames
    —What will you do—she asked—Go there—Pi'ilani said
—Alone—Anne asked—Yes alone—she answered—By myself—
    —I am sure somebody up here with me could go with you
at least for the most dangerous part——I have been back there
    several times once Kua went with me into the valley
and came out with me and I have gone in with others
    at different times but I am going by myself this time—
—I will say prayers for you—Anne said—I was alone—
    Pi'ilani said—when I came out the first time—
—How long will you stay there in Kalalau—Anne asked—I will wait
    to see what I find there—Pi'ilani answered
—When they told you the same thing those other times

and you went back were there signs that someone had been there—
—All my life—Pi'ilani said—I have known about it
    I heard about them trying to find where the chiefs
were buried or where any of us had been hidden
    I heard about what had been found with the bones and taken away
gold and canoes and carvings and spears thieves have been taking them
    for a long time and there were many burials in those valleys
and in the cliffs going up and many are still hidden there
    and after the soldiers took everybody out of Kalalau
and burned down the houses nobody was left to see
    who might crawl in over the rocks like crabs to steal the dead—

16.

How utterly still she sat as she was saying it all
    Anne thought and then Pi'ilani went on—There was
so much talk and talk   When I came out of the valley
    back to Kekaha the first time they had been talking
ever since we had left and they believed themselves
    each of them telling something else that meant nothing
playing cards with their own stories that they said were us
    so the bets got big and they asked me one thing or another
and I would not know what they had inside their heads
    that had been growing there while they knew nothing about us
when we were in Kalalau talking to nobody
    except each other those years while day by day there were
more things that we did not have to say or that we
    did not want to say again and what we said lasted—
—Did you see no one at all—Anne asked—After they were all taken
    out of the valley—Pi'ilani said—sometimes we heard voices
sometimes maybe voices of people we had known sometimes
    calling our names sometimes talking about us but
never seeing us they always sounded like echoes
    even when they were close to us and I have learned since
that friends came looking for us at the beginning
    bringing food for us and clothes but they did not find us
it was only our own voices that made no echoes—

17.

I remember Ko'olau's voice even now—Anne said
    —Clear and strong one time when we were outdoors singing hymns
it was shortly after you were married I heard
    one voice riding above the words and I looked sideways
and it was Ko'olau and I have heard him sing in the good days

other songs——He always sang—Pi'ilani said
—Everyone used to sing as we rode up here—Anne said—Valdemar
     always loved singing even when he had no voice left
still teaching all of us songs he remembered from Norway
     and songs from here *Oh Kaili leaf of the koa*—she hummed
—Flute words—Pi'ilani said and Anne nodded—I am sure
     I was not supposed to know what all of them meant—
she smiled—But we knew—Pi'ilani said and she went on
     —Kaleimanu's voice was very small from the beginning
but it travelled it knew its way he was a quiet child
     even when he was playing with all the others
he kept listening for something and he wanted to hear stories
     he was a story catcher he said and if a story
flew by him he would catch every word and keep it
     alive and later we would find that he knew it
all the way through but he wanted to hear it again
     to be told it again and he said he knew that stories
were hiding all around him in places telling themselves
     and he said that each of them knew where it was going—

18.

—We had named him for his grandfather for Ko'olau's father
     Kaleimanu who used to work for Mr Gay
on the ranch and my son wanted to know why his grandfather
     had been named Kaleimanu The Wreath of Birds
and how the name happened—And where did that name come from—
     Anne asked——Out of a dream his own mother Keawe had
She gave him that name because of something she knew
     in the dream but her son said he had to ask her
for years before she would tell him any of the dream
     and when our son asked his grandfather it was the same
for a long time he would say only that it was a dream
     of birds and I saw how our son Kaleimanu
kept his eyes on the birds running by the water the shore birds—
     Anne thought of the stilt that Valdemar shot to study
and the species had been named for him the thought made her feel
     far from everything—And staring at the stilts in the pond—
Pi'ilani said—*Kyip kyip* I would hear him around
     the house so that I thought there must be a bird there
and his eyes went with the lines of birds over the sea when the sun
     was going down he could make that high sound of them as they went
that cry so thin a thread too fine to be seen not beginning there
     one day he told me that flowers and leaves in the leis
had all been picked and ended but that in bird leis
     the birds were flying only they were birds from before
and from afterward so that nobody could see them—

19.

—He said that when we hold a bird what is in our hands
    is not the bird any more and that when we look at birds
we see only a little of them——Did his grandfather tell him that—
    —I do not think so—Pi'ilani said—but I do not know
Only Keawe had been in her dream and nobody
    ever heard all of it but maybe it was a dream
that could not be told   He wanted to hear bird stories
    from back before about people from then who were birds
in that time and he kept asking all of the elders
    for stories and then when no more words came he would say
Is that all but later he knew where each of the stories
    stopped so we went on telling him stories he knew
and he would ask us about them as though the stories
    were still there even when we thought he was asleep
he might ask us about something now in the story
    and we would not have the answer and would have to say so—
Pi'ilani looked out the door to the lanai
    —We were all asleep out there that morning when we went
to the valley—she said—and when Ko'olau picked up
    Kaleimanu to go on he asked the child Do you remember
Lahi and Kaleimanu said Who ate nothing but birds
    We are going to the place on the mountain where Lahi lived
Ko'olau told him and the child said Is the giant up there
    Lahi and his uncle killed the giant Ko'olau told him
That was that time Kaleimanu said But I want to see
    We will go and see Ko'olau said and carried him half asleep—

20.

—All the way going up from here to Kilohana
    I think he was talking to Kaleimanu in front of him
on the horse and still asleep I heard Ko'olau
    at the turns of the trail telling stories in his night voice
floating over the rocks and he stopped when we rode close
    to the spring where Nawaimaka comes out of the ground
that low cave that you could pass without seeing it there
    and the clear pool that keeps moving into the Brook of Tears
he told Kaleimanu asleep in his arm about the spring
    and the child asked is this where Lahi waits for the soldiers
and Ko'olau said—No we are not there yet—and we rode on
    up the trail then all at once I heard a raw voice
above me *'uwa'u 'uwa'u* like one bird
    crying like one sea-bird 'uwa'u the petrel
then I heard Kaleimanu laughing and he said—I know
    it is no 'uwa'u it is you then I heard it

again farther up and again Kaleimanu
    laughing and he said—I know it is you Kua you are not
'uwa'u but the sound came again and Kaleimanu said
    —It is you Kua it is at night the 'uwa'u calls
and still Kua and Ko'olau kept making that sound
    and Kaleimanu laughed but he said—Lahi will eat you—
and he told us he was awake now and kept asking what
    bird he was hearing because birds were all around us
he sat up watching them until we came to the high edge
    at Kilohana where the trail climbs on but the whole
world falls away in front through the clouds and the valley
    of Kalalau appears to be as deep as the sky—

21.

—And on the edge I thought I was hearing nothing
    the wind kept rushing at us along the cliff face
hitting us and shaking the trees and the voices
    of the birds must have been still calling around us
but it seemed cold with silence and we came to Kilohana
    where we would separate and Kua would go back
with the horses so we all dismounted there and Kua
    walked to a place on the edge hanging out over the clouds
so bright they were hard to look at and the rusty cliffs
    rising around them and he pointed to one rock
out on a cliff fold where there was another like it
    close to it and he said—Kaleimanu see
that one there That one is Kua——It is not—Kaleimanu said
    —You are Kua I know you—But Kua said—That is spirit Kua
Do you remember the story of the two spirit children
    the boy and the girl whose father was lazy and sent them
to the spring every night for water—and Kaleimanu said
    —That was Naiwi The Bones and one night at the spring
children like us who die found those spirit children and they
    stay playing all night because they forget and the day starts
to come so that it is too late for them to get back
    before the sunlight turns them to stone——There they are—Kua said
—Do you remember their names—The girl's name has leis in it
    so I remember she is Hikimaunalei
and the boy is Kua——And so now—Kua said—you will
    look up at that rock some time and say that is Kua—
but the boy kept looking at Kua without answering—

22.

Pi'ilani remembered them all saying good-bye then
    on the mountain and she looked out the doorway at the morning
with its sunlight glittering on the green dripping branches
    and she said—Makuahine down there in Kekaha
they tell me now that I never talk to a soul
    they tell my mother I never say anything any more
and it may be true but see how I have been talking
    up here—Anne said—I am happy you will tell me
these things that must be in your mind all the time now
    I have known what happened only as most people do
in parts and all of them hearsay and then for a long time
    I heard nothing whatever and you had gone back to Kekaha
and had been there for a while before I was told of it—
    Pi'ilani said—At first I would not go out at all
Only the family in the house knew I was there
    I was still hiding but everyone let me alone
Now they do not ask me anything they move farther away
    from asking anything—Then she saw that Maka'e
had been standing in the doorway behind her listening
    and she stood up and Maka'e came over to her
her voice choked with crying and said to her I would never
    have asked you anything that I wanted to know about that time
but when I heard you talking I could not go away
    do not be angry with me Pi'ilani—and she put
her arms around Pi'ilani and stood with her eyes
    shut and tears running and Pi'ilani embraced her
and after a moment said to her—It is a little thing—

23.

She stood with her arms around the older woman
    rocking her as though she were reassuring a child
until Maka'e turned to Anne and said—Forgive me
    Makuahine—and she went out with the tray
Pi'ilani said to Anne—It is so long since I saw you
    I know you lost your husband and it is late to say it
but I was sad to learn of it——Thank you I remember
    what admiration he had for Ko'olau in the days
when your husband worked at the ranch he would boast about
    Ko'olau this Ko'olau that Ko'olau was
the best he had ever seen Ko'olau could do
    anything—Pi'ilani said nothing—They came up here
together I cannot say how often with Kua
    and maybe Kapahu and some of the others looking for

wild cattle they said but he always hoped to discover
     a new wild flower for the museum Almost every trip
he brought back something new—Pi'ilani nodded—Sometimes
     Kua or Ko'olau or one of them would have told him
a name for a plant and what sickness it might be good for—
     Pi'ilani said—Ko'olau told me about
a spear at the doorway of your house—Anne said—That was
     a present from long ago——He told me about that
before Kaleimanu's first birthday—Pi'ilani said
     —And that was a long time ago and now I am glad
to have seen you Makuahine and thank you
     and I ask you to excuse me it is time to go—

24.

—You walked all night—Anne said—There is still a long way to go—
     Pi'ilani answered—I want to be down there
in the valley before it gets dark—She took off
     the borrowed shawl folded it on the bench and lifted
her old black steaming wrap from front of the fire
     and slung it around her shoulders Maka'e came in
and embraced her again and then Pi'ilani
     turned to Anne—Good-bye—she said and they kissed near the cheeks
with the distance in place between them like a pane of glass
     that had always been there and Pi'ilani stepped out
into the sunlight that changed her into the color
     of a shadow and she went down the nine steps like a shadow
and up the trail among the old trees and was gone and there were
     only the trees as Anne stood looking and she could almost
see what she had known there and would not see again
     faces and garments in the sunlight of the early days
husband children friends certain that it was all theirs
     the certainty swelling their voices as they sang
their hymns under those trees on the mountain repeating
     their claim to the wilderness she kept holding off
memories of Valdemar who knew so much Vally
     so much older than she was showing her the skulls
he had dug up at Manaulepu many years
     before he had known her it had all been for science
she recited a psalm Blessed is the man she said
     stiffening slightly as she stood there becoming the severe
bony old woman her grandchildren would not like
     she heard a step on the boards and nobody was there
and she remembered the time soon after they were married
     when he was away from home at the legislature
and she heard footsteps that the servants told her

were the sound of a spirit but she had gone out
with a lantern and seen the night heron fly off over
the garden and she smiled because she took no stock in such things

25.

Pi'ilani had never meant to stay so long
at the bird house fluttering in words in the net of words
she had planned to be farther up the mountain by the time
the rays of the sun were leaning at this angle in the mist
through the gray 'ohias here the net was the braided
tracks of wild cattle leading away into ravines
a few of them freshly churned in the black mud of the forest
and more recently used than the trail she was remembering as
she came to it the hoof-prints frayed out full of sky
into thickets and concealed clefts and she was careful
of her way that looked different each time with branches fallen
low growth taller she hurried listening for the sound
of cattle in the woods it was along through here
that she had heard Ko'olau telling Kaleimanu
to be listening for wild cattle and Kaleimanu's high voice
asking why they were wild and Ko'olau saying that all
the cattle came with the haoles and some of them ran loose
on the other face of the island from the beginning
But they got around here to the west of the mountain
in my own lifetime he said in the year I was born—
—How wild are they—Kaleimanu asked—Oh they are wild
as lightning—Ko'olau answered—How big are they—
—They are bigger than any bulls you saw down below there
They can pick up a horse and rider and throw them both
over their shoulders——How did they get there—the child asked

26.

Then Kua who had been old enough to be riding
with hands from Valdemar Knudsen's ranch at Waiawa
at the time it all happened joined in the story and told
Kaleimanu how Makua Valdemar Knudsen
had been able to lease all the land from Waiawa westward
to the wide plains beyond Mānā and first he ran
what they called Texas Longhorns and goats on that whole pasture
and later because it was the tallow and hides
that made money he put in a number of Durham Bulls
to get weight on them and that made an easy strain

grazing wherever it suited them along the hills there
          and into those dry valleys but not very far
so at round-ups it was no trouble to herd them down
          into the pens—I can remember that time and then
they tell me one day this young Englishman turned up
          rode all the way around the island from Hanalei
where he had some kind of ranch set up and as I heard it
          a letter had come from his brother in Australia
with bad news and he had to go as soon as he could
          but he had this hundred head of cattle and nobody
he could trust with them and he wanted Makua Knudsen
          to pasture them for a year at Waiawa and offered
a hundred dollars well Knudsen told him he did not
          want his cattle but he would do it and he sent a few hands
half way to Hanalei for them and we met them
          up almost to Kilauea they were miserable
half dead worn out starving we could hardly get them
          to move at all and the Hanalei hands helped us
bring them across the Wailua River the ones
          that did not lie right down in the water and die
and there were a lot of those floating toward the sand bar
          it happened at each of the rivers we had to cross
and we crept so slowly that they sent Kapahu along
          to see what had become of us and we all doubted
whether any of them would make it to Waiawa
          I think in the end there were twenty-five that did
and it was all they could do to stand up but Makua Knudsen
          said turn them into the grasslands so that is what we did
they walked out like that as though they would simply die
          but when some from the ranch went out to round up cattle
a few months later they found the red Hanalei ones
          in with the good ones but when they tried to round them up
the Hanalei ones stuck up their tails and headed
          up into the valleys and knew their way onto the mountain
later we heard that those cattle had been wild to begin with
          and were caught and fenced up but they could only be herded
when they were starved half dead and we never knew more than that—

27.

Pi'ilani thought of riders coming back from the mountain
          when she was a child the horses suddenly there
with leaves in their manes and the raw meat slung
          behind the saddles the polished horns swinging and a vast
blackening crater dripping in her mind the red cliff
          where the neck had been and the hacked off bull's head riding

upside-down with its tongue dangling and its eyes staring
        at the ground and then after the trips how they sat
late eating and chewing over the whole story
        and then the old stories again the surprised meetings
the bulls charging on unchecked by bullets that barely
        dented their skulls the huge hearts driving them on even
with holes torn in them and always Meʻeawa
        saying he knew that those wild cattle had been crossed
with the same power on the mountain that made the giant
        men of the cliffs with the one red eye it all lit up in her
again for a moment each time she started through these woods
        listening knowing that there were almost none of them
left on the mountain any longer but she listened for them
        without thinking more about them watching the trail
ahead of her always following that first time
        startled when she looked up to see that now there was
nobody in front of her and the sun was already high

28.

She came to hills of bright cloud rolling up out of the valley
        and before noon she had arrived at Kilohana
where they had all dismounted that first time and had stood
        in silence looking around them at the stream slipping
toward the edge and at the falling away and away of the cliffs
        fin after fin drifting among clouds the great bay in the air
as deep as the mountain the valley of Kalalau
        its measureless hollow Kalalau The Straying
they could see through white clouds threads of surf unrolling
        slowly into shadow the cliffs hung steep as blankets
on a fence she could see that Kepola her mother
        was frightened looking over past the edge and Kua
said he would say good-bye now and Kaleimanu
        went to him and embraced him laying his head against
Kua's stomach and then asked him if this was the stream now
        where it happened—Where what happened—Kua asked him
—Where they met the soldiers—Kaleimanu said—This is
        the stream—Kua told him—but this is not the place—
Kaleimanu said—Will you tell me the story once more
        right here—and they stood in a ring in the wind listening
to Kua tell of Lahi the boy who ate birds
        and his uncle who was Kanealohi Slow Man

29.

He said—After they came up here to eat the ʻuwaʻu
        that live in the cliffs first there was the giant who tried
to kill them and Kanealohi told Lahi When the giant
        comes you hold out a bird to him but when he reaches
to take it you back up into the tunnel and he will
        follow you and since you are smaller than he is
he will get stuck in the rocks and then I will kill him
        so they did it that way and then the great chief heard about them
up here eating birds and he said Those birds are mine
        and he called together four hundred of his soldiers
to come up here and kill Lahi and Kanealohi
        but those two moved up this stream to a smaller one
that runs into it and if anybody steps
        in the stream anywhere along it even far below here
the surface away up there begins to ripple and they would know
        there was somebody coming and one day it began
to ripple so they came out and could see the whole army
        climbing up to kill them and Kanealohi was frightened
but Lahi went to where the rocks almost come together
        with the top of the trail between them and there only
one man could climb through at a time and he killed them as they came
        one by one and they fell all the way down from the cliff
and the last one was the chief himself and they say that
        he recognized that Lahi was his own son and he said so
and asked Lahi to spare him and the boy let him pass
        and it was Lahi who became the chief later in the story

30.

It was then that Kua had led Kaleimanu
        to the edge of the cliff where the light rose from the valley
and had showed him those two rocks that were the children
        of Naiwi and said to him—That is where the right trail
goes down—and he pointed to a thread like a goat track
        following the knife edge of one of the fins out in the clouds
—That is the one that goes all the way—he said—The others
        end in nothing—And he hugged the child and told him
—But it is not good to look back—Then he went to help them
        load themselves with the few things they would be carrying
Piʻilani stood looking down at the clear water
        gliding in front of her toward the fall its surface
not appearing to move she knelt in the wet moss
        to put her mouth to the cold pane and drink from it
with her eyes open at first and then she closed them

and plunged her head and hands into the unseen current
for a long breath overhearing the voices in the water
    talking and then she sat up and ate a few pieces
of taro and drank again and lifted her head to stare
    at the face below her in the stream with the sky
under it and the eyes burning from their dark places
    she looked at it feeling that she knew nothing about it
and then stood up in the day and walked to where the right trail
    disappeared over the edge into Kalalau

31.

At first there were small trees rooted in the crevices
    above the shallow groove descending the flank of the cliff
groping the folds and strung around the ribs of rock
    and there were the tops of bushes reaching up just below
the faint path that plainly was little used now and was blurred by
    rains and by the wind that struck at her the moment she stepped
down and it came at her again around every corner
    but there was nothing to hold onto bare rock on one side
and on the other beyond the tops of the bushes
    empty air and her eyes crept along the snaking path
that twisted downward ahead of her she set her feet to it
    like hands she did not look up to see nobody there
she pulled her mind back even from that first time when
    Koʻolau had been in front with Kaleimanu
slung over his shoulder and she kept hearing him
    saying Hold still Keep your eyes closed Keep your eyes closed
Lie still and every part of the path seemed longer
    than she remembered it then the bushes were behind and there was
only the drop of the cliff beside her and after
    Koʻolau there had been Kinoulu her mother's
sister and the little girl Ida who had wanted
    to come to be with Kaleimanu and then Kepola
Piʻilani's mother who gasped at the corners
    to begin with but the wind took away the sound
most times and Piʻilani pulled her mind back to the path
    in front of her and the wind rose as she followed it
out onto the top of the long fin like a crooked
    log with the drop disappearing on both sides into
shadows and out in the margins of her vision
    white flecks came and went small as dust in a sunbeam
tropic birds the size of gulls soaring in circles that far
    below her then almost at the end of the fin the path
tightened around a corner to double back downward
    so that the curtain of rock hung again beside her

32.

The wind had lashed at them here as it lashed at her this time
        the sky had filled with dark cloud and the rain had found them
they had leaned against the cliff wall in the racing fog
        the water spilling over them as they crept forward
scarcely able to move but afraid of being caught there
        when the light went so they inched ahead until the rain
let up and at last it stopped and the clouds tore apart
        over the drop and they could see the gaunt buttresses
towering around them out of the depths of the valley
        and she had tried for a moment and had not been able
then or ever to conceive of what Ko'olau
        had told her about them carrying Judge Kauai
into Kalalau some time earlier taking him
        down that same path when the old man was already
too sick to walk and too heavy to stand on his feet
        so that it took four of them just to lift him she could
not see how four of them with him slung between them
        could have found footing on this draped hair of trail and the Judge
had been dressed up for the journey in his town clothes
        wrapped in his robe and wearing his blue spectacles
and the broad hat with the peacock feathers around it
        and she had come to know all the men who had carried him
one of them Kilohana who went back to the top
        again and again by himself to carry down others
whose feet were gone or withered and no use to them

33.

She had been sure before she set out that nobody
        had found where he was buried and she had been sure of it
all the way up the mountain through the night and she had kept
        seeing the grave as she went the fur of moss around the black
branches above it in the deep shade back among
        broken rocks with the cliff looming far overhead and the stream
leaping across the stones below it a place from which you could see
        anyone coming and never be seen and it appeared to her
to be untouched the ferns and bushes grown over it
        unbroken undisturbed unnoticed how could it
be taken away from him when it was what he had
        always been it was where the cold touch had come from
that ran down between her breasts at their wedding when
        Reverend Rowell carefully pronounced Ko'olau's whole name
—Do you—he had said—Kalua i Ko'olau
        Do you The Grave at Ko'olau Do you The Grave

on the Windward Side take this woman Piʻilani
        Climbing Heaven to be your lawful wedded wife
from this day forth—and the rest that he had sworn to
        and that she had sworn to with that cold still running on her
Only once near the end she had asked him about his name
        and he had told her what she had already known about it
how Kawaluna his grandmother Kawaluna
        The Age Above had been there when he was born and she
herself had delivered him and when she held him up
        she had announced—He is Kalua i Koʻolau—
and if anyone dared to ask her later she always
        answered the same way saying that she had known it in the night

34.

And it was in the night that he had died just as
        the Iʻa The Fish The Milky Way was turning
and Piʻilani after his breath had stopped when his pulse
        was no longer there had put her head down on his chest
with her hair across his body and had listened
        to the darkness below her and the darkness above her
while the last embers of the small fire among the rocks
        at their feet went out and the cold of his hands deepened
and her tears kept turning cold when they ran down onto him
        she heard the darkness of the mountain under her
all the way to the underside of the sea floor
        and through her hair she heard the night winds high in the valley
rising and leaving and she heard ʻuwaʻu ʻuwaʻu
        the cry of the petrels echoing in the cliffs
the stream whispering over the rocks and the faint sounds
        some said were crickets and others said were land snails
singing and they were spirits and when the wind was quiet
        she could hear the sea far below her where all the waves ended
she sat up in the dark and saw where the stars had come
        she picked up a shell and started to pat it rocking
slowly forward and back chanting under her breath
        first she chanted to him by name by the name that she
had called him all her life and already she could hear
        the difference—Koʻolau Koʻolau you are going
you are going now you are still here you are going
        you are not sick any more you are not dying now
but if you want to come back Koʻolau come back come back—

35.

She had chanted the same words until she heard them
     go out like the fire and she patted the shell rocking
without words and then began again—Koʻolau
     it is the time of your going I hear the sound of it
but I go on trying to think of something to give you
     where you are on the mountain that keeps turning away
and all that is left here now is that you are gone—
     She chanted until the stars at the top of the cliff
began to grow faint in the ghost dawn and she stood up then
     and slowly climbed down to the stream and washed her face and hands
When they had been sure that he would not live many more days
     they had moved for the last time together back to the hollow
where they had taken Kaleimanu when the child
     was dying and where they had buried him in the low cave
at the foot of the cliff and when it began to be day
     she pushed farther back in the narrow among the rocks and found
a place deep among them not far from Kaleimanu's grave
     and there she knelt chanting her husband's full name—Kalua
i Koʻolau Kalua i Koʻolau—and as she chanted
     she began to pull back the ferns and pry up the stones
but she had only the stones and sticks and the kitchen knife
     to dig with and she dug all day but at sundown
it was not deep enough and she slept that night beside him
     and all the next day she dug the grave knowing nothing
but what she was doing until late in the day she thought
     it must be deep enough and she lined it with ferns
and hauled Koʻolau's body to it and settled his gun
     on his chest and then filled the grave and rolled stones
onto it and closed the bushes back over it

36.

Then it had been dark and once more she had chanted to him
     —Koʻolau now it is night for me and it is night for you
now we are in the night Koʻolau there is only night where we are—
     When the chant had ebbed in her breath she had got to her feet
and gone down to the stream again stepping like a stranger
     as though she were feeling her route through a rolling cloud
she had come to the water running cold from the cliff
     she had heard it come up to her talking to itself
not to her not to her even then not to her yet
     she had stepped down into it and knelt among the big stones
slipping between them she had lain down among them letting
     the breathless touch glide over her until she could feel it
no longer while the colorless syllables still

    hurried past her she had got to her feet and followed
the stream through the dark knowing her way down the valley
    It had been years since she had spoken to anyone
except him and in an earlier time Kaleimanu
    but some who had lived in the valley had come back
people they had known once had come back a few of them
    at a time she had seen one or two of them approaching
the floors of ashes that had been their houses
    had seen new grass roofs later and backs in the taro ponds
she had heard the voices and slipped close to listen
    and that night she could see small fires down in the valley
near the east headland and she had wanted to be with people
    but she had gone past the fires to where the current rattled
across the shingle she had felt the canoes drawn up there
    she had walked slowly along the rocks to the white streamer
unfurling on the tops of the low breakers and she had sunk down
    into the night surf to be washed clean in the darkness

37.

As she came down the dry cliff in the heat of the afternoon
    into the smells of rock dust and lantana that rose
like a breath out of the gorge she thought of standing
    in the sea that night in the cold of Kanaloa
the hand of the dark pulling her pushing her she had felt
    what it was taking away and what it was leaving
what it was leaving her darkness darkness and she came
    to the top of the side valley and the smell of ginger
where the thin cries of the tropic birds were no longer
    far below her she began to hear water and she went on
and here was the lap of ferns where they had rested
    that first time and then farther down where the dim path
wound among rocks at the foot of a high wall of stone
    she stepped away from it into the shade of kopikos
she was sure that nobody had found the grave as she
    opened her way through the branches in the narrow cleft
she was sure as she had been sure each time the rumor
    had reached her and she had gone just the same to tell
Kawaluna what she had heard and ask what Kawaluna
    thought of it and each time the answer had been the same
there had been the day when Ida had brought her the page
    of the Commercial Advertiser where it said
that Deputy Sheriff Coney and Police Officer
    John had dug into a mound in the upper valley
and found a couple of rough boards and then a body
    wrapped in a coarse gray blanket with a raincoat around its head
buttoned in the back the hands folded over a rifle

a Mauser with a woman's satchel full of cartridges for it
and the brigand's revolver since they were certain
    that the body which they estimated to have been
four or five months in the ground had once been Koʻolau

38.

Everything on the torn tongue of paper had told her
    that they were wrong and she had been sure of that to begin with
all of it she said to herself reading it over
    nobody had found him but just the same she had gone
to Kawaluna to read her the scrap of paper
    and that massive woman sat looking down at it
without moving and then Piʻilani had seen
    that she was shaking and when she looked up she was laughing
she said—You know that nobody has found Kalua
    i Koʻolau—and she held up the paper as though
it had mud on it and Piʻilani began
    to wonder whose grave they might have found she kept
thinking it might be Mamala it might be Mamala
    who had got away into Wainiha when the soldiers
had rounded up everyone they could find in the valley
    and who had lived back there taking wild cattle and goats
after Koʻolau had stopped using the rifle
    Mamala she thought but then who would have buried him
whatever he died of a friend must have buried him
    to have left him his Mauser and the revolver
and ammunition and wrapped him so carefully
    and brought the boards from some ruin there had been others too
living in the other valleys they had known there were others
    but as she thought of it she wanted to be able
to say that she had been back to the grave and had seen
    that no one had found it and she decided that this time
she would go over by herself into Kalalau

39.

She was sure now as she lifted the tangle of branches
    guava and then ʻohia and kopiko remembering
Kawaluna looking at her steadily each time
    and then shaking her head and saying—You know that nobody
has found him—and yet Piʻilani had come each time
    to see what she knew the litter of moss and brittle twigs
undisturbed the russet fur along the fern fronds

untouched the sunlight floating on patches beyond
reach she saw it all in her mind as she came up
        between the rocks and there was no path there were no
footprints or broken shoots and then the hollow in the crag
        and the corner into it and she saw the place before her
almost as she had seen it in her mind only
        a little changed in itself in a little estranged
giving off no sign that it knew she was standing there
        the shadows whispering among themselves the cliffs
with their backs to her the new growth on all sides not
        knowing her it was what she had known and been sure of
she stood watching the ragged light scattered across the leaves
        tears were running down her face and under her breath
from the center of her body she chanted to the place
        Kalua i Koʻolau nobody knows where you are
nobody has found you nobody has found you

40.

She moved cautiously to the grave breaking nothing
        making scarcely a sound until she could kneel beside
the flat stone in the shadow of ferns and touch the green
        moss just above ground there she waited birds were speaking
in branches close to her elepaios curious
        not singing and she waited and then she lay down
breaking nothing and put her ear to the ground and listened
        as she did each time she came and in one ear she heard
the leaves and the birds in the branches and in the other ear
        the one note of the mountain of Kane the silence
under the forty forms the darkness under the day
        it had not changed and she closed her eyes and was filled
with it and at last she stood up slowly and with the same care
        went along to the cleft in the rock wall and the bushes
of ʻulei that had grown over the mouth of the low cave
        at the foot of the cliff where they had buried Kaleimanu
the small green leaves were shining like eyes and the white flowers
        were hiding among them and slender branches were swaying
slowly out over them into empty air and she
        put her ear to the warm stone and stood listening there
then sat against the rock wall beside the ʻulei
        and saw the shadow rising on the cliff and heard
the birds that were not the ones Kaleimanu had listened to
        telling their day and its passing and when she felt the shadow
she unwrapped the last of the cold taro and ate
        and then she lay down and heard the sleep of the mountain

THE MOUNTAIN

The mountain rises by itself out of the turning night
    out of the floor of the sea and is the whole of an island
alone in the one horizon alone in the entire day
    as a word is alone in the moment it is spoken
meaning what it means only then and meaning it only
    once with the same syllables that have arisen
and have formed and been uttered before again and again
    somewhere in the past to mean something of the same nature
but different something continuing and transmitted
    but with refractions something recognized in its changes
something remembered from what is no longer there
    and behind it something forgotten as the beginning
is forgotten and as the dream vanishes the present
    mountain is moving at its own pace at the end
of its radius it is sailing in its own time
    with the earth turning away under it as the day
turns under a word and it came late as a word comes late
    with a whole language behind it by the time it is spoken
its fire came late among the fires in the dark of space
    its burning plume rose late through the plated shell of the globe
it formed late at the end of the old plume unfurling into
    the black depth of the sea and it burst up at last into
the air higher and higher collapsing sliding away
    and pressing anew from beneath splitting open lifting
and finally moving away from the fire-plume and cooling
    almost twice as high in its youth as the scored peak
in the story and setting out in that giant time
    following its elders the earlier usages
already invisible beyond the late day

There it towered where each of its antecedents
    had stood in a cloud-hidden unremembered past
barren and farther from land except for each other
    than any coast in the sea that circled the globe
and already there had been ages when the engendering
    plume of fire had fallen back into its own darkness
for so long that the earliest craggy intimations
    looming and cloaked with clouds and commanding the currents
of the ocean had washed crumbled and subsided
    and had sunk in succession under the breakers

76

until none was left rising above the water
    and beyond the most ancient surviving reef that scarcely
showed through the waves a submerged convoy was continuing
    the voyage consonants of an archaic language
all their high sayings returned to sand and each of them
    had once faced the rain and wind the sun and the night sky with
bare rock and the shining black drapery and jagged
    stone salients of lava and across them the weather had broken
measureless all through the time before time and before
    the first waifs of life had found their way to those surfaces
solitary travellers lifted by storms and long swells
    to a naked place where one day they found company

3.

Some came from the invisible islands sinking
    already far ahead into the past some had become
what they were only there on one island in the waning
    course of its age and then had been carried backward
into the future on an island from afterward
    where they went on to become what they would be only there
and then were ferried in turn to this mountain to continue
    themselves some from the sea cast up on the surprising shore
some from the air in a dream of roots so from one branched
    coral polyp waving far off in the unanswering
night before the gods the family of coral and its white choirs
    came into being so from one star in the shallows
the constellations of starfish moved outward so
    from the mussel its child the hermit crab emerged
at the foot of the mountain so from the fronds floating in
    on the waves the ferns were formed that woke on the mountain
after the night ran through the narrows of changing
    in the darkness without eyes and some were born in the sea
some in fresh water or on land so in the caves were born
    the crickets of each cave ground crickets and when there were trees
tree crickets swordtail crickets and the sound they made
    that in time would be called singing ran through the mountain
born only there were flowering trees and lobelias
    and birds that discovered them and were changed when they tasted them
born was the plover into flight born were the birds
    each from the wingbeats of the others born were the guardians
the noddy at sea guarded by the owl on the mountain
    birds passed the peak in high streams that blacked out the sun
and at daybreak the wet hollows of the earth opened wings
    and flew up in answer into the light and the infant
shoots of the taro uncurled and reached for the morning

4.

It had all come late to the first age still without measure
        except for the turning in which it was turning
the longest age the age of origin the aeon
        through which processions of islands rose and were washed away
without names the aeon before the gods which the gods
        who came in time to take all the names of the light
and of what appeared in the light for themselves would call the age
        of unbroken darkness and empty night but the whole
day of the world had hung there in a drop of rain on a leaf
        with no need to fall and the mountain had been sailing
away from its source through sunlight and starlight far longer
        than the age of all the gods that were yet to come
the next mountain had risen into its following
        tree of smoke behind the horizon and it was as long
again before the next and the next and still the gods
        knew nothing of the light and the waifs of life drifted
back into the future and again into the past
        coming to be made by where they woke so that the offspring
of seeds of shrubs here and there grew into tall trees
        and so little menace and pursuit was there
that toxins and thorns were given up and generations
        of insects and birds forgot flight and the use of their wings
then came the day when fear found the edge and fell into
        the age of night fear and day fear and the hiding and crawling fears
the time of the hairless ones and of blood on the leaves
        and of standing figures arriving from their distance
from the night the time of people coming the time of time

5.

They came on a wide cloud with three separate floors
        they appeared on an island that turned as it flew
so it was told later when there was no one alive
        who could remember any longer the way it had happened
and it was all true in a way only the way kept changing
        they had become their journey which was the tale they repeated
they told where they thought they had been and thought they remembered
        they told of the faces of death they thought they had left
one after another so that their own shadows
        were its shadow now and they claimed that they were the heirs
of the root of the earth the source of the earth they had it
        with them wherever they went it was the fire they were carrying
before which there had been nothing and their own footprints were names
        which they had given to the stars they had followed
out of the night of Asia into the islands new names

for the sky as they went from Newe and Kauana lipo
under Haku po kano to Hoku pa'a and their wake
  was what they had almost forgotten broken shells on a house floor
a bed pile in a dark corner and bones of a half-eaten child
  they came from beneath the stars of the south that brought
the bad weather they came in the fever of a sick wind
  on the hot flailing air some called themselves Take
and the islands from which they had sailed they called Hiva
  but when they saw the mountain they said it was theirs

6.

It looked to them like the world they had come from
  or like the way that world might have been there were steep valleys
formed like the ones they had seen inhabited crowded
  tended and fought over foot by foot but here they found no one
at first except big birds that could not fly away
  and feared them so little that it was easy to catch them
so they feasted on them until there were none of them left
  and they set up houses and others came and joined them
it was a land of crags and rocks and slopes veined with water
  where they moved immense stones into vast masonry
giant walls and waterways platforms causeways that would be
  their monuments rising out of silence when they themselves
had become legends after they had been overrun
  by others in waves among them those from Tahiti
called Manahunes who had been invaded and had sailed
  north to pass on their defeated name to those they conquered
who withdrew into the cliffs or sailed into the northwest
  to the old islands taking with them the old tongue
and all certain knowledge of themselves and they grew
  small in the distance and were belittled in stories
where they appeared as dwarves knee-high with arts of their own
  great powers the strength of giants the cunning of sorcerers
and were still claimed as forbears long after they had vanished

7.

And from the southwest in that age came the goddess of fire
  Pele following the source of fire to make her home there
some said she was born in Tahiti some said she was born
  in Kaui helani a land floating like a cloud
some say she was driven away by her stern sister
  the sea goddess Namaka who predicted that Pele
would set fire to everything and they say that when Pele left

she had with her in the canoe her brothers the gods
and under her arm her small sister Hi'iaka
    they sailed to the ancient syllables the line of faded atolls
in the northwest and then journeyed back to the mountain
    which the inhabitants by then had named Kauai
and since that was the way she came her prow grounded
    on the shingle near Hanalei and Haena and she
found everyone dancing there and Pele fell in love
    others say she had travelled the length of the islands digging
for the well of fire and was settled at Kilauea
    on Hawai'i when she heard in a dream the sound
of the nose flute coming from somewhere on the mountain
    on Kauai and first she thought it was old Pohaku
her grandfather but when she followed the sound she found it was
    coming from Haena beside Kalalau where they were
all dancing and she fell in love as a fire would
    fall in love and she loved a young chief named Lohiau
and she emerged into the firelight and the chanting
    with her back like a cliff and her breasts proud so that everyone
thought her the most beautiful woman they had ever seen

8.

The story was so old that everyone dancing
    there at Haena that night had always known it
it was the same story that they were dancing and it led
    into holding and losing into absence and rage and ashes
and into returning and it was rising out of Pele's dream
    far away on the island of Hawai'i and in her dream
with her eyes on Lohiau she chanted *Hanalei*
    is overcome by the great rain as the flame leapt
between them and it told of her biting his hand
    as she turned to go home and of his sister finding him
when he had hanged himself from the roof-tree after Pele went
    and of his dog refusing to leave his grave and of Pele
waking and persuading her sister Hi'iaka
    to bring Lohiau to her and of Hi'iaka
coming at last to the coast below Kalalau
    and seeing in a cave high in the cliff the ghost
of Lohiau and of her bringing him back to life
    and of love waking between them in turn and the barriers
their love came to one after the other and triumphed over
    and then of Pele's own fires burning up Lohiau
and his return to life one more time and reunion
    with Hi'iaka it was all there in the chanting
in the sound of the drumming at the base of the mountain

9.

With Pele had come her brother the Chief of the Sharks
        and the shark rock was there at the headlands of Kalalau
the dragon had arrived from the birthplace of Pele
        the owl of the mountain commanded from the cliff
people had settled in all the long valleys running
        in from the sea on the steep north slope of the mountain
they had terraced the green gorge of Nualolo
        with its broad table high above the surf they had taro growing
in Wainiha that narrowed climbing toward Kilohana
        and while they were dancing the darkness went on wheeling
so that they came to nights in which the stars over them
        burned in places where a few hours earlier
they had been seen higher above the horizon
        by Arthur sailing for Iceland and by Merlin
versed in the turnings of western islands and by Brendan
        and the animals with him in the small ark of his summer
and then by Charlemagne's veterans in the dark of Europe
        still furred in its forests that harked back to the ice
with their roots in amber worn faces had looked up through woods
        that they had been given for the felling and later
far north where the nights were blank the Norse followed secrets
        in search of somewhere it seemed they must remember
with a name like time and in time farther west they cheated
        the Skraelings for furs a first touch of a flayed new world

10.

Farther west and later past currents and tracts of ocean
        so crowded with fish that in some places a hull
might have trouble forcing its way among the braided backs of them
        beyond the coast of the continent and inland through forests
of spruce hemlock and birch there were eyes at night watching
        those same figures glittering between the auroras
others were watching from farther south by the low tones
        of rivers in a land full of the lives of animals
beaver in the streams bear in the forests wolves deer and moose
        their ways forming the fabric through which the colors
and charactery of the human lives were continued
        season by season and in that wholeness remained whole
believing that they might draw from the life around them
        from the senses and quickening of the animals
what they truly needed and no more and that in return
        for their restraint and compunction the creatures around them
who they knew were their elders and were spirits and powers

would protect them from the evils of sickness and pestilence
it was an understanding that sustained them until
        fishermen out of England came upon that coast with
diseases carried from Europe and with offers of iron
        for furs and then epidemics in waves erased villages
and the survivors believed the animals had betrayed them
        and they took the guns and cloth and treatment they were given
and set out into the three centuries of screams
        and dismemberment the piled scalps parades of zeros gross fortunes
far away and the bleeding across the continent from the constant
        skinning familiarly known as the fur trade that finally
arrived at the sea which by then was called the Pacific

II.

It had been a long time since anyone on the island
        remembered some name from the south for a bay or a narrow
fold in the Hivas that the ancients had once clung to
        and then had sailed from and later the Spaniards came to those
steep coasts but finding no gold there they christened
        the constellation of peaks the Marquesas and sailed on
leaving little except the diseases they happened to have
        and some of them vanished in those seas and planks from their
wreckage rode the currents northward and from time to time
        beached on the island and someone picking shellfish from the rocks
at Lawai or Kapaʻa or even at Kalalau
        might find them and take them home and they would be
passed around and touched and the shapes and surfaces
        discussed and the red and black on the iron spikes
hammered in Spain with ends that could cut would become
        treasures and were indeed prophets generations after
anyone had arrived from Tahiti or had sailed there
        and come back to tell and the name had come to suggest
mirages and clouds or another life before
        or after and by then stars had dropped out of their knowledge
below the southern horizon Hokuloa and Kaʻawela
        and other lights had never been known as beacons
only the ancients had told of the stars of Kuanalipo
        that were leading the floating forests to Tahiti
directing strange sails to the islands of the ancients

12.

An age of passing with nothing appearing to change
      a succession of comings and goings of the moon
a history of tides generations of calendars
      families seeing themselves pass in running water
an aeon when the chiefs had divided the round island
      among themselves and agreed that it would remain
under a spell set apart from the other islands
      a cradling a kind of calm that ripened around the mountain
days for planting returned and they planted by the lower streams
      nights for fishing returned and the nets came up full
more than once they were invaded by chiefs from other islands
      and drove them off and were left at last unmolested
though drawn step by step into the bloodlines woven
      through the island chain but still the horizon was their own
as in their eyes it had always been and would be
      for that long again and then one morning in the season
of rains the time of Lono the days when the Pleiades
      had risen and the year had become new again
when the high chiefs of Kauai were Kaneone
      and Keawe in the gray moment of the ghost dawn
at Waimea on the shore by the canoes Kauiana
      thought he saw parts of a forest out on the ocean
which had not been there the evening before when the sun
      had gone down and these were like no forests he had ever seen
so that for a moment he was not sure they were there
      then the others with him saw where he was looking
and caught sight of the same things and one of them shouted with fear

13.

For three days the sick wind had been reeling into them
      from the south bringing these things closer to Waimea
Kuimana the chief had heard the shout from the shore
      he came down with Aimaku both of them with spears
and saw the black shapes out past the surf there was more light then
      and the low parts were rocking like canoes in the water
the trees on them rocking with the rest and gray things like dead rays
      were swinging in the branches Kuimana stood watching
while the others talked without knowing and then he said Take out
      the canoes and see what they are and Aimaku
went out with seven canoes at first but people
      kept coming down to the shore when they saw those things
and the canoes kept going out and by that time
      there was daylight so they could see that the things were

part island and part canoe and could see pieces of iron
    all over them on the outside many shapes of iron
of different sizes some very large and they said
    to each other that the iron that they had been sharpening
into knives must have come from islands like these and they saw
    creatures on them with three-cornered heads and white faces
like human faces their skin dark blue and white hands like real hands
    which they kept raising and voices like voices calling out
something that sounded like the word iron so the people
    called back going closer until they saw steps being lowered
from the canoes to the water so that they could climb
    up the black sides and see the iron waiting everywhere

14.

These creatures had long hair tied back so that at first
    they appeared to be women and there was smoke blowing
out of the mouths of some of them they had wrinkled skin
    with treasure holes in it that went far inside them
and they could reach into those and bring out knives and nails
    beads and a kind of white tapa and many other things
and they talked the way people talk but what they said
    was like pebbles going around in a gourd they babbled
noises *blither blather jabble jumble rumble*
    berry love Tahiti love baby love woman
Moku saw a roll of rope with an iron club on it
    lying in front of him and picked it up and when they
pulled him by the arm he broke loose and jumped over the side
    and Kaleo was looking into everything
like an eel and he came out of a doorway laughing
    holding up a big knife with a square blade and they
tried to catch him but he stood up on the wall laughing
    and as they reached for him he jumped too and Aimaku
said it was time to go and they left and went back
    to tell the chiefs and others about all this
they kept telling it over and over talking about
    what to do and by then people who had seen those things
out to sea from Kekaha and Makaweli were coming
    until there were many sitting watching along the shore
by the time the sun went down and they saw a row
    of fires all at once jump from one of those black islands
all the fires the same like fish and in a moment they heard
    thunder coming from there and then it happened again
and then it was dark and they sat trying to see

15.

Some stayed there all night watching and others sat
    beside fires talking some said they were sure the strangers
must be gods and insisted that the fires jumping from the island
    and the thunder afterward proved it but others
did not believe it and some said they needed to see
    whether the strangers would bleed and they went on talking
until the fires sank and the voices came more slowly
    then the woman chief Kemalia who was very old
reached over to a drum that a friend was holding
    and patted it with one finger like a heart beating
until that and the thin wave spinning out along the sand
    were the only sounds and then she said as though
she were sitting there alone—No they are not gods
    One time after Umi had died on the island
of Hawai'i and while his son Keali'iokaloa
    was chief in his place a thing like one of these came there
and we thought it was an island and called it an island
    but they are not islands they are only a big kind
of canoe and that one was named Konaliloha
    and it broke into pieces on the rocks at Palemanō
we were told and many died there but one man and one woman
    reached the shore alive and they stayed on the sand a long time
on their knees so the place is called Kneeling even now
    everyone wanted to help them and people brought them
into their houses and gave them food and the man's name
    as they remembered it was Kukanaloa
and they thought the woman was his sister people asked what they
    ate where they came from they ate fruit and everything
no one could understand them but they lived there after that
    and were people and had children and died like anyone—

16.

By then the sick wind had come to an end and they let
    the fires go out and slept or sat watching the darkness
in the darkness out to sea listening hearing
    over the low brushed syllables of the water
the calling of plovers across the night the two notes
    leaping up and then from out on the water a hollow
knocking and at times other notes in pairs not rising
    echoes of a pebble on a beach or a bird voice
but not a sound of a living person and then for a long time
    they would not hear it and suddenly it would be there again
clear and thin but so faint that they would ask each other

whether they had heard it they sat watching the flying stars
and each of them there began at some point to remember
    sitting beside someone who had died and watching listening
to what was not there and to what still seemed to be there
    in the last night some remembered that the death had been
heralded by a ringing in the ears and they found
    themselves trying to tell whether the night was still breathing
and not knowing what they were groping to remember
    and now they would not know it until they themselves were gone
but everything else was still the same the night sky
    constellations in their places the sea stroking the sand
the shore onto which they had been born and where they had
    been who they were then the stars began to leave them
growing smaller disappearing and a breeze woke
    just as it used to and they no longer heard anything
from out to sea but as the darkness faded those dark
    spider shapes of it remained and as they went on watching
into bare day they saw from one of those islands
    a smaller darkness born a canoe coming toward them

17.

Black prow broad in the water paddles far to the sides
    like the wings of a chicken they could not tell as they watched
whether it was scarcely moving or was approaching them
    like a thrown spear and for a moment when they looked
it hung still in the gray light like the thread of white
    water suspended in the high falls at Moeloa
far up in the gorge of Waimea at that hour of the morning
    after the months of rain that late in the winter
while the shout of the water was echoing in the cliffs far
    behind them out of their hearing as they edged down
along the sand saying again the same things they had said
    in the night and some of them were holding offerings
standing in the water with pigs in their arms chickens
    dogs bananas taro such gifts as might be offered
to any stranger a few were carrying spears
    they talked faster louder as the canoe came closer
and they could see the black heads and blue skins of the strangers
    who were paddling backwards they were coming backwards
they must be coming from afterwards or from somewhere
    that was already gone and people started to laugh
girls were laughing arranging the flowers on themselves
    Kapupu'u who had come back with the big knife
was laughing and said—I am somebody who will pick up
    what I can—until Kemalia heard him and told him

—That could be stealing and you know what happens to you
        if you steal from people—He said—Maybe they are not people
at all not people—and he laughed and went on laughing
        as the canoe came closer and they all crowded toward it
and caught hold of paddles a stranger was standing
        in the prow holding a pole with an iron hook
and Kapupu'u snatched the pole and the other
        would not let it go so they both pulled back and forth
and another one standing in the canoe pointed
        an iron rod at Kapupu'u and it flashed
and roared and Kapupu'u fell back in the water
        kicking and from a hole in his chest his blood began
to flow around the canoe until it was all around it

18.

The soundless white thread had not moved in the waterfall
        everything had stopped but nothing was stopped they let the canoe
go and saw that it was something else it was not a canoe
        and the figures with blue skins looked to them like things moving
under clear water they heard the voices coming from them
        echoing echoing while the echo from the iron stick
still circled in their ears they heard in the sharp rattling
        syllables of the strangers the habit of seizure
and the rush of fear and the paddles rose all together
        from the sides of the canoe and then fell together
into the red water but now the strangers were paddling
        forward and away and Kapupu'u was floating
face up with his eyes looking at the sky but he was dead
        some of them picked him up feeling the warmth of him
and carried him up the sand with the blood dripping
        all the way to his house and the wailing going with them
and some stayed to watch the strangers turn at a distance
        of several spear throws when their voices and the hollow knock
and creaking of the paddles could still be heard as they moved
        saw them paddling on toward the left following the shore
to the river mouth and across it and on past
        Makaweli and Koloa and a few of the men
followed to see where they would go and the rest gathered
        in the shade at Waimea where they could watch the islands
of the strangers out in the dazzling sea with the crying
        and the chanting for Kapupu'u close upon them
some wanted to face the strangers now as enemies
        and recalled the alien armies that their ancestors
had driven off and how many of the invaders
        had been left dead along the shore at Kekaha and Mānā

and they shouted but then some spoke of the thunder
    and the fire at night from those black islands and said maybe
the strangers were gods after all and at last Aimaku
    stood up and they were silent and the wailing seemed louder
He said—It is not in my mind that they are gods but for now
    we should act as though they were gods and had taken
their sacrifice and we will watch everything they do

19.

So it was still their day their light their shore with those trees
    they knew and the same birds running in lines along it
like shadows of threads lifting off and alighting
    it was still they who said who were gods and who were not
and the spirit of Kapupu'u was still somewhere
    not far away perhaps listening to the wailing for him
and shuffling softly among the old leaves then from the sea
    a sound came to them like rocks rolling in a stream bed
and one by one they stood up shading their eyes watching
    those black islands turning slowly in their places
and three more canoes appeared and were coming toward them
    the paddles out to the sides flashing too slowly for wings
and again they went with offerings the same ones
    they had been holding the first time and they stood along the sand
waiting pointing out things to each other and they saw
    in one of the canoes strangers with brighter colors
and one of them kept telling the others what to do
    then when the prows were near shore strangers jumped out and began
pulling the canoes to land and still the people stood watching
    until the stranger who seemed to be the high chief
swung his white legs over the side of his canoe
    and set his black feet down beside the water's edge
then they all knelt down and lay on their faces touching
    the hot day in the sand and heard the stranger say
something that sounded far and calm and Aimaku stood up
    and saw the stranger slightly below him hold out
his empty hand and repeat what sounded like a greeting
    and Aimaku swept his own hand toward the shore behind him
and turning to the stranger said—You have a house here—

20.

If the stranger were a god he would understand
    Aimaku was sure of that and it was clear to him
in a moment that the stranger did not understand
    Aimaku waved to the people with offerings
and they came forward holding out the gifts they had brought
    reaching out to the strangers and staring at them
both the men and the women watching them as intently
    as a heron with its eye on the water but the men
and the women were watching them differently and the strangers
    kept looking at the women's breasts as they took the gifts
and turned to pile them in the canoes and they turned back
    to look at the women and go on looking and then their chief
said something to them and facing Aimaku he made
    a gesture as though he were drinking and the strangers
rolled out a round wooden box with iron circling it
    and raised it so that water dripped out and it was empty
as water gourds are empty after any trip
    and Aimaku had the men help unload more of those boxes
and he and Kanalu led the strangers' chief to the pool
    of good water and he directed the men to help
fill the containers with water while he took the chief
    and the chief's companions up the valley to the place
of the gods with many of the people following them
    and everyone lying face down as they passed by
there Aimaku showed the strangers the enclosure and altar
    and images watching them all and listening to them
and he could tell that they thought they understood what was there

21.

Three times during those days the small canoes came ashore
    from the tall ones that kept turning and moving closer
in the daytime and farther out at night and the men filled
    many of the round boxes with water and handed the strangers
more and more pigs to carry away and sweet potatoes
    often giving them for nothing or exchanging them
for the pointed sticks of iron that the strangers had with them
    the strangers wanted to touch the women and many
of the women wanted to find out what the strangers
    would be like to lie with and they managed to slip away
into houses or through the bushes and the women
    found out how the strangers hid in their skins and they gave
themselves to discover it and for the pleasure and for
    nothing at first and then they learned to ask for those

sticks of iron and to bargain sometimes for more than one
       so that many of them had handfuls of iron by the morning
when the black islands had vanished from the horizon
       and they shared the iron with their fathers and brothers
but after a number of days some of the women had red
       swellings where they had welcomed the pleasure and then sores
opened discharging yellow rot and the smell of dead things
       and pain spread through their limbs and on some the flesh around
the sores began to die and drop away and the men
       with whom they had lain since they had been with the strangers
began to show sores of the same kind on their bodies
       and on some of the men and women growths emerged in the shapes
of fruit or fish while the sores spread to their faces
       into their mouths and throats and along their bodies
many of them had pain passing water yet they felt
       a need to do it all the time and little water came
but occasionally a green fluid and there were rottings
       of the face bit by bit the nose falling into itself
and a stabbing in the bones a fire burning in the bones
       all day and hotter at night and the same troubles kept touching
others one by one and they would begin their dying

22.

While some were dying the heat was rising around them
       as it does from stones on a shore after the sun has gone down
but some were shivering and twitching the way a fish
       shudders at the moment of death while the chief of the strangers
whose name as they knew then was Tapena Tute
       or Kapena Kuke was eating a part of a pig
from a family garden by the river at Waimea
       having guided the two black islands northward into a winter
that did not retreat before them when the calendar
       said it was time to be planting peas in England
they had sailed up blue canyons between towering forests
       deep in snow the silence ripped by the swirling screams
of eagles and along cliffs of ice with their own radiance
       while echoes from the crags creaked and thundered around them
the hollow thump and scrape of floes crowded up to them
       never leaving through the fog halls and the frozen nights
when they could not see the stars or the black water
       mornings when they could see nothing and never
the passage that they thought they had glimpsed again and again
       believed they had come to and had found it and it was a ghost
in the future that word before language that northwest
       passage that did not exist ice hung in the rigging

solid with the sails he was rheumatic from the waist down
     he turned back south toward the islands to which they had given
the name of a person of position and influence
     on the other side of the world an earl named Sandwich
and Cook sailed to the island of Hawai'i and the bay
     named the Road of the God where he found the diseases
that his crews had brought had travelled ahead through the islands
     and were waiting for them there and there he was killed trying
to recover something that had been taken from them

                              23.

Late in the month of tangled waves a little more than a year
     after the first appearance one morning off Waimea
the black islands were there again and no one was
     surprised and no one was happy to see them the surf
was high it was dangerous getting in and they wanted
     everything again as they had wanted it before
a welcome and every provision and comfort
     at that moment and for the time to come and all of it
for nothing or almost nothing as a kind of tribute
     but the chiefs had been talking about it in the meantime
and the greeting was stolid and the prices were prices
     that grew with discussion and Kuke was not there with them
where was Kuke but his successor in the command
     Clarke spitting blood by then with consumption had cleared out
the women they had on board from the other island
     to keep the news of Cook's death from travelling with them
the people showed the strangers the sores and deformities
     on their persons urging the strangers to take away
what they had brought a few parted with pigs or salt but the chiefs
     bargained for firesticks indicating with gestures
that they required those for conflicts on the island
     and a single musket was worth the days of many pigs
and though the strangers were not gods they had powers
     known and unknown and racks full of strange possessions
glinting with the suggestion that even their touch
     would relay some of their hidden substance and the women
gathered the strangers as before and a few of them stayed out
     on the black islands and were gone when those islands were gone

24.

In his heart Cook had known there was no such passage
        but it was the kind of knowledge that is not a thing for words
and since that was what they had been sent for Clarke continued
        the commission sailing northwest the way of succession
coughing his orders keeping more and more to his cabin
        arriving at Kamchatka and there as he considered it
unlikely that his vessels could survive the voyage
        and was certain that he himself would not he confided
Cook's journal to a Russian major who had become
        his friend asking him to dispatch it across Russia
to the British Admiralty and so the Imperial
        Academy in St Petersburg knew of Cook's
landfalls and his death before anyone did in England
        and Clarke turned once more to the search along the walls
of ice and found only a route to extend
        the peeling enterprise that by then had crossed the continent
marked by mounds of rotting animals born into fur
        considered only as skin trapped for it and screaming
into a time of contagions until they were all but gone
        from the lakes and rivers from the forests and the forests
in turn were going and even in dreams the animals
        were harder to see and by the time Clarke was groping
along the Aleutians island by island the sea cows
        the Russians had found there thirty-odd years before
already were nearly extinct the meat was like beef
        the fat of the calves could hardly be told from fresh pork fat
they fed upon seaweed they had no fear of humans
        a hunter could walk to them in shallow water and lay
a hand on them large hooks were put in them and rope parties
        of thirty dragged them ashore with those in the boats
beating on them to exhaust them while they groaned
        and the blood shot up in fountains and the others
would come to try to help by unhooking or breaking the ropes
        floundering after them and staying near them even when
they had died and all with no voice but the breath they groaned with

25.

It had been said that they were there merely for the taking
        so they had been taken but Clarke's crews came upon
sea otters sitting in the waves and families of seals
        easy to kill and they kept the furs and recorded
the locations to come back to though Clarke on the way south
        died before they reached Cathay the goal which the Genoese

had sailed for the true China they anchored in the crowded
        harbor of Macao and found that the furs they had with them
were treasures commanding prices they could scarcely credit
        because those in power in that country and those with wealth
dreamed of draping their persons their families their
        concubines beds saddles all that betokened them
with furs of other animals and the English officers
        Portlock and Dixon could see the fur trade crossing
the Pacific by way of the Sandwich Islands
        where ships could stop for provisions of food and water
salt and firewood and in Macao they smelled wood dust burning
        with a fragrance they thought familiar and then they remembered
a similar fragrance from the fires beside houses
        in Waimea and the merchants in Macao inquired
whether the English could bring them wood of that kind
        which they valued highly its name proved to be sandalwood
so that when they came back to Kauai with their first cargo
        of furs they let the chiefs know that they were looking
for the fragrant wood and the payment could be in guns

26.

Along the river above Waimea the English
        admired the family gardens laid out with great skill
and judgment the trenches bringing fresh water to the fields
        the taro ponds intersected by embankments
stands of bananas fences of sugar cane the houses
        set among mulberry trees with a designing sense
the English said was almost scientific and all tended
        with care and diligence that would have reflected credit
on even a British husbandman and the cane
        was fine and equally cheap the taro the finest
obtainable anywhere superb roots for an eight or a tenpenny
        nail their industry in supplying us with everything
in their power was beyond example their eagerness
        to do acts of kindness and their hospitality
were unbounded But each visit seemed to leave new
        sickenings invisible spells against which they had
no defences epidemics that overtook them
        like flood waters each one arriving with its own
alien heat its cold shakings aches and eruptions
        smells discharges scales constant incontinence
unexampled discolorations and deformities
        starings wild speech chokings and blackenings before
death and still the people flocked to the shore welcoming
        each visit and paddled out to the vessels to hold up

offerings wanting to go with them to see that Britain
        where it was coming from and one who left with them was a chief
Taiana taller than the English a handsome man
        and shrewd who went with the furs to Canton where the English
colony made much of him dressing him like one
        of themselves having his portrait painted he found there
a Hawaiian woman Waineʻe who had sailed
        from another island as a servant to a captain's
wife but had taken sick and stayed and he remained there
        for some time to the great pleasure of the English
and bought knives axes saws carpets cloth iron entire sets
        of china and guns and ammunition to take home

27.

The English supplied him besides with whatever might be
        useful to his country such as bulls cows sheep goats rabbits
and when in his time on a later vessel and with
        a different captain Taiana attired and cheered by
His Majesty's subjects in Canton sailed east for the islands
        he insisted on taking with him that sick woman
Waineʻe having promised that he would see her home
        but she died at sea and they wrapped her in a sailcloth
that had seen the world turn and dropped her over the side
        and the captain told Taiana that he would repeat
a prayer to the true god in English and Taiana
        looked at the clouds and the horizon and from the depths
of his voice called softly to Kanaloa older
        than all the names he had survived Kanaloa from whom
all worship and all forms had washed away Kanaloa
        the beginning and the end death and the west and the sea
the rays of the octopus the sleep inside the shell
        of the coconut riding the currents of himself
—You Kanaloa Kanaloa—he called under his breath
        —I have returned your fish to the ocean and said go back
take her back to Ulukaʻa to the island turning
        out of sight in the night sky where there are women waiting—
Then once again he was the only one with his words
        and since when he had left there had been threats from other
chiefs his enemies he feared they might be in power at home
        and when they arrived at the island of Hawaiʻi
he learned that it was so but a young chief of that island
        named Kamehameha who was already a favorite
of the war god welcomed Taiana's knowledge daring
        and all those possessions and weapons into his own ambition

28.

When a sorcerer is projecting harm in secret
        small fires are seen at night sometimes flying across the sky
as Taiana knew and he knew that it is not fortunate
        to see them but even more dangerous are those fires
whose flight cannot be seen like trains of powder smoldering
        he had been troubled in Canton when first he saw beggars
he had wanted to feed them all and he was shocked by the deformities
        and mutilations among them and at Macao
around the fringes of the marketplaces he was looking
        at one of the hidden fires burning there among the Chinese
some of whom were taken as crew carpenters shipwrights
        even purchased by the head from India to sail
to Alaska for furs and among them they carried another
        disease to Hawai'i that would bloom like blood in a stream
he had seen that fire and not known it but now he kept
        close watch on the way of Kamehameha who tried first
to procure from the same captain who had taken Taiana
        two Chinese carpenters to build him a warship
and failing that he had them construct on his double canoe
        a platform and mount on it a small swivel gun
which he would use in the coming invasion and conquest
        of Maui and all that time the women were kind to
the carpenters wherever the ships went but as for Taiana
        before long he had had enough of Kamehameha
and left him and joined the forces gathered against him
        but the swivel gun followed him and Taiana was killed
at Nu'uanu when they were all driven over the cliff

29.

In a time of blood fountains when the chiefs were at war
        on all the main islands Taiana with his imposing
presence evident gifts and knowledge of the world
        and an audacity that had frightened Vancouver
into thinking that the young chief might seize the Discovery
        perhaps was hoping through alliance and strategy
to make himself ruler of his own disputed Kauai
        where the rightful high chief was scarcely more than a boy
whose regent after repeated struggles had many
        enemies but the cliff battle left Kamehameha
and the small reverently sequestered carving
        of his war god in dark red kauila wood in command
of all the main islands except Kauai and he was hungry
        to invade at once despite the exhausted state

of his own army the wreckage and the starvation his wars
  had left everywhere and the reluctance of his own chiefs
and he brought together the largest army and fleet
  there had ever been in the islands and he offered
human sacrifices on the altars of Kū
  before that midnight in late spring when they pushed off
to attack Kauai and its young chief Kaumuali'i
  his superior in birth and in every grace
but the night wind struck the invading fleet in mid-channel
  sinking so many canoes and drowning so many
that Kamehameha in bitterness gave the order
  for the remnants to turn back and that was the first time
and then for years he gathered forces and wrung the islands
  to provide a still larger fleet for another attempt
and as they were about to embark from Oahu
  they were hit by a sickness that would kill a man in the time
it took to go and fetch water and the bodies turned black
  his army was dropping all around him and he was sick
almost to death and lay thinking of Kaumuali'i's
  mother who was known to have a prayer of such power
that it was spoken of in a whisper all through the islands
  and he knew in his fever that it was she who had done this

30.

Whatever allowed him to recover did not leave him
  the same ever afterward and he would not again
attempt an invasion although the armed men who might
  have opposed him on Kauai could not have withstood him
but he could not rest without Kauai numbered among
  his holdings and he fell back on ruses and offers
made with one hand and on promises he whose name was
  The Lonely One he of whom no one could be certain
whom no one could trust he who on his own island
  of Hawai'i had invited his last rival there
Keoua to a meeting to talk about ruling
  the island in peace and as Keoua landed
he was speared and then all his companions speared except one
  and Kamehameha had soon married the daughter
of the man who had speared him and that was Ka'ahumanu
  and so Kaumuali'i had neglected to answer
Kamehameha's proposals for him to rule
  Kauai as an untroubled island tributary
of The Lonely One and when the invitations came
  from Kamehameha he had replied by sending
emissaries with gifts and garlands of fine words

but had stayed home with his faithful friends and felt the looming
of that Other with the islands lined up behind him
          and the nature of a moray waiting and it took
two brothers from New England named Winship a brace
          of sea captains to bring Kaumuali'i to meet
Kamehameha in Honolulu and set foot ashore
          after both chiefs had performed a duet of accord
but an Englishman in that place warned Kaumuali'i
          of a plot to poison him and he left for home at once
and they poisoned the Englishman yet the brothers Winship
          had arranged enough peace for their own purposes
which involved cornering the traffic in sandalwood

31.

Most of twenty years it had taken to assemble
          that fragrant pyre from which there would be no returning
it had been hard to deal with the chiefs during the fighting
          when they needed men for raids and were unreliable
about schedules and contracts with one eye all the time
          on the next step in the match and the first sandalwood
sent to China from the islands had been of a kind they did not
          esteem there so the price had been low and the merchants
in Canton kept it down by insisting that all the wood
          that came from what their shipwrights already were calling
The Sandalwood Islands was of poor quality
          but of some ten species of santalum found from eastern
India through the Pacific four distinct kinds
          were native to Hawai'i in the drier forests and once
they were common varying in shape from tough bushes
          and in some places vines to trees fifty feet tall
always occurring in symbiotic relation
          to a host tree often the Hawaiian acacia koa
and of the kind prized for commerce it takes forty years
          for a tree to acquire down near the root a core of heart wood
where the sweet smell is housed and the whole tree must be cut
          at or below the ground to obtain a short length of it
all the rest for the most part they left where it fell
          and as long as Kamehameha lived he and Kaumuali'i
enjoyed the profits thus taken from the islands under them
          while the ruin went before them and climbed the mountains

32.

The chiefs bought on credit to be paid in sandalwood
  and the chiefs' collectors dug the commoners out of their
family gardens and sent them farther all the time
  into the steep forests with axes to fill the quotas
of sandalwood notching tallies but even the records
  lasted no longer than smoke although in some places
a unit of measure remains a hole in the mountain
  that the men were told to dig there at the beginning
its shape and dimensions those of the hold of a ship
  which they would fill with heartwood for the next cargo
the men were given little or nothing to eat
  and they ate whatever they could find in the forest
they were given nothing to wear on the mountain
  nothing to cover them when they lay down after dark
on the ground in the cold some were weak with the new
  sicknesses and their farms went to ruin while they were gone
famines followed in waves named for the bitter roots
  they learned to eat each time near starvation and when the cut logs
carefully stacked filled the holes the wood was loaded
  onto their backs held in place by a rope that ran
across the shoulders and under the arms each load
  weighed one picul a Chinese measure of one hundred
thirty-five pounds and the scars from the rope and the bark
  remained on the men's backs for the rest of their lives
but some died there among the trees some on the trails some reached
  home for a while as the demand for the wood quickened
and the debts mounted and it is legend that the cutters
  pulled up every sandalwood seedling they could find
but Kamehameha bought sailing vessels and cannons
  and assorted merchandise Kaumuali'i bought a brig
sets of china uniforms more things than he could keep track of

33.

Even so there were those who lived to look back upon
  that time as a last moment in their own bodies
a familiar face falling away far below them
  no one could have measured how much waited upon the life
of the opaque Kamehameha with his heart
  of kauila wood until all at once he was not there
and Liholiho his son the heir to his imperium
  at twenty-two had his father's demanding manner
without his authority whereas Ka'ahumanu
  the dead chief's favorite of his twenty-one wives

had will enough for any deed and made for herself
        the post of prime minister enlisting others
among the widows to play Liholiho like a fish
        in the shallows until he sat and ate with them
and with that one meal ripped irrevocably
        the merciless web of caste and ceremony
of ritual and dread and sacrifice and coherence
        the kapus that maintained the power of the war god
and of the chiefs themselves a fabric that had been
        decaying for longer than anyone could remember
but much faster since the foreigners had first breathed on it
        and the widows may have imagined that the rending
of this fretwork of fear and distinction would allow
        women access to further power but the power
even as they held it turned into a ghost and escaped them
        appearing out of reach while the god of the powerful
foreigners appeared to many in the strangers' wealth
        and their impunity long before the year when the chief died
and the grip of the kapus was broken and many were
        curious about this stranger god by the time the first
boatload of missionaries embarked from New England
        summoned late in time to save unknown souls from their lives

34.

They were allowed to stay for the time being at least
        perhaps they would be permitted to set up permanent roofs
for teaching their lessons in righteousness and reading
        though nothing in their gray probity pleased the widow-in-chief
and on Kauai Kaumuali'i welcomed two of them
        mainly because they brought back his son George who had been
sent to school in New England as a boy though the money
        for his schooling had vanished along the way and the heir
to Kauai had apprenticed as a carpenter
        worked on a farm joined the US Navy held a job
in the Boston Navy Yard acquired a reputation
        for outlandish behavior but was homesick and ready
for the ride back with the bearers of glad tidings
        and the missionaries to Kauai raised their tabernacles
and George who of course had been named for the King of England
        moved up a valley with a random following
of hopefuls to pursue a good time and then one morning
        two years later an open boat appeared offshore
bearing the young chief Liholiho and his retinue
        and he and Kaumuali'i exchanged fulsome assurances
and after Liholiho came his sumptuous brigantine

with its own history as Cleopatra's Barge bringing
his five wives and the two chiefs sailed around the island
        sightseeing and feasting for forty-two days and nights
until one evening at Waimea after more than two months together
        at the end of a feast on Liholiho's yacht
the anchor was quietly weighed and without a word
        the vessel set sail for Oahu with Kaumuali'i
given no answers all night as they crossed the channel

35.

In Honolulu he was treated as a guest of state
        he assured those who asked that he was returning a visit
but this time he could not leave and the abduction
        apparently had been planned by the ruling widow
Ka'ahumanu who put the island of Kauai
        into the custody of her brother and forced
Kaumuali'i four days after his arrival
        to marry her then soon afterwards made his son
by his royal wife become a husband of hers also
        and having thus tied up the family line she toured
the islands showing off all her pets on their strings
        taking with her a retinue of a thousand or so
her vast self borne on occasion in a whaleboat held high
        on a grid of spears in the fists of seventy warriors
but when she fell sick the missionaries ministered to her
        with a certain success which they nursed without sleeping until
her conversion whereupon she kept Kaumuali'i
        as her only husband and he then sickened and grew weak
he was dying and delirious and the will taken down
        in his last days left what he owned and what he owed
to Ka'ahumanu and Liholiho and then he died
        to be buried in the uniform of a British hussar
with foreigners saying that he had been handsome courteous
        dignified honorable and beloved and on Kauai
the news of his death released a ground swell of disaster
        there was wild mourning and the succession was dubious
nobody could be certain about keeping the land they lived on
        some feared the chiefs from the other islands the cabinet
of Ka'ahumanu and some hoped that Kauai
        might be left to itself again as it used to be
after the summer solstice that year came an eclipse of the sun
        and the missionaries kept saying that it meant nothing

36.

Kaumuali'i's son George after he had returned
        with the missionaries from his hand-to-mouth education
was a disappointment to his father from the beginning
        a shiftless abusive arrogant drunkard who burned down
a whole building in Waimea when the shopkeeper declined
        to give him a bottle of gin but he soon acquired
a large like-minded following of those who had nothing
        after the diseases and the sandalwood ordeal
had torn up families and left the terraces untended
        and they listened as George ranted after the kidnapping
of Kaumuali'i and more of the disaffected
        of the island more of the uncertain and the covetous
the gamblers and holdouts gathered around him and made him
        their figurehead although George himself had no great
mind of his own and when the first governor came
        from Ka'ahumanu George would have been willing
to get along with the fellow but his own followers
        talked him out of it and a week later at first light
a party of them attacked the company from Oahu
        quartered in the fort near Waimea and they called upon
the whole island to rise—It is ours—they shouted and then
        retired to sit in the shade some miles away leaving ten
of their own and six from Oahu dead and they did
        nothing more as the reprisals began and schooners
brought troops and volunteers in growing numbers to rub out
        what they called the rebellion and after a single skirmish
they began a slaughter that did not spare women or children
        shot bayoneted speared mutilated left to rot
and they caught George drunk and shipped him to Oahu to die
        and went on with a meticulous hunt for the families
of the chiefs of Kauai to root them out entirely

37.

It was not an impromptu havoc but an ancient
        rancor whose moment had been heating for a long time
children of the chiefs on the other islands had grown up
        hating the chiefs of Kauai who had once claimed
the entire chain except Hawai'i itself and they all knew
        that the genealogy of the chiefs of Kauai was older
and loftier than that of the recent leaders
        of the younger islands to the east and the latter were never
allowed to forget it even the legends often
        began on Kauai and ended there and Kamehameha

was one of the later chiefs with whom the others
> had aligned their fates so that the failure of two
giant invasions of Kauai was beyond forgiving
> and besides Kauai for generations had given refuge
to those running from battles or feuds or shifts of power
> on other islands and the pursuers remembered and went on
caressing their weapons and waiting for the day
> to cut down Kauai and so it was accomplished
and afterward the island was carved up and given
> to the kin and followers of Kamehameha and some of them
drew the income in absence and some moved to Kauai
> and established themselves as the missionaries
had been doing and other alert and enterprising
> foreigners merchants ship chandlers in the early days
of the whalers and one of the missionaries began
> to make sugar and molasses at Waimea
and encouraged the Hawaiians to grow sugar for their own good
> and thus the sugar business became part of the Lord's work

38.

Since the missionaries on O'ahu had managed
> to coax the widow-in-chief Ka'ahumanu
into the fold before Kaumuali'i died
> at his funeral everyone sang The Dying Christian
in Hawaiian and a flock followed after her
> into the faith so that the day of righteousness seemed
to be breaking upon the heathen or what was left of them
> after four decades and more of falling like leaves
of being carried off by new sicknesses that kept coming
> from the horizon first the venereal that began
in welcome and grew like gossip mutilating
> and repulsive then the varying succession
of fevers poxes boils and of running at every
> orifice the swellings sores coughing breathlessness
blackening and emaciation and the constant pain
> and foulness the bewildered burials when everything known
in heaven and earth every cause and expectation
> and the gods themselves were suddenly insubstantial
like smoke or the air clutched in falling a time when those
> who still had strength for growing taro and mending terraces
and sluices and cleaning the channels were compelled to travel
> far into the mountains for the receding sandalwood
nothing to them but costing their lives and when the land
> that had been theirs without ever belonging to them
seemed to be slipping away through their hands like water

and on Kauai the chiefs of the island whose word
had been the way the world was and whose ancestry led back
    into the nights before creation had all of them been cut down
even their infants dismembered and the hacked pieces
    desecrated so that nothing was left of the past
or of the future and they had come to where they had nothing
    this was the moment into which the missionaries
translated their promises of lands beyond death
    and in this life the substance of the island began to pass
into the keeping and plans of strangers whom the Lord
    had led there to make something out of the waste places

39.

Not all the new landholders from the islands to windward
    were retainers of Kamehameha's who had shared
his long coveting of Kauai the ancient the aloof
    the island apart there were those among them who were mere
fringes on the skirts of the reigning widow watchful
    idlers happy to join in the hunt when the cry went up
and to flail in the battue of the chiefs and carve up
    first the limbs then the spoils among themselves but later
when the destruction had unstrung the common survivors
    around the island and weeds wrapped up the taro terraces
famine followed sickness and the lands themselves rendered
    grudging return to the alien claimants some of whom
moved in among the ruins and tried to resume
    a semblance of the old life and it came to be part of them
others listened to foreigners and picked up the parlance
    of leasing while the hungry who could do a day's work
were taught to labor and be paid in credit and the streams
    were turned out of their former veins into alien
enterprises there were plantations of coffee
    wide marshes of rice and the irresistible poison
and imperial promises of sugar with the volcanic
    sounds and smells of its mills the lands around them flowed into them
all that had lived in those places flowed into them and the taste
    was sweet nothing and meanwhile on the mountain the cattle
that the first captains had brought as presents for the chiefs
    ran wild trampled and multiplied and the horses
that had come in those early years grew in numbers
    and the ranches of the foreigners spread like a change of climate

40.

While the sandalwood trade was shrinking during the years
        after the death of Kamehameha the debts
of the chiefs continued and they climbed like the stakes
        of hapless gamblers until foreign warships arrived
insisting upon collection and the government
        assumed the debts and levied taxes to pay them
then the landed chiefs' sole remaining wealth was the land
        which no one but they could own but they could allow
the use of it as they had always done for payment
        of some kind agreed upon verbally at first
and the enterprises of the foreigners were based
        upon such agreements at the beginning but as more
was invested in them greater security
        was demanded by the speculators there were contracts
in writing of course and for lengthening terms and then
        no more than a single lifetime after the masts
of Cook's vessels had appeared off the coast at Waimea
        a commission was appointed at the insistence
of foreigners to determine the real ownership
        of all the lands in the kingdom which thereafter
foreigners would be able to purchase outright
        on the same terms as Hawaiians but it was a manner
of thinking about the land which only the foreigners
        understood and after ten years when the commission's
Great Division went into effect the control
        of the lands of Hawai'i was in the hands of foreigners
who had title to the greater part of them allowing
        a portion for the chiefs and their overseers though that might be
further reduced upon claim and then there remained
        fragments for the people still living in the valleys
whose ancestors had built the walls of the terraces
        and who had been lucky and had been told what they
had to do and what building they had to go to
        what room to find what table to stand in front of and there
had said what their names were and described the stones and marks
        by which you would know the places where they had been born

BORN

Born in a dark wave the fragrance of red seaweed
    born on the land the shore grass hissing while the night slips
through a narrow place a man is born for the narrows
    a woman is born for where the waters open
the passage is for a god it is not for a human
    the god is a gourd full of water and vines climbing from it
there the forest rises to stand in the current of night
    with time moving through it and the branches reach out
into darkness the blue darkness at the sea's root
    it reaches up through the current of time and holds
the night sky in its place while in the sea the child
    of the hilu fish is born in the night under the tides
the child floats through the seven currents it is already
    someone to bow to in awe born is the sandalwood tree
on land the guardian of the whale in the ocean
    born Kanemahuka to remember the sound
of the stream at Poki'i and voices by the low fire
    talking about a killing born is Keawe in the valley
of Waiaka whom he would hold in his arms Keawe
    to remember crying above the rushing water
the burials along the valley the mourning from doorways
    born to them both Kaleimanu to remember
the smell of oxen and of crushed sugar cane in the mud
    born is Nakaula to remember spears stacked by the door
and whispers about canoes at night born Kawaluna
    to remember the cave her grandfather showed her alone
where he had hidden the sacred images and to remember
    the sound of guns close by and shouts of strangers and screams
and blood on bodies under the trees born is Ho'ona
    to remember the island of Hawai'i the sea cliffs
at Onomea and the donkey trail to the landing born is Kukui
    to remember drums and her mother dancing born is Kepola
to remember the shadow of smoke born is Ko'olau
    to Kaleimanu and Kukui in a new year
a month of long waves born is Pi'ilani to Ho'ona
    and Kepola in the spring in the time of the flying fish

2.

When the stream from the falls at Waipao wound among rocks
     all the way to the sands at Kekaha there were still
a few thatched roofs beside banana trees half a lifetime
     after the chiefs of Kauai had been hunted down
and after the age of murders and dying from hunger
     and from unknown sicknesses and the going for sandalwood
and after the great distributing of the lands
     for the sake of the foreigners a few of the old
terrace walls were still in repair along the watercourse
     with the sluices cleared and taro at different stages
as though everything were the way it used to be
     and the children thought that was how it had always been
but it was all made out of pieces salvaged from ruins
     hauled out wept over huddled among for years shored up
with the old knowledge but not the old assurance
     families still fished when the nights and the seasons were right
and when the first ranchers tried sheep on the plains toward Mānā
     Kanemahuku and Nakaula and their sons all went
as shepherds rather than work in the cane fields or the mill
     Kukui's first child was born in those days a daughter
they named her Kamaile but she lived only one day
     then in a few years Kukui was in labor again
and it seemed she was dying the midwife was her mother
     Kawaluna who kept massaging her moving with her
telling her to think of red seaweed and that the child
     would come when the tide turned and as she was saying it
the preacher Rowell was riding past on his way
     to a house where someone had died and he heard the moaning
as he passed the door and he stopped to ask whether
     he could help and Kukui thought he had called her by name
he said a prayer over her and left and when the tide turned
     she gave birth to a second daughter Niuli
and Kukui was sure she owed both lives to his prayer

3.

Kawaluna was of an older mind than her daughter's
     but she said nothing and she watched over Niuli
with unwavering tenderness from the day she was born
     the child's name came from Kukui who said she had heard it
during the red hours in labor and she told everyone
     about the preacher appearing in the doorway
with his black clothes and white hair and saying her name
     she talked about him with friends of hers who knew him

he had lived in Waimea since she had been a child
        she remembered the times she had seen him at burials
and people in Kekaha whom she had known all her life
        had gone to his church but she had never spoken with him
she decided she wanted to take Niuli
        to his church in Waimea for him to put a blessing
on the child as he had done for some of the others
        in the village and one morning they put on
their best clothes Kukui with the baby and her husband
        Kaleimanu and her father Nakaula
and her mother Kawaluna and family and friends
        they walked along the cart road with the sun in their faces
toward Waimea hearing the terns toss their grace notes
        over the surf and then the note of the church bell
and they stood in the shade outside the building and greeted
        people they knew and showed them the baby and went in
to stand up and sit down when the others did and they heard
        the loud singing and went up for the blessing when they were called
and Kawaluna watched it all like an owl in daylight

4.

It was the new church that had just been finished the one
        they all called the foreign church although there had been
a foreign church at Waimea since Kukui's parents
        were young and they had told her of the missionaries
first arriving and bringing the high chief Kaumuali'i's son
        home to him and they had told her of the house the chiefs
had them build for the foreigners and of the white faces praying
        toward their feet that was long before Kukui was born
Nakaula and Kanemahuku had guided ox carts
        that brought the cut coral limestone to build the first church
and the big house for the missionaries that seemed to be one
        house on top of another and they had driven other oxen
when their hair was white to bring the stone for the new church
        and the broken coral to burn for plaster and whitewash
and the church walls still smelled of lime with the procession
        of sunlight squares moving over them slipping down to the sounds
of the voices but none of the family had been
        inside the church since it was finished Nakaula
pointed out to them down there in front Valdemar Knudsen
        who they knew had the big ranch at Waiawa now
and near him the new Judge Kauai whom they had all heard of
        a Hawaiian with his wife beside him and their clothes
looked so beautiful to Kukui that she thought they were
        shining people and after the service when they all went out

and stood under the trees talking to friends the Judge
     and his wife came over to them to see the baby
and how handsome the Judge was the women thought and how lovely
     his Hawaiian wife was they agreed and on the way back
Nakaula said there was land above Makaweli
     that was hers from her father who had been given it
by Ka'ahumanu herself and that was good land he said
     and Kukui smiled without thinking about anything

5.

That evening they set out a feast and the village gathered
     bringing food and they sat looking across the terraces
toward the sea after the sun went down and the wind dropped
     they recalled building the church and the oxen the mules
mule stories and the way Nakaula talked all the time
     to animals—Oh yes—he said—you have to keep them
listening to you and they listen in different ways
     so you speak to them differently as you speak to
foreigners differently—then they considered Kauhiahiwa
     the old man in Waimea who had been there when the first
goats and pigs that Kuke brought had been put ashore
     on Ni'ihau and when the first cows and horses
had been brought to Kauai for the chiefs and Nakaula
     showed how Kauhiahiwa imitated the animals
coming from the ship onto this strange land where there had been
     only dogs and little pigs and rats until then
so when the new animals came people were glad to see them
     and Kauhiahiwa had followed them watching them
he was the one who looked after Reverend Rowell's
     cows and horses and talked them down to the river
in the mornings and told them to swim across to the pasture
     and called them back in the evening and Nakaula
said that as a child he had followed Kauhiahiwa
     and listened to him and learned to speak with the animals
which he would rather do than hoe in the fields toward Mānā
     when the tobacco was there or bend in the cane fields
or work in the mills and they sat late around Niuli
     talking about what had gone on before she was born

6.

Then they talked about the new Judge Kauai and how old
    he might be for he had not been born on the island
and he was still a young man and they considered the story
    that he was descended from the high chief Kaeo
the old ruler of Kauai and half-brother of Kahekili
    and Nakaula turned to his father Kekiele
who kept the times straight in his mind the time when they
    hunted the chiefs of the island in the valleys
above Koloa the time when they built the fort
    the time when they erected the gallows at Waimea
and hanged three men and one woman north south east and west
    and buried them beside the platform while old Father
Whitney stood by the graves reading prayers from his book
    the time when the coughing came over them and Kekiele
repeated to them how Kaeo and Kahekili
    had ruled before Kamehameha and how Kaeo
had ruled Kauai until the death of Kahekili
    and how Kaeo on his way home from Maui
had been attacked by Kahekili's son on Oahu
    and the foreign ships had joined in and killed Kaeo
he told of the mourning when they had learned that the chief was dead
    Kekiele had been a young man then and he had seen
the sky turn dark and then they considered the Judge's
    kin on the island and what lands each of them had
and the Judge's wife Kaenaku and her lands
    at Makaweli and then the lands at Mānā
that the Norwegian Knudsen had come to take over
    a few years back after the tobacco failed there
and of the cattle he had and the horses he had brought in
    they talked about Knudsen and about his horses

7.

Nolewai Nolewai some of them had heard him say
    Norway the land he came from wherever that place was
somewhere in the great cold and different from Scotland
    or England or America which people from the island
had sailed to Norway was farther than any of them
    and colder and Valdemar Knudsen laughed much more
than the missionaries and he sang songs from Nolewai
    that were not like the hymns and Eleao who had been working
for Knudsen planting foreign fruit trees and diverting water
    through Waiawa said they all liked Knudsen who asked them
what the name was for everything and older men came

to see Knudsen and stay at his house and they picked flowers
not to wear nor for medicine but to talk about
    and draw pictures of and pull apart and write about
they shot birds not to eat but to measure and draw
    and count the feathers and they asked their names and Knudsen
rode out with some of his guests to the shore and to caves
    where they dug up bones and whatever else they found there
they asked about them in Hawaiian and talked about them
    in other languages and took them away and the people
at Māna had told him they did not want him to dig there
    for the bones of their ancestors but old Puako
took Knudsen to Keoneloa and other sands
    where there were bones to dig and he told long stories
about fleets and battles and Knudsen wrote all that down
    and not a word of it was true and they wondered how Knudsen
could believe Puako who had always been happy
    to lie to anyone who would listen to him
one more reason they said why Knudsen needed a wife

8.

One of the sounds that Niuli would remember
    from her childhood when that time had vanished behind her
a sound that she could not name when first she recalled it
    and could not be sure she had heard while she was
awake and could not tell when it had come to her
    for the last time before it was only remembered
was the light hollow patter of small hooves running on stones
    and the crying of sheep the same few cracked notes making
question and answer somewhere between bird and child
    and she remembered hearing them talk about sheep
and the smell of sheep and the sight of them like pale shadows
    shifting in the glare out toward Waiawa and the cliffs
and then they were not there and had not been there a long time
    and nobody spoke of them and the one time she asked
her father Kaleimanu about them he said only
    that they were gone and it was just the cattle now
out there and the horses and the talk was of cattle and horses
    and of work in the sugar mill at Kekaha and she thought
the sheep must have been in a time before Koʻolau
    was born and that sound like water on its way over pebbles
they told her that she was three almost four when he was born
    she remembered the rain drumming at night and her mother's moans
and the baby crying and Koʻolau as a small face
    in Kawaluna's lap and the sounds of horses then
and a crowd of people standing out under big trees
    then Koʻolau's voice later when he was a child

9.

Through those years Kukui always spoke of the Reverend
        George Rowell as a kind of guardian spirit
partial to her in particular though he never again
        rode past their door and she had been back to church only
when a friend of theirs took a child to be baptized
        and one time for a wedding but her mother
clearly went there with reluctance and her husband Kaleimanu
        explained that the foreigners in the congregation
disapproved of the natives calling The Reverend
        Father Rowell the way the men who worked for Knudsen
called him Father Knudsen the foreigners were afraid
        that with a minister it might be mistaken
for the way the Catholics at Koloa who were Christians
        but the wrong kind of Christians called their priests Father
but the natives at Waimea went on calling Rowell
        Father he was George Berkeley Rowell who had come
from Cornish New Hampshire and Andover Seminary
        sailing in the Tenth Company of Missionaries
with his wife Malvina Jerusha and his brother
        Edwin on the brig Sarah Abigail a voyage
of one hundred forty-three days and had watched his brother
        die almost at once upon their arrival and when
they had settled on Kauai had listened while his wife
        gave birth to seven living children he was something
of a doctor and helped with the deliveries
        something of a carpenter and oversaw the building
of the big church at Waimea something of a farmer
        and kept cattle and a mixture of stock and he
had a big garden up the river at a place named Kakalae
        where he grew mangos and loquats oranges bananas
even peaches by the bucket and for an outing
        the family rode up the valley to the garden

10.

After Ko'olau was born Kukui wanted
        to take him to the church in Waimea to be baptized
but her father Nakaula who drove mules most days
        into Waimea and back told her it might not be
as easy as she imagined because he had heard
        angry talk from members of that congregation
about the pastor's behavior Nakaula
        was a close listener and he said there were many
who would hear no complaints against Father Rowell
        and grew heated in his defense but there were others

who insisted that the pastor was breaking the church laws
    they said he was neglecting his duty to perform
the ceremonies including The Lord's Supper
    that he welcomed as members of the church anyone
who wanted to come without examining their belief
    and kept no church records and had said in public
that too much reliance had been placed upon matters
    that were formalities and that he saw no reason
to question his congregation about their faith
    or to insist on church ceremonies but thought it enough
sometimes to play to them on the melodeon
    and let them sing if they wanted to so the trustees
with Judge Kauai and Valdemar Knudsen among them
    were announcing that Rowell was not fit to be called
a minister of the faith and Nakaula
    told Kukui he would have to ask whether the pastor
was still performing baptism and he seemed surprised
    some days later to inform them that Father Rowell
had said he would not refuse baptism to anyone

II.

By then there had been a church at Waimea for most
    of four decades and long before Kukui was born
first there was the grass shelter by the beach standing open
    toward the sea and then the wooden room with its echoes
dwarfing the sounds that made them and its hollow darkness
    and odor of mortality then the stone upon a stone
set in sand in the salt smells of sweat and mules and unkindness
    world without end as they sang at the time and then
what they called the great stone church that was more of the same
    but its name was still the Foreign Church and it represented
somewhere else it was a long walk from the Kekaha house
    that Nakaula and Kaleimanu had built
from boards they had fished out of the harbor for Knudsen
    that had come from New Zealand as ballast and glittered
with salt where the sun bleached the top ones on the loaded
    mule cart that dripped half way up the mountain toward the house
Knudsen kept adding to and he gave them enough
    for the two rooms and roof and porches near the shore
where Koʻolau was born it was too far for Niuli
    to walk or to be carried and they took the mules
and the wagon and some of them rode and some walked behind
    with friends and when they got to the church this time they were
all watching somebody some were watching Father Rowell
    to see what they could see some watching Judge Kauai
and Knudsen and the ones that Nakaula pointed out

    as the trustees and when the pastors announced the sacrament
of baptism they all stood up and walked to the front
    with two other families and Kawaluna answered
first when Father Rowell asked the name of the child
    to be baptized and she watched his face as she told him
the whole name beginning with the grave and he looked up
    and asked—Is it a night name—and she said—It is his name—

12.

When she turned to the rows of faces she looked directly
    at Judge Kauai and his eyes were on Koʻolau
awake in Kukui's arms and gazing up at the sunbeam
    that crossed the room and when they filed out of the church
to the playing of the melodeon and stood talking
    with friends who had gathered to see the child Judge Kauai
and his wife Kaenaku came over as they had done before
    both of them tall and stately in their beautiful clothes
and Kukui was sure the great chiefs must have looked like that
    moving the way clouds move and they paused in front of Kukui
to admire the baby and Kawaluna listened
    to the Judge's voice asking Kukui—What do you
call him yourself—and she watched his face as Kukui smiled
    and said—Koʻolau—and then the Judge said—Koʻolau
Aloha Koʻolau—then the melodeon
    stopped and they heard the leaves stir at the end of it
and the terns calling out past the sand and the Judge waved
    good-bye to his friends all around them and was gone
and they were on the wagon bench going back to Kekaha
    and they caught up with Kepola whom Kukui had played with
when they were children and Kepola was with a stranger
    they were going along more slowly than the mules so they
fell behind and Nakaula said over his shoulder
    that the man was Hoʻona who had come from Papaikou
on the island of Hawaiʻi something to do with sugar
    but whether it was the sugar or Kepola
that was keeping him on Kauai nobody seemed to know

13.

Niuli looked after Koʻolau from the beginning
    and they all said it was Niuli who taught him to walk
she put his clothes on him and she took them off and they talked
    to each other when no one else understood the sounds he made
they splashed in the shallow lagoon where the stilts waded

and she washed him and dried him as her mother had done
they touched and clung to each other and he followed her
        wherever she went and Kaleimanu watched them
play with the dogs and he taught her to be careful
        around the mules but he caught them both up on the oldest
mule and took them riding in the summer evening
        friends calling to him from the end of the day and the first
owls gliding out from the ravines over past Waiawa
        where he worked most days for Knudsen and later when
he could understand what both the children were saying
        and they wanted to ride the mule by themselves he settled them
astride the warm withers and for an instant that was gone
        before he could grasp it he breathed the day of the mule
with no age to it no story no reward and he led them
        along the sand toward Mānā where old friends he seemed
not to recognize with the late day shining on their shoulders
        were casting their nets in silence and drawing them back
intent and moving like waves with sometimes a call coming
        across the water and the gulls flashing and shrieking
Koʻolau shrieking to the gulls and smoke climbing far behind them
        from the sugar mill and fading upward and Niʻihau
its own shadow on the horizon he came to wish
        those evenings had been every evening and when he came
home from one of them after Koʻolau began to talk
        Kukui told him that Kepola had come to visit her
to let her know that she was going to have a baby

14.

And they stood smiling in spite of everything they knew
        and could not know and Kaleimanu asked her—Is it
the one from the sugar mill from Papaikou there
        from Hawaiʻi the one with the clothes—because they had
noticed the way he was dressed that day on the way home
        from church those clothes that looked as though they had never been
worn before and had nothing to do with a place like this
        the dust and the midday glare that bleached the colors
out of the day on all sides like a white shadow
        in which those clothes remained bright as a fire and stayed
in everyone's minds when they had ridden on out of sight
        and afterwards whenever they had seen him he was
dressed that way like somebody with news and maybe
        he had been going each time to visit Kepola she had
been a quiet one when they were children Kukui said
        not wild with the boys like the others and she laughed
—His name is Hoʻona—she reminded them for

the future and Kepola had said that he wanted
to marry her in the church and he had been taking her
      to church every Sunday and Kepola said she liked it
—I like it too—Kukui said laughing and Nakaula
      and Kaleimanu were sitting listening as she
told them all that Kepola had said Hoʻona
      was important—No—she said—not important I mean
he is serious—and she pronounced the word slowly
      like a new thing to admire—Well—Nakaula said
—I suppose that is all right maybe he will take care of her—

15.

Nakaula wondered whether Father Rowell
      was performing weddings now and Kukui said
she was sure he was because he had married Keoniki
      only a few months back—And it is important—she said
and Nakaula said—I remember Keoniki's baby
      was nearly born then——Maybe Kepola's will be too—
Kukui said—Just as long as they are married in time
      that is what matters——Two eyes and a nose—Kawaluna said
—and one mouth—and they let it rest there until some weeks later
      when Kukui announced that they were all invited
to the wedding which she said Hoʻona himself
      had arranged with Father Rowell and they took the mule wagon
to Waimea on the eleventh day of the moon
      called Huna or hidden because the horns then are hidden
it was the day Kepola's mother Nahola had chosen
      and it was clear that Hoʻona was well acquainted
with Father Rowell and with Mrs Rowell who played
      the melodeon for the service—There was none of that
when we were married—Kukui said to Kaleimanu
      —We just stood there and said what he told us and held the pen
while he pushed our hands on the book and that was that—
      —This is more like his clothes—Nakaula answered
and afterward on the beach when they were all eating
      pig and fish Kepola told them that Father Rowell
had made Hoʻona a member of the church and one
      of his close assistants—When is it coming—Kukui asked
looking at Kepola's waist—In two months maybe—
      Kepola answered and it was a night in spring
the night of Hua the egg the moon almost full
      when she went into labor and Hoʻona wanted
Father Rowell to be there because he was a doctor
      but Nahola sent for Kawaluna to deliver
the baby a girl whose name would be Piʻilani

16.

—You hear the owl just when the baby was coming—
        Kepola's father Kapahu asked Kawaluna
—I did—Kawaluna answered looking at his eyes
        which she had known at every stage of his life—Good thing maybe—
Kapahu said and she nodded and gave him the baby
        —She is a good thing—Kawaluna said—Look after her—
and she took away the umbilical cord and as
        the stars were fading she hid it in a hole in the rocks
then she walked down to the sea and in the light before sunrise
        she stood in the water chanting as the waves broke
—You mountain of Kane island of the ancestors
        I have washed away the blood now you wash away the blood
it is for the spirit to watch over her it is time
        for the spirit to come with wings and watch over her—
Then in a few days they brought Niuli to see the baby
        and Niuli began right away to take care of her
as she had taken care of Ko'olau and the three
        children grew up together and when they were playing
with the other children they stayed together it was less
        than ten years since the last wave of sickness the fever
and weakness the skin breaking out in pustules they called
        smallpox had killed so many of them and had taken
it seemed all of the children then and Kaleimanu kept thinking
        of that time as he watched them playing and he felt
that he was holding his breath as he saw them rolling
        in the edge of the sea and as he looked at Ko'olau sitting
up high on the old mule and felt the reins in his hands

17.

Nakaula and Kaleimanu picked up threads
        of news from Knudsen's ranch at Waiawa and Hofgaard's
store in Waimea and from friends coming and going
        and they followed the game of land trading between
Knudsen and Judge Kauai who had his family
        out Makaweli way and up toward the mountain
not a convenient location for his work at the courthouse
        he owned land here and there on the island some of it
through his wife Kaenaku and some that he had acquired
        in his days as tax assessor and the way that he
and Knudsen worked it out Knudsen got the land up toward
        Makaweli which was where he finally settled
and Kauai got the stone building and the land surrounding it
        at Kekiaola in the middle of Waimea

not far from the church and he moved his family into town
      Knudsen and the Judge remained friends and both attended
the church where they got along worse and worse with the Reverend
      Rowell who managed to have Judge Kauai removed
from the Board of Trustees and publicly demanded
      the return of the church keys which the Judge refused
arguing that Rowell's proceedings were in violation
      of the laws of the church which he quoted as the voices
rose into the koa rafters and the congregation
      took sides some with Dr Smith but most of the natives
whom the pastor had admitted without examination
      siding with Rowell and the pastor put new locks
on the front and back doors of the church and denied entrance
      to Judge Kauai and his party which included
several foreigners and many who were members
      of the congregation in good standing first he shut
the door in their faces and they heard the new locks close
      and the next time they came they found the doors boarded over
and the pastor standing there holding a hammer and nails

18.

And then there was the matter of the melodeon
      which the pastor had ordered to be sent out from Boston
some years before and Ho'ona had learned the details
      from Pastor Rowell himself one day when Ho'ona
was whitewashing the walls inside and the pastor explained
      that the melodeon was his own property purchased
upon his order by a congregation in South Hadley
      Massachusetts which had recently installed one
of the same make in their own church the price of the organ
      was two hundred and fifty dollars and the dealer
in Boston deducted the sum of twenty dollars
      because it was being bought for the mission field
and the gentleman who selected it a Mr
      W R Wright of North Hampton waived his commission
and a Mr Harford collected fifteen dollars
      to contribute to it and a Mr Smith another ten
and a further three seventy-five for the insurance
      and the pastor had sent a hundred and fifty
of his own money and the balance later which sums
      were never repaid him so it was his melodeon
but Judge Kauai et al sued him on the question
      of who owned the church itself and who was entitled
to lock up the property and Pastor Rowell
      lost the case and appealed and the supreme court then ruled

that he had neglected church ordinances and The Lord's Supper
        and had regarded baptism as unnecessary
the covenants as useless and for aught that appeared
        had disregarded even a declaration
of belief in the Holy Scriptures and he therefore
        had forfeited his relation to the church altogether
as had those whom he had encouraged and who sustained him
        the church was not his nor was the melodeon
and the doors were opened but by then Pastor Rowell
        had resigned and he and his own congregation
were building themselves a church nearby independent
        of the Board of Foreign Missions and there he started his school

19.

Nakaula and Kaleimanu had been using
        Knudsen's mules and their own to move Judge Kauai's household
to the stone house in Waimea on the days when the rains
        that year allowed them to make the journey through the mud
and the swollen Waimea River and they were hauling
        loads for Pastor Rowell for the new church the sandstone
foundation blocks cut with axes each stone the length
        of the yardstick and half as wide and a span thick
they drove the wagons up near the smoking lime pit
        and they took the mules without the wagons up the mountain
to drag back the tie-beams and rafters and they and the children
        were present for the Judge's house-warming and again
when Pastor Rowell held his opening service in the new church
        the foreigners were divided over that but Knudsen
the Gays the Robinsons of Waimea and Dr Smith
        of Koloa had stayed with the pastor in the end
and Ho'ona had heard them agreeing that Pastor Rowell
        had views far ahead of his time and they spoke with approval
of the new school for native children which Mrs Rowell
        was planning to teach and Ho'ona said he wanted
Pi'ilani to go to that school and he asked
        Kaleimanu about Niuli and Ko'olau
but they were all too young and Mrs Rowell could not
        manage the rough children so that Pastor Rowell himself
was the teacher by the time they were old enough to attend
        Niuli liked the company Ko'olau hated the school
Pi'ilani did her lessons without a word

20.

Whatever the pastor pronounced to them in that voice
        that was not the one he talked in and not the one
he spoke in when he stood up during the church service
        and not the one he used for English with other foreigners
whatever words the pastor uttered from the moment
        they walked through the door onto the dead wood each syllable
of their own language articulated so carefully
        that it did not sound like their own language at all
not only because every sound that he uttered
        with that round deliberation was always wrong in his
particular way but because it was coming from those
        particular clothes that face mouth regard that way of turning
and staring at them and because those words although they
        were like the words of their own were really arriving
out of some distance that existed for him but not
        for them and they could hear it echoed in his children
who went to Dr Dole's school in Koloa with
        the rest of the foreign children and who were never
allowed to play with the little natives as they
        had heard themselves called but who spoke the language without
that foreign wrongness and even so they were only
        partly in what they were saying and the rest somewhere
out of sight like hands making shadows the air in the room
        was hard to see through like water but they repeated
the names of the solitary letters that they
        said every day the threads of a seamless garment
and he showed them what each letter looked like it was
        white whether large small straight or flowing and it was
in itself silent in a black sky where his hand drew it
        and it stayed there meaning a sound that it did not have

21.

They learned to draw the white lines themselves and repeat
        their names in the order the pastor said was the real one
they learned to pray with their eyes closed and say together
        that they believed in the only god and his son who was killed
back when nobody remembered and he taught them
        that the old gods had never been and he taught them names
of numbers and how numbers behaved with each other
        Niuli stared at him but she saw the white dog lying
under the back step when they left for school and they
        were laughing about something as they were going past
the wet canoe dripping onto the sand and she smiled

trying to remember why they had been laughing
and Pastor Rowell asked her to answer his last
    question and she said—I believe in one god and I
believe in my father—and she stopped with the pastor
    looking at her pebble to pebble and he told them all
that other foreigners would not be so patient with them
    as they would find out if they had not yet learned it
then he pronounced the word Indolence in English
    three times very slowly and then molowa molowa
molowa and told them that is the source of vice
    and of misery and death it is the mother of disease
he said improvidence brings on decay and is rotting
    your people you must learn to want more than you have
it will elevate your characters I have seen your beds
    on the damp ground in the dirt the dirt Koʻolau had stopped
thinking about punching Makuale with whom
    he had been having fights on the way home from school
and he was thinking about disease and what he had heard
    from the boys in Waimea about a sickness
as close as Koloa that was different from the others
    it had got into a man whom one of them knew who lived
down by the harbor and if they said you had this sickness
    they arrested you no matter what you told them
and they put you on a boat and you never came back

22.

He forgot about Makuale on the way home
    and when they were almost there he saw his father
Kaleimanu down by the canoes with somebody
    he had never seen and he thought they were going fishing
and he wanted to go out with them and when he got there
    —This is Kua—his father told them—You remember
me talking to you about Kua Papiohule
    who works with me at Father Knudsen's at Waiawa
and trains the horses for Father Knudsen—they looked
    up at a tall thin man who smiled and repeated
each of their names in his quiet voice taking his time
    Kua said—You are going to school can you read books yet—
and Niuli looked at her feet—What are you learning—he asked
    and Piʻilani wrote an A in the sand and stood up
pointing to it and said A and he nodded—You are
    teaching me now—he said—And I would like that—and turning
to Koʻolau he said—Your father tells me you like horses—
    —I like horses—Koʻolau said—But mostly I know mules—
Kua said—Maybe some day we can all go out

to Waiawa and you can see what you think of the horses—
Kaleimanu said—We have been talking about the news
     from Waiawa Father Knudsen is going to be
married at last it took him a long time to find
     the right one and we used to wonder whether he
would ever do it—and the men laughed—Who is she—Niuli asked
     —Miss Anne Sinclair—he said to her—And her mother
is Mrs Sinclair who owns the island of Niʻihau
     and two years ago bought most of the land division
of Makaweli from Victoria Kamamalu—
     and Kaleimanu said—It appears that Father Knudsen
had Miss Sinclair picked out years ago and all those trips
     to Niʻihau in the whaleboat looking for birds
and eggs and flowers he had Miss Sinclair in his mind
     and all through those land arrangements with Judge Kauai
out toward Makaweli he had his eye on her—

23.

—The right one—Niuli said—What does she look like—
     —Oh she is a beautiful young woman—Kua told her
—and plenty of men have been hoping to marry her
     and she loves horses she is good on a horse she rides
like a cloud——Is that why he wanted to marry her—
     Niuli asked and Kua said—I think there may have been
some things besides that although the sight of her
     at a gallop out there on the sands would not be
soon forgotten but there were some who were trying
     to catch her who I think have no eye for horses
there was more than one of those studying men who visited
     Knudsen and went over to Niʻihau with him
looking into books and drawing pictures of the plants
     growing over the rocks who were watching her their voices
would change when they talked to her and they say that when
     she first came with her mother from New Zealand and they
sailed into Honolulu in their own vessel—
     Kua spoke to Niuli as though he were telling her
a story in which anything was possible
     and he said—they had sailed all the way to Vancouver looking
for land enough for themselves and had found nothing
     to their liking but wherever they went the young men
all wanted to marry Miss Anne from the time they stopped
     in Tahiti at the beginning and the British Consul
begged her to marry him and in Honolulu
     the King and Queen Emma invited them to all
the banquets and dances and she could have married

just as she pleased and her mother could have had
the lands at Kahuku or Ewa with the island
    in the harbor but she chose the island of Niʻihau
and Miss Anne gave her hand to Valdemar Knudsen
    though he is older than the others and they talk about that
but Knudsen says they can talk if they like for the choice
    was hers all along and that is how it looks to me—

24.

—When can we go and see the horses—Koʻolau asked him
    —I will come and tell you—Kua said to him and they all
walked with him to the shade of the milo tree two horses
    stood there one a handsome bay with saddle and bridle
gleaming and Koʻolau stood staring at that one—Is he
    yours—he asked Kua and Kua said—Yes—lifting his hand
to the black mane—Knudsen gave him to me when he was born—
    Kaleimanu said—And the saddle Kua made himself—
—Could I learn to do that—Koʻolau asked Kua
    —You could if you want to—Kua answered—I want to—
Koʻolau said and Kua told him—When we go to Waiawa
    we can talk about that and we will see what your father says—
Then he said good-bye and mounted leaving the other horse
    under the tree behind him it was a fine chestnut mare
—Whose horse is this—Koʻolau asked—Mine now—his father said
    —Kua brought her down from Knudsen's where I was riding her
when I worked up there and Knudsen says I am going
    to be working there most of the time so I should have her—
—And keep her here—Koʻolau asked—In the family—
    Kaleimanu told him and he unhitched the reins and said
to Koʻolau—Go on then—and nodded toward the horse
    and Koʻolau got his bare foot up into the stirrup
and scrambled into the saddle with his feet swinging
    and his father led the horse on home but Niuli
stood watching Kua riding out toward Waiawa
    and then Piʻilani started home and Niuli went with her
they kept asking each other questions about getting married

25.

Niuli questioned her mother quietly about Kua
    where did he come from and grow up where was he living
did he have any family any sisters a woman
    —Ask your father—Kukui said looking sideways

at Niuli—He knows more about Kua than I do—
    but it was Niuli's grandfather Kanemahuka who said
—I knew his family out there by Kaumakani
    his grandfather was with the chiefs of Kauai
he was alone with Deborah Kapule at the time
    of the slaughters at Hanapepe and he was killed then
by mistake they said some kind of mistake——And his
    parents—Kaleimanu told Niuli—both of them are dead
they died in one of the foreign sicknesses long ago
    and he had an older sister die at the same time and then
he was alone when he was younger I think than you are
    and he was out at Hanapepe down near the harbor
trying to help when they were fishing and help with the horses
    that is how he managed then with the fishing and taking care
of the new horses and that was his school he picked up
    as he went he knew old Kauhiahewa who calls
the animals for Father Rowell he seems to know
    everybody on the long road he has been to the house
of the chief Deborah Kapule he can sing
    a song he has heard once Archer had him looking
after his horses and then Knudsen kept those horses
    and Kua with them when Knudsen was just beginning
and now the Waiawa horses and the horses at Makaweli
    there are so many you will never see all of them
and Kua knows them—Kaleimanu said and Kukui
    was smiling at Niuli—He is too old for you—she said
Niuli looked at her feet—Father Knudsen is older
    than all the others who wanted to marry Miss Anne—
—she said—But he is the one she wanted to marry—

26.

Ko'olau was doing badly at school the fighting
    was more interesting than the learning and he listened
from farther and farther away when Reverend Rowell
    started over the numbers or the words of the Bible
Pi'ilani and Niuli were doing better but he
    wanted to leave though now it was Kaleimanu
his father who wanted him to stay—What will you do then—
    he asked Ko'olau—If you stop school—and Ko'olau said
—I want to work with the horses and make saddles
    and Kua will teach me——What have you learned in school—
Kaleimanu asked him—You have not learned how to learn
    Can you read yet can you write yet—and Ko'olau answered
—I can read and write now—and Kaleimanu asked him
    —What can you read now——A little—Ko'olau said—That is not

enough—his father said and when he was next at Waiawa
　　　he talked about it with Kua—The boy should be able
to read and write—Kua said—He is going to ask me
　　　whether you can read and write—Kaleimanu said
—I learned what I could here and there—Kua said—and I can read
　　　a little but it is not enough and I can write my name
and a few words but not easily and it is not
　　　enough tell him and so when he can read and write
so that Father Rowell says it is good then I will
　　　teach him other things—and when Koʻolau heard that
he astonished Reverend Rowell with his attention
　　　and before long he was reading and writing
better than most of the others at school and the pastor
　　　said to him—That is good that is good—and Koʻolau waited
until Reverend Rowell was saying it without
　　　surprise as something that he expected and then
he said to Kaleimanu—Go and ask Father Rowell—

27.

It was when the still days of summer were gone and the light
　　　at every hour held the reflection of something never
visible as the glaze does in the eyes of someone
　　　remembering a time not there the good winds were back
the trades out of the northeast coasting along the ridges
　　　cool and lifting the heart and it had been raining
at night as it does most years during the autumn
　　　in the time named Hilinama a season returning
to an old happy way of doing things that had been
　　　forgotten for some reason now vanished at last
and in the clear sky of morning bright clouds were racing
　　　westward across the mountain where at every turn
of the climb streams were splashing down among the black rocks
　　　though the trail was not yet muddy with the long rains
of winter and as they wound through the woods and along
　　　the edge of the canyon picking their way on the path
threads of voices a phrase here and there flicked past them
　　　like the flutter of wings in the trees and they were caught up
without seeing that it was happening to all of them
　　　in a moment of beginnings unrepeatable
and brief as when a number of planets seem to burn
　　　in the same place though the depth of the sky is around each one
so the beginnings were with them unnoticed as their breathing
　　　Anne Sinclair was seeing the vast cloven green-towered
mountain that she would soon love as fiercely as any place
　　　on earth and would summon up as she lay dying

in the dry light of a distant continent but as she
        rode there at the start of her life with this inquisitive
viking she had chosen for a husband she was gazing
        again down at the bay at Craigforth in New Zealand through woods
on the hill before they had been cut all the way to the sea
        and Knudsen whose youth seemed to have returned entire
saw himself climbing through the high fjords as a boy
        in Norway hearing the glacier streams and the birds of a short
far summer and Kua who could sense a new time arriving
        in the life around him felt the light hands of those he had
watched dying one after the other when he was a child
        and pain rose up without faces and at moments the faces
without the pain and Ko'olau to whom the day
        the mountain the horse under him the presence of Kua
the occasion the company the forest were a complete
        world was surprised to catch sight of himself sitting
in Father Rowell's schoolroom and what startled him most
        was the feeling he had of watching a fish escape him

28.

He talked of it afterward as though it were what he
        had grown up to do and to know the riding and the sound
of the forest the learning from Kua the kindness
        of Knudsen and of Miss Sinclair her face and her voice
that made English sound new and easy and the gun
        that Kua taught him to hold when they hunted the wild bull calf
the fire beside the cabin at Halemanu and after the hymns
        that Knudsen got them all to sing there then the other songs
they went on singing in the dark of the trees he told
        Niuli and Pi'ilani about it the echoes
followed him into the winter when he rode to Waiawa
        with Kua and Kaleimanu to work with cattle
and with horses and to hunt goats and to go with Knudsen
        and sometimes with Knudsen's guests and Miss Sinclair riding
far up on the mountain looking for birds that Knudsen
        and his guests wrote about in notebooks and for flowers
that they picked and shut into the books and he saw what Kua
        meant about Miss Sinclair riding like a cloud and he
taught Niuli and Pi'ilani small as they were
        to ride and when the date was set to announce the engagement
between Miss Sinclair and Valdemar Knudsen Kua told them
        that they were all invited to Waiawa to the party
and they all took the wagon up there on the day before
        and helped get things ready and they slept there in a cabin
and sang after dark again and Knudsen had been planning

a parade on horses in the morning and when he learned
from Kua that Ko'olau had taught Niuli and Pi'ilani
        to ride he came over to them to invite them
to ride in the parade and he told them he would find
        beautiful cloaks for them and they looked at each other
—Say you will—Ko'olau said to them and first Pi'ilani
        and then Niuli nodded but they lay awake most of the night

                              29.

Ko'olau kept to himself like a secret Kua's telling him
        that he looked as though he had been born on a horse
and that what he had to hold in his head was to stay with it
        stay with it and Kua let him ride more of the new
horses and then help with the patient training
        of the colts even though he was still a child and always
small for his age and the boy learned to handle the lariat
        until it seemed to rise into the air by itself
and wait there for him to let it come down and he treasured
        the old Harpers Ferry rifle that Kua had let him
take care of telling him that it had been through a war
        showing him how to empty it and clean the bright tunnel
touching the long cold of the barrel and smelling
        the oil the hard scent of the metal the old fragrance
of burnt powder coming through itself like a small wave
        along the sand with the whole ocean behind it
that winter Kua let him shoot goats twice on the ridges
        back from the edge of the canyon where they would be able
to get to the bodies to take them home and Ko'olau
        was learning the trails webbing the mountain the hidden
entrances and after the wedding on Ni'ihau
        there were processions from Waiawa and Makaweli
and a service at Pastor Rowell's new church at Waimea
        it was too small for everyone but they could all hear
the new melodeon that had come from Boston
        bought by the congregation and they joined in the singing
and Ko'olau helped Kaleimanu and Kua keeping
        an eye on everyone's horses and on the carriage
that Eliza Sinclair had brought from Makaweli
        and on Judge Kauai's carriage and after the service
when they rode up to Waiawa for the banquet
        Ko'olau listened to Kua and the Judge talking
like old friends and later at the ranch they were standing
        together and Kua saw Ko'olau watching them
and he pointed the boy out to the Judge who nodded
        and Kua told him good things about Ko'olau

and when the Judge spoke to Koʻolau the boy told him
       how his mother remembered the Judge at Koʻolau's christening
—Maybe I saw something good from the start—the Judge said

30.

Niuli and Piʻilani were helping Kukui
       over by the kitchen and Koʻolau saw the children
of the foreigners the Dole children from Koloa
       Dr Smith's older children and Reverend Rowell's and others
he did not recognize talking on the far side of the house
       they all appeared to be in white clothes moving there
in the sunlight but when he looked at them one by one
       he saw that was partly a trick of the light and he caught
Reverend Rowell's eye watching him and the pastor nodded
       —Are you one of Reverend Rowell's students—the Judge asked him
—I used to be—Koʻolau answered—and I learned to read there—
       —A very good thing—the Judge said—I learned to read
from a missionary on Maui when I was a boy there
       it is good that Pastor Rowell started that school of his
so you know how to read and I hope you go on reading—
       —I am working now with my father for Father Knudsen—
Koʻolau told him—You can still go on reading—
       the Judge told him——Have you ever read a newspaper—
—All we read there was the Holy Bible—Koʻolau told him
       —You should know that of course—the Judge said—but you must not
stop there I will give Kua things for you to read
       if you will read them but will you read them——I promise—
Koʻolau told him and saw that the Judge was looking
       at Reverend Rowell—Are those Reverend Rowell's children
over there—he asked Koʻolau who told him that they were
       —Do you know them—the Judge asked—They are older—Koʻolau said
—Do they go to Reverend Dole's foreign school in Koloa—
       —Some do—Koʻolau said—They have to wear shoes there—
the Judge said and he laughed—Did you and the pastor's
       children ever play together—the Judge asked—We used to—
Koʻolau said—But they were not allowed to and he gave them
       beatings when he caught them and he will not let them speak
Hawaiian because they speak it better than he does—
       —Do you think that is the reason—the Judge asked—Keep reading—

31.

In a while they would look back wondering where that
        time had gone which seemed to be theirs and to be staying
the children growing up the Knudsens at home at Waiawa
        then the big new house at Makaweli where the Knudsens
moved and their children were born and Koʻolau listening
        to the men talking in Hofgaard's store in Waimea
where he went first with Kua and Kaleimanu
        and Father Knudsen at the time when Mrs Knudsen
was expecting their first child and Koʻolau listened
        to every word there about sugar and about changing
the courses where the streams ran and about cattle and horses
        and the King and debts the place was a second school for him
and the Judge came in there and Koʻolau heard him talking
        about reducing the King's salary and about postage
and the legislature and he heard them arguing
        about whether the Chinese disease had come from China
or whether the Hawaiians had carried it all the way
        from India if they had come from India
where the disease had always been a fact of life
        and this was the same sickness Koʻolau had heard of
there at school in Waimea and the thought of it had been
        like a stain in daylight the sickness that was
a crime and if someone was accused of it that person
        would be arrested and taken somebody had been taken
from Kauai lately put on the schooner at Koloa
        in a stall with a bucket and cup to go to be judged
in Oahu and then to Kalaupapa on the island
        of Molokaʻi at the foot of the high cliffs by the sea
the place they never came back from it was the Hawaiians
        who had the disease the men said in Hofgaard's store
the Hawaiians mostly and the men more than the women
        and then they talked about whether there was ever a cure
and whether removal was the only thing to be done

32.

At Kekaha the children had outgrown playing
        together at the edge of the water although they supposed
that they had simply been busy for a while with other things
        Niuli had always been quiet serious affectionate
helping her mother with everything and Kukui
        needed her because she suffered from shortness of breath
which left her exhausted and all at once everyone was agreeing
        that Piʻilani would be beautiful that she was

already beautiful and Koʻolau heard them say the word
 and it echoed through him like a bell and he recognized
the name for part of what he had been staring at
 and he had known something of it even before they started
school when they ran naked with the other children
 and rolled in the small waves and touched each other everywhere
he had liked to touch Piʻilani more than the others
 and when they were older they would meet after dark
and lie down between the canoes then Piʻilani's father
 Hoʻona was away more and more of the time
at work at the sugar mill and in Waimea helping
 Reverend Rowell with the church work he seemed to be
wearing new clothes each time Koʻolau saw him and he brought
 clothes home for Piʻilani's mother Kepola
and for Piʻilani and sometimes they were new clothes
 sometimes they had belonged to somebody else and her father
said Reverend Rowell had given them to him
 but sometimes at night he did not come home from Waimea
and said Reverend Rowell had let him sleep there but people
 in Kekaha knew he had a woman in Waimea
and they told each other what they had heard about her

33.

At the mill Kaleimanu had heard the men laughing
 with Hoʻona about women and about what they had learned
of him when he was over at Papaikou on the Big Island
 of Hawaiʻi before he found his way to Kauai
women at Onomea women all the way
 from Hilo to Waipio wherever his errands
directed him and his good reasons for leaving
 that island just in time like the old chiefs in flight
and Kaleimanu heard it at Hofgaard's store when Hoʻona
 rode by one day in a new hat and Koʻolau heard it
in Waimea from boys he had known at school it was
 what Hoʻona was known for the usher in church on Sundays
and dressed for it Koʻolau never mentioned her father
 to Piʻilani but whenever he went to her house
he watched her mother who seldom spoke and her grandmother
 and grandfather and helped them and Piʻilani
saw what he was doing and she understood why
 and she could see that her family was proud of Koʻolau
and that they liked the two of them being together
 and wanted them to stay together she looked at other boys
all of them watching for any hint of welcome
 and she thought they were all missing something that she

had always known in Koʻolau it was already so
     when they both found themselves lifted up as when a wave
arches itself under a canoe and the whispering hull
     pauses like a caught breath and then is flung forward racing
down the blue slope that keeps curling out from in front of it
     they felt themselves hurtling in a single rush with no thought
of anything else no sense of before or after
     yet it seemed to them that they were not moving at all
and everyone around them could see what was happening

34.

Then whatever they were doing they found that they were
     singing and Piʻilani remembered the words
of the songs her grandmother kept starting again
     as she worked around the house and Koʻolau kept up
with the songs the men sang at Waiawa as they were riding
     or sitting with guitars in the evening and when they
spread out feasts at Kekaha for birthdays there would be
     a moment when they all began singing whatever
came to their minds there were chants from the old stories
     with somebody's hand beating on a hollow gourd
there were chants that were addressed to the gods there were songs
     about lovers in the rain and the wind in the cliffs
and the names of places and songs about places and the love
     that had once been there and they sang the foreigners' hymns
and songs of foreigners who had come with the cattle
     and had brought guitars Piʻilani and Koʻolau had been
hearing that singing all their lives but not as they were
     beginning to hear it on the wave that was running with them
and around Kekaha and even at the ranch those who knew
     Piʻilani and Koʻolau were overtaken by pleasure
at the thought of them and a sense that something was turning out
     right at last and that all of them were reflected in it
and when they repeated the stories they thought of Piʻilani
     the face and presence of Piʻilani and of Koʻolau
who could have been a chief they thought and one of their own
     they gathered more often as they said they used to do
in other times and in spite of all that had happened
     for a while they imagined they believed their own stories

35.

At the ranch at Waiawa and at Hofgaard's store
        and wherever else Koʻolau went they would be talking
sooner or later about the Chinese sickness
        sometimes they called it the chiefs' sickness and Kua explained
that as a child he had heard of a sickness before his time
        among some of the soldiers in the King's bodyguard
and it was said that carpenters had brought it from China
        when they came to build ships for the chiefs but no one was sure
and the talk would turn to the law now and how many
        had been arrested so far on Kauai and taken away
there was no way of being certain of that either
        for sometimes the signs of that sickness had been found
by Dr Smith or the doctor in Hanalei
        when they had been examining some other complaint
and there were those in Hofgaard's store who insisted
        that all the natives should be examined without wasting time
and they longed for the means to do it but no one wanted
        to be sent away and those who feared they might have
the disease stayed out of sight of the constables
        both native and foreign who prowled through the villages
and around the edges of towns and there were rumors
        of someone or other having been seized somewhere
on the island and carried off by the constables
        with no one to stop them and of others who had
disappeared when they had been left alone in their houses
        Kaleimanu knew one of the constables who haunted
all the settlements from Koloa to Mānā
        who said that his name was Nali but they all knew him
as Iole the rat and even when they could not see him
        they could tell when he was around by the way the dogs barked

36.

Kaleimanu had heard that this Iole came
        from the valley above Hanapepe and Kua told him
that the rat was someone like Kua who had no family
        but this one had been living by stealing before they
made him a constable and then Kawaluna began
        to talk about the people called Mū who had been there
on the island before the first Menehune arrived
        maybe it was the Mū people who set the rock at the top
of the mountain to be the altar of Kane long ago
        when they were as tall as trees and lived in the forest
and the Menehune fought with them and believed

that they had killed them all but the Mū people lived on
and from time to time someone would go into the forest
        and disappear because the Mū people had caught them
and then in the time of the war chiefs it was Mū people
        who watched for those whose faces were not on the ground
when the chiefs passed or whose shadow touched the shadow
        of the chiefs or whose arm dropped when it should have been held up
the Mū people saw them and laid hold of them and dragged them off
        to be sacrificed and Kawaluna said that those
people could disappear or turn themselves into shadows
        but they were still there and this rat might be one of them
Kua told them that at Makaweli Eliza Sinclair
        who owned the island of Niʻihau had let it be known
that the constables would not be welcome there and that she would
        not send from her island anyone who had leprosy
but would keep them clean and bathe them and nurse their sores herself

37.

When Koʻolau heard the men in Hofgaard's store talking
        about the Chinese sickness he tried to listen
without being noticed and he saw that the subject stopped
        if Judge Kauai came in as he did many days
unless he was busy in the courthouse or away
        in Honolulu at the legislature and Kua
told Koʻolau that Judge Kauai made no secret
        of his opposition to the government's policy
of seizing victims of leprosy or those suspected
        of having it and sending them away from their families
for the rest of their lives and he said that the judge
        had been trying to learn what happened to those people
at the leprosy station in Honolulu
        and at the settlement on Kalaupapa from which
they never returned and Kua said that Knudsen himself
        had spoken against the government's way of dealing
with leprosy and had told Kua that he had seen
        that sickness in Norway when he was a young man and that he
had been angry in his own country at the way the lepers
        were treated and he said the sickness was dying out there
but not because of separating the sick ones
        and hiding them away to rot and Father Knudsen
had told him that some of the best doctors now believed
        that sending the sick ones away did no good at all
Koʻolau noticed that it was the foreigners
        whom the sickness almost never attacked who feared it most
and what the Hawaiians dreaded most was being taken

away from their families he thought of that while he rode
to Pi‘ilani's house as the sun was going down
        beyond Ni‘ihau and he remembered his father
in that same light setting him on the mule when he was a child
        he could still feel the mule's warm shoulders and the bones moving
and then he walked with Pi‘ilani down to the canoes
        and she told him that she was going to have a child

38.

Pi‘ilani said that her mother had understood
        what was happening long before she did and her family
all knew before she knew and she laughed and they lay down
        on the sand laughing and watched the light go out of the sky
she said—Now I want to tell Niuli—and when she did
        Niuli cried and said it was because she was happy
and Kukui when she heard it threw her hands up and shouted
        and Kawaluna sat watching Ko‘olau and smiling
then Kaleimanu began to talk about where the children
        could live and whether they could build another room
and he was smiling and they all began to say
        good things they were thinking about Pi‘ilani
Niuli was cleaning a fish and said she remembered
        Pi‘ilani as a baby and Kawaluna said
—Your finger is bleeding—and Niuli said—Yes it is—
        and put it in her mouth—Is it bad—Kukui asked her
—I do not even feel it—Niuli said—I was thinking
        about that time then and remembering how we were all
round and small—and she stood there with her finger in her mouth
        looking at them as though she had just been asleep
then Kukui asked when they had known about it
        over at Pi‘ilani's house and when the baby
was supposed to come and she started counting on her
        fingers and started over and they laughed at her
—I am trying to see when would be good for the wedding—
        she said and she asked Kawaluna when it should be
and Kawaluna asked—Have you decided where it will be—
        —In Waimea—Kukui said—at Reverend Rowell's church—
—What about Pi‘ilani's family—Kawaluna asked
        —Do you know what they want to do and does Pi‘ilani
want to get married at all—and she looked at Ko‘olau
        —A wedding—Ko‘olau said—We never talked about that—

39.

Koʻolau thought Judge Kauai had forgotten saying
        that he would give him things to read and when he saw
the Judge now and then at the store in Waimea
        the Judge never mentioned it so that Koʻolau
had forgotten it himself when he saw the Judge one day
        near the courthouse and the Judge said to him—Come
to my office by and by—and Koʻolau found his way
        to the right door which was open—Close it behind you—
the Judge said and he took from his desk a bundle
        of papers with a string around them—You can read
Hawaiian I know—he said—Can you read English too—
        —If I have to—Koʻolau said—You have something
to thank Reverend Rowell for—the Judge told him—I have been
        saving these for you from the papers in both languages
and a few things from the legislature but I preferred
        not to pass them to you at the store and when you have
read them we can talk about them somewhere in private
        maybe here if you find my door open and now I am told
that you are going to be married——How did you know that—
        Koʻolau asked and the Judge smiled—You are a little bit
famous around here—he said—You and your beautiful
        Piʻilani that is good that is good——If you please come
to the wedding—Koʻolau said and the Judge answered—I will—
        and on the day when they came in by horse and by wagon
from Kekaha the Judge joined them in front of the church
        and they were still more surprised when Kua pointed
to Father Knudsen and Mrs Knudsen by the church door
        there had been a meeting of church officers that morning
and the Knudsens had stayed for the wedding and Doctor
        Smith of Koloa had been standing with them and was
at the door of the church as the shy faces filed in

40.

After the wedding the Judge and his wife Kaenaku
        came to the feast in Kekaha and when the singing
began they sang with the others and they stayed a while
        when the old dances started though some hesitated
at first to dance the hula in front of the Judge
        but when the Judge learned of that he laughed and clapped his hands
and waved them on to dance and Kaenaku sat talking
        with Piʻilani and with Niuli and Kukui
and then a few days later when Koʻolau was working
        with a young horse at the ranch at Waiawa he turned

to see his friend Kaʻaka from Kekaha ride up to him
      at a gallop shouting—Koʻolau Come Hurry Come—
and he rode on to Kaleimanu and Kua shouting—Come—
      and as they mounted he kept calling out—Sister Sister
they are taking her to the doctor—and as they were riding
      they tried to understand what he was telling them
the sheriff's deputy had come to Kekaha to the house
      to take Niuli away to the doctor in Koloa
and they had cried but he said she had to go with him
      the men galloped to Kekaha where Kukui and Kawaluna
were still at the house and friends had gathered there crying
      but Niuli was gone and Kaleimanu got the wagon
to drive them all to Koloa and Koʻolau and Kua
      rode on ahead and arrived at Dr Smith's house
and knocked and the deputy sheriff opened the door
      and told them that the doctor was with a patient
Koʻolau said—I want my sister—and the deputy said
      —If you create a disturbance I will put you in jail—
—We will wait here—Koʻolau said and they all stood on the steps
      until the doctor came out and they heard Niuli crying
as the wagon drove up and then the doctor told them all
      that Niuli had leprosy and that his duty forced him
to send her away on the schooner—Let her come out—
      Koʻolau said and the doctor went in and led her
out through the door she was holding her hands over her face
      then she stopped and stood looking at them while they were there

THERE

I.

There was very little there was probably nothing
 that he could promise them the Judge said there was probably
nothing that he could do once the doctor had decided
 and he explained that he was opposed to the way the problem
was being dealt with but that he could not alter the law
 and Father Knudsen told Koʻolau and Kaleimanu
much the same thing he said most of the foreigners
 in the legislature and most of the Board of Health
believed in having the lepers taken away
 from everyone else by force if need be and he told them
that their one hope for Niuli was that the doctors
 in Honolulu might disagree with the judgment
of Dr Smith or might say that she had the sickness
 in a mild and curable form and send her back
when they believed she was better perhaps in a year or so
 you can write to her he told them you can send her things
the schooner had not yet sailed but she was on it
 and as he rode from the ranch Koʻolau looked at the horizon
that he had always seen and he knew nothing there
 at the house in Kekaha they put Niuli's things
in a box and took it to Koloa to the schooner
 where she had been locked in a cabin and a constable
was talking with some men on the wharf and stopped them
 they told him the box was for Niuli and he said
—I will take it—but Koʻolau would not give it to him
 —We will give it to the doctor—he said but Dr Smith
was not at home and they found no one they could trust
 with the box for Niuli by the time the schooner
was ready to sail and Dr Smith did not come down
 to the wharf and when they called Niuli there was no answer
and then they could hear her crying coming from inside
 as the lines were cast off and the schooner began to move

2.

Twice after that Koʻolau rode to Koloa
 to Dr Smith's with the box but once the doctor
was somewhere else and once he was with a patient
 and sent the woman who was doing the housework to tell him
to leave the box there but he carried it back to Waimea
 and to the Judge's office where the Judge told him

that he himself was not the best person to arrange matters
    with Dr Smith and the Judge advised Koʻolau
to take the box to Reverend Rowell since the doctor
    was an important member of the pastor's congregation
and Niuli had been a pupil of his—But be sure
    not to tell him you came to me first—the Judge said
and Koʻolau watched his smile pass like a breath of the trades
    over the lagoon and it was Kua who reminded
Koʻolau later of the time when the pastor
    had nailed up the church doors and locked the trustees out
the Judge among them and then the melodeon business
    in the years when Koʻolau was a child and those things
are still awake in their faces Kua told him
    and you should recognize what you are seeing there
Koʻolau was thinking of that as he knocked at the Rowells'
    big house with the deep lanais and railings around
the two floors and he stood waiting holding the box
    it was Mary the Rowells' youngest daughter who
opened the door she was older than he was
    and had always seemed to him to be one of the grown-ups
even before he went away to school and now since she
    had come back he saw her sometimes at Makaweli
where she looked after the Knudsens' children
    he could tell from her face that she did not recognize him
and she told him that Reverend Rowell was not there

                                    3.

He set the box on the horse again and rode around
    to the church and tried the front door and the latch opened
he walked in and saw Hoʻona arranging flowers
    in a milk jug in front of the church and Hoʻona
turned and saw him and waved and said his name and the empty room
    echoed stirring the smell of dying and Koʻolau
wanted not to be there but he walked up to Hoʻona
    hearing the soles of his bare feet and he tried to keep
his voice small because of the echoes as he asked
    where the pastor was and Hoʻona as though he were
confiding kept his voice low too as he told Koʻolau
    that Reverend Rowell had gone up to his garden
and then he said—Your sister how terrible terrible—
    Koʻolau answered nothing and finally nodded
—I have to see the pastor—he said and turned to go
    —What is in the box—Hoʻona asked—Niuli's things—
Koʻolau told him—For the pastor to send to her—
    Hoʻona said—You can leave them here and I will give him

the box when he comes—but Koʻolau said—I will take it
    thank you—and he turned and walked back through the echoes
and rode up along the river bank beyond the village
    to the terrace walls and plots of the old days and the garden
in the place called Kakalae where the pastor grew his
    mangos and loquats bananas oranges even peaches
the pastor was alone there hoeing when Koʻolau
    rode up and he straightened at once and came over and said
—I was shocked and grieved to hear about your sister
    something so painful it is hard to understand it
but Dr Smith tells me that this has to be done
    for the sake of everyone and there is no other way
and I do not know what I can do but pray and I pray
    I pray for your sister——These are her things here—Koʻolau said
—They took her away without them and I have brought them
    to you to ask you to give them to the doctor
to send to her we do not even know where they have put her—

4.

—I will give it to him—Reverend Rowell said—and we will
    make sure that it reaches her—and he walked to the shed
under a mango tree and put away the hoe
    and picked up his black coat and hat—Will you follow me
to the church—he asked as he mounted and they rode
    in file down the path along the river where Koʻolau's eyes
kept returning to the black coat moving ahead of him
    under the black hat and he saw nobody inside them
while they passed the broken terraces and the tethered goats
    on the way to the lane in Waimea where they turned
toward the church and he saw the pastor's thin face again
    white foreign old and remote from him and he hitched his horse
beside the pastor's and carried the box once more
    into the church hoping that Hoʻona had gone home
but his father-in-law was still there and Koʻolau stood
    by the door as the pastor walked on and talked with Hoʻona
he could not hear their words until the pastor turned and said
    —Come come—and Koʻolau carried the box toward him
feeling that now he did not want to give it up
    —Have you put a letter inside for her—the pastor asked him
Koʻolau shook his head—Would you like to write something
    to send to her—the pastor asked and Koʻolau stood
silent for a moment and then nodded—You can write
    to her here—the pastor said and went to a table
behind the pulpit and took out sheet of paper
    and a pencil—Sit there and write—he said to Koʻolau

and Koʻolau was thinking that he did not want
    to untie the rope and open the box in front of
Hoʻona or the pastor either but he sat with it
    on the bench beside him and laid the paper on top
and wrote slowly—Niuli we were all there in
    Koloa we heard you on the boat we were calling you
we are all sad sad and you are here in our minds
    we love you Niuli write to us tell us what
we can send to you with the love of your brother Koʻolau—

5.

—You must fold it and put her name on the outside—
    the pastor said—Write Niuli from Kekaha
and is her name on the box—Koʻolau shook his head
    —It should be—Pastor Rowell said—It should bear her name
in large letters and not just in pencil—Koʻolau sat
    looking at him and then drew his knife from his sheath
and began to carve her name on the box in capitals
    Hoʻona watched him for a while and then said to him
in that same low voice—I will be going out to Kekaha
    some time later and I want to see Piʻilani
tonight or tomorrow if you wait we can go out
    together—but Koʻolau said—I want to go home early—
and Hoʻona said—Until I see you then—and Koʻolau
    stood up to embrace him and said goodbye and then went on
with the carving while the afternoon sunbeams crept toward him
    across the benches—I am going over to the house now—
the pastor said—You can bring the box when you have finished—
    then he went to the front door and Koʻolau heard the lock turn
—Come out by the back door—the pastor said—and lock it
    after you and bring me the key—and he held it up
and laid it on the table and then Koʻolau heard the door close
    and after that only the sound of the knife in the wood
the same wood that Knudsen had let them have for building
    the house even the whisper of the carving echoed
in the empty room and her name when he mumbled it
    under his breath and then it was finished and he scraped off
the shavings and put them in his pocket and untied
    the rope and lifted off the lid and a kind of darkness
rose over him like a wave as he opened the box
    and let the light touch the worn folded clothes that he knew
and nothing else there for her to hold and remember
    he creased the paper and set it on top and then he tried
to think of something he could put in to send to her
    but he could think of nothing else and he closed the lid

6.

Then he was at the door on the Rowells' lanai again
          women's voices from the back of the house and the smells
of cooking and when he knocked he could tell that no one
          heard him so he knocked louder and heard feet coming and the door
opened and he recognized Lali who worked there
          but she did not know him—Who is it—she asked him
he remembered Ho'ona telling how she sang the hymns
          louder than anyone with her voice somewhere up
in a tree he used to do imitations of her
          getting caught in the higher notes—This is for Reverend Rowell—
Ko'olau told her—What is it—she asked—It is for him—
          Ko'olau said—What is it Lali—he heard Mrs Rowell's
high foreign voice call from another room and then she
          appeared behind Lali the white sunken face and she said
—Are you not a student of Reverend Rowell's are you not
          from Kekaha you have grown so that I scarcely know you—
—Yes I am—Ko'olau answered—Yes your name is Ko'olau
          I remember you—and he said—This is for him
for Reverend Rowell——What is it—she asked—It is
          my sister's clothes to send to her——Your sister—she asked
—Niuli—Ko'olau said—She was a pupil of his too—
          —Was she the one they just sent away the poor child—
Mrs Rowell asked and put her hand over her mouth
          as Reverend Rowell appeared behind her—There you are—he said
—Bring it in—but Mrs Rowell turned and said to him
          in a voice like a whisper—Maybe by the other door—
—No No—the pastor said—It will be all right bring it in—
          and Ko'olau carried the box into the house
—Where do you want it—Mrs Rowell asked her husband
          and Ko'olau saw that she was afraid of the box
—Come with me—Reverend Rowell said—Yes of course it will be
          all right—Mrs Rowell said and Ko'olau followed
Reverend Rowell through the house to a room with a table
          papers spread on it books on shelves—Leave it there on the bench—
the pastor said—How beautifully you have carved her name—
          Ko'olau held out the key to him and said—Thank you—

7.

Kawaluna asked him that evening—What did you do
          with the box—and he told her he told them all and she went on
asking until he told about the doctor's house
          and then Judge Kauai and Reverend Rowell and writing
the letter and carving Niuli's name on the lid

and as he answered her he could hear his words fall with the sound
of a net dropping where there were no fish and Kawaluna
    went on asking him what else was in the room what else
was on the bench what had he seen through the window
    what were they talking about in the kitchen did the pastor
lead him out through the back door or return the same way
    they had come in and then she stopped asking and looked at him
nodding and Ko'olau said—The pastor told me
    that the doctor would be coming to church on Sunday—
—That is good—Kaleimanu said and Kukui was crying
    to herself turned away from the firelight and Pi'ilani
was putting things away and Kaleimanu told
    Ko'olau what he had done that day on the house
that they were building for him and for Pi'ilani
    he said they could almost start putting the roof on you will see
in the morning and Ko'olau and Pi'ilani
    went out to the back lanai where they were sleeping then
the child was already growing big in her and they
    talked about that and what she was feeling inside there
and they talked about Niuli and Pi'ilani told him
    that she kept thinking of when Niuli had seemed
to be so much older than they were and Ko'olau said
    that there were times when he could remember Niuli
clearly and then he would look and not be able to see her
    they fell asleep talking and there was a line of dark cliffs
and below the cliffs but above him in the light
    that came through young branches there were some people standing
against the bright sky so that he saw only their shadow side
    they were playing some game that he did not understand
passing something around among themselves that asked
    the person with whom it stopped—Who are you—and a man's voice
said—The new arrivals go on playing that game—
    and he saw that the one with whom it kept stopping was
the new arrival who was not a woman but a man
    who turned in anger and pulled a young tree to the ground

8.

Through those days Pi'ilani and Kawaluna
    grew closer together they recognized some likeness
in each other a way of looking at daylight and darkness
    and when either of them laughed everyone paid attention
Kawaluna told Pi'ilani about things
    she never spoke of to anyone else and she taught her
something of what she knew of the healing powers of plants
    ways of touching the life in the body and of hearing it

and breathing strength into it she showed Pi'ilani
    bright designs to watch in the night sky lights that her father
had pointed out to her from the time before the tide of slaughter
    and Ko'olau and Kaleimanu put the roof on the new house
so that Ko'olau and Pi'ilani could move over there
    but when Ko'olau was away at Waiawa Pi'ilani
went over to spend the day with her mother or to be
    with Kukui and Kawaluna and when Ko'olau
went to Waimea he stopped to see Father Rowell
    who told him that he had given the box to the doctor
and the doctor had sent it on to Honolulu
    to the hospital and he had heard nothing since then
then one day as he stopped at the church to talk to the pastor
    there was a foreigner by the door watching him
a man taller than he was and thin with eyes like metal
    maybe about as old as Kua he remembered seeing
that man in Koloa fixing a door on the doctor's house
    and later at Makaweli with the foreigners
the pastor saw them looking at each other and he said
    —Louis do you know this young man he was a fine student
of mine when he was much smaller and now everyone says
    he is one of Valdemar Knudsen's most trusted men
his name is Ko'olau—and to Ko'olau he said
    —You must have heard of my son-in-law Louis Stolz
my daughter Mary's husband you know—and Stolz let his eyes rest
    on Ko'olau's bare feet and then raised them to his face
nodded and said—I am glad to meet you—speaking
    in English which he pronounced so that it sounded
to Ko'olau the way those foreigners spoke it
    who brought in new cattle sometimes from the boats in Koloa

9.

Once he had met the man Ko'olau kept hearing
    about him Ho'ona told him how helpful that
Mr Stolz had been to the foreigners in Koloa
    working as a carpenter with his brother when they first
came to the island a few years back they had made
    that balcony on the doctor's house with the shaped railings
and those upstairs windows toward the harbor on the Doles' house
    and he had become friends with the Pastor who took
pleasure in making furniture and had all those tools
    arranged in his workroom where he kept them as bright
as the spoons in the kitchen and the Pastor let Mr Stolz
    work with him there making arches for inside the church
that was how Mr Stolz met Mary when she came home

from Makaweli on Sundays she was already
old enough for people to be wondering whether
        she would ever be married and that was the way
it happened that Mr Stolz became one of the family
        he even built the bed there for when they would be married
then Kua told Koʻolau that this man Stolz had
        some cattle of his own now that he kept out there between
Waimea and Makaweli and he called himself
        a rancher in Hofgaard's store and Koʻolau met
Judge Kauai on the street in Waimea and the Judge
        asked him whether he had been reading and he said yes
and the Judge said—I have more for you but never mind coming
        to my office this time for I have retired in favor
of my son who is now Judge Kauai the second and I am
        the Judge in name only so if you come by the house
out on Koloa Road in a while I can provide you
        with some more to think about Have you heard from your sister—
—No—Koʻolau said—We will talk about that too—the Judge told him

                                10.

A house still unfinished in a grove of mango trees
        half a dozen dogs barking as Koʻolau rode up the lane
the Judge was sitting at a table on the deep lanai
        in his hat with the broad straw brim and the band of pheasant
breast feathers around it that he seemed never to
        take off now that his hair had turned white and Koʻolau
saw how heavy he was becoming the chairs complained
        when he sank into them and the floor gave when he stood up
—You have been out here before the house was here I expect—
        the Judge said and Koʻolau said—There used to be cattle—
—It used to belong to Eliza Sinclair—the Judge said
        —We exchanged years ago you know I have been playing
peck and peck with land for years and now there is this Stolz
        got the land next door before I knew it was going
must have been Rowell passed him the word and he was quick enough
        do you know him——I met him—Koʻolau said—Keep an eye
on that one—the Judge said—Came here from California
        with his brother a few years older who took himself
away to Maui up country to Makawao where I
        come from so I hear about him I feel as though I had
bugs in my shirt with the two of them this one would like
        to carry the whole island in his pocket and the natives
should thank him for honoring them with his presence
        California is not where they started from they went there
with a cargo of hides I believe have you heard how

he talks with that accent from South America they were born
in Argentina and grew up there and his parents
　　came from Germany so he is a foreigner
among the foreigners and wants them to believe
　　that he is the same as they are Well did the Doctor send
the box to your sister——Pastor Rowell told me he did—
　　—And where is your sister now——We have not heard He sent it
to Honolulu where they take them but we have not heard
　　anything from her or about her since they took her—
—You will learn something about the place from these papers—
　　the Judge said—and I will see what else I can find out—

II.

—I cannot say whether I will be going over
　　to the legislature in Honolulu again—the Judge said
—I have made my troubles here and there I have not agreed
　　with all the agreements and there are those who have not
forgotten the time a while back when I stirred up
　　that commotion over the manner in which the voting
was conducted and I threatened to have the ballot boxes
　　called into court and opened and counted in public
you can imagine that some were displeased with that idea
　　and in this matter of leprosy I have listened
and have read what I could find about it ever since they
　　talked the old king into signing the law that was supposed
to get rid of the sickness by getting rid of the sick
　　rounding them up and shipping them somewhere out of sight
they were afraid that having the occasional leper
　　in full view would upset the delicate feelings
of foreign visitors and discourage them from bringing
　　their money here but it was never foreigners
who suffered from the law they were not the ones who were taken
　　by this sickness and deformed by it and lived with it
and died of it no from the start it was the people
　　of the islands the blood of the islands that were being
got rid of it was our families that were being
　　broken up once again and we had been disappearing
into the sand ever since the foreigners came here
　　right here to Waimea hardly more than a hundred
years ago and now leprosy and this law and many
　　now keep insisting that this is the only way
keeping the lepers apart from the righteous but it is not
　　getting rid of the sickness they keep finding new cases
they say that by this means the lepers will get the best
　　medical treatment but they are not curing them
Gibson himself says they are simply herding them together

and feeding them but even the Queen now believes
that it has to be done and they sent her cousin
    to Kalawao for a while and still there are doctors
who argue against doing this and say there are better
    ways to deal with this and why should you know all this
I am not sure what can be done but if it did not matter
    for us to know they would not keep us from finding out

12.

—The schooner goes whether I am on it or not—
    the Judge said—and there are many ways of inquiring
have you spoken about this to Mr Knudsen——He knows
    that they took Niuli and afterward he told me
he was sorry to hear it but he knew it was the law
    and there was not much that he could do about it
and then he told me about Mrs Sinclair over
    on Ni'ihau refusing to let the government
send over and take the lepers off the island—
    —Yes I have heard about that too—the Judge said to him
—and it may be true or was true once but she is not young
    and these days she is over here most of the time
up there at Makaweli and the government cares
    little about Ni'ihau since the foreigners never
go there anyway unless the Sinclairs or their
    relatives invite them over there I expect Knudsen
is sympathetic and will go on trying to learn
    it was a doctor in Norway who found the germ
too small to be seen that makes leprosy and I know Knudsen
    reads medical papers from Norway—Ko'olau stood up
and thanked him—A fine horse that one you have—the Judge said
    —He is—Ko'olau said—but he really belongs
to Mr Knudsen though he is mine for now—and he rode
    back through Waimea and on out along the shore
toward Kekaha thinking as he went that he had just heard
    the voice of Niuli coming from inside the schooner
in the harbor at Koloa and he told himself
    that it was the stilts crying across the sand but it was not
the voice of stilts and yet it flew along beside him
    like the stilts with their long wings flashing into the light
and as he came to Kekaha he saw Kawaluna
    sitting looking out to the west toward the blue shadow
of Ni'ihau and she heard him come up behind her
    and stop and when he spoke to her and dismounted
she did not look at him at first and then she said
    that she was sitting between Niuli and Pi'ilani

13.

He told her of his asking and learning nothing
    about Niuli and then of the voice just as he was riding
toward home though he thought it had been only the stilts calling
    before sundown and Kawaluna nodded—It may be—
she said—You see the birds now flying all around us
    the shore birds and the terns out over the shallows and the owl
down from the valleys in the daylight Pi'ilani
    is near her time——Has it begun—Ko'olau asked
—Not yet—Kawaluna said——Maybe tomorrow
    maybe tonight sometime she does not know it yet
or maybe she knows it and has not said anything
    you know how she is there she is with Kukui do you
see the owl now—Ko'olau turned to where she was looking
    and saw the gray wings sailing along the edges
of the lagoon like a shadow through the dry notes
    of the insects shrilling the hour and the long quavers
of the toads the heron's bark the low hushing of the surf
    the owl swung through them and circled back without a sound
Ko'olau noticed that he had stopped breathing as he watched it
    as though the owl had held his breath and when he turned
to Kawaluna whose eyes were still following it
    he thought that she herself was the owl sitting there and when he
looked back he could not see it but as he looked for it
    Kawaluna was standing beside him—Time to go—
she said and they walked out from under the branches
    toward the houses and he thought how lightly she walked
his grandmother his mother's mother how she floated
    over the sand he heard his own footsteps and the horse
behind him and he looked at her as he had turned to her
    all his life to feel sure at the sight of her and she was
looking out ahead of them and said—Pi'ilani—
    and then he saw Pi'ilani in his parents' doorway
watching them come it was that night she went into labor
    not for long and the child was born before the ghost dawn
it was a boy and small and cried with a small voice

14.

In the morning shadows Pi'ilani and Kawaluna
    filled the room with a slow undercurrent of comfort
Pi'ilani remembered the way a canoe coming in
    rides at last the front of the wave toward the sand
the baby lay still and looked like a hatched bird lying
    asleep against her breast as Ko'olau stood over them

—Get out of the way—Kawaluna kept telling him
        and when she had gone out and walked down and into the sea
and stood there as she had done after each life that she had drawn
        into the daylight she came back with sea water running
from her feet and she took the cord from the navel
        to the place where she had hidden Pi'ilani's
and Ko'olau's years before and she came back and bathed the child
        again and Pi'ilani bathed herself and put on
a new dress as Kukui stood holding the baby then Pi'ilani
        asked Kawaluna—Did you find a name for him in the night—
and Kawaluna shook her head and Pi'ilani asked
        Kukui the same question and Kukui shook her head
Kaleimanu was in the doorway smiling at the child
        —I want him to be named for your father—Pi'ilani said
to Ko'olau—I want his name to be Kaleimanu
        so that he answers to the same name as his grandfather
and if he grows up to be like him that would be a good thing—
        and they cared for the baby so that their friends laughed and said
that the boy would never learn to walk if his feet
        never touched the ground and each of them holding him
was overtaken by thoughts of Niuli of whom they
        heard nothing but for all Pi'ilani's nursing her child
he stayed small as a fledgling and never put on weight
        his bones remained thin and nothing about him grew large
except his head and his bright eyes which soon followed them
        and lit up at the sight of any of them and he would
laugh and call out to them and he seemed to be a happy child

15.

In the year after Niuli was taken away
        whenever Ko'olau went to Waimea he would stop
at the Rowells' big house and ask whether there was any
        word about his sister until not only the pastor
but whoever answered the door knew why he was standing there
        and when she had been gone for a year he rode on
to Koloa to the doctor's house where they told him
        that the doctor was with patients and so he waited
until the woman with whom he had spoken came and asked
        what he had come for and then stared at him and went away
and came to tell him that the doctor knew nothing more
        and as he rode from there Ko'olau went to see the Judge
who told him that he had written to the hospital
        about Niuli and the answer from Honolulu
was that they had no record of anyone by that name
        but that he was pursuing the question and would do so

when next he went over to Honolulu in a month or so
       for it made no sense and he had no explanation
except that he had learned that patients when they were taken
       were told that they did not have to give their real names
if they were ashamed or were afraid of bringing
       shame on their families—But she would not do that—
Ko'olau said—She knew we were not ashamed of her
       she knows we are not ashamed of her she would not be ashamed
she was never ashamed she never did anything
       to be ashamed of——It is the foreigners who are ashamed
of us—the Judge said—and the sickness lets them show
       what they feel about us——Did they give her the box—
Ko'olau asked—Nobody knows—the Judge told him
       —I have been asking the authorities and now I am
turning to other sources both on Oahu and at
       Kalawao in the leper colony and I have been
finding out about both places and have saved more things
       for you to read but I still have no news of your sister—

16.

The Judge said—When nobody knows it does not prevent
       many of them from being sure and I listen
to the arguments in the legislature and at meetings
       in churches and among doctors and every one of them
is right and now the saints of the Board of Foreign Missions
       whom I have served as a trustee are as one supporting
this policy of seizing lepers and hiding them away
       as they have done now for fifteen years and upwards
trying to sweep them under the matting and meanwhile
       those who have gone to minister to those bewildered
souls in their separation and helplessness have been
       Catholics speaking French which scandalized the righteous
ministers from New England to whom God gave us first
       and who are content to know better at a safe distance
and who say such terrible things about the French priests
       that I decided I had to find out about it
and got to know the priest at the church in Koloa
       and the one over in Hanalei and they did not tell me
how the disease was God's judgment upon the natives
       for their sinful sensuality and the way they are always
touching each other there was none of that and they told me
       about the Catholic mission at Kalawao
and this priest Damien in particular who lives
       among the lepers not apart from them but eating
with them working with them through the days listening to them

helping them bury each other and these people
have ways of their own for finding someone among
        the lepers there and they tell me stories of Kalawao
that have never been published and then there are still other
        kinds of inquiry that the foreigners do not know about

17.

In Kekaha they knew that Ho'ona and the woman
        he had been living with some of the time in Waimea
whose name they knew was Malukauai had a daughter
        and it was said that there was another daughter
but whether she was theirs or was Malukauai's child
        by another man or Ho'ona's by another woman
nobody was certain and they all talked about it
        in Pi'ilani's family and in Ko'olau's
and Pi'ilani's mother Kepola heard part of it
        from Ho'ona whose answers always left a door swinging
what was the daughter's name she asked him and he said
        that her name in Hawaiian was Kealia
but they never called her that and her name in English
        he never told her but he said the girl's mother
had taken her to Pastor Rowell's school without saying
        who the father was—But they all knew—Kepola said
and laughed and asked—How old is she now—And Ho'ona
        told her he could not remember—A little younger
than Pi'ilani I believe—Kepola said—Yes younger—
        Ho'ona said—If I saw her one day in Waimea
I would not know her—Pi'ilani said—Do they go
        to the church—Kepola asked—Sometimes—Ho'ona answered
—Do you sit in the same bench then—Kepola asked
        —I am the usher you remember—Ho'ona said
—so I stay by the door—Kepola said—I think we
        should go to the church more often—and she laughed again
Ko'olau thought of it as he rode home through Waimea
        and there on the street was Ho'ona walking with a young girl
then Louis Stolz rode past them toward the Rowell house as the bell
        in the church began ringing and Ho'ona looked up
at Stolz and saw Ko'olau and he stopped and when Ko'olau
        came up to him he said—Reverend Rowell is dead—
he was crying and then he added—This is Kealia—

18.

So that girl who looked up at him and then looked away
  was Pi'ilani's half sister and he searched her face quickly
for anything he could recognize he stared for a moment
  and said her name and again she looked up at him
and mumbled something and turned away and he told her
  he was glad to know her and when she nodded he thought
he saw something familiar—When did the pastor die—
  he asked—Just a little while ago—Ho'ona said
—I was at the church and Lilia ran from the house
  to tell me—and Ko'olau looked at the tears on his face
and said nothing and for a moment none of them moved
  or spoke on the dirt street in Waimea late in the day
with the news spreading its shadow through the buildings around them
  and then Ko'olau said good-bye and rode on home
and when he told them in Kekaha about the pastor
  Kukui gasped and started to cry and his father
Kaleimanu said that they must go to the funeral
  and Pi'ilani went to tell her mother Kepola
who said she would go with them and in the evening Ko'olau
  told them of meeting Kealia and they asked their questions
and he told Kepola he thought the girl was about twelve
  but it was hard to tell Pi'ilani what she looked like
so as they rode together to the funeral
  they were wondering whether they would see her this time
now that Ko'olau could point her out and there she was
  with her mother outside the church as they arrived
and Ko'olau told them which ones they were and they all watched
  as the woman and the two girls went into the church
and they followed and saw where the three sat down and they
  took a bench where they could look at them and Ko'olau
saw Stolz beside Mary up in front with the family
  the Knudsens were up there and the Judge arrived with his wife
and sons and went up to his bench and there were all
  the foreigners from Koloa and from the foreign church
nearby and the bell rang and Valdemar Knudsen stood up
  and raised his hands like a preacher and announced a hymn
and then each of them was standing and singing the same words

19.

The singing itself took Ko'olau by surprise
  he had never liked the hymns back at the time when they
had to sing them in Pastor Rowell's school they were different
  from the songs and chants that he had grown up hearing

from Kawaluna and Keawe and Nakaula
    and the elders in Kekaha in the evenings
the hymns had felt to him like obeying a stranger
    and whenever the Pastor was not looking at him
he stood silent watching the others and watching Pi'ilani
    as she sang and Niuli as she sang and then
he would begin singing with them and as he stood there
    at the funeral the schoolroom that he had longed
to get away from woke up inside him burning through him
    and he looked at the Pastor's body in its box
white faced under the flowers this dead foreigner
    who had seen him born and whom he had looked up to
and had disliked most of the time until the day
    he had ridden up to the garden with the box
for Niuli and then back down by the river seeing
    the Pastor's back riding ahead of him and knowing
from watching the back of the Pastor's head under its black hat
    what the man was feeling about Niuli it was there
in the lines across the back of the neck then Ho'ona
    whom they had not seen slipped in at the end of the bench
beside Pi'ilani and Kepola and in the second
    verse of the hymn Ko'olau out of the corner
of his eye saw Ho'ona standing there and he saw
    tears on the man's face again and then he saw that Kepola
had her head bowed and there were tears running on her cheeks
    and he saw that Pi'ilani was singing and her face
was wet and shining and it startled him to see her in tears
    and between them their child Kaleimanu was gazing up at her
reaching up to her and at the sight of her tears he started
    to cry and Ko'olau picked him up and held him
to his shoulder and stood not singing looking at the lid
    of the coffin and he thought that he felt nothing now
for the man whose body was lying in it but only
    a strange ache that had come from the schoolroom and he began
to sing with the others and suddenly his throat grew tight

20.

At the end of the service when they had filed past
    the coffin and out the back door leaving the family
and the ushers and pall-bearers behind them in the church
    they went and took up places in the cemetery
facing the waiting grave and Pi'ilani as she
    gazed at the piled earth and the long hole beside it
kept hearing the word for that dark pit that was Ko'olau's
    first name her hands were cold and the shadow of a kukui tree

moved like cold hands over the pile of fresh earth it was all
    coming to pass in whispers the trees stirring the words from
the bowed faces she saw the Judge's wife on the far side
    of the grave and the Judge and their sons and then her father's
arms loaded with flowers arrived at the mound and he
    set wreaths carefully on the grass to one side of it
and stepped away as the bearers came with the coffin
    slowly around the church from the front door she saw Valdemar
Knudsen with his wide beard and she supposed the tall
    old man beside him might be Reverend Dole from Koloa
and there was Doctor Smith who had taken Niuli
    and she saw a strange younger man with a long closed face
whom she had noticed in church standing beside Mary Rowell
    they were all foreigners and the preachers standing
beside the grave were foreigners and most of what they said
    had been in English so that she had let it float past her
the bearers let the coffin down onto the boards and stood back
    the men who held the ropes were Hawaiians and she saw
the way the man with the closed face was watching them
    as the man on the horse did when he was overseeing
the backs bent in the sugar fields then they lowered
    the coffin and the preachers all read from their black books
and she heard Valdemar Knudsen pray in a loud voice saying
    that this man's mind had been broader than most
and ahead of his time and later she tried to think
    what he had been talking about as she watched the family
come one by one to pick up earth and flowers and drop them
    into the grave the Pastor's wife the grown children and their
wives and husbands and last the one with that hard face

21.

That night Pi'ilani and Ko'olau lay awake
    recalling those who had been there at the funeral
and after a time they began talking about Niuli
    and where she might be and whether they believed she was
on this side of the grave or on the other side
    and Ko'olau said Now that the Pastor was gone
she seemed farther away and there was only the Judge
    left for him to ask about her and Pi'ilani
wondered who the man was next to Mary Rowell
    and Ko'olau said that was her husband and he told her
what Kua and the Judge had said to him about
    this Mr Stolz and his origins and ambitions
and she listened as Ko'olau said—He goes sometimes
    to Makaweli when Mary does and I see him there

but we never talk and now he runs some cattle
    of his own closer to town than Mr Knudsen's
and he calls himself a stockman—Then Kaleimanu
    woke up and they lulled him back to sleep with stories
but the next time Ko'olau stopped to see the Judge
    it was Louis Stolz the Judge wanted to tell him about
and how the man was getting his friends onto the Water Board
    and writing to the offices in Honolulu
for concessions and water rights that could give him
    advantages over his neighbors who had been there
since before he ever made his way out of Argentina
    the Judge said it seemed as though Louis Stolz had minded
his manners as long as the Pastor was alive
    but that once Reverend Rowell was out of the way
he began to show what he was like there were no
    Hawaiians at Stolz's place the men who handled
the cattle there were Mexicans but the Judge had heard
    of Stolz having his way with Hawaiian women
Married women—the Judge said—and I cannot be sure
    what truth there is in the stories but I keep hearing them—

22.

Then Ko'olau asked about Niuli and the Judge
    said that the priests in Koloa and Hanalei
had written to friends of theirs over at the mission
    at Kalaupapa and inquired about Niuli
but they had no record of her there by that name
    nor of any woman of that age admitted from Kauai
and they had found no trace of her at the hospital
    in Honolulu where she would have been taken
but they said that patients found many ways to hide
    and that they would keep trying to find her and the Judge said
that the priests had given him papers about Kalaupapa
    which he had saved for Ko'olau and they had confided
stories about the colony that were not public knowledge
    —We should learn what goes on in that place—the Judge said
—It has been happening in our own lifetimes and to
    our own people however the sickness first came here
first they got the old king to sign the law that would let them
    treat the lepers as criminals and they chose Kalaupapa
because it was isolated all the way out
    on a peninsula on Moloka'i cut off by sea cliffs
thousands of feet high and with the surf breaking around it
    it is there in the ancient legends and the histories
of the chiefs a promontory of spirits on an island

of spirits with a lake of spirits in the middle of it
and when they chose that peninsula for their outcasts
      there were families who had been farming and fishing there
since the time of the legends and ships used to sail there
      straight from California just for the sweet potatoes
for they were the finest in the world and those families
      were never told of the plans for their rocky leaf
of land which was the world they had known all their lives
      they met the first twelve patients who were pushed into the surf
some of them with limbs crippled and shrivelled by the sickness
      and they helped them into their own houses and took care of them—

23.

—But that was long ago at the beginning—the Judge said
      —back when you were at the Pastor's school and at that time
none of us knew what went on there and the constables
      kept rounding up lepers and shipping them over
dropping them off at Waikolu along the coast
      to find their way to the grass roofs at Kalaupapa
some of them scarcely able to stand and they say that in less
      than a year two hundred of them had been thrown out like that
and the inhabitants could not feed them or shelter them
      but were crowded out of their own fields and houses
with lepers everywhere lying sitting hobbling begging
      until those who had lived there left the peninsula
where they had been born and they shipped out or climbed the cliffs
      into the rest of the world when it seemed that the world
was gone and the lepers moved into their empty houses
      and ate up whatever had been left there and they brewed
alcohol from the sweet potatoes and lay around
      naked so that the place became known on the island
as the crazy pen but the Board of Health kept sending
      more of them from Kalihi in Honolulu
putting up shelters and buildings sending a doctor
      and rations of meat and taro root so much a head
and not much of either and as for anything else
      they wore their rags while those lasted and were lucky
to have one scrap of blanket on that rainy coast
      and I hear the crippled were given nothing to eat
unless they did their share of the daily grave-digging
      and when it came to coffins those who had no money
were buried without them and this priest Damien says that
      he has seen a body dug up by the pigs and eaten
some died alone and unnoticed for days some forgot
      who they were and wandered into complete mindlessness

but now they tell me that with the mission it is better
    with more food and a hospital but just the same nobody
would go there willingly and now there are hundreds of them
    dragged away by the constables as your sister was—

24.

—And besides the priests—the Judge said—I have been talking
    with two brothers from Moloka'i who work on the schooner
Waiola and a friend of theirs on the steamer Pele
    they are all sons of the families who were crowded
out of Kalaupapa and now they go back to the place
    for a different reason there were always kahunas
all kinds of sorcerers at Kalaupapa and the lake
    in the middle of the peninsula has no bottom
but goes all the way down into the house of Pele
    and the sorcerers make their way at night to the water's edge
and talk with the darkness these men may be sorcerers
    they have kahunas in their families who return there
and among the patients at Kalaupapa there is one great
    sorcerer who was sent there years ago a woman named
Paniku Hua she has visions she talks of a dark cloud
    coming toward us reaching for the throne she has seen it
for years drawing closer I have sent messages to her
    and those men brought one back to me she says Less Than Ten
whatever that means Less Than Ten I asked them what
    she could reveal about your sister and she told them
nothing at first but after a time she said Shorebird
    and that was all and they tell me she is a healer
though her own sickness is one that she cannot cure
    they will be going back there soon and talking to her
asking the questions again and maybe she will have seen
    something more and there are sorcerers here who may
be able to tell us something we want to know
    but remember there was no word for this sickness
in our language before the foreigners came here——
    the Judge fell silent and Ko'olau saw him
staring down through the trees toward the sea and he thought
    it was time to go and he stood up but the Judge said
—I cannot say I cannot say and the older I get
    the less certain I am about how things come to be
and now there is Rowell taken we could never get along
    he was hard in the head and a foreigner in his heart
and I made trouble for him but I am sorry he is gone—

25.

Kaleimanu stayed small and they kept him home at Kekaha
    where Pi'ilani taught him to read and write more or less
he wanted to know the exact name of everything
    and then why it was called that and what its story was
he coaxed the stories together believing that they
    would recognize each other and have things to tell each other
and as he walked he repeated the stories to himself
    and confided them to other children Pi'ilani
would find him with the others listening to him
    for him all the stories were parts of one tale and he would
follow Kawaluna and Nakaula and all
    the elders of the village holding them in his wide eyes
begging for more stories and asking questions about
    the ones he knew and the people in them he was
little and funny and everyone liked him and he loved
    his girl cousin Ida whose mother Kinolou
was Pi'ilani's sister the children were almost
    the same age they were together most of every day
they could recite some of the stories together
    or one would go on from where the other had stopped
when Ko'olau came home early he would lift Kaleimanu
    onto the horse in front of him and ride along the sand
and he told stories of the village and the legends
    so that it sounded as though there was no difference between them
Pi'ilani's father Ho'ona spent less time at the church
    after Reverend Rowell died but he still brought back news
from Waimea telling how Mary Rowell now Mary
    Stolz seemed unhappy as everyone agreed and they said
Louis Stolz was high-handed and rude and they all knew
    which Hawaiian houses he visited by the back door

26.

Pi'ilani watched her father when he was with them
    behind his face she could not tell where his mind was
but he had settled into his own custom of passing
    like the tides back and forth between his two houses
and two families and at Kekaha everyone
    was used to it Pi'ilani heard him use one voice
to talk to Kepola and to others in the house
    and a different one to talk to men on the steps
dealing out bits of news from the mills and from Waimea
    one by one like a game played with Ko'olau's father
and Ko'olau and sometimes Nakaula and Kua

who told what they had heard at Hofgaard's store and Makaweli
in those days they were talking about King Kalākaua
    how much money he was said to be losing and how angry
the foreigners were because of it and Koʻolau told them
    of the Judge saying for years that this king would ruin them
and that David Kalākaua was not the rightful king
    in the first place but it was one more bought election
and Queen Emma was the one who should have been on the throne
    he said that Kalākaua would run them into debt
until the foreigners had all the excuses they wanted
    he said Knudsen was guarded in his words but it was known
that he had no faith in Kalākaua and at Hofgaard's store
    they talked about Rice and Isenberg from Kauai
and the younger Mr Dole working aginst the king
    they called themselves The Hawaiian League with their own
militia The Hawaiian Rifles but they were
    all foreigners or the children of foreigners
and Piʻilani listened to the talk eddying
    around the king with bits of rumor circling in it
his gambling his drinking but his faults as they talked
    seemed small beside the fact that he was their own king
and they would rather have him than be ruled by foreigners

27.

—A new day is upon us—the Judge said to Koʻolau
    —Louis Stolz has become a notary public
I suppose it is a kind of distinction for him
    and I am sure he intends to turn it to account—
they had met on the street in Waimea and Koʻolau
    noticed that the Judge was walking now with a cane
and had grown ponderous and sounded as though he were tired
    and the next time he saw him the Judge said—Now Mr Stolz
so I am told has had a suit brought against him
    for falsifying land records and I hear that Holi
is going to sue him for adultery with his wife
    or keeps threatening to do it—and as the Judge went along
Koʻolau was troubled to see that it was hard for him
    to walk and then one day that winter in Waimea
his father rode up to him and said there had been
    an argument at Hofgaard's store and the Judge had told
Louis Stolz that he had sworn falsely upon oath
    and Stolz had struck the older man and shouted at him
to keep his mouth shut and had knocked him down bleeding
    and when the Judge tried to stand he hit him again
and a woman had called out—Louis is trying to kill

Judge Kauai—and they finally dragged Louis away
and now the Judge had brought a complaint and Ko'olau
        rode down to the Judge's house and saw the bandage
above his eye and heard the story in detail
        and the date of the hearing before the present Judge Hardy
and when the case had been tried he learned from Judge Kauai
        the program of that day in court witness by witness
foreigners and Hawaiians and how Judge Hardy had found
        Stolz guilty of assault as charged and had fined him
but Judge Kauai said—Dignity is not so easy to restore—

28.

The Knudsens had gone up to Halemanu for the summer
        Valdemar's beard entirely white by then and the children
growing tall he rode out less often into the forest
        with Ko'olau and Kua and the others when they
were all up there together and Ko'olau and Kua
        were out by themselves again and again that summer
tracking wild cattle which were harder to find each year
        as they traced the paths over the mountain skirting
the Alakai swamp and climbed to the sharp ridges and down into
        the steep green clefts where water was running on the rock walls
through curtains of fern within arm's reach as the horses
        slid down the muddy trails written over with the split prints
of cattle washed dim rewritten gone and the tracks switched back
        and clung to steep ravine sides coming out at the edges
of canyons with white wings circling a vast distance below them
        drifting across blue shadows and the far red rock face grooved
stained split with age where the white threads of waterfalls
        hung swaying in the silent sunlight then one day above
Kalalau they came to where a young man was watching them
        from under the trees but he came out when they called him
and told them that he was Iwa and that he had come up
        out of Kalalau down there where he was living
and they told him who they were and asked about the valley
        the families they knew there and Iwa asked them
how long it had been since they had been down there and they
        did not answer at first but looked at each other and then Kua
said—I have heard of the new people who have gone to live
        in these valleys—and Iwa looked down at his feet and said
—My father's brother Nihoa came home and they had taken away
        his wife for being a leper and had left the two babies
just screaming and they took away my friend Kuhi
        off the cane wagon he never came home we heard how they
went and got him and now some of us live down there

where we hope it would be harder for them to find us—
—Did you come up looking for something to eat—Kua asked him
        nodding toward the gun in the shadow of a tree
and Iwa said smiling—Maybe a goat or something—

29.

As they were riding back down to Halemanu
        Kua said—Knudsen has known about them for a long time
longer than I thought he may have known they were there almost
        from the beginning hearing from friends out by Hanalei
or people at Haena and Wainiha they all knew
        and the canoes that go around Mānā and bring
word back to the ranch at Waiawa whenever Knudsen
        asks me about them I can see how much he knows
he wants them to be let alone there he told me and he said
        he saw it all happen in Norway when he was a boy
he does not want the rats from the Board of Health prowling
        out at the ranch or coming up here he was talking
about the three of us going down into the valley
        to find out what he could do for them maybe later
in the summer when it dries out some more we could
        go down the way we used to when he was looking
for birds on the cliffs I think he is as strong as ever
        only more quiet—and Koʻolau watched Knudsen
those next days with Kua's words in mind and he watched him
        on the day when Knudsen left his family there
with Makaʻi and the others and he and Kua
        and Koʻolau rode down to Makaweli and on the way
Knudsen said he was anxious to hear what was happening
        over in Honolulu he told them he had been hearing
rumors of coming change there and as they were riding
        beside the house it was silent without the family
hens out in the back field the voices of doves in the trees
        Meʻeawe came around the corner and stopped in surprise
and stood stiff as though he had been caught at something
        he stood still until they were close to him—What has happened—
Knudsen asked him—What is it—Knudsen repeated
        —It is the King—Meʻeawe said—It is about the King—
Kila brought the mail for you it is in the house there—
        and Knudsen thanked them all and went in by himself

30.

—Now they have him tied down hand and foot—the Judge said
        —it is what they have been wanting to do from the start
he will not be able to waste money now or command
        any troops at all the foreigners will do the voting
they will let him sit there on the throne in his uniform
        and will tell him how lucky he is not to be in jail
because of this money or that money while they let
        the Americans take Pearl Harbor for their warships
in exchange for making the sugar planters rich
        and we will see what it all means to the likes of us
we will still be their problem their embarrassment
        on the one hand the King and on the other the lepers
and the same voices that profess to be horrified
        at any resistance to authority are the ones
that are shouting to be rid of the King and the last
        remnants of rule by Hawaiians in Hawai'i
they believe we are here for the profit of foreigners
        I hear my neighbor Stolz was there at the legislature—
and Ko'olau saw the sweat trembling on the Judge's cheeks
        heard the shortness of breath felt the waves of anger like heat
from the baking pit—What will they take from us next—
        the Judge said—The last of the dirt under the houses
or whatever we still think is ours you can be sure
        they will clean out the lepers now once and for all
they have a thousand lepers over in the settlement
        but that number will multiply and no more of these
lepers kept hidden by the rest of the family
        those will be dug out one by one and there may be others
up there in the windward valleys before long—and Ko'olau
        saw his hand fall in despair onto the table
and it seemed to him that he rode home through a shadow
        Ho'ona was there in Kekaha and Kepola
and her parents came over and that evening they all sat
        talking and trying to understand what had happened

31.

Pi'ilani woke in the dark and lay listening
        Ko'olau was sleeping Kaleimanu was sleeping
she got up and went out the door touching nothing
        knowing the feel of each board underfoot she slipped the latch
without a sound and stepped onto the lanai smelling
        the air above the sea before morning and there beside
the post at the top of the steps was a dark form

       and she stopped breathing it did not move and she saw
it was Kawaluna sitting there and an arm stirred
       a hand came out onto the step beside her and turned
upward in welcome and Pi'ilani sat down next to her
       and they stayed there without a word looking toward the sea
Kawaluna put her arm around Pi'ilani
       and after a while Pi'ilani leaned her head
on Kawaluna's shoulder and they sat hearing the whisper
       of the small waves finishing along the sand as the first light
of the ghost dawn began to seep into the darkness
       and Pi'ilani saw a wave beginning to
lift and move in toward them on the flat sea it rose
       higher with the face of it dark and beyond it
in the dim light was Kekaha out there and the whole coast
       that had been her world since she had been born the wave kept rising
until she could not see over it and it had cut off
       everything she knew it kept growing as it came closer
until she thought it was going to break over them
       there it stopped and stayed where it was and blacked out half
the sky darker than a night without stars and she stared at it
       but there was nothing to see she opened her eyes and the light
before daybreak was spread on the calm sea all the way
       to the horizon there was not a wave nor a cloud
she felt Kawaluna's arm around her and it was the next
       of the days in which they were learning how little
they knew about how their lives were being directed
       from somewhere out of sight and by decisions they never heard made
then from the capital came word of a rebellion

32.

Ho'ona came back from the mill in the morning
       to tell them what he had heard and Ko'olau and the two
Kaleimanus his father and his son were down
       at the canoes with the fish that they were bringing in
the news had come from Koloa when the Pele
       docked at daybreak but it was a tattered story
and what seemed to have happened was that somebody
       in Honolulu by the name of Wilcox who was part
Hawaiian had marched to the palace wearing a red shirt
       he had his own army behind him some of them Hawaiians
or part Hawaiians all wearing red shirts and armed
       they had their own constitution for the King to sign
instead of the one that the foreigners had forced
       upon him and this one would take back the power
from the foreigners and return it to the Hawaiians

and would let them decide whether Kalakaua or his sister
Liliuokalani would sit on the throne but the King
    was not at home and the government troops in support
of the foreigners had killed no one knew how many
    of the red shirts and driven them out of the palace grounds
then it was all over and the foreigners were still
    in control of the government and the King had done nothing
and could do nothing and through that day and the days
    that followed as they talked about it there were foreigners
in Hofgaard's store who laughed at this Wilcox or growled that he
    deserved to be hung and there were Hawaiians at
the mills and the ranches who said less and who sensed that
    one more wisp of hope had just blown away from them
before they knew it existed and there were other Hawaiians
    who said it was shameful to show so little respect
for those in authority and it brought shame on all of them
    and the Judge told Koʻolau that he supposed Wilcox
had his head in some cloud and never knew what he was doing
    but he said he wished he had been in the legislature
to hear the big Hawaiian Bipikane roaring like a bull
    shouting that he would gore them all until they charged him
with contempt and threw him out—he was a clown—the Judge said
    —but there are times when that is the best you can hope for—

33.

When Koʻolau told his family in Kekaha
    about the encounter with Iwa on the cliff top
and about the lepers hiding in Kalalau Valley
    and when they had asked him question after question
and had fallen silent it was Kawaluna
    who began to ask her own questions as though her voice
were coming from somewhere else so they could hardly hear her
    she asked when he had first gone into that valley
what path he had entered by and where he had gone the first time
    which stream he had followed who had been with him and what
he had seen then who had spoken to him and what they had said
    what sounds he had heard in the valley that time that were
still clear to him so that if he shut his eyes now
    and heard them he would know them and he answered her
as well as he could Piʻilani had crouched to listen
    they were all listening and Kawaluna asked how often
he had gone there how well he knew the valley and when
    he had been there last and he told her everything
as well as he could remember and then he asked her
    whether she had ever been there but instead of answering
she sat looking straight at him and said nothing at all

then in the morning at Waiawa Knudsen and Kua
were talking and Knudsen waved and called him over
        and asked them both about Iwa and what they knew
about the people hiding in Kalalau and told them
        that they had written asking him to request the Board of Health
to allow them to remain where they were and they wanted
        him to be their doctor and he had written to the Board
and they had said that in view of the isolation
        and inaccessible situation of that place
they would consent but they warned that this exemption
        was temporary and that their intention was still
to remove those fugitives on some future occasion
        when weather and other circumstances favored it

34.

—It did not mean much—Valdemar Knudsen said to them
        —the Board of Health is not making any real promises
and as for my being able to provide those souls
        with medical attention that suggestion may be
there in the hope of quieting the official
        contention that the lepers must be rounded up
to be given proper treatment for their condition
        and of course with only two doctors on the island
neither of whom approves of allowing victims
        of leprosy to remain at large and neither of whom
could include the fastnesses of Kalalau within
        his practice there could be no pretense of medical care
for those who have chosen that place as a refuge
        but on the other hand all of the treatment we have now
in the hospitals is inadequate at best
        there is nothing that could be called a cure and the means
of delay sometimes seem more cruel than the sickness
        except for whatever hope they permit but these people
who have chosen to manage without any of that
        should know that my medical qualifications are too
limited to deserve the name and that I could not promise
        regular visits into the clefts of Kalalau
how many years has it been since the last trip we made there
        but I will spend as much time as I can at Halemanu
where they can reach me and I will send them medicines
        and perhaps for some emergencies I might be able
to go into the valley but no one must count on that
        I understand that most of the time there is one of them
somewhere along the edge of the cliff above Koke'e
        would you be so good as to tell him what I have said—

35.

Ho'ona arrived in Kekaha one day with news
        he had brought from Waimea while Ko'olau was away
at the ranch and they all saw that Ho'ona was burning
        to tell them something but he was having trouble
saying it right out and he knew he would have to repeat it
        when Ko'olau came home Kepola was beginning
to find it funny before she even heard it
        and he saw the way she and Kawaluna and Pi'ilani
were looking at each other and he said—You remember
        what they have been saying about Holi's wife——You tell us—
Kepola said—But you know it—Ho'ona said—
        Everybody has known it now for a long time—
—What do you know—Kepola asked—And how do we know we know
        if you will not tell us what it is—and Ho'ona who was
the only one in the family who wore shoes every day
        and who had not yet taken them off when he got home
shuffled his feet and then unlaced his shoes and set them
        up on the lanai beam out of reach of the dogs
and stood looking at his feet—I never met Holi's wife—
        Kepola said—Does she have a name of her own—
—Holi has brought suit—Ho'ona said—against Mr Stolz—
        —I remember Mr Stolz—Pi'ilani said
—He was standing beside Reverend Rowell's grave
        and I can still see the small top of his head with his hat off
and that thin woman next to him in church——Holi has charged him—
        Ho'ona said—with what is termed Mischievous Sleeping—
—Mischievous Sleeping—Kepola said—Now what is that—
        —You know what it is—Ho'ona said—I am not sure
I do—Kepola said—You will have to explain—
        —It means adultery—Ho'ona said—With Holi's wife—
—The unnamed one and is that what we know—Kepola asked him—
        Ho'ona said—And it will be tried in the court
and Judge Kauai's son will be one of the witnesses—
        —Mischievous Sleeping—Kepola said—What a shameful thing—

36.

When Ko'olau came home they lost no time telling him
        that Ho'ona knew something and they got everyone
together to hear it and made him say it all over again
        —With a jury too—Ko'olau said—Who is to be
on the jury——They have not been named yet—Ho'ona said
        —But they say six foreigners and six natives—It will be
nothing but shame—Ko'olau said—And maybe they will not

even find Mr Stolz guilty he is a foreigner
and she is only one Hawaiian woman and married
       to one Hawaiian man and Mr Stolz has made important
friends there is Dr Smith who sent Niuli away
       and then never could say what happened to her and there is
Reverend Dole who surely would not let it be said
       that a friend of his had been doing things of that kind
with some native woman——But everyone knows—Kepola said—
       —And there are witnesses there is young Mr Kauai—
—Wait and see—Ko'olau said and he added—I think
       Judge Kauai will have something to say about it
Holi kept announcing that he was going to do this—
       But it was the summer then and Ko'olau was away
much of the time up at Halemanu or between
       the ranch and Makaweli and once Pi'ilani
and their son Kaleimanu whom Ko'olau still carried
       half the time and held on the horse in front of him
went along up to Halemanu and stayed there with him
       for days and Ko'olau and Kua went several times
to meet Iwa at the top of the cliff beyond Koke'e
       carrying medicines and they went in with him
and went in by themselves all during that summer
       down the razorback ridges the steep crumbling ledges
along the cliff walls above the bottomless chasms
       through clouds and then up into side clefts in the buttresses
to the caves and grass houses and the lepers and their
       families who were living there with them and they took in
tools for them and clothes and bedding and chalmoogra oil
       for the sickness and it was late in the summer
before Ko'olau rode back to the harbor at Koloa
       and turned aside in Waimea to see the Judge again

37.

—No of course it was nothing like justice—the Judge said
       they were sitting on the lanai looking out through the trees
toward Koloa Road and the Judge's wife Kaenaku
       had come and joined them—And of course I never went
to court—the Judge said—On that day it would not have been
       proper for me to be there for the purpose of watching
my neighbor on trial for furtive activities
       that everyone in the courtroom knew he had committed
and to hear the questions and hear him lie under oath
       to them all as I have heard him do in the past
and all of them listening and knowing that he was lying
       you know one of our sons was the lawyer for the plaintiff

though Holi has no money and another of our sons
    was a witness for the plaintiff but they got former Judge
Hardy a successor of mine and Mr Hofgaard
    who had heard me tell that man to his face that he
had borne false witness and who had seem him try to kill me
    and each of them in turn stood up to profess their esteem
for their fellow foreigner's character and to deplore
    the distress such a case must cause to a decent man
and his wife and that was more or less how the court
    viewed it and encouraged the jury to see it
and nothing different was to be expected I think
    with the present complexion of the government and with
the foreigners in power I wonder how much longer
    they will let us go on pretending to be ruled
by a king from our own people—and Ko'olau was thinking
    how his face had changed in the course of the summer he searched
the shadows under the broad brim and they seemd to be melting
    Kaenaku said to him—You told us you had been
into Kalalau and had seen the people who have gone there
    because of the sickness I would like to know about them—
and Ko'olau looked at her and saw that she meant it
    and he tried to answer her question about them

38.

The Judge had been sitting there in that same position
    when Ko'olau walked up the steps that day and he did not move
when Ko'olau got up to leave as Kaenaku's
    questions about Kalalau seemed to be ended
and she was silent and stared off into the leaves
    then she said—My father knew that coast and he left me
the land over there near Wainiha and Hanalei
    I remember him talking of Haena and Kalalau
and Nualolo he called them the owl's valleys
    but I do not know what he had seen there what they did there
or how he went there a whole life ago and the one
    story he told me of that coast was about a ship
the most beautiful ship that anyone ever saw
    it drifted ashore there and ran aground and an old chief
Kiaimakani got the people to make ropes of *hau* bark
    and tie them to the mast and crouch down in silence
while he chanted to Lono and they held their breaths staring
    and he blew the conch shell and then they pulled and the mast
broke and the ship rolled away onto the rocks and sank
    and they stood with the ropes they had made slipping over their feet
out into the waves and that is what my father told me

I am not sure why but perhaps because it always made me
be quiet—and she laughed—But I know you do not go
        along the coast to that valley you go down over the cliff
it is hard to imagine that—and she looked away toward the road
        and the Judge said—It is getting harder for me to walk now
I suppose it is age and my weight there comes a time
        when everyone starts complaining about some part
of the poor body and it is my feet that are failing me
        I mention it only because I can scarcely pretend
it is not so and I see you have a fine pair of feet
        I think they will take you anywhere you have to go
how foolish to come to notice such things out of envy—

39.

The Judge had always liked riding in a carriage
        and they had a small family of carriages
out in the stable one of them dating from the days
        of Kaumuali'i and the sandalwood trees
and all of them too delicate for most of the roads
        most of the time but he and Kaenaku had taken
one or another of them into Waimea
        to church on Sundays or into Hanapepe
or Koloa for celebrations or weddings or funerals
        their carriages were well known along that coast and their
horses and their clothes and the Judge surely had never
        driven barefoot in any of them but he could
no longer get his feet into the tops of his boots
        and at last he stood up without them and waded down the steps
with the cane and heaved himself into the waiting carriage
        beside Kaenaku they were dressed as though they were
going to a birthday party and they rode to Koloa
        and tied up outside Dr Smith's and made their way
to the railing at the foot of the steps and up the steps
        where the door was opened to them by a young Hawaiian girl
who looked at them with surprise that turned into something
        like fright and showed them into the parlor and left them
sitting in the high-backed chairs and the Judge began
        laughing to himself recalling the arguments
in the church more than thirty years earlier and how he had
        cited church law to the foreigners and how the pastor
had nailed the doors shut and all that melodeon business
        and the Doctor always long-faced as the spine of a book
he thought of their muttered civilities all these years
        when they met in some doorway and then the Doctor came in
and greeted them with unsmiling correctness keeping

his eyes away from the Judge's feet and the Judge said—We have
come for a medical examination so perhaps
　　　I should come into your office when you are at liberty—
and the Doctor looked at him as though he were an object
　　　and said—Of course although it may not be necessary—

40.

—It appears to be some kind of dropsy—the Judge said
　　　as the Doctor showed him into a room heavy with
the smell of disinfectant upon former disinfectant
　　　with sheets at the windows—Please sit there—the Doctor said
pointing toward the end of a long table I can give you
　　　an examination in the usual way
listen to your heart sound your lungs and so on if you so desire—
　　　—It is my feet—the Judge said—But I believe you know—
the Doctor went on—I believe you have known for some time
　　　what this ailment is and it is common to cling to some
other explanation as long as possible—
　　　He paused and the Judge said nothing and the Doctor said
—Do I have to tell you——No—the Judge said—You have told me—
　　　—But you knew—the Doctor said—The Chinese sickness—
the Judge said and the Doctor as though he had not heard
　　　said—It is still called leprosy but that name may change
since a doctor in Norway a man named Hansen
　　　has determined the cause of it in a minute form of life
too small to be seen——Has he found the cure—the Judge asked
　　　—Not yet—the Doctor said—but we can delay the course of it
chalmoogra oil corrective surgery you need them both
　　　and I am afraid you will have to be sent for treatment
to Kalaupapa I will give you some time of course
　　　to make preparations——Not everyone goes—the Judge said
—The law requires it—the Doctor said—You are a man
　　　of law some have to be taken by force——There is
a resistance growing—the Judge said—Armed resistance—
　　　—That is true—the Doctor said—Police officers have been
threatened and have resigned I think Knudsen has made it
　　　worse by encouraging that band that has gone into hiding
over in the windward valleys——They have permission
　　　from the Board of Health I understand—the Judge said—I have
read it—the Doctor said—and it is regrettable
　　　but temporary—The Judge hauled himself to his feet
—Did you ever learn what happened to that girl from Kekaha
　　　named Niuli who was sent to Kalihi ten years ago—
—I have no recollection—the Doctor said—I believe
　　　Pastor Rowell asked you about her——Did he—the Doctor said

41.

As they went out the door the Doctor said—Your wife will be
        able to go with you——But I heard the law was changing
about that—the Judge said—She will go as a patient—
        the Doctor told him—The marks of the sickness are obvious
on her face I will let you tell her in your own time
        if she does not already know—and he escorted them
out to the lanai and when they were in the carriage
        they rode off in silence until they had left Koloa
then he put his hand on her arm and looked at her face and nodded
        and they drove on home where their sons were waiting for them
they all sat around the big table on the lanai
        and the Judge told them what the Doctor had confirmed
and told them which boxes to bring from his office and he
        and Kaenaku signed over to their sons all of
the lands in Kikiaola and in Haena
        and in Hanapepe and Koloa and they drove to town
to register the changes in the courthouse and then
        they began the last days in the house there packing
boxes and bundles going through papers and the messages
        went out to Kekaha and up to Waiawa
and then the morning came when they got up in the dark
        and the lamps were lighted on the tables and the pack horses
were loaded by lantern and Koʻolau rode in
        long before daybreak and three of them helped the Judge
into the saddle and set his feet in the slings
        they had made instead of stirrups and they turned
at the end of the drive and looked back at the house with the lamps
        burning and the figures crying and waving and they
rode out and up the mountain—The house will be ready
        they tell me—Koʻolau said to the Judge and Kaenaku
as they paused after the sun rose and ate and drank
        without dismounting and then they rode on toward Kokeʻe
stopping no more than they had to and arrived late in the day
        where a camp was ready for them and the Judge's family
those who would stay and those who would go in sat up talking
        and slept and at daybreak the men who had come up
out of Kalalau to make the camp helped them to the cliff's edge
        where they said their good-byes and four men from Kalalau
picked up the Judge and started down into the valley

THE VALLEY

The valley is the mountain split open to windward
        to the northwest to the sea to the horizon
where the ancient peaks sailed away sinking before there was
        anyone before the archaic words were first uttered
and from the crags at the head of the valley to the winding
        stream beds and the drapery of forest tumbling into
the braided ravines it is so far down that only
        sections of that carved land can be seen glimpses caught
between drifts of clouds as they travel in to the cliffs
        along the pinnacles and the waved fins of buttresses
and through gaps in the stone facades cloud shadows pass
        across blue slopes all the way below and in the partings
of the clouds waterfalls spring white from distant scars
        high in the rock walls beyond the chasm and the silent plumes
descend slowly through the air of another time until they
        melt into mist but the veins gather somewhere below them
and down toward the rocks along the shoreline stone terraces
        had been stepped some of them raised in the remote past
fanning out from banks of the main stream like bones of a fish
        toward the cliffs and a scattering of thatched houses
was settled among banana trees near the taro ponds
        the roofs of families that had lived there for longer than
the stories told and now their boats waited on the shingle
        their donkeys and goats were tethered near the houses
and up in the head of the valley on the ledges
        in the steep gorges were the caves and shelters of those
who had come in recent years because of the sickness
        and the police raids breaking without warning into
the houses of the poor to hunt for those with the sickness
        up there the fugitives had improved what they called The Big House
when they heard that Judge Kauai was coming to live among them
        it was not as big as Koʻolau's house in Kekaha
but it had two rooms and a good roof and a door
        and a sheltered outhouse tucked back against the cliff
and a stream ran a few steps below the front door

2.

When the word spread from Koloa and from Hofgaard's store
        that Judge Kauai and his wife Kaenaku and others
of their family had gone over into Kalalau

rather than let themselves be sent to the hospital
at Kalihi in Honolulu and the settlement
        at Kalaupapa everyone had something to say
about the sickness and the manner of dealing with it
        and the constabulary and the tales of those who had
driven them off with guns and the growing bands of
        fugitives in the upper valleys of the islands
the tearing apart of families the persistence
        of the disease the torments of the treatment and the failure
to find a cure the way that leprosy seldom
        attacked the foreigners the fact that it was costing
so much even to try to confine it for treatment
        everyone had something heated to contribute
over and over some exhibit of fear and shame
        Damien had died of leprosy at Kalaupapa
and the photographs of him on his deathbed had been published
        in the American papers as far away as New York
and those of the missionary persuasion were so
        unhappy about the choir of praise carolling after
this Catholic that in Honolulu the Reverend
        Charles McEwen Hyde wrote to a fellow preacher deploring
the extravagant laudations as though this man
        had been a saintly philanthropist when the simple truth
was that he was coarse dirty headstrong and bigoted
        had no hand in the reforms and improvements and was not
a pure man in his relations with women and his
        death resulted from his vice and carelessness and Hyde's friend
arranged for this corrective statement to be published
        in San Francisco and a copy was sent from there
to Robert Louis Stevenson who had stayed at the settlement
        not long after Damien's death and as he taught the patients
croquet he had learned how they remembered this man

3.

In Hawai'i on his way to Samoa and the hill
        at Vailima Stevenson had observed for himself
a precarious moment and had made the acquaintance
        of this minister with the echoing name of Hyde
he remembered clearly the comfortable neat pastor
        in his pleasant parlor on Beretania Street
and courtesies for which he could have been grateful
        except this letter of the later Hyde absolved him
as he put it from any bonds of the kind and instead
        he was impelled in the cause of public decency
to right the name of Damien and deal fitly

with a letter so extraordinary I conceive you he wrote
to the Reverend Doctor Hyde as a man quite below
        the reticences of civility one of those
missionaries who in the course of their evangelical
        calling had grown rich until the cab driver commented
upon the size the taste and comfort of the minister's home
        he thought readers should be aware that the letter maligning
Damien had been penned in a house that could raise
        the envy of passers-by and your sect he wrote
which had enjoyed in Hawai'i an exceptional
        advantage when calamity befell its innocent
parishioners and leprosy took root in the islands
        had been sent an opportunity by God which they
had failed sitting and growing bulky in their charming mansions
        while a plain uncouth peasant stepped into the battle
brought succour to the afflicted consoled the dying
        was afflicted in his turn and died upon the field
of honor and the battle could not then be retrieved
        as the Reverend Hyde's unhappy irritation
suggested but it was lost forever and such rags
        of common honor as remained to him he had made haste
to cast away and Stevenson wrote on concerning
        Damien and cleanliness and life at the settlement
and adversions in the clerical parlor to misconduct
        with women and is it growing at all clear to you
he asked what a picture you have drawn of your own heart
        the man who tried to do what Damien did is my father

                                4.

His open letter was published on Kauai in
        the newspaper 'Elele The Messenger and its message
ran like the burning of a cane field the heat and smoke
        soon rolling far away from where it had started
there were the missionary offspring for whom the document
        was an outrage rendered particularly shocking
by the author's descent from elders of their own persuasion
        there were the functionaries of the Board of Health
already nervously revising inadequate
        budgets and justifications and they took public
objection to the use of the leprosy question
        as a political lever while at the same time urging
stricter enforcement of the segregation of lepers
        which was adding to the growing civil unrest
and accounts of Kalaupapa re-echoed like choruses
        two small orphan girls from Father Damien's orphanage

at the settlement had been ordered by the Board of Health
        to be sent to Honolulu on the schooner and they
had been met on the causeway after nightfall by native
        police officers who dropped the trunk containing
one girl's belongings into the water and a fight
        broke out between the officers and two patients
who had escorted the girls that far and two officers
        were stabbed and died a third barely survived the patients
were given ten years and then on the island of Hawai'i
        when the police went to arrest a certain Kealoha
assumed to have leprosy he refused to go with them
        and when the police shot him in the leg he returned fire
with a Winchester killing the sheriff and wounding
        one officer who ran away with the others
Kealoha himself died in jail not long afterwards
        the tales summoned others and recommendations
for dealing with the situation multiplied
        in the newspapers in the legislature in statements
issued by the Board of Health and in Hofgaard's store

5.

It depended to some degree on who might be listening
        in the store but there was recurrent low-rumbling
assurance of no-nonsense in the new directors
        of the Board of Health and persistent speculation
as to whether the disease was not in fact a form
        of syphilis and so a visitation of the wrath
of a too-patient God upon the natives a sentence
        which they had brought upon themselves with the abominations
of their behavior their dirty sensual ways
        their touching and their sharing of food as they licked it
from their fingers and all their doings from their infancy
        many of the regulars at the store could remember
the papers raging after Little Big Horn most of them
        had stood there discussing the hunt for Geronimo
they had shaken their heads over what they understood
        of the Ghost Dance and had agreed that Sitting Bull
deserved what he got and they had hoped that Wounded Knee
        had driven home the lesson at last they supported
their men from Kauai Rice and Isenberg over
        in the legislature in Honolulu and they approved
of the new constitution rendering the King helpless
        and depriving most natives of the vote and they sympathized
with American expansion in the Pacific
        spoke of annexation as the way of progress

but meanwhile there was this unpleasant situation
    that would not go away and a crumbling government
a constabulary unequal to its duties
    one day in Kekaha Pi'ilani heard the dogs
sounding serious in front of the house and she stepped out
    and saw the tall man whose long face she remembered
from beside the open grave of Pastor Rowell he was
    sitting his horse looking down at the dogs in front of him
and she could see what he thought of them but when he looked up
    he smiled without raising his hat and he called out
—Is this the house of Ko'olau—and she nodded
    —I wanted to have a talk with him—Louis Stolz told her
—I will tell him when he comes home what is your name—
    —Tell him Louis Stolz thank you—he said—I may find him
myself—and he rode off with the dogs barking after him

6.

As she turned in the doorway she saw Kawaluna
    watching her from the steps of Ko'olau's parents' house
she felt a chill along her arms and she went to talk
    with Kawaluna but kept watching that man's back
and the older woman said nothing but stood looking after him
    by the time Ko'olau came home it was almost sundown
and she told him about the visit and he said—Yes he came
    to the ranch looking for me and father and I were there
with the new horses I met this man years ago
    in his fine boots and all he could look at was my bare feet
I think I know what he wants but he told me he had heard
    that I was good at making saddles he told me
there were those in whose opinion I was the best but I said
    Kua was the best and he should go talk to Kua
he said he had heard about Kua and he might just do that
    but that he wanted to talk to me first he had heard a good deal
about me he said and that was true I heard Pastor Rowell
    speak to him about me and I know things Mr Knudsen
has said but this Stolz never paid attention before
    all that time and now he wants to get me to make
a saddle for him he says of my best work I told him
    that was the only kind of work I did he said this
saddle was a matter of importance to him
    to mark his new duties as Deputy Sheriff
looking at me as though he had caught one big fish
    and this saddle he said was to be made like one
that some officer in the American cavalry had

I said I could only make saddles of the kind
we use here and then he said I can show you a drawing
        I said no this is the kind I make the kind I am riding
he said with that strange way he bites the words I understand
        that it will cost more if it is made to a design
that is unfamiliar here but that will present no problem
        and I sat there making no promises watching
Mr Knudsen's horses the young ones and waiting for him to go
        and he said you can look at the drawing and think about it—

7.

Up beyond Halemanu riding the mountain with Kua
        that summer there were turns on the trail where Koʻolau
could see all the times he had passed there every step that he
        had ridden among those trees along those rocks through that light
they floated in front of him and then in a moment
        they had moved on and it was a day like any other
they were getting meat for the people at Halemanu
        for Mrs Knudsen and the children and the guests who would
be coming up from Makaweli with Valdemar Knudsen
        and they rode up along the cliff edge at Kokeʻe
looking for someone from Kalalau with news of the Judge
        they had been talking about Stolz and that visit of his
to Waiawa to find Koʻolau and of what he had said
        about a saddle and his being Deputy Sheriff now
and what that was really about and Kua said
        nothing on the subject for most of the day and they
met not Iwa this time but Puhipaka under the trees
        above the rocks where the Piliwale sisters
were turned to stone and Koʻolau gave him newspapers
        for the Judge and his family and Puhipaka
said they were all right it was a good house and the people
        took care of them and went to see them and sat talking
they had enough to eat and the Judge had those books he read
        but his feet were getting worse there were others down there
like that—With me—Puhipaka said—it is my face
        but you can see that—and when they had left him Kua said
—I think Mr Stolz wants a saddle that he can say
        you made for him a saddle like nobody else's
because I think he wants to make use of you in some way
        in this new position of his and it has to do
with how close you are to the Judge and to the others
        in Kalalau—and Koʻolau nodded—That is
what I thought too—he said and Kua said—One of the guests

who is coming up with Mr Knudsen is Dr
Campbell who says that the people in Kalalau
     should be let alone and he is a government doctor
but others never thought that way and Stolz is one of those—

8.

—It is better if they go out in the evening—
     Kawaluna said to Pi'ilani as they stood watching
the two Kaleimanus the child and his grandfather
     taking their canoe down the sand to go fishing
—For that child the sea is good but the midday sun is not—
     Kawaluna said—I know—Pi'ilani said
—I see how his eyes look in the sunlight—Kawaluna said
     —and the brightness hurts them——And he loves to go fishing
with his grandfather—Pi'ilani said—but I know
     it is true about the brightness though when it is night
I lie awake until they are back——Next week the moon
     will be right on the third night and we will all take the net out
and nobody will sleep—Kawaluna said and they laughed
     seeing the canoe reflected on the calm sea as the light
widened between them and they sat on the steps while the stilts
     waded along the water's edge lifting in flight
a little way with the white flashing as the wings rose
     then gliding back down onto their feet to run and stand
vanishing into their shadows and then appearing again
     It was after the night when they all took the net out
with Kawaluna herself directing the fishing
     a night when the net came in heavy with fish and they
ate fish on the beach before the sun was up and then began
     to clean and salt some and dry some and in the afternoon
they slept and the next day Ko'olau went back to Waiawa
     and the young horses and again Mr Stolz turned up
and sat watching him work with them and when Ko'olau
     had stopped for a moment he went over to talk to him
and told him he had brought the drawing for the saddle
     —There is only one kind I can make—Ko'olau told him
—and that is my kind—and Mr Stolz said—I have also heard
     that you are the best pig hunter on this part of the island
I would like a chance to go hunting pig with you—
     —I have not hunted pig for a while now—Ko'olau said
Mr Stolz said—I expect you have not forgotten
     anything could we go the day after tomorrow—
—It would have to be later—Ko'olau said—some time later—
     but before Mr Stolz left he had agreed on a day

9.

The dry still days of later summer and the beginning
    of autumn had already gone and the rains were coming in
again along the upper valleys—He thinks I will
    help him talk big about what a pig hunter he is—
Ko'olau said at home at the end of the day
    on the steps of the house looking out past Mānā
to Ni'ihau—But maybe we will not see one pig
    in a whole day—he said and he told Pi'ilani
what Kua had said and what they both thought Mr Stolz
    had in mind—He wants to get up in the world—Ko'olau said
—and it may be the Judge he is after so he can say
    I am the one who arrested the Judge I brought him in
I cleaned out that place and maybe he thinks I will help him—
    —What makes you think that—Pi'ilani asked and he sniffed
—That rope is rotten—he said—I know it—Pi'ilani agreed
    —But I wanted to hear what you said—and Ko'olau took
Kaleimanu onto his lap and sat looking out
    to the far island darkening with the sun beyond it
and the red seeping into the light and after a while
    he looked at Pi'ilani sewing beside him and he said
—Do you see anything different about my face look at
    both sides—and she looked up at him and looked closely and said
—No there is nothing different about it maybe some little
    red there from the sun you should not spend so much time in the sun
and you should protect yourself better and wear your hat—
    But he said to her—We did not work in the sun today
we have not been much in the sun these last days run your hand
    over my face there do you feel anything—and she said
—No it is smooth do you think you rubbed it too hard
    when you were washing—and he said—I saw it in the mirror
these red places they go away and they come back—
    —Wear your hat—she said—You should have been wearing it
all summer long and now the summer is gone but you
    should be careful wear it when you go out tomorrow—
—We should all be wearing hats—Ko'olau said and they laughed

10.

In the early morning before he left when they were alone
    in the house she felt how silent he was and she said
—You will be up in the forest today and the sun
    will not be so hot and the winter is almost here
but try to be careful—and he said—What if it is not
    the sun—and she put her hand on his arm and said

—We will watch it and we will hope and you know you are strong—
     He put his arm around her and drew her against him
and said—I did not want to talk any more about it
     last night with our Kaleimanu there but I have seen
red patches like that on him too on his legs and his chest
     then I did not see them and then I saw them again—
—Yes—Pi'ilani said—I have seen them and I know
     that Kawaluna has seen them too but she talked about
his eyes and the sun hurting his eyes and keeping him
     out of the sun and maybe it is only the sun
how dry and hot it has been these last months I cannot
     remember such a hot summer—Ko'olau stood looking away
—What stays with me—he said—is that I think I remember
     red places like that on Niuli on her arms
and on her neck that patch that Kukui pointed to
     as an old birth mark that had come back do you remember—
—They never told us about those—Pi'ilani said
     —They never told us anything they simply took her—
—They never told us anything—Ko'olau said
     —but we know more now although not about Niuli—
and they stood together in their house without a word
     with their arms around each other and then she reached up
to the rack by the door and took his hat and put it on him
     with the cord under his chin and handed him the gun
from behind the door and he laughed and swung a belt
     with a few cartridges over his shoulder and picked up
a saddle bag and then turned and embraced her again
     and stepped out the door—A fine day for it—she said

II.

She stood watching as he saddled his horse and she saw
     Mr Stolz come riding between the houses and he
called out—Good morning—to Ko'olau and looked around and saw her
     and this time he raised his hat—Good morning—he said again
—I thought I would save us some time and ride out here early
     to meet you—and Ko'olau said—I am ready—and mounted
Mr Stolz waved to her and she nodded and they rode off
     she knew it would be late when Ko'olau got back that night
and the lamps had long been out in the houses she could see
     when he rode in on the tired horse and she thought how he
never seemed tired himself but this time he looked tired
     as he took off the saddle and led the horse to the paddock
and came and put his arms around her and stood still
     then he went and washed and sat down at the table
where the lamp was burning—Today no pig—he said

    with a laugh—Lucky the pigs safe tonight—he sat looking at her
with his hat still on and she brought fish and poi over
    to the table and bananas and he caught her hand
as she was passing—Where did you go—she asked him
    —I took him up Ka'awaloa all morning
not many pigs there you know but I heard one and told him
    One pig there and he spent some time trying to find it
then we came back down and up Niu a way toward
    Pu'u Opae I showed him tracks and we followed them
but we never saw anything—Ko'olau stopped talking
    and she asked—And was that all—and he said—As far as pigs go
But after a while he started to ask me about
    the Judge and others in Kalalau little rain questions
little by little you know and I had nothing to tell him
    then he comes out and tells me it is a bad situation—
—Is it—I asked him he said—Yes and it cannot go on
    it is unclean—he told me—and against the law—and I said
that I understood that the Board of Health had given
    permission for those people to stay where they were—
Where did you hear that—he said—I work for Mr Knudsen
    I told him—And I work for the Board of Health now—
he told me—as a special agent—and so I said nothing
    and at the end he said that I appeared to be sunburned
but that he thought I should show it to a doctor

12.

—If he comes out here again—Ko'olau said to her
    —try to keep him from seeing Kaleimanu—and she said
—He is over at my aunt's most of the time these days
    playing with Ida they spend the whole day together—
—But you saw the way that man comes shadowing around
    looking at everything——Yes I saw that—she told him
—And that low voice of his if he talks to me I will make sure
    that people hear us and what we are talking about—
But for some time nobody came out that way except
    those who lived there Ho'ona came from the mill
and said he had heard that Mr Stolz had been out
    hunting pig with Ko'olau and Pi'ilani said nothing
then one day when Ko'olau was at home a man they knew
    named Pokipala whom Kua had known for years
and who was working for the government one of those
    they called rats who slipped around behind the houses
looking to see whether someone was living back there
    trying to hide came riding along with his head up
out in the open and up to Ko'olau and showed him

a paper he had that was an order to go with him
to the doctor to be examined because someone
        who had seen him suspected that he had leprosy
—The sickness—Ko'olau said—that separates people—
        and he said—You stay there—and went to his horse and Pi'ilani
caught his arm at the corner of the house—Whatever
        they tell you—she said quickly—I want to stay together
if you have to go away I want us all to go—
        then his father Kaleimanu came and asked where he was going
and when he told him his father said—I will come with you—
        and as they rode off Ko'olau asked Pokipala
—Who was it who said they thought I might have that sickness—
        —I am not supposed to tell you—Pokipala answered
and Ko'olau said—I know who it was he says he works
        for the Board of Health——And he does—Pokipala said
—It was Mr Stolz—Ko'olau said—is he afraid that
        people will know——He is not afraid—Pokipala said
Then Ko'olau said—You do not have to ride along with us
        we know the way——It is my duty—Pokipala said
and they rode on to Dr Campbell's office in Waimea

13.

At night on the schooner coming back from Honolulu
        Valdemar Knudsen sat out on the deck for a while
in a sheltered corner against a bulkhead with a blanket
        and a piece of sailcloth over him and watched the masts
waving across the dark clouds and the stars behind them
        and as the wind crossed his face it seemed that he had never
ceased to be the child bundled up in his wooden carriage
        with the blanket tucked under his chin and he could feel
somewhere near him out of sight warm figures who loved him
        then he remembered that they had been dead for years
in Norway far back in the frozen ground which he did not
        think ever to see again and there was his beard lying white
on the shadowy sailcloth and he felt alone and felt age
        rushing across dark water and he growled a few bars
of a hymn low to himself and then a phrase of Norwegian
        from a hymn he had sung as a child recalled to him
a moment from the book he had been reading on this trip
        on which he had come alone this time it was a new
edition of Ibsen and he had been reading *Ghosts*
        again and pondering these incurable afflictions
and the judgments that echoed from the mouths of the spared
        Reverend Dole preaching to the natives about the Lord's
vengeance upon their sins and his son Sanford Ballard's wife
        Anna never touching a doorknob in her own house

without covering it with a handkerchief for fear
    that a native might have touched it before her and he thought
what I feel is not age yet for I am as strong as ever
    but in him was a new distance an alien floating sadness
and he went over to Honolulu much less often these days
    than in the years when he had sat in the legislature
and when he and his own Anna had gone there together
    and each time had felt young again but he had taken this trip
to try to arrange some improvement however
    tenuous some more practical and kinder way
of providing for those found to have leprosy
    because at present he saw nothing but useless cruelty
but he was coming back reaching for hope in the empty dark

14.

He had managed to obtain one tentative permit
    to take care of those on Kauai whom the doctors there
were convinced had leprosy and already he was providing
    care for them at Kekaha while those who had gone
across into Kalalau to whom he had been sending
    such medicines as existed had signed petitions
asking for his treatment to be made official and their
    refuge sanctioned by the government but the Board
kept sending him letters urging the segregation
    of lepers and insisting upon their removal
from contact with their families then a notice arrived
    stating that unless doctors pronounced those in his care
cured in a matter of months they would have to be sent
    to Honolulu and Moloka'i and Sheriff Wilcox
on Kauai was resorting to increasingly rougher
    tactics surprising native houses searching and seizing
everyone even suspected of harboring
    the disease and the cases of violence the shootings
and rumors of shootings multiplied and that summer
    the Board had informed Knudsen that he would be allowed
to keep his patients at Kekaha only for three more months
    and in Honolulu he had learned that his friend George Trousseau
whom he considered much the finest of the doctors there
    best informed and most clear and gifted was on the point
of resigning from the board of examiners because
    his own findings and the conclusions of the latest
Indian Leprosy Commission had left him convinced
    that the policy of enforced segregation
had always been useless and impossible and that there were
    more effective and humane ways of dealing with this disease

15.

But then there was that colleague of Trousseau's Moritz
    one of the predominant medical authorities
at the leprosy settlement of Kalaupapa
    who made it obvious that he alone understood
this disease in its sources and shifts both pathological
    and racial and who would discourse exhaustively
on the unclean eating habits of the Hawaiians
    and in his view the segregating of those with leprosy
was an unquestionable necessity and his voice climbed
    as he described the improvements that had been effected
at Kalaupapa the facilities the expenditures
    the misconceptions while at the Board of Health
under its new director Knudsen heard heavy rumblings
    about a policy of no nonsense and of smoking this
thing out at last and he might as well know that Sheriff Wilcox
    was disgusted at what he called the incompetence
and cowardice of most of his native constables
    who he said frequently let people know in advance
when they were coming and were easily frightened off
    and that the Sheriff's grumblings had been echoed respectfully
in letters and then a visit from Louis Stolz
    who now had the confidence of the Board where a friend could
quote his letters of application for the post of deputy
    not for the sake of the office as there is neither
money nor glory in it for me but I would like
    underlined to see the laws a little better
enforced in this district than they are at present
    and believe I can say without boasting that I can do
better than the present incumbent and they had given him
    special authority for dealing with the lepers
on Kauai those now cared for at Kekaha those still at large
    and the fugitives at Kalalau whom the Board
fully intended to clear out by force if need be
    as soon as a vessel was available and the weather
allowed a landing for the waves there along that coast
    would make it dangerous to anchor and go ashore
during the winter months and in the meantime the plan
    was to remain a secret for obvious reasons

16.

The night wind was rising and the sea was growing rough
    he went below feeling stiff and damp and his sleep was shallow
he kept running over it all sensing the fabric

of what he had known and been sure of dissolving
under him and sliding out like a tide to the sound
      of the creaking of the vessel that was taking him home
then it was the morning and they were coming to anchor
      off Koloa and then the whaleboat reached the ramp once more
and he saw it all as though it were under water
      and as he stepped onto the wharf he heard his name called
a voice like an unwanted touch and he looked around
      and saw it was Stolz himself with that smile and his arm raised
he was pushing through the others toward the ramp and there he stood
      the extended hand the pleased face the opportune greeting
there was something they were to deliver to him here
      this morning he said but what a pleasant surprise
and so on into questions which Knudsen found himself
      diverting and he managed to divulge nothing at all
about the trip except the weather on the way back
      and then Stolz told him of the special authority
granted him by the Board of Health which Knudsen said
      he had known about—and in that connection—Stolz said
—Dr Campbell informs me that your employee from out past
      Kekaha there you know that Koʻolau has been examined
and found to have leprosy and I am afraid I will
      have to send him to the settlement—Knudsen looked at him
and watched the moustache and Stolz said—I have been thinking
      of urging you to use the influence you have
with Judge Kauai and those lepers now evading
      the law over in Kalalau and perhaps between us
we could resolve this disgraceful situation
      in a civilized manner——This is scarcely the place
nor the moment to talk about it—Knudsen told him
      and he turned to his son Eric and the Hawaiians
from Makaweli who had come down to meet him
      —I may call on you then—Stolz said and Knudsen nodded

17.

Anne had come down from Halemanu and the children
      were away at school and she and Knudsen lay talking
in the big bed at Makaweli and when he had told her
      what there was to tell they were both silent for a while
then she said she wondered what would become of Koʻolau's
      family they had that little boy and she asked whether
they would go away to the settlement with Koʻolau
      and Knudsen said he did not think so but she said
—But you remember there were some who were allowed to have
      their wives or husbands go with them if they wanted to

as helpers—and Knudsen said—The Board has not been
    consistent about that and recently they are set
against it in general and of course they will not
    admit children there unless they have the disease—
Anne said—I keep seeing them when they were younger and how
    beautiful Pi'ilani was do you remember
when was that day when she was wearing the head lei and standing
    in her white dress outside the church in the sunlight
I seem to have forgotten all but the happiness
    and how she looked with that stillness she has—and Knudsen
said—Yes—and kept trying not to let his mind go on
    turning back to Stolz he did not want to mention the man
and he said nothing until at last she said it for him
    with a kind of laugh—You never did like him did you
from the beginning that Louis Stolz—and he said—I did not—
    and took her hand and said—I never could abide him
not when he came here to see Mary Rowell when she was
    taking care of the children and not when he married her
not when he went on toying with Hawaiian women
    threatening them if they ever told I could not bear his wiles
and his overweening and he makes me ashamed of myself
    because I think I disliked him before I even knew him—

18.

A man came to Makaweli one morning with a note
    for Knudsen from Dr Campbell and the next morning
the doctor himself came and asked to see Knudsen alone
    He said—I wanted to tell you that I have been informed
by the President of the Board of Health that he is
    proposing to come over here shortly perhaps next week
to go out to Kekaha with Dr Smith and I believe
    Dr Emerson and me to examine the leprosy patients
now in your care would you prefer to be present
    at the time of the visit——I would not—Knudsen told him
—and I would not want those helpless people to suppose
    that I was one of your party and I shall make it
clear to them that your visit has nothing to do with me—
    —In that case my calling upon you this morning
may be an embarrassment—Dr Campbell said—I thank you
    for your courteous intent—Knudsen said—And I respect your own
difficulties—Campbell looked at the floor for a moment
    and then at Knudsen—You are a man of science—he said
—And I have admired you for years and hope that you will
    understand me when I tell you that not all members
of the medical profession entertain the same views
    of the present methods of dealing with leprosy cases

and the policy of segregation and removal
        for treatment away from their families——Yes I know that—
Knudsen told him—And I believe you delayed having
        Pake and Keola sent over from Kekaha
to Honolulu after their diagnosis
        some months ago I sympathize with your position—
Campbell said—I should warn you further that the Board
        plans to elicit the help of one of your wife's
family Mr Gay to persuade the fugitive lepers
        in Kalalau to put themselves in the hands of
the authorities—Knudsen said—I would be rather
        surprised if he did that and still more if they agreed to it—
—It was young Mr Rowell on the Board who suggested it—
        Campbell said—And he proposed taking part in it himself—
—Did he now—Knudsen said—It would be worth watching
        one of the Rowells charm Judge Kauai out of his tree—
and they both laughed at that and bowed and said Good Morning

19.

Knudsen was at the ranch at Waiawa with Kua
        watching the foals running when Louis Stolz rode up
and fingered the brim of his hat and when they had traded
        civilities Knudsen asked Stolz what his errand was
he allowed Stolz to see that his arrival had stalled
        a conversation and he followed the way the man's eyes
slipped over the ranch and over Kua and the men
        working there that morning and Stolz said—I hoped I would find
you here—and there was a pause with the sound of hooves
        drumming through it and then Knudsen said to Kua
—We can go on with this later—and Kua nodded
        and rode off and Knudsen considered moving into the shade
but decided to stay where they were and he sat waiting
        until Stolz said—The President of the Board of Health
has been to the place in Kekaha where you house the lepers
        he took three doctors with him to examine them there—
Knudsen said—I know of the visit—Stolz said—They inform me
        that two of those you have living there are confirmed lepers—
—That conclusion was reached months ago—Knudsen said
        —They have been pronounced incurable—Stolz told him
—And they are to be sent to the settlement——So that they
        can die there—Knudsen answered—I have heard that too—
Stolz said—It is my duty to see that the law
        is carried out——Ah—Knudsen said—your duty—and Stolz went on
—And we have spoken of that other who lives in Kekaha
        your cowhand Ko'olau and I have learned from the Board
that Mr Rowell wants Mr Gay to support him

in bringing the lepers in Kalalau to their senses
but I think you and I would be more likely to manage that—
        —You mean—Knudsen said—because Judge Kauai was your neighbor—
—Because they trust you—Stolz said—and they trust this Koʻolau
        who could bear a message from you and I could offer him
concessions of some kind perhaps——Do you think so—Knudsen said—
        —What concessions could you offer considering your duty—
—I can talk with him—Stolz said—We hunt pig together—
        Knudsen said—I can see how it might serve your purpose
but I must talk this over with my relative Mr Gay—

                                20.

On a Sunday in the autumn when the big mill at Kekaha
        was all but silent with the wind echoing in the slatting walls
Hoʻona was over there part of the day checking
        shipments and storage and talking story with whoever
came along with nothing to do but Piʻilani's
        and Koʻolau's families were spending those days
together around the house on the way to Mānā
        preparing too much food and talking talking as though
there was not a trouble that they knew of in the world
        Koʻolau and the elder Kaleimanu his father
and his son Kaleimanu were cleaning and salting fish
        that they had brought in that morning and Hoʻona walked in
and sat down in the shade looking sick and Piʻilani
        asked him what was the matter—That one Pokipala—
—Where is he—Koʻolau asked and stood up—He is not here—
        Hoʻona told him—He came to the leper house
I saw his horse there and heard crying and then I saw him
        come out and ride away going toward Waimea
he said he is coming back in two weeks with the wagon
        to take Pake and Keola off to the settlement—
Kukui began to cry and the rest were silent
        —Only those two—Koʻolau asked—That is what he said to them—
Hoʻona said and Koʻolau asked—What about Nalu
        who was taking care of Pake he told me that if she went
he wanted to go with her are they going to take him too—
        —He will not be allowed to go—Hoʻona said
—And Keola's sister who he lived with——They will not
        let her go either—Hoʻona said—And you know
Keola has almost no fingers left to feed himself
        cannot reach his mouth right and then it was Malea
who started to laugh when they were all crying and she said
        We going to make one big dinner once and for all
with our friends and we all get drunk for our own funeral—

21.

—Do you think he will come back here then that Pokipala—
      Kukui asked and none of them answered—The doctors
only went to the leper house—Hoʻona said at last
      —And so did Pokipala——That was this time—Koʻolau said
—What can they take when they go—Piʻilani asked Hoʻona
      —One box with their things and you know they do not have much
there in that house——More than they let Niuli
      take with her—Koʻolau said and the child Kaleimanu
started asking his questions about Niuli again
      and about the settlement and then he too gave up
and they ate in silence and when they had said good-night
      and gone to bed and the house was still Koʻolau
slipped out and walked down between the canoes to sit
      on the sand looking out toward the dark rim of Niʻihau
and in while Piʻilani came and sat there beside him
      without a word and they lay back as they had done
years before and for a long time they said nothing
      hearing the small waves breaking along the shoreline
Then Koʻolau said—That Keola has lived there a year
      more than a year and that Pake was there for that long
they thought they could live like that doing nothing wrong
      and their friends could see them they thought they would die there
all that time they thought so and then he just came for them
      and he will come again you remember the doctor told me
they would send me away—Piʻilani said—Yes—in the dark
      —And I want us to stay together—she said—But I
do not believe he will let me go with you——If Kaleimanu
      did not have the same kind of red places on his skin
I would want you to stay here and be with him—Koʻolau said
      —But they will find him too and I do not know where they send
children where did they send Niuli—and Piʻilani said
      again—I want us to stay together—and they sat there
in silence and then Koʻolau said—I will not let them
      take me to the settlement and I told Pokipala
that day the doctor examined me that I would go only
      if we could all go together after what you said to me
but I do not trust them and I know the time has come
      to go away and to go over into Kalalau
and live with our friends there—Then we will go together—
      Piʻilani said—We will be there together—

22.

Hoʻona and Kukui hung ti leaves around the doors
        as the church did at Christmas and Kawaluna watched them
as she helped with the food and Hoʻona said that the neighbors
        were going to the leper house for the good-bye dinner
—We could send them food—Kukui said and they packed up
        baskets of things to eat and to take to the leper house
and Hoʻona and Piʻilani and Koʻolau's father
        carried them and Hoʻona took an old cloth runner
the women at the Waimea church had sewn years before
        which Reverend Rowell had given him one day saying
it was too faded to put up again and he wondered
        whether Hoʻona might like it the pale words read Peace
On Earth Good Will To Men Hoʻona took it
        to the leper house and they hung it up though few of them
could read it and by that time they were afloat in cane liquor
        and ʻawa It was the next day when the eating and drinking
and the visits were over that Kawaluna was sitting
        on the front step as the sun went down and only family
still there and Koʻolau went to Kawaluna
        and sat at her feet and leaned his head on her knee
and she laid her hand on his hair and then he said to her
        —I will not let them take me to the settlement—
and when he looked up at her she nodded without answering
        —I am going over into Kalalau—he told her
—Yes—she said—Koʻolau—and then she said his name again
        —Koʻolau—so that they heard it mean the windward cliffs
and the time of trouble that name that she had known was his
        before he was born the others were all listening to them
as he said—Piʻilani is coming with me and we will
        take Kaleimanu with us——Yes—Kawaluna said
and Piʻilani's mother Kepola said—I could come
        if you want me with you——Yes—Piʻilani said
and Kepola's sister Kinolou was there with them
        and Kinolou's little girl Ida who had grown up with
Kaleimanu and Ida said—I want to go with
        Kaleimanu——Oh no—Kinolou said but Kepola told her
—I can take care of her if she comes—and as they began
        to cry Koʻolau stood up and said to Kawaluna
—When you decide what night would be good for us to go
        I will tell Kua and we will get the horses for it—

23.

That first time that she had climbed down the steep crumbling
        narrow path along the top of the ridge that flared out
into the clouds over the valley when she looked back on it
        afterwards the way came and went in the braid of
later times when she had travelled down that trail something
        of each emerging just as the trail would appear
where the clouds parted and then they would cover it again
        There would be nothing below her and small echoes drifting up
through deaf cloud and always it was hard to balance and always
        she was carrying something although that first time
when the horses were unloaded they had hidden
        some of the bundles and the rolled blankets back under
the bushes for someone to come up and get them later
        She remembered the rain the first time it caught them
with the wind whipping it cold against them and pushing them
        toward the cliff but then she thought how the rain had found her
somewhere on that trail every time going up or down
        but that first time it came as the clouds were turning
into shadow and the daylight was going she could still feel
        the first touch of night in the valley but by then they were
down from the screen walls of the cliff and the trail twined
        between broken rocks and across scree down to the first
small clutching trees and she knew that the sound she had come to
        under the wind was a stream running below her
then as they went in among the branches it was darker
        and ahead of her she could see Ko‘olau’s shirt
which she had not seen up in the white cloud and she knew
        that he had taken off the cloak he had been wearing
and had wrapped it around Kaleimanu over his shoulder
        at last she heard him call out a strange sound that was a signal
and a moment later she heard the answer to it
        coming from below and they picked their way down through the dark
until she saw a lantern flickering up through the woods
        like a burning insect and Ko‘olau called out his own name
and a voice shouted—Ho—with pleasure and the lantern swung
        and rose toward them and it was Iwa carrying it
who laughed to see them and reached to take everything
        he had arms for and he led the way through the trees
to Naoheiki’s house in the lap of the mountain

24.

—We were hoping you would come over to us—Iwa said
    —That Pokipala talks and the ripple goes all the way
you never told me about the doctor in Koloa
    and Kua never told me but we heard all the same—
Ko'olau said to him—I have been thinking about it
    but when we made our decision there was no time
to find you and tell you and besides it was better to have
    no more ripples going around   They sat down by a small fire
between rocks behind the house and Iwa said—If we
    had known what day you were coming we would all have been here
the ones who could get here and we would have the pig
    all baked and the dinner ready——We have plenty—
a voice said from the side of the house and Kauila
    came around the corner laughing and walked to Ko'olau
and embraced him—You remember me—Kauila asked
    —I think now I am wearing another face and I am
still younger than you are Naoheiki is up here asleep
    and the Judge and his family over there they will all
be glad you people came but maybe you should go see them
    tomorrow because they would all be asleep now
and here we have plenty to eat only it is cold—
    Ko'olau said—I think mostly now we are tired—
Kauila said—And thirsty I am sure and must be hungry—
    —My my—a woman's voice said and it was Kalaina
limping into the firelight—I know they are thirsty—
    and she held out a big water gourd to Kepola
—I am Kalaina—she said and then she was gone
    and as they drank she came back with baskets of fruit
—Wait there—she said and turned to get more—Thank you—
    Kepola said—But the children are too tired to eat
they are both asleep——You eat a little—Kalaina said
    —and then we can all sleep and start new tomorrow—
and she kept bringing more food cold fish cold taro
    she went for more water and then she took Kepola
by the hand and Iwa picked up Ida and led the way
    into the house and Ko'olau stood up with Kaleimanu
still asleep on his shoulder and Kalaina led them all
    one by one through the low unlit doorway

25.

Kalaina drew them through the dark to a soft pile
    where they could lie down and Pi'ilani saw the doorway
behind her lighter than the darkness around her

there were paler shadows out there above the fire
Kaleimanu made distant sounds in his sleep as they put him
        between them and she lay gazing up at the black
above her in the smell that kept soaking into her
        smell of damp and dirt smell of decaying wood and moss
smell of rags age mouths with no teeth old food incontinence
        rancid and bottomless so that she felt hot in there
though she had been cold out by the fire and as her back
        sank into the pile she was half asleep but when she looked up
she was awake again and thought she could never sleep
        and kept seeing her feet moving down through the fog again
ahead of her and then she woke hearing the owl very near
        and she thought it was Kawaluna but the smell told her
where she was and she lay listening to the child's breath
        and when she opened her eyes again she saw the doorway
filled with the first gray of the ghost dawn in the silence
        before the birds were awake and she tried to imagine the place
now that it was day and she could make out the matted grass
        and the poles of the ceiling and she saw that she was lying
on a heap of rags and moss with a crowd of baskets
        and gourds watching her from beyond her feet and then they were
all outside with Kalaina limping ahead to show them
        the stream for washing and for filling water gourds
and telling them to eat and she looked up to where the cliffs
        disappeared in the cloud and Kauila was telling them
that the Judge said he needed a while to be presentable
        and Kauila laughed as he said it and told them to eat
and she saw that Koʻolau who had carried the gun with him
        down the cliffs along with the roll over his shoulder
and Kaleimanu on top of the roll now took the gun
        with him wherever he went and set it next to himself
when he ate and when she raised her eyes from the children
        and looked at his face she saw that he was watching her
and then she heard the unbroken sound of the stream flowing

                            26.

—Not too clean in there—Naoheiki announced to the world
        as he hove around the corner still half asleep
—If I had known you were coming we would have got it up
        like a wedding for you with flowers and all that kind
makes me ashamed now—and he embraced them one by one
        as he talked—But we can still do that today—he said
—This is my mountain house and I let my friends stay here
        in the lean-to when they are up here and sometimes
they let it slip for a while the front of the house is around here

where we were sleeping when you came and this whole place now
above the stream with the rocks around it they call
        the Big House where the Judge and his family are staying
and now there are other houses around some you can see
        from here some wood houses some grass ones since you leper friends
started coming with your families and there are more
        down through the woods that you cannot see from here they are even
growing some taro up here now I am happy you have come—
        he said it to Koʻolau and embraced him again
calling him brother and then he said it to all of them
        then Kauila reappeared to say—The Judge says come now—
and they filed over with Naoheiki as the host
        leading the way and found the Judge sitting up in a chair
as big as a throne made out of planks with blankets
        folded around him for cushions he had his broad hat on
and a dark coat buttoned like a man in a picture
        and as they came in from the sunlight he looked like that
like a faded page or a shadow his feet were wrapped up
        and propped on a box but he raised his arms—Come in Come in—
he called—How glad I am to see you and I see you all know
        Naoheiki but you cannot know what a friend
he has been to us like a son to us and I think you know
        Kaenaku and my family we are all here all well
more or less—and he laughed and looked around at his wife
        and his older sister Mere and as they embraced
he went on asking questions about their coming over
        and their health and what news they brought and Koʻolau
when his eyes had settled into the room was shaken
        to see the Judge's face wrung and crumpled with the skin
by his mouth like the rind of a dry orange and he looked
        at the Judge's wife Kaenaku and could scarcely see
through the knotted features before him the woman he had admired

27.

Kepola was looking at Kaenaku out of
        the corner of her eyes not wanting to appear to be
staring and she was thinking back to Kaenaku
        coming out of church wearing ginger leis her elegance
her hats her fragrance the way she sat in the carriage
        her manner of speaking and inclining her head she looked
at Kaenaku's mouth like a chicken's foot and she wondered
        how much older Kaenaku might be than she was
and Kaenaku caught her eye and they both looked away
        thinking that they would be neighbors and the Judge praised
the children and then told Koʻolau that they had been

preparing another petition but Koʻolau
    told him of the Board of Health doctors and Sheriff Wilcox
        going to Valdemar Knudsen's house for the lepers
in Kekaha and about them sending Pake
        and Keola off to the settlement after that
Piʻilani and Kepola took the children outside
        with Naoheiki going ahead to make them all at home
and Koʻolau talked with the Judge about Knudsen saying
        to Kua that this was a bad time when the best doctors
at the Board of Health were on the point of resigning
        and the harsh voices were having their way and proposing
sending a vessel to Kalalau to take off the lepers
        Knudsen had said they kept discussing the matter
what boat to charter and when and kept putting it off
        but he was afraid that some day they would do it
and the Judge said—It sounds as though there is not much hope
        of their favoring a new petition and perhaps less now
than there was with the others but I am for sending it
        even so to have it on the books and make it plain
that our intentions were serious and honorable
        though they may choose to make light of them and ignore them
but they will have trouble making light of me if they come
        I suggest a sedan chair—he said laughing—If they can find one—
Koʻolau said—I will not go with them and I know
        Pokipala told everyone I had the sickness but he
never knew that our child Kaleimanu is sick the same way
        and I will not let them take us with them—and the Judge looked
past Koʻolau's head and saw the gun leaning by the door

28.

Piʻilani would look back on those first days in the valley
        first days first weeks she could not tell how long it lasted
that time that season that age in itself and it would seem
        to be a sound ringing all alone that she had not
heard before and could not call to and even when
        she could no longer hear any echo of it there was
its silence and she went back in silence to something
        she thought had been there even in the new strangeness
of whatever she had touched and even in the cold
        and the missing Kekaha and the bed and voices back there
and in those moments of nothing but cloud and wet and not
        knowing with the knowing waiting under them even
there she knew it had been and she had breathed it and looked
        through its air for however long it lasted and she
could turn to it in her mind afterward and see it as a clear

suspended time when she had once had everything Naoheiki
showed the children a pool up along the stream where small fish
 swam straight up the rocks inside the waterfall and he took
Kepola and Pi'ilani to his house and told them
 that he would be staying at his place down near the shore
so they were welcome to the whole of his house up here
 and he started to clean it out saying he had to make it
right for them and he told them that he would take them all
 down to the lower part of the valley where people
had always been living and they would have a big feast there
 so they would get to know the ones who lived there now
he went on talking as he swept and carried and they worked
 together and he told them who they would meet down there
stories of the families who was who and who they
 were descended from until Pi'ilani and Kepola
could no longer tell who he was talking about and they
 were all laughing drawing out threads of stories while
the Judge was trying to tell Ko'olau what he had learned
 of those living down in the valley now—You knew it—he said
—long before I came or any of the lepers up here
 and I know it only from up here where they had
the house ready for us and were glad to put me down at last
 I have not managed to get down there yet and I know
only the ones who came up here to see us bringing us
 things we need but I have never known such kindness—

29.

—It has been that way since before I came—the Judge said
 —Word arrived that they would have a house ready for us
and that we would be welcome and by that time there had been
 lepers living in hiding up here for years some of them
and with their families so those people knew what to expect
 they had seen something of the sickness by that time
the helplessness and the dying and they knew how lepers
 are regarded by the foreigners and the government
and what the law is and although I decided to come
 even then I believed only a part of the welcome
they extended and I thought it came only from
 the lepers here in the upper part of the valley
the ones for whom Knudsen has been getting the medicine
 for you to bring and even when I had let them know
that I was scarcely able to walk any more
 and would never be able to climb down the trail and they
said they would carry me I set out only partly
 believing and thinking that if I fell it would be

better than rotting away as a favor to those
    who pray for a world without us and then they picked me up
and started down and it seems that I must have been
    in a fever perhaps or something like it with the fear
cold in me shaking me and the sickness so that I
    felt nothing in my body at all which I had been
prudent enough to empty before we started
    but part of the way down I did not know who I was
I looked into the clouds and slipped out into them
    I looked up through tears but I was not weeping I was
not there and then they were heaving me over the rocks
    at the foot of the cliff and it was beyond believing
but I learned that they had carried down others before me
    though maybe no one so heavy and still they treat it
as no big thing and some go daily to houses
    to move those who cannot stand up but what has surprised me
almost as much is the way those who were here before us
    in the lower valley have behaved toward us and how
good they have been to us we have heard in the stories
    that people once treated each other this way but I thought
that was long ago and probably was made up—

30.

—They keep telling me that we are their family—the Judge said
    —the word makes me feel more like a foreigner the more
I would like it to be true and after what I have known
    and what my family and Kaenaku's have known it seems stranger
that they should all welcome us in that way without question
    I know that some have seen leprosy in their own relatives
and some have seen people taken away with it
    but most of them know simply that this is an affliction
that has befallen us and those of our own blood
    recurring like an inheritance how many of those
with my name have died of it these last years I cannot tell
    and in this valley everyone knows of the household
by the wet cave outside Hanalei where they grow taro
    who were cursed and one child in each generation
has been claimed by leprosy nobody understands that
    but here they treat us as their own kin think of Naoheiki
who got his house ready for us and has given his own to you
    and Kaumeheiwa down by the shore is another like him
some of our people up here who have the strength for it
    go down and work in the taro beside the friends there
and Puheliku has restored a small taro pond
    that had been abandoned down there a long time ago

and they all went and planted the first taro with him
    and then ate and drank and danced that was after I came here
some go out fishing together and they bring fish up here
    they bring it to me and what good am I to them
they sit and listen to me as an elder and what they ask
    I answer as well as I can but the best of it is
their own stories—Koʻolau said—Our boy Kaleimanu
    has always loved stories——This is a place for them—
the Judge said—Will you bring the boy over to see me—
    —That will make him happy—Koʻolau said and he took the rifle
to leave at Naoheiki's house and he told Piʻilani
    that he was going down to the valley to see about fish
and he followed the stream path all the way to the shore
    and there he saw a tall imposing man and a beautiful
boy standing by the water and he knew the man who was
    named Pā from a family that had always lived in the valley
where everyone knew that this gentle figure was a shark spirit
    —Koʻolau—he said and embraced him—You have come to stay—

31.

She remembered that it was only a few days after
    the great feast of welcome that Naoheiki had planned
and brought together for them at his house down near the sea
    to which everyone in the valley who could walk
or was not too sick or too old or taking care
    of someone who needed them came bringing what they could
they came with fish and fruit with taro shellfish seaweed
    fern shoots chickens a goat from the cliffs and Koʻolau had gone
with Kala up a ravine toward Nualolo and they
    had brought back a pig there must have been more than a hundred
who came and they chanted part of the ceremony
    for the new year in a procession along the water's edge
and there were other chants there were love songs and dances
    and the children played by the water until dark
and Piʻilani kept remembering the feast
    at the lepers' house in Kekaha only a month
behind her and that woman's drunken voice shouting
    —Come and eat and drink we are celebrating our
funeral and now this was Kalalau and after that day
    he went out fishing with Kala and the Pā's and sometimes
took Kaleimanu with him and Kepola and Kaenaku
    liked spending time together talking and it was into
that time toward the end of one day filled with the luminous
    green of the year's beginning that Iwa arrived
at the Judge's and stood in the doorway catching his breath

—They have taken the Queen—he said and the Judge said—What—
Iwa gave him the bundle of papers that he could not read
    saying—You have to tell us what is in there they have taken
the Queen maybe she is dead because they said there is no more Queen—
    and the Judge opened the bundle and groaned as Koʻolau
and others who had seen Iwa running to the house
    pushed through the door and stood listening and the Judge
groaned again as he read—They have taken the kingdom—
    he said—They have finally taken it from us
that stiff-necked gang those partners in foul play they have
    got the American Navy to help them and they
have locked up the Queen in the palace and taken over
    and who do you suppose is the ringleader in all this
but our own Sanford Dole from Koloa that ruthless prig—

32.

—My son is a good boy—the Judge said—He has sent all these
    Commercial Advertiser The Friend and in Hawaiian
Ka Leo o ka Lahui I cannot trust one of them
    and a letter here saying he will send the rest and it is
as bad as it sounds—he read on with all of them asking
    question after question and they stood in tears listening
some unable to comprehend it and some understanding
    only too well—And who will be playing the footstool
for Sanford the Great—the Judge asked——But Lorrin A Thurston
    born to know better I remember him telling at length
of how his admiration for Sanford went back
    to the days of their youth when they went out walking together
with their guns and one day as they were passing
    through a native village a native dog barked at them
so Thurston shot it and they walked on but when that
    village was behind them Sanford said he was thinking
that trouble just might result from that which was one thing
    I doubted about the story so according to Thurston
in the next native village they came to Sanford
    shot the first native dog he saw and turned to Thurston
with that righteous look he has made his own and said Now
    I cannot be required to testify against you
and Thurston said I thought here is a man of foresight
    the kind of man we need which is what he was
for the mission boys the annexationists
    whatever they will call themselves next it is
in their pockets now—and Piʻilani saw that there were tears
    on the Judge's face and on all the faces in the room
and for a moment then they all stood there without a word

and then one and then another slipped out through the door
and some talked later asking the same things over again
        some said nothing and worked in the taro looking down
at their faces in the water and knew nothing to say
        she worked among them and listened and in the days
that followed more papers came and more of the story
        and the Judge read to them about the Provisional
Government and its proclamations and about the Queen
        but nobody knew what to expect and it seemed
to Pi'ilani that nothing had changed except in their voices

33.

In the new year at the new roll-top desk in his office
        Louis Stolz was reading of new things in the papers
among them a new Krupps Howitzer the latest
        thing of its kind manufactured in Germany
newly arrived the performance it promised its caliber
        weight of projectile range number of rounds possible
in a given time accuracy all of it on paper
        the gun scarcely uncrated the crew not yet named
Pokipala was standing in the doorway—I have told you
        to knock—Stolz said turning—I knocked—Pokipala said
—Then you wait—Stolz said—I waited—Pokipala said
        —I came to say I think Ko'olau has gone——Gone where—Stolz asked
—I was over Kekaha way to the leper house and I
        went out Mānā side and the Ko'olau house looked to be closed
his mother was next door watching me and Where is Ko'olau
        I asked her Not here she said You know where he works
Is his wife home I asked She is out his mother said
        Ko'olau's father came out and walked to Ko'olau's front step
and sat down on it facing me and I came back asking
        whoever I saw where Ko'olau was and they told me
they did not know—So the next day Stolz rode over
        to Kekaha and asked about Ko'olau and they all
said they did not know where he was and Ko'olau's father
        went again and sat on the steps next door—And where
is his wife Pi'ilani—Stolz asked and Kaleimanu
        answered—Has she some sickness why do you ask about her—
—I am looking for Ko'olau—Stolz said—And you have been told
        that he is not here——And his wife is not here either—Stolz said
—We do not tie her up—Kaleimanu answered—And nobody—
        Stolz went on while the dogs kept barking at him
—nobody knows where she is and is the little boy
        with her—Kaleimanu stared at him—Are these dogs
all yours or are they his——They get along together—

—When he is away you feed all of them do you
how long has he been gone——Piʻilani is with her mother—
    Kaleimanu said looking across to Niʻihau
and the year was some days older before Stolz could be sure
    where Koʻolau had gone and when and who was with him

34.

So whatever thought he might have had of using Koʻolau
    to talk the Judge and the rest of the fugitive lepers
into leaving the valley in some semblance of order
    and putting themselves in the custody of the Board
represented by Louis H Stolz who would be given
    credit for the operation he would have to
go about it in some other way now and no doubt
    he would have to go into the valley himself at some point
and try to arrange to speak to all of them there
    but he had no authorization for going in there
and his supervisor Sheriff Wilcox who never stopped
    trumpeting about wanting to clean out that valley
kept telling him to wait until the weather was right
    and they had the right boat and enough men to do it
for there would be deaths on both sides so Stolz wrote to the head
    of the Board Dear sir a leper belonging to
this district after having been examined by Dr Campbell
    and notified that he would have to go to Molokaʻi
asked for and received permission to stay a week
    in order to settle up his affairs this request
as has been our practice here was granted upon his
    promise to be ready and willing to go
upon the return of the steamer Pele he has broken
    his promise and has gone over to Kalalau where
so many other lepers are as this is the first
    person who has escaped from this district while I have been
deputy sheriff I am anxious to bring him back
    and have requested Doctor Campbell to get out
a warrant for him which he will do Unless I receive
    positive orders to the contrary it is my
intention to proceed shortly to Kalalau
    and endeavor to arrest the person in question
who is a man named Koʻolau I think it is quite
    probable that unless I happen upon him
unawares resistance will be shown as almost
    every man in Kalalau is armed and much as I
should regret it and endeavor to avoid it
    somebody it may be myself or a constable

may be hurt or killed and as the Board has tacitly
 tolerated the lepers in Kalalau the man being
therefore justified to a certain extent in going there
 I would be pleased to receive any orders or advice

35.

But other questions of authority were occupying
 the capital and before Stolz received an answer
news came of the takeover and the dismantling
 of the kingdom by the annexationists and he nodded
as he read of the new Provisional Government
 name after name that he knew and thought well of so that
he was elated and rushed around to Hofgaard's store
 where they were shouting and drinking toasts but he wondered
how all this might affect his own position and duties
 Wilcox was there and assured him that nothing of that kind
would change—It is just that our friends have taken over
 which is something they should have done a long time ago
and ended the circus—he held out a bottle of Hofgaard's
 best iron-bottom cane liquor and they cheered but Stolz
still received no answer to his request and the winter
 slipped away and the President of the Board of Health was changed
and in the spring Stolz wrote to the new president starting
 over again Dear sir allow me to respectfully
call your attention to the fact that if it be
 the policy of the Board of Health to remove
during the present year the lepers now residing
 in Kalalau it would seem necessary that steps
in the matter be taken shortly as the months during which
 a steamer can effect a landing at Kalalau
are at hand if a system of segregation is to be
 carried out undoubtedly these people should be removed
it cannot be otherwise than that healthy persons will
 and are at the present time becoming infected
with leprosy and this time the Board replied telling him
 that An attempt to remove the lepers from Kalalau
simply means reducing the place by force of arms
 and they requested Stolz to send them a full report
of the number age and sex of all lepers at Kalalau
 also if possible a like list of other people
residing in the valley and it would also perhaps
 be interesting to the government they told him
to know the quantity and kind of firearms in their possession

36.

Stolz sent an answer by the next steamer respectfully
      begging to differ with the view that removal
of lepers from Kalalau would probably lead to men killed
      on both sides and suggesting that effectual work
could be done before force of arms was resorted to
      but he called their attention to the fact that at present
he was merely agent for the district of Waimea
      with no authority in Kalalau and he was not
hankering he assured them for any work in connection
      with lepers but the work ought to be done and somebody
twice underlined must do it Should the Board desire me
      to act further in this matter I suggest that
a commission be sent me as Agent for the Islands
      of Kauai and Ni'ihau then a few days later he wrote
urging that before further steps were taken
      in regard to the lepers in Kalalau should the Board
decide to remove them first a stringent quarantine
      be placed on the valley allowing no communication
either for lepers or non-lepers between Kalalau
      and other places boats are engaged in taking taro
to Ni'ihau and other places and presumably
      taking visitors should this source of income and communication
be cut off and the well people told plainly that this quarantine
      would not be lifted until the sick people were removed
I am sure that it would have a salutary influence
      on the non-lepers and cause them to assist
in the removal To carry into effect such
      a quarantine three stations would in my mind be necessary
one on the Hanalei trail of two white men and four natives
      one on the Waimea trail of like get up and strength
and one on the beach at Kalalau as soon as the Board
      decides on the removal of the lepers a good man
should be sent into Kalalau to urge and persuade them
      to give in peaceably my only object in giving
my poor views to the Board is that time is flying
      he wasted none himself but went to Mānā and hired
a canoe to take him around under the cliffs to the valley

37.

It was cold up at the head of the valley among the rocks
      at the foot of the cliffs with the winter rains beating down
and the streams crashing around the small mountain houses
      tucked up in the cloud much of the day and while they were

still numb with the news of the Queen and the kingdom
        some of the people who lived in the valley and some
of the lepers who worked with them built a few more houses
        lower down where it was warmer and they gave the first
and biggest of them to the Judge and his family
        and brought him down gathering to welcome them all
and then other families and lepers living alone
        moved down nearer the taro and the beach and Koʻolau
and Piʻilani and their household moved down under
        a small new grass roof and were out most days in the taro
or along the shore and it was turning to spring with the days
        passing like clouds until they began to imagine
that they had been forgotten but Piʻilani kept watching
        the red spots swelling on Kaleimanu's body
always new ones appearing and one eye looking strange now
        not shutting right and tears coming from it when the other
was not crying and sores on his feet getting worse
        though he said they did not hurt even when the rocks cut them
she saw the same swellings coming on Koʻolau's body
        and she washed the sores and swellings with the powder
that was kept at the Judge's house and they swallowed
        the bad-tasting oil and then one day when she was
alone in the house and the valley seemed peaceful she looked
        over to where the two main streams come together and there she saw
that man Louis Stolz who had come to Kekaha
        to hunt pig with Koʻolau and who had seen the red spots
on his face and with him was the one called Penekila
        the steel pen and she thought they had come down the cliff trail
from Kilohana and she saw Penekila point
        to the house where she was watching them and they came along
and Stolz put his head in the door and looked around
        for a long time before he saw she was there and then he
spoke to her like the feel of a fish asking her
        how she was and how she liked it over here and did she
miss her friends in Kekaha asking her who her friends were
        in Kekaha who her friends were here and telling her
what he thought was news of Kekaha and she kept saying
        yes yes as he stood there looking at everything

38.

—And where is Koʻolau—he asked finally and she said
        —He is working down below there——When will he be back—
—Sometimes he comes at noon sometimes at the end of the day
        you can come in and wait for him—she said with Stolz
already standing inside the door—No—he said

    —Please tell him that I would like to speak with him down there
near the beach when he comes home today and how are those
    red spots on his face that I noticed at Kekaha—
—About the same—she said—They come and go and most of the time
    they are hardly there——Please tell him that I will be
down at Kaumeheiwa's house by the beach tonight
    I want to see him at any time—She said—I could
make you two something to eat here while you wait—but he thanked her
    in that sliding way he was talking that day and then he told
Penekila to stand up and she watched them go
    down the trail by the stream and she slipped around toward the cliff
and down the banks of the terraces to the one
    where she knew Koʻolau had gone to work and she saw
that he was not there but she watched Stolz and Penekila
    come to the far end of the terrace and talk to those standing
below them in the water and she turned at a sound
    and saw Koʻolau and Kaleimanu under a tree
smiling at her and Koʻolau said—We saw them coming
    and we said to our friends Nobody has seen us for some time
and Makuale said I never saw you all morning
    only this face of mine in the water—and Koʻolau saw
that she was crying and Kaleimanu buried his head
    in her skirt and cried and they stood watching the others
across the water and then she saw Stolz go on down
    toward the Judge's new house and the others climb out
and go off and the surface of the water was empty
    except for the small shoots of taro the delicate arching
stems the green heart faces of the leaves waving together
    in their youth and the three of them stood under the tree
with tears on their faces and Piʻilani said—He has come
    to take you—and Koʻolau answered—Whatever happens
he will not take me and now we can go down to the meeting
    and hear him tell us that he will take all the lepers
to Molokaʻi and will not let you come with us—

39.

    —It is some time—the Judge said to Stolz—since you lit up
    my doorway come in come in word of your arrival
went before you——How are you—Stolz asked—It depends—
    the Judge said—As you may have noticed in your own life
some days only lack of music keeps me from dancing
    some days I do not stand up and this is one of those
you must excuse me and you must lower your head
    not to strike it on the beam there a gesture worth
bearing in mind—The Judge was enthroned in his plank chair

with his broad hat on and a bright fabric far from its
original purpose drawn around him like a shawl
    his bandaged feet were propped up on a long box and his hands
trembled gripping the arm of the chair but the rest of him
    sat motionless as he deflected Stolz's phrases
and then said—Can we tempt you with something to eat—
    —Oh no—Stolz said—I am going—and there the Judge stopped him
—Of course—he said—I never imagined that you had come
    for old times' sake—Stolz said—I have come for your own good
I have been making a survey of Kalalau—
    We know that—the Judge said—why else have Penekila
and Sam Ku been turning up asking their long-nose questions—
    Stolz said—And now I have come to tell you that the time has come
for the lepers in this valley to go to the settlement
    on Moloka'i and I want to know whether you will
agree to go willingly—The Judge said—Do you think I became
    sick willingly——You will get medical treatment there—
Stolz told him—How many have they cured by now—the Judge asked
    —And those others who are sick in your family can go
with you—Stolz said and the Judge looked around at Kaenaku
    and at Mere—When are you planning this move—he asked Stolz
—In a week or two—Stolz said—When we have what we need
    by way of men and equipment which is why I am asking
these questions—and the Judge laughed—Willingly—he said
    —willingly and forever Well as you have not come
for us yet I see no reason to say no today—
    —You are being sensible—Stolz said—I am continuing
to act as though I had a choice for as long as I can—
    the Judge answered—Watch out for your head as you leave—

40.

Hon W D Smith Pres Bd of Health Honolulu
    Sir in accordance with your request herewith a complete list
of the residents of the valley of Kalalau there are
    twenty three households four of which consist of only
one old man each In nine households no leprosy
    is visable sic to a casual observer
in three households all the inmates are afflicted with leprosy
    while in eleven underlined households the inmates
are part lepers and part non-lepers the population
    numbers one hundred and two with seventy four apparently
non-lepers and twenty eight lepers eighteen of them male
    eighteen adults ten minors only six rifles
could be heard of and only three of these are available
    one of them belongs to a non-leper the lepers do not wish

to be taken away as they believe the new Japanese
doctor at Kilauea may be able to cure some of them
J Kauai and Paoa are the two lepers most likely
to give trouble it is my belief that if these two
and perhaps one or two others were removed most underlined
of the others would go voluntarily I also believe
that these leaders could be taken with a small force
two or three men like Sam Ku with what material
we have here would do Two weeks later after Stolz's own visit
he wrote again to Hon W D Smith now
Attorney General Dear Sir in accordance with your
instructions I went to Kalalau and interviewed
most of the lepers six of the reported cases
I would not undertake to move some of them I am sure
being non-lepers As for their going peacefully
my trip was only a partial success the majority
among whom is J Kauai desire to go and will
make no trouble but about four or five of the young
strong fellows say they will not go while as many more
were non-committal the amount and kind of intimacy
existing between lepers and non-lepers at Kalalau
is simply abominable I believe there will be fifty cases
of leprosy in consequence of lepers having been
allowed to remain in Kalalau Then three weeks later
he wrote again that eighteen of the lepers had decamped
for parts unknown including J Kauai They had vanished
into the tangle of ravines up at the foot of the cliffs

THE CLIFFS

The cliffs rose before him straight into the summer sky
 it was a week after the solstice and along the headlands
the trades were blowing Stolz stood at the mouth of the valley
 looking up into it and in the sun it all seemed to be white
the glittering on the leaves and across the blank taro ponds
 the water running over the rocks and the frayed clouds
slipping behind white crags with the tropic birds wheeling
 around them and thousands of feet above him the cliff faces
appeared to be white against the white sky that was falling
 upward behind them nobody in this place would give him
a straight answer to anything he asked he opened the white
 page again with the sun on it and wrote I will
hurry up things as fast as possible and report
 the progress as it occurs folded it over and addressed
the envelope to send at the first opportunity
 he had sent word early in the morning for everyone
in the valley to come down to Kaumeheiwa's house
 and as he waited he kept seeing Koʻolau's face
at the last meeting when Stolz had told him that no one
 except those with leprosy would be taken to Molokaʻi
and Koʻolau saying in a low voice that when they married
 they had promised they would never be separated
and that no man would separate them now Penekila
 and Peter Nowlein had unloaded the canoe
while Stolz questioned Kaumeheiwa about Judge Kauai
 and the others who were hiding in the upper valley
and while he waited he had Penekila and Peter
 set up the tent on the hill above Kaumeheiwa's house
where he could see up the valley and he told them
 to carry the chest of guns up the hill behind the house
and hide it in the rocks there and by the end of the morning
 when they had gathered for the meeting there were only three
lepers from the lower houses though there was one then
 who could not walk and all of them including Kapaheʻe
the famous swimmer had decided to go to Molokaʻi

2.

They gathered a few at a time and sat in the shade
 at the foot of the bank waiting until Stolz decided
that he had waited long enough and that no one else

would be coming it was already past noon and a hush
seemed to fill the lower valley with the sound of the waves
        brushing the shingle those who told of the meeting later
said it was not like the first one at which he had spoken
        as though he wanted to be kind to them this time
all but three of those gathered in front of him were
        residents of the valley and most of them had lived there
all their lives and he threatened them like a preacher
        promising Hell He said that anyone helping
the lepers who were in hiding was breaking the law
        and that if they did not help him their lands would be taken
and they would have to leave the valley and go to jail
        —And as for this Ko'olau—he said to them—You see
how he has run away from me into the mountain
        you will see how his head becomes bigger but the rest of him
grows smaller and smaller and I will capture him
        I will take him alive if I can but I will take him
living or dead he has brought this trouble among you
        all the ones who are hiding have brought this trouble among you
and they are making you sick with their own sickness as long
        as they are here in your valley—and he waited
to see whether anyone else was coming and they watched him
        and turned away and he told Penekila and Peter
to pick up their guns and the three of them started
        along the main stream toward the head of the valley
by then Puhiliku had reached the mountain houses
        and the caves in the cliffs and told everyone there
about the meeting Stolz had called at Kaumeheiwa's house
        and Ko'olau said—We should go down there and hear
what he has to say this time—and he picked up his gun
        whose name he said was Death Winks Far Away and Pi'ilani
went with him down the trail by the cliff and as they went
        they kept stopping to listen for someone coming

3.

—Because I think Louis Stolz may try to wait for me
        out of sight—Ko'olau said—And take me from ambush—
and when they were down by the taro ponds they saw
        the tent on top of the hill and they stood watching it
for a while to see whether anyone was there
        then they went on down the stream to a place called Kahali'i
where they found a raincoat with the name Louis Stolz
        stitched into the collar and a package of soda crackers
inside it rolled in a blanket and Ko'olau said
        —He seems to have dropped these we had better not leave them here—

and they went on down to the trail behind the houses
    and Koʻolau held up his hand and in a moment
Penekila came along the trail and Koʻolau stepped out
    and greeted him and asked him where he was going
and Penekila said he was looking to see
    who was in the houses and Koʻolau asked him where
Louis Stolz was and Penekila said he did not know
    but he thought Stolz had gone off to Hanalei on the trail
—That surprises me—Koʻolau said—Because we were told
    that he wanted to speak to us down here by the houses
and so we came down to see him—and he began to ask
    Penekila about his family because he had known him
for years in Waimea and he said it did seem strange to him
    that Stolz would ask them to come to the beach to meet him
and go off to Hanalei—But the meeting is over—
    Penekila said as Peter Nowlein came up the trail
and Koʻolau asked Peter where Louis Stolz was
    and Peter told him that Stolz had gone up the valley
hoping to surprise Koʻolau somewhere on the trail
    and capture him up there—You see Penekila—
Koʻolau said—I thought you were my friend but it is Peter
    who has told me the truth—and he and Piʻilani
went down through the houses to Kaumeheiwa's house
    where they found friends waiting and others came from the houses
and the ones who had been hiding were carrying their guns

4.

Koʻolau said to them—I have heard what this Stolz told you
    about how he is going to capture me and I have come
to meet him here We have all been friends up until now
    but if any of you is afraid you should not stay with me
because nobody knows what will happen and I understand
    he means to take me alive or dead—then he turned
to Penekila who had followed him down and he said
    —Penekila you are no friend of mine you lied to me
you told me Stolz had gone to Hanalei when you knew
    that he is up there now somewhere lying in wait for me—
Penekila said—I saw him take his raincoat
    so I thought he was going to Hanalei—but Koʻolau
was studying a few strange faces along the beach
    new constables whom Stolz had brought with him and posted
to guard the lepers he planned to take away with him
    and Koʻolau and Piʻilani and their friends who had come
down from the cliffs with their guns spent the night above the houses
    out of the sound of the surf with two of them always awake

listening to the darkness and they stayed there all the next day
    keeping watch in turn and talking with their friends who brought
fish and taro and the rumor that Stolz had captured
    Paoa and that he was coming that night for Koʻolau
and Koʻolau said—We will be here Everyone knows where I am—
    Iwa and Kala had been there with them and they went down
to the trail below and it got dark but the moon rose
    and Koʻolau and Piʻilani watched from behind a rock
listening to the leaves until Koʻolau breathed to her
    I hear two of them coming—and then they saw Kala
and Iwa running down the slope and they heard Stolz
    shouting after them—Halt Halt I warned you Halt—and then
the click of a gun and at that Koʻolau took aim
    and fired and they heard Stolz groan and in the moonlight
they could see that the man with Stolz was Paoa who turned
    and began to beat Stolz with his handcuffs and they heard
the chain each time he struck and Koʻolau shouted to him
    to stop and he stood up but Paoa called out to him
—He is going to shoot—and Piʻilani saw Stolz
    on one knee and the gleam of his rifle and Koʻolau fired
a second time and they saw Stolz fall over and roll
    onto the rocks and they went down and found him dead

5.

Paoa said to Koʻolau—That was my rifle
    that he was going to shoot you with when you stood up there
in the moonlight so we could see you as though it was daytime—
    And Koʻolau said—I thought you were killing him
with that piece of chain——My handcuffs—Paoa said
    —He put them on me he was hiding up there in the rocks
and I came out and he put that pistol in my back—
    Paoa reached across the body and with both hands
drew the Colt from its holster and stood up looking at it
    —And when he had these on me Sit there he said and he went
all through my house turning everything over and took my rifle
    and said Now we are going to find Koʻolau and we came down
to where we saw Kala and Iwa and he said
    There he is and when they ran he was going to shoot
but you shot first—They turned the body over and saw
    the blood glittering as though there was a sound in it
which they were not hearing and Koʻolau patted the pockets
    until he heard the clink of keys and he fished them out
and found the one for the handcuffs and then put the keys
    into his own pocket and found a box of cartridges
for the Colt and by that time Kala and Iwa

had crept up the path and Ko'olau said to them—Come
He is dead He was going to shoot you when you ran
        He thought one of you was me Now pick up the body
and bring him down to the lanai in front of the house
        and they came to one of the lepers Kapahe'e
the swimmer waiting by a rock and Ko'olau
        told him what had happened and said—You can go ahead
and say we are coming with the body—and then they saw
        Wahinealoha who said Penekila had sent him
after they heard the shots and they all carried the body
        down to the house lanai and Kapahe'e said
—We were frightened when we heard the shots and we knew
        that the trouble had come——There will be more—Ko'olau said
Kapahe'e said—When Kaumeheiwa heard what had happened
        he ran to that old rotten canoe of his and said
he had to go and tell them and that he was paddling
        to Mānā if that canoe gets there—And they put the body down

6.

Even in that light Pi'ilani could see how frightened
        many of the gray faces were as they gathered
at the top of the steps like seaweed moving in the waves
        and stared up at the body she saw that some of them
were afraid of Ko'olau and some were simply afraid
        of whatever was before them the constables were afraid
the eyes were afraid and the whispers and Ko'olau
        told them how it had happened and said they should not be
afraid of him they were still his friends and he reminded them
        of Stolz insisting that he was going to take Ko'olau
alive or dead—And he did not come here with orders
        from the Queen—Ko'olau said—But from those others
who took the Queen away from us they stole her from us
        what they call now the Provisional Government
he came from them—And now more trouble will come from them—
        a voice said with a silence around it and it was
the tall man named Pā and Ko'olau said—We will leave
        the body here and if they do not come for it we will
come bury it ourselves—There were seven lepers with guns
        down there with him and he motioned them to come with him
and whispered to Iwa—Come—and in a low voice said
        —Show us where the guns are—but Iwa said—Penekila
is watching——Then tell me—Ko'olau said—Up in the rocks
        only a few steps in back of the tent going
toward the cliff—and Ko'olau was looking away from Iwa
        as though he was not listening and he said—Good night—

to them all there and went down the steps with Pi'ilani
        and the friends with guns went with them as they started
up the trail and climbed to the tent in the moonlight
        and stood looking inside it and Ko'olau told two of them
to search among the rocks until they found the chest and he took out
        the keys and opened the lock and they lifted the rifles
out into the ghost dawn and then the boxes of cartridges
        and they handed them around whispering until the chest
was empty except for one metal box which Ko'olau
        held up and opened and he could see that it was packed
with bottles and bandages and he turned to Pi'ilani
        and gave it to her and then they closed the empty chest
like a coffin and went on up the dim trail carrying the guns
        through the valley which seemed to have become a different place

7.

Kaumeheiwa the gentle Kaumeheiwa the smiling
        Kaumeheiwa who had always been happy when
anyone asked to stay at his house above the beach
        near the Pā family and Naoheiki's big house and the others
who had always lived in that valley Kaumeheiwa
        who had welcomed the lepers and then Stolz and the constables
felt the cold breaking over him heavier than the waves
        and he was used to the night sea in the old kukui canoe
that leaked so that he had to keep hitching the paddle
        under his leg while he scooped with the baling gourd
and he seldom felt the cold but however hard he paddled
        this night his teeth chattered and as he rounded the white
headlands of Nualolo he kept saying to himself
        Trouble trouble as the paddle bit and went by
Like the Pā's and Kapahe'e and many of the others
        in the valley he had been able to swim before he
could stand and the deep water was like his own sleep
        that he could float into but the cold kept climbing through him
in the moonlight as he paddled outside the white surf on the cliffs
        past Mākua'ike and Miloli'i Keawanue
where the valleys ran out from under deep shadows
        Mākaha Kauhoa Mākole Ka'aweiki
Polihale of the springs and the temple walls and the underworld
        Kapa'ula and then the long sands before Mānā
and he ran the canoe ashore below a dark house he knew well
        making the dogs bark and rush down the beach as he climbed
calling and his friend came to the door hardly awake
        and Kaumeheiwa breathing hard told him he needed
a horse right away and told why as they saddled her

behind the house and he galloped off to the mill and shouted
at Mr Faye's door with the dogs barking around him
         and then one light appeared and the door opened and they telephoned
to Sheriff Wilcox for a long time before anyone answered
         waiting to the sound of Kaumeheiwa's breathing
with the dogs barking on and on around them and then
         Kaumeheiwa telling the story and Mr Faye
repeating it into the receiver and the buzzing of flies
         coming back out of the earpiece and he said what his name was
and mounted and rode back to the house and they took off the saddle
         and he pushed the canoe back out into the same night
and paddled home to Kalalau as the stars were fading

8.

All the way it had seemed to him that if he could tell
         what had happened it would be gone then gone away
and not be there afterward wherever he was
         and not be still coming wherever he looked but when he
pulled the dead weight of the water-logged canoe from the surf
         onto the shingle below his house and heard the muffled groan
of the wood dragged over the stones he knew it was there unchanged
         all of it whatever it was and he saw the first light
welling up in the valley and the tent limp on the hilltop
         and along the beach in that light friends of his by the whaleboats
he saw neighbor after neighbor from the valley and they were
         bringing things of their own to take away with them
he saw that they were putting them into the whaleboats
         getting ready to leave and Penekila and Nowlein
were up at his own house watching them from the step
         he did not at first see the body lying behind them
by that time Wilcox had sent the news from Waimea
         to Deverill his deputy in Hanalei
and Deverill had taken the steamer Waialeale
         with Captain Smythe and was making for Kalalau
to get Stolz's body and Koʻolau and Piʻilani
         and their friends watching later from the head of the valley
standing on ledges above the mountain houses could see
         the steamer arriving and anchoring inside the headlands
and the boat making for shore and they watched as it
         went out again and returned three times before it was finished
and more smoke rose from the funnel and the steamer turned
         and moved out and away and Paoa went down
to see what had happened and late in the day they gathered
         at the Judge's house and from there they could see that the tent
was gone and Paoa said that the four lepers
         who had already decided to go and one other one

had been taken on the steamer he said Kapaheʻe
  had gone and Kamali and Hakau and Pauwahine
and Mele and besides there were nine from the valley
  who were not sick but were afraid now women living alone
Kapoli and Puahi and Kahalehei
  some who had relatives they could go to in Kilauea
or Kapaʻa and that Kaumeheiwa had gone
  Deverill and Smythe said they wanted him to tell
his story again and they asked him about everything
  and promised that he would be famous and had him sit with them
by the head of the body and as the boat steamed out
  the father and the boy named Pā were watching from the headland

9.

—Well now they have two heroes—the Judge said—and you can be sure
  they will make the most of them dress them up for a little while
and wave flags over them blow their horns and Kaumeheiwa
  will tell them again about how he carried the news
of this catastrophe through mountainous seas at night
  to the proper authorities and for a while he will be
the good Hawaiian and Kapaheʻe who I know is
  as old as I am and has been improving upon
stories about himself all that time will bring them out
  in up-to-date versions The Society of Stranglers
he belonged to in his youth and the man he passed one day then
  up in the forest above Kalalau following him
but walking backward so they both stopped to fight and when
  a twig fell on the man's shoulder and he looked aside
Kapaheʻe caught him in the Stranglers' Hold and killed him
  and the one where he sailed from Kalalau in the whaleboat
with a load of taro and two old people who were hoping
  to visit Niʻihau and a fierce storm hit them halfway
the waves pounding the old whaleboat until it broke apart
  and they were all hanging onto the wreckage and swimming
and he tried to keep the old couple afloat and then swam on
  for help and heard them singing a hymn the way he tells it
and he swam all night and woke up on the reef at Lehua
  and then got up and swam on to Kiʻi that one has
gained with fond repetition and then there was the time
  when Valdemar Knudsen decided to swim ashore
from the whaleboat past Nohili and the surf had him
  helpless and as you might have guessed Kapaheʻe
arrived just in time to rescue him and then swam back out
  to the whaleboat to wave and so on I expect that he
seldom revived those stories here in the valley
  where they knew him and he had the Pā family

as neighbors who are said to swim with the sharks and have sharks
     for guardian spirits but he will recall the stories now
wherever he is taken and the reporters will make notes
     and nobody will have heard those tales in Honolulu
or on Moloka'i and so for a matter of weeks
     he will be the good leper unlike the rest of us
when voices are rising about this news from Kalalau—

10.

Ko'olau said—I think now they will be back soon
     for the rest of us this Louis was going to take us
all by himself big man but after the way it turned out
     they will not let it pass and they will send others for us
but I have said from the beginning that I will not leave here
     alive I said that to the haole and what I did then
is what I still think I had to do and I will be buried
     in this valley as my name says and some of you
have said that you would fight to stay rather than be
     taken away from here but I think you should all consider
once more what you will do if they come with a large force
     maybe soldiers to take us or kill us and if you want to go
you should try to decide now before they are there in front of us
     Pi'ilani has told me her mind but I will not
say it for her—And then Pi'ilani said—I came here
     with my husband and our son so that we could stay together
this is the only place where we can stay together
     and I will not leave them no matter what happens to me—
Then the Judge said I could scarcely leave on my own feet
     but Mere has already gone and I doubt that I
could fight off many of them I hope they will not find me—
     and Kaenaku said—Now I keep thinking about
things my father told me when I was a child and they all
     used to say how beautiful I was how beautiful I would be
he came to this island when it was mourning and bleeding
     with grief and under everything I remember
going to see old Deborah Kapule and her answers
     to my questions and her huge sadness and my father
seemed to me far away from the people on this island
     so I did not know and then I would find myself crying
and now it seems to me that I have turned into the grief
     I did not touch then and my father never showed and into griefs
that I know nothing about for things that I never knew
     I will hide here and stay with my husband if I can
I am not afraid of their guns but I cannot keep them
     from taking me away—And then the seven who had taken
rifles from the chest with Ko'olau one by one said they would

stay and fight to the last but Ko'olau said to them
—Wait and see what comes and if they arrive in force
heavily armed there will be no reason for staying
unless you would rather die here than go with them—

II.

In Hofgaard's store the news of the shooting of Stolz
brought out the bugles a rehearsal of rising notes
in the brass choir of unquestionable righteousness
the refrain returned to having been soft with them
the lepers and the natives and this is what comes of it
and suggestions grew violent before several of the more
seasoned champions of order composed a letter
to W O Smith Pres Board of Health and Att General
in red ink Sir We the undersigned request and demand
that every effort possible be promptly and diligently made
to bring to justice and punish the murderer
or murderers of the late L H Stolz and to clean out
the valley of Kalalau of its leprous population
or we will take the matter into our own hands and promptly
revenge the death of our friend murdered in cold blood
T H Gibson Professor English niceties
be damned Th Brandt E E Conant C B Hofgaard
H P Faye who was happy to recapitulate
for new arrivals the appearance of Kaumeheiwa
at his door in the dead of night gasping out the news
and they all expressed satisfaction in the strong wording
and the red ink and made copies for themselves before
going in a band to present it to the captain
of the steamer to Honolulu announcing to him
that this outrage was a challenge to the new Provisional
Government in which all their hopes were invested
and by that time something of the same view of the matter
was awake in the capital assembling a military
expedition under Special Order 67
dated on the second day after Stolz's death
boarding the steamer Iwalani with twenty four
privates under Sergeant-Major Pratt Lieutenant
G W R King and Captain W Larsen
and as they were stowing their gear around noon a carriage
drove onto the wharf and a uniformed courier
from the president's office introduced to Captain Larsen
with ill-concealed embarrassment Prince Kunuiakea
representative of the deposed royal family
who had offered his services for addressing
the insurgents and persuading them to leave peacefully

12.

There were reporters from the papers standing around
        the gangplank and the emissary in his gold braids
and his piping explained in a low voice to Larsen
        that the man had presented himself at the governor's
office in a public manner and because of
        the recent overthrow and the American hesitations
about recognizing the Provisional Government
        it had seemed politic to accept the proposal
with a certain flourish of welcome however
        belated and awkward and the official hope
was that the man's presence on the expedition
        could be utilized as a kind of symbolic
accompaniment however unnecessary
        —I think you understand Captain—he said and Larsen
saluted and the salute was returned and the courier
        drew from the gloved hand of his attendant a roll
of something like parchment which he unfurled and began to read
        announcing the full name of the heavy man in the carriage
and the principals in his genealogy beginning
        with his forbear Kamehameha I the courier
picking his way with evident caution through the names
        getting them right in his dead voice and then turning
to the carriage and introducing Captain Larsen
        who stepped forward as the Prince's two attendants
and then the Prince himself stood and stepped down to the wharf
        Larsen saluted with a sidelong glance at the courier
the Prince bowed slightly and Larsen told the Sergeant-Major
        to show the Prince to his cabin in the officers'
quarters and he watched as the Prince's attendants
        carried his trunk aboard and then the Prince followed
Larsen watched the top hat the black coat with its tails
        the trousers and shoes that he supposed were the garments
of an ambassador and he saluted the courier
        and went on board and the steamer Iwalani sailed at three
that afternoon with its contingent of reporters
        the men working up jokes about the Prince and his entourage
the officers raising their eyebrows to the reporters
        and Larsen and the officers came on deck before daylight
at five thirty off Hanalei to find the Prince
        and his pages clad more simply in white gowns facing the coast
where the day was about to break above the mountain

13.

From the landing at Hanalei Larsen telephoned
        to Wilcox and then on the wharf read a proclamation
of martial law in the presence of those who could
        be summoned to the place then they boarded and sailed on
and one of the Prince's attendants said to Captain Larsen
        that the Prince requested a word with him—It is about
the landing—the Prince said—and the conduct of it
        I propose to go ahead and meet with the lepers first
with as little threat as possible and I prefer
        to approach them simply and without pointless formality
I will be dressed just as I am but on the other hand
        it is important that they should be aware of who I am
and have some idea of who I represent
        in the traditions and story that are theirs and mine
I shall require to go ashore with a guard of honor
        such as befits and will indicate my position
I think four men might be enough one at each of the four
        corners around me and my own two attendants in white
going in front without arms—Larsen said—I will allow you
        a boat when we get there for yourself your companions
but if you intend to speak with the lepers you will have to
        introduce yourself to them I have no intention
of sending men ashore in the way you describe and there is
        nothing in my orders that suggests it—Larsen
was aware that the reporters had been listening
        and he continued—You have heard my offer Prince
will you go in the first boat or will you not we have heard
        that the lepers are resolved to resist any force
sent to capture them—and the Prince said—I thought I had
        made it clear that what I requested was not a show of force
but a guard of honor indicating my heredity—
        —Fall in—the Sergeant-Major shouted to the men on deck
and the flag was run up for sunrise—There will be
        no guard of any sort from my command—Captain Larsen said
—Will you go or not——I will not—the Prince said and turned
        to the rail and the passing coast and Larsen muttered
to the nearest reporter—Did you see how the Prince turned
        a little white when I told him he would have no protection—

14.

—Fall out—the sergeant major shouted and the men sat around
        smoking and polishing their rifles and whispering behind
the Prince's back and Larsen said to Lieutenant King
        —Once he learned that we would not cover him he decided
not to play the part after all and I had been thinking
        before we were assigned the privilege of transporting
royalty of sending one of the native constables
        ashore first to find out from the ones who are there
how things stand now but I have decided simply to land—
        At nine-fifty off Haena Point they saw a group
of several families on the beach around whaleboats
        whom they learned by sending a boat had come from Kalalau
rather than be caught in a battle between lepers
        and soldiers and when they were asked whether they thought
the lepers would resist a landing no one would answer
        they steamed on to an anchorage off the beach at Kalalau
there the men were lined up on deck and Larsen addressed them
        concerning the objects and duties of the expedition
and the possible risks saying that some were convinced
        that the lepers were resolved to resist any force
that was sent for them and then with a glance at the reporters
        he asked for volunteers for the first boat and each
of the officers later reported proudly
        that All of the men volunteered underlined and they loaded
the first boat with as many as it was meant to carry
        there were sixteen and they landed without opposition
forming at once into a column of twos and marching
        quickly across the beach and climbing to take possession
of a tableland overlooking the lower end
        of the valley where they halted until the others
came up to them and then they marched on up the ridge
        to a point where one of the native police informed them
that they were some three hundred yards above the place
        where Mr Stolz had been killed and there they pitched their tents
and hoisted their flag over what the reporters
        were told was Camp Hitchcock and the sergeant major
noticed as one man handed it to another
        a tattered yellow copy of a book he had noticed
on deck that morning something about Geronimo

15.

Early that morning Kaleimanu and Ida
  were playing along the stream above the mountain house
and Pi'ilani was talking with her mother Kepola
  saying that perhaps Kepola should take Ida
and go back to Kekaha now before more trouble arrived
  but Kepola said that she wanted to stay with them
and Ida wanted to stay and Kepola said
  she kept thinking of Kaenaku and wondering whether
she would see her again and they heard the children's voices
  high with excitement and went upstream and found them
bending over a clear pool before a cleft in the rocks
  Ida was saying maybe it was only the fish
swimming upstream—Look at the fish—she said but Kaleimanu
  said—It is the water too—and she said—Maybe it is
just turning around—and he said—Yes it is turning
  but it is going back up look there—and he pointed
—It is going up—he said—The soldiers are coming—
  and Ida started to cry—It is going up—he shouted
and then he looked at Ida and said—You must not cry—
  and he put his arms around her—They can never come up here—
he told her—It does that so that we will know about them—
  and he saw Kepola and Pi'ilani and told them
in his high voice and they all went down and found Ko'olau
  sitting in the doorway with his rifle on his knees
and Kaleimanu ran and told him about the water
  and Ko'olau asked the children about it and then said
as though it were part of the children's game—There is a steamer
  down in the bay I have watched it come in and anchor
and a boat has left it for shore it may be the soldiers—
  And Ida was crying again and Kaleimanu
kept telling her that they would not come up past the waterfall
  but they all went out and sat among the rocks at the end
of the ledge where they could see down the valley and at last
  they saw Paoa hurrying up the trail by the stream
when he got to the ledge he said before he had caught his breath
  —They are here soldiers a lot of them—then he gasped and said
—I hid behind Kaumeheiwa's and heard their officer
  read from his paper shouting and he is going to kill us
is what he said unless we let him take us away—

16.

After a moment sitting there hearing him
        breathing heavily Koʻolau asked Paoa
—What will you do then—and at first Paoa said nothing
        staring down into the valley and out to the steamer
and the whaleboat going out to it almost too small to see
        —I will stay with you—Paoa said—and fight if they come—
—You are frightened—Koʻolau said—Yes I am frightened—
        Paoa answered—The captain said they will hunt for us
and if we do not give up before nine tomorrow morning
        they will shoot us on sight but I will stay and he will
not catch us up here only now I have to go down
        one more time to bring my wife—and Koʻolau said to him
—That is how Stolz caught you when you went back to your good house
        and he took you away from your wife it is not long
since the time when we lived down there one by one we moved down
        closer to the beach and the rest and it was good then
all the children together it was there that we lived
        just down there and it is gone since the day he came
now you should go down and let them take you and your wife
        you do not want to stay up here and she would not like
having the soldiers come—Paoa looked down the valley
        then he stood up—I will try to come back—he said
—A few are ready to go with them and I hope
        the Judge escapes this time the same way as the last time—
then they watched Paoa picking his way down the trail
        and at the mountain house they began to pack up the things
they would want to take with them if they needed to move
        to some other shelter in the cliffs and the things they meant
to hide and come back for and Piʻilani watched her mother
        who she thought had always seemed to find every trouble
from her own ailments and her husband's multiple life
        to the coming of the sickness and the setting out
from Kekaha and all that came after at once familiar
        and amusing and she saw it again as her mother
folded and packed and went out with the children to find
        hiding places in the low cellars under the cliffs
as though they were playing a game she had grown up knowing

17.

Captain Larsen had lined up his own men on the beach
        and sounded a bugle to call what inhabitants
might be within hearing and had read the proclamation
        of martial law following it with his statement

that his men would shoot on sight lepers who had not surrendered
        within forty-eight hours he was maintaining the conduct
of the campaigns in the western states which he had studied
        then he sent out parties to begin searching the houses
those near the beach first and by mid-afternoon three lepers
        had emerged saying they were ready to go away with him
one was badly disfigured one a woman with deformed hands
        one an older man who had been living by himself
they were herded into the neatest house near the beach
        which was said to belong to that same Kaumeheiwa
who had carried the news of the murder of Stolz to Māná
        though accounts varied as to where Mr Stolz met his death
some said there near the house and some said it was farther up
        on the way to the cliffs but that house was requisitioned
and the lepers left there under guard until such time
        as they should be removed supplies meanwhile being ferried
from the steamer by whaleboat and stored there and the night
        passed quietly then after reveille the searching
of the houses continued Neil Boyle and Louis Toussaint
        coming to the closed door of the house where they had been told
former Judge Kauai had been living though Mr Stolz
        on his last visit had found no one there and the neighbors
told him the Judge had not been seen there for some days
        and may have gone up to the cliffs somewhere Boyle and Toussaint
struck the closed door with their rifle butts and then
        opened it and found the house empty but went on looking
pulling down tearing open poking with bayonets
        Boyle jabbed at a pile of blankets and tent halves and heard
a muffled sound and dragged out a woman who told him
        her name was Kaenaku and admitted to being
the Judge's wife but said she had not seen him and turned
        her back on them as they went on searching the house
until a bayonet under the bed touched something yielding
        and Boyle and Toussaint put their heads to the floor and found
themselves looking at a dark roll of sail swaddling
        a wad of dirt-colored bandages that they discovered
were protecting the feet of the retired Judge Kauai

18.

—If you burst in upon us so rudely—the Judge said to them
        when he had managed to crawl out and sit up with his back
propped against the bed—You will have to allow some time
        for us to make ourselves presentable and if I
am to go anywhere I can tell you that I shall require
        considerable assistance since I can no longer walk

—We want no more of your tricks—Boyle said to him—And this house
        will be watched until I receive further instructions
for dealing with you—He stood looking down at the Judge
        —We know about you—he said—We call you the Archleper
It is your fault that all the rest of these lepers are here
        and all this has happened and Mr Stolz was murdered—
—Still wearing the King's old uniforms I see—the Judge said
        smiling up through his mat of hair—Hand-me-downs they too
were young once upon a time—and Boyle and Toussaint
        left the door open when they went and Kaenaku closed it
The search continued and the number of lepers huddled
        in Kaumeheiwa's house grew and another three were brought
out of a beach cave and meanwhile the tents at Camp Hitchcock
        were struck and moved a mile farther up the valley
to a place on the ridge overlooking the stream
        They named the new site Camp Dole and put up their flagpole
while a search party found the grass house of that same Paoa
        who had been arrested and with Mr Stolz when he was killed
inside they found a rifle and cartridges several issues
        of the newspaper Holomua in Hawaiian
with Koʻolau's name on them two baskets packed ready to go
        and outside in the undergrowth they found Paoa
and his wife and arrested them and took them to the beach
        where one Wahinealoha had also been arrested
though later he turned out not to be a leper at all
        and he and the tall man named Pā both said they knew
where the stronghold was that the lepers had in the cliffs
        Pā said he would not go up but Wahinealoha
and Paoa were sent to talk with the outlaws and before
        sundown they were back saying that eleven lepers
were coming down behind them which Wahinealoha said
        was all of them except Koʻolau—Is that true—
Larsen asked Paoa who answered that he did not know

19.

—And what will Koʻolau do now—Larsen asked Paoa
        —He will never come down—Paoa said—But what of those
who are with him does he not care about his family—
        —His wife says she will not leave him—Paoa answered
—and their child is a leper and does not want to leave them—
        —What are you smiling at—Larsen asked him—Something
the boy said about you—Paoa answered—No he will not
        leave them——And what if we corner them——Koʻolau
will fight to the last—Paoa answered and Larsen said
        —You are telling me that he will allow them to be

killed I expect a man like that might kill them himself
        if it came to that——Those are your words—Paoa said
—I believe he would—Larsen said looking at the Lieutenant
        and the reporters—But I am happy that the rest of them
are being sensible though I am a little surprised
        we had been told that they were a strong force heavily
armed—and as he said it the first of the lepers
        from the cliffs appeared on the trail sick and weak and crippled
Paoa said—Some of them want to speak with the Prince
        before giving up—and the Captain laughed—Oh the Prince—
he said—I am not even sure where he is this is martial law
        we do not have time to waste on nonsense——And some of them
wanted to speak first with Sheriff Wilcox—Paoa said
        —It is too late for that—Larsen answered—I am in command here
put them all inside—and a soldier guided them
        to the doorway and turned back for the rest
—And our hunt—Larsen said—has scarcely begun——Tomorrow—
        Lieutenant King said—we can begin to shoot on sight—
—And out of sight—Larsen said pointing to the beached whaleboat
        from which the new Krupp howitzer was being unloaded
They watched and the reporters watched as it was turned
        and rolled up the beach to sit facing up the valley
—Give the ones in the house there something to eat—Larsen said
        —and tell them that they will leave on the steamer tomorrow
along with the other residents of Kalalau—
        and he started up toward Camp Dole leaving the reporters
taking notes around the gun crew before they went off
        to their own camp on the beach complete with jester Marmont
government detective and dandy who returned from his own
        explorations with long yarns about naked hobgoblins
which that evening offended his more earnest companions

                                    20.

In the ghost dawn Pi'ilani heard the owl and she reached
        and touched Ko'olau's arm—I heard it too—he whispered
—I think it is Kala—but he put his hand down
        on Kaleimanu's lips and as he rolled from beneath
the blanket he was holding the rifle and he sat up watching
        Then they heard a whisper—It is a friend Ko'olau
it is Kala—and Kala slipped from the bushes
        —I came down last night—he said—I have been out there
I did not want to surprise you in the dark—and Ko'olau
        put the gun down and stood up and embraced him—They have
caught Kilohana—Kala told him—I had to tell you
        They have four men hiding up there on the top of the cliff

where the trail from Waimea starts down and Kilohana
  was ahead of me and they caught him they never saw me
I heard them talking he was good he answered them
  he never told them anything and now they think
they have everybody except you they have a mirror
  up there on top and one down at their camp and they flash
messages back and forth and tomorrow morning
  they say when the signal comes they will start to shoot on sight
They do not know where you are yet but they have brought
  a big gun and they will come trying to find you
They say that this morning they will take away everybody
  from down in the valley so that nobody will be left
except you by then—Pi'ilani and Kaleimanu
  and Kepola and Ida were sitting listening to him
—I would stay here with you Ko'olau and fight against them
  because we are friends and my own chiefs are all gone
but I was thinking about Pi'ilani's mother
  and the little girl if they want to go now I can take them
we can take the pig trail up that side that these people
  do not know exists we could start in a little while
and go up that stream and get behind that rock wall
  and they will not see us—Ko'olau looked at Pi'ilani
and nodded and Pi'ilani looked at her mother
  and said—you have to take her now—and they stood up
and embraced crying silently and made a small bundle
  saying nothing and the children stood facing each other
and put their arms around each other and then Kala
  embraced Pi'ilani and Ko'olau and said
—I will get them home—and Kepola and Ida followed him

21.

In the morning the soldiers of the Provisional Government
  got the lepers down to the beach and gave the remaining
residents of the valley one hour before sending them
  to the steamer named for the mountain where they had lived
and as the whaleboats were taking them out a man on a horse
  with an entourage of rough-looking dogs rode down
from the ridge and the sergeant major challenged him
  informing him that the valley was under martial law
the man told him that his name was Kinney Wili Kinney
  and said he had land over Haena side up into
Wainiha and cattle there and he said no he had seen
  no lepers anywhere and the sergeant asked him
how he had passed the sentries—What sentries—Kinney asked
  then the sergeant major told him that they were hunting for one

Koʻolau the murderer of Deputy Sheriff
        Louis Stolz—Oh I know Koʻolau—Kinney said
—but I have not seen him for a long time now—and the sergeant
        asked whether he had known Louis Stolz—I have met him—
Kinney said—But not here though I heard about his visits here—
        —What did you hear—the sergeant asked and Kinney answered
—I understand that the last time here he was angry
        and he told the lepers that those who did not go with him
he would hunt down and shoot them——Who did you hear that from—
        the sergeant asked—From some of the women when I was
over here looking for cattle——We are clearing out
        the valley now—the sergeant told him—and I am
ordering you to leave it at once—and Kinney
        called his dogs and rode off without another word
glancing once at the steamer before he disappeared
        The last whaleboats reached it and the Waialeale
got under way and rounded the point toward Haena
        and Kalalau seemed empty in the morning sunlight
under the white tropic birds wheeling far up toward the cliffs
        They drew the howitzer up from the beach and fired it
toward the distant rock face five rounds the sound crashing
        and rolling like a storm around the stone buttresses
and the crags and pinnacles thousands of feet up the echoes
        falling over each other before they sank and then nothing
and one search party went up the west side of the valley
        taking Paoa and they found nothing and they burned each house
after looking inside it and another party
        under Lieutenant King went up the east side of the valley
and found nothing and burned each house as they left it

22.

The largest group in the hunt fifteen of them under
        sergeant major Pratt began by burning the beach houses
and then started up the stream burning and late in the morning
        where two streams flowed together they found fresh tracks
in the mud showing that a number of people had passed there
        shortly before but they grew uncertain as they traced
the marks along the stream because they seemed to continue
        in several directions finally they decided
to follow tracks leading up toward the cliff and they crawled
        through a dense tangle Pratt said it seemed like a pig trail
they picked up a broken gourd with some taro in it
        and came up from the thicket onto a level patch
that they saw was a campsite with sleeping places
        for at least eight and it appeared to have been used

until some time that morning they found fresh pieces
 of orange peel and a bundle of food including fish
wrapped in ti leaves bags of taro and of salt and a coat
 with two cartridges in it and Miller said either they
had left in a hurry or they planned to come back
 it was Pratt's belief that they had just abandoned
the site when they heard the soldiers and the tracks led on up
 crossing the stream between rocks and went on climbing
several hundred feet to the base of the straight rock face
 where they could see what might be a way up and Pratt ordered
one or two to volunteer to see whether that was
 the trail and Anderson and Evanston said they would go
and they started up with McAulton and Johnson
 and McCabe and Herschberg and Reynolds and the others
behind them they had been climbing then for hours
 Anderson was from Norway a village in the mountains
and Herschberg was from Sweden from a stony farm
 McCabe was almost fifty and said he had been
at Gettysburg thirty years before and in the long campaign
 that ended at Appomattox and that he had seen action
in the west and he would mention things from those times
 in the army before he shipped to the islands
and married a Hawaiian woman and settled down
 —And if you settled down—they would ask him—What are you doing
back in the army again after everything
 and no advancement for all that—they said that was hard
to understand and he would tell them it was a living

23.

Of the seven who had come up from the valley
 with Koʻolau and Piʻilani bringing the rifles
two had gone with Paoa when he was sent up to talk
 and the other five had moved into the clearing
in the thicket below the cliff where Koʻolau
 and his family had been staying since the soldiers landed
They sat watching down through the trees and when the steamer
 got under way and left the five had made up their minds
that there were too many of them to hide in such a small place
 and they had decided to move across the valley
to a cave they all knew and if they were driven from there
 they would take the back trail to Wainiha and they were packing
to leave when a spur of cliff over to the east
 and some way above them seemed to burst all at once
and broken pieces of rock clattered down and then they heard
 the hollow boom of the howitzer and the echoes

began rolling up around them into the cliffs overhead
      five times it happened while they crouched waiting and when
the stillness crept back again Koʻolau said—Go now
      they are sure to be coming up—and the five picked up
what they had ready and made their way into the thicket
      Then Piʻilani looked down through the trees toward the sea
and saw the smoke rising and said as though she could
      not believe it—I think one of the houses is burning—
They stood watching then and saw another smoke start to bloom
      and then another and Koʻolau said—Now they are coming
It is time for us to go up and we may not be able
      to take everything—but they picked up what they could carry
the three of them and went up beside the stream to the cliff
      and Koʻolau showed them how to go up the rock face
then he came back for their belongings and they settled
      on a ledge under a deep overhang with big rocks
out in front and between these they could see the valley
      and the columns of smoke rising into a spreading cloud
and the dark fold of the stream and then the glint and flash
      of metal the flicker of soldiers on the trail
there was the sound of water back under the overhang
      a cool breath from the cliff as they waited until the first
soldiers emerged from the trees below and started toward the cliff
      and they could hear the voices and Koʻolau stood braced between
rocks with his rifle raised and then a soldier's head appeared
      in front of the ledge and he shouted—I have found
the trail—and Koʻolau shot twice and the man was gone

24.

No one was looking up at that moment their eyes
      were on the rock face in front of them when they heard Anderson
shout—I have found the trail—and the two shots rang out
      the echoes ricocheted through the sounds of bodies
thudding down and rocks rolling and the scree sliding around them
      no one saw where Anderson fell from the ledge overhead
Evanston climbing below him was knocked from his handhold
      and slid down onto Aulton who in turn fell onto
sergeant major Pratt and Miller fell onto all of them
      Johnson who had been poised on a loose rock fell onto the scree
to one side dropping his gun and he rolled down they guessed
      six hundred feet and they were all sure he must be dead
and they picked themselves up cautiously covered with blood
      barely able to stand and Pratt said—We will retreat now—
and they crawled along to where they could see Johnson
      caught by some bushes and when they reached him they found

him still alive but scarcely conscious a long head wound
          shoulder seemed broken and knee badly pulped and Miller
started trying to bandage him while Pratt said—We will
          return fire before we go—and he ordered the others
to aim just above the ledge and they propped themselves up
          against trees and bushes and fired until they were low
on ammunition and then they limped and crawled
          over the scree looking for Anderson's body
but they could not find him and Johnson was bleeding and they
          had to take turns helping to carry and drag him
down through the thicket to rest in the empty camp site
          the afternoon clouds filling the valley had become
an acrid fog and the smoke of the day's burning
          kept them coughing as they slipped down through mud with light
beginning to fade out of the day and it was dark
          long before they saw lights in the tents and groped toward them
and there Pratt made his report beginning with the statement
          that they had located Koʻolau's stronghold and then
that Anderson was presumed dead and the body not found
          then they all began going over their wounds by the light
of the kerosene lanterns turning three of the tents
          into a field hospital for the night and Johnson seemed
to be in bad shape and would have to be shipped off
          when the next steamer got there and Captain Larsen
announced that they would go at first light to find the body

25.

At first they heard nothing except the echoes and echoes
          of the rifle and then the sounds of falling and slides
and shouts from below them and then only the cries
          of white birds sailing circling the cliffs and then voices again
smaller and farther down in waves like rain blowing
          then bullets began banging into the rock over their heads
bounding away screaming and pieces of stone spattered around them
          as the rattle of the shooting climbed over the ledge
and Koʻolau drew Kaleimanu and Piʻilani
          back under the steep overhang and said—Stay in here—
and he crawled along the ledge to where he could watch
          the shore until they stopped shooting at the cliff
and he saw them carry and drag one man from the scree
          along into the trees but it was not the one he had shot
who would not have fallen over there and he waited
          until they had gone and then crawled back to Piʻilani
and said—I have to see—and he slipped over the edge and down
          below the cliff to where Anderson would have fallen

found the man rolled far down and checked for signs of life
    took off cartridge belt shirt necktie to look at the wounds
still bleeding and he plugged them with ferns from the woods
    started to haul him to where they would be sure
to see him and left him in plain sight with the hat
    under the head and he noticed a bayonet by itself
off on the scree and no sign of a rifle and went back
    up the cliff where Pi'ilani had unwrapped fish and taro
and held some out to him—There is water back there—she said
    —a little and some in the gourds—and they ate and Ko'olau
took one of the rifles and gave it to her and said
    —You remember when we would go shooting there behind Māna
this rifle is better than the one you shot in those days
    if you need it—And she said—Why did you go down there—
Ko'olau answered—I wanted to be sure he was dead
    I saw them carry away somebody I thought
was not the man I shot and I went down to see—
    —You knew he was dead—Pi'ilani said—They never
went near him—Ko'olau said—I needed to see—
    —Would you have gone if you had thought he was not dead—
she asked—And left us up here—He answered nothing
    Kaleimanu whispered to him—Is it the story now—
—What story Ko'olau asked him——Where the soldiers
    come up the cliff one at a time and he throws them down—
Ko'olau said—It is like that story in some ways
    as you are like Kaleimanu your grandfather
but not all the same—And he felt the child shivering

26.

Larsen and King and Pratt sat up late in the tents
    at Camp Dole writing their reports in the night heavy
with damp smoke and the aftertaste of smoke Larsen
    fought it off with cigars and each of them at some point
looked up at the shadows in the tent wall and heard
    the owl hunting down along the valley over
the charred remains they all slept badly Johnson was moaning
    they were awake before the bugle and the morning gun
and Larsen and Reynolds led a party up to the fork
    in the stream and on up to the cliff where Anderson
had been shot and they looked for his body and found it
    finally shirtless the hat under the head the wounds
plugged with ferns the cartridge belt off to the side and they
    carried him down to the woods and Larsen examined
the ledge through his glasses and ordered an attempt
    to climb the cliff to one side to a place where they

would be able to fire onto the ledge and the men
        started up through the woods to a crevice in the rock face
Larsen was watching and there was not a sign from the ledge
        McCabe was climbing up the rock face and when he appeared
to be almost high enough two shots rang out and he fell
        and then another shot but this one came from the edge
of the woods where Herschberg's rifle had caught in a vine
        and Herschberg had been killed by his own gun
they took the bodies down into the campsite that Pratt had found
        every man in the expedition who was not wounded
was there by then several of whom claimed to have seen action
        against the Indians on the plains and they stood smoking
agreeing that this beat anything they had ever seen
        they knew where he was now but they saw that he could not be
approached except by one man at a time and would be sure
        to pick him off before he himself could be seen
it would be suicide to try to get him that way
        so they took the bodies down to Camp Dole and buried
all three together Mr Hoogs reading the service
        and fired three rounds over them and kept a detail
on watch up under the cliff and that evening a message
        came from Sheriff Wilcox saying that he had five lepers
who they knew had been somewhere in the upper valley
        they had been out near William Kinney's above Haena
and it seemed they had given up for a good meal

27.

From the ledge they could hear the voices before daylight
        and at dawn the shooting began again a few bullets
at a time and they heard the voices coming closer
        they could look down through the rocks to the edge of the woods
and again a man was climbing up toward them Pi'ilani
        could see him moving up with two others behind him
and then Ko'olau's rifle fired and she saw the man
        fall back and it fired again and another man fell
and the rest went back into the trees and the shooting
        kept on and then stopped and they stayed there looking down
through the rocks trying to move around into the shade
        as the sun rose higher and Pi'ilani brought a gourd
she had left in the cave to fill and gave it to Kaleimanu
        and in the middle of the day as they sat waiting
Ko'olau said—There may be more of them coming
        and what will you do if they kill me—And Pi'ilani
picked up her rifle and said—I would rather die
        than be taken by them—And then she said—But what would they

do with him if he was alone It would be best
        to die all together—Koʻolau said—If it seems
that there is no other way I will try to kill us all
        quickly and we will not see the rest—And they pulled the child
to them and sat with their arms around each other
        Piʻilani said—Yes that would be best—And she felt less
frightened after that and the sound of the bullets
        troubled her less striking the rock above them all that day
a few at a time then stopping then coming again
        she watched Koʻolau studying the cliffs and the valley
and she sat in the shade rocking Kaleimanu
        and looked up to see tears on Koʻolau's face and he
said to her—Let us take off these dirty clothes and put on
        the clean ones in case we are killed They know where we are now
and there are three places up on the cliff and one place
        on the trail from which they could shoot into the ledge here
and they will find those and find a way to train
        the big gun up into the ledge here so I think we must
go down to the cliff after dark taking only what we have to
        we will have to get past the sentries and wade down the stream
and up the stream on the other side to a place I know
        I think it will be some time before they can find us there

28.

They ate the rest of the food and Koʻolau took two rifles
        and Piʻilani one and they took all the cartridges
and a few things in two blanket rolls tied to their shoulders
        Piʻilani knew that the sores on Kaleimanu's feet
were getting worse every day and it was not easy
        for him to hold things because his fingers had grown stiff
and were twisting up tight but Koʻolau told him
        to follow close behind him and they started down
a foot at a time feeling the rock in the dark
        slowly as snails over lichen and came at last to the foot
of the cliff face and the treacherous scree and Koʻolau
        picked up Kaleimanu and put him on his shoulder
while they skirted the trail and went down into the steep dark
        under the trees to where they could hear the stream running
and when they came to the water he put Kaleimanu down
        and told them not to step in the mud but on the rocks
then they knelt and drank and felt their way down the stream
        until they began to hear the soldiers talking
above them in the campsite where they had stayed before
        they went up to the ledge and they slipped past the soldiers
down through the water between the rocks where the current

    pulled them they hung on and slid down rock by rock
and came to where a stream flowed in from the other side
    and they inched their way up that stream to a leafy hollow
with walls of stone on three sides and Ko'olau drew them out
    under the small trees there onto a beach of shingle
and then moss and they lay there in the dark holding
    Kaleimanu who was shivering again and she asked him
whether his feet were hurting and he told her no
    They lay there and slept some until it began to be light
and Ko'olau said—The name of this place is Koheo
    and it always seemed to be a good place but now we must go on—
and they slipped back into the stream and up the valley side
    and Ko'olau left Pi'ilani and Kaleimanu
part way up and went off to see whether his friend
    Kelau who had a house at a place called Kaluamoi
was still there and he crept to where he could see the house
    and saw PG soldiers sitting in front of it
laughing and playing cards and other people around there
    he thought it must be one of the guard posts now and he left
and they climbed farther up to a place called Limamuku
    with a cave above a waterfall and banana trees

                              29.

Pratt wanted to use the howitzer Larsen opposed it
    saying it took too many men from the scouting parties
King wanted to send a contingent up to a corner
    on the Waimea trail and fire down into the ledge
and Larsen opposed it saying that at that distance
    they would accomplish nothing and he sent a note
down from the mountain to Pratt asking for six men
    for the Wainiha trail adding that there was no danger
over there which King read by mistake and as both men
    had been finding Larsen's temperament hard to endure
his lofty moods and caprices the note as they construed it
    led to heated words at Camp Dole later in the day
and a rivalry dividing the expedition
    with Special Police on one side and Provisional
Government troops on the other became more deeply entrenched
    and after relieving the guards up at the clearing
which they now called the lepers' campsite or the police camp
    King returned to Camp Dole to find that Larsen had left
in a whaleboat with instructions to do as he pleased
    with his plan for firing down into the ledge but that he
would take no responsibility for it and Pratt rolled
    the howitzer farther up the ridge to a flat spot

where they could aim it above the ledge and after signals
    to the men at the camp they fired several rounds but as they
could barely see the ledge above the trees they withdrew the gun
    and resumed the occasional rifle volleys around it
during the day and that evening Larsen came back
    from Kekaha by whaleboat bringing with him two natives
a woman he said was Koʻolau's sister and a man
    who was her husband and he said they would go next morning
up to the ledge to talk to Koʻolau they were frightened
    and were kept under guard that night and before they left
in the morning he told them that any treachery
    would cost them their lives and then he started them up the trail
with soldiers behind them bayonets fixed and Larsen
    had never pronounced her name and was not aware that the woman
was not Koʻolau's sister but a cousin who was called that
    and they had scarcely set out before she began pleading
—Koʻolau Koʻolau do not shoot it is only Palila
    sister Palila sister Palila—At the police camp
a skirmish line was formed to move up behind them
    and Palila and her husband climbed to the empty ledge
where they found old blue overalls a pair of boys' trousers
    a cotton shirt some dried eel and empty cartridges

30.

Through one tree above the waterfall they could see
    framed in leaves Waimakemake the ledge that they
had come from and when they heard the rifles begin
    again in the early morning they looked across
and saw here and there a splash of stone where a bullet
    struck the cliff and then later in the morning they heard
the crack and roar of the big gun again and the echoes
    reeling around the cliffs they could see the puffs of smoke
rising from down in the valley at a place Piʻilani
    thought must be the ridge at Puneʻe and they saw rocks
shatter above the ledge at Waimakemake
    and fall onto where they had been lying and she thought
they would destroy it all but then the shooting stopped
    and they could hear voices from far down in the valley
but then it was quiet for the rest of that day
    and the next morning a long way off they thought they heard
a woman's voice calling very faintly and they moved back
    from the waterfall to try to hear it and at last
Piʻilani said—Yes I think it is Palila—
    and Koʻolau said—Yes they have gone and brought her and made her
come up how frightened she must be they must be with her

just behind her the soldiers and that is why we heard
those signal shots from the top of the cliff this morning
    and they sat hearing the frail sound and whispering
about where she must be now as she called—Sister Palila—
    —Poor thing—Pi'ilani said—They went to Kekaha—
Ko'olau said—Frightening everybody with their
    guns and their uniforms and those faces Provisional
Government or whatever they told everybody they were
    and made her come with them—Pi'ilani said—They are going
up onto the ridge—and they kept trying to hear her
    and then far over on the ledge they could just see her
and someone with her a man and then soldiers and then they were
    all gone and bits of voices floated up from the valley
but for the rest of the day they heard no more shooting
    except signal shots from the cliff top and they found food now
fern shoots and shell fish and small fish out in the stream
    and bananas and after another day of hearing
nothing from below Ko'olau climbed to where he could see
    the whole valley and there was the steamer in the bay
but the next day the bay was empty and from farther on
    he saw that the tents were gone and there were no boats on the shore

31.

He sat for a long time looking down into the valley
    watching the shore the sides of the far headland the glint
of the taro ponds and the ridges as far as he could follow them
    he looked across at the ledge at Waimakemake
and the cliff above it but he saw no one no sign
    of anyone there and as the light began to go
he went back to the green hollow above the waterfall
    and they ate and drank and began to ask each other
whether the soldiers could have left Kalalau hardly daring
    to say it at first but they asked whether it could be
possible and if the soldiers were gone whether they would be
    coming back and whether they had left guards on the trails
or at the cliff top and after a while Ko'olau said
    —They made Palila go up onto our ledge over there
and they saw we were not there and the shooting stopped after that
    maybe they think that we have climbed out of the valley
there is that trail up from Waimakemake that they
    might have heard about because Mr Gay had it cleared
a few years back and there is the way Kala went up which they
    would never find under the deep ferns they would not
think we could have come down at night past the sentries
    and if they believe we have left the valley they would have

no reason to stay but they might have left guards hidden somewhere
        or send in spies or offer rewards to get people
to come into Kalalau looking for us and even if they have gone
        they could be planning to draw us into the open
so we must watch carefully all the time and see whether
        anyone at all is still in the valley and if they are
we must not let them know we are here because someone
        may be watching them or someone may visit them
and look for us and so for days they slipped out carefully
        from Limamuku and the banana trees by the water
and down the stream and they left Kaleimanu to watch
        the cliff top and the upper ridges when they climbed down
along the rocks of the stream to get food and when Ko'olau
        made his way silently farther and farther
from the waterfall to look up the side valleys and down
        to the trail and climb to crevices where he could see
the ridge where the soldiers had camped already the mark of them
        was disappearing under the green and that night
back under the shelter where it could not be seen
        they built a small fire of dry sticks and cooked a meal

32.

Then for a quarter of the moon they lived that way
        going out from Limamuku in the morning
together sometimes and sometimes Ko'olau alone
        scouting the valley farther and farther from their hiding place
sometimes Pi'ilani and Kaleimanu would wade
        down over the slippery rocks catching shellfish
and the little fish that climb upward through the current
        sometimes Kaleimanu would stay in one place listening
he seemed better now that their life was quiet again
        but the seizures of cold and the shivering kept returning
he would go to sleep and wake with his teeth chattering
        and then he would sleep again and she would lie awake
One morning when he was asleep she went with Ko'olau
        to the old campsite on the other stream below the ledge
they found pieces of clothing boxes that already
        seemed to have been there for lifetimes and out on the rocks
there were empty cartridges everywhere and under bushes
        another rifle some more rags and nothing else
they did not climb to the ledge for fear it was still being watched
        but they stayed for a long time looking down through the trees
to the valley below and the shore and up to the cliff top
        they stood where the soldiers had been talking that night
when they had slipped past below them in the sound of the water

and after all those days they were still whispering
 She said—The medicine that we brought up from the Judge's house
  was all gone by the time we came up here and the leaves
that I have been putting on the sores on Kaleimanu's feet
  seem to be doing no good now maybe they were only
for the old sicknesses before the haole came bringing
  all the new things to die from and turned them loose on us
to get rid of us but I keep putting those leaves on him
  the right way with the prayers and still the sores are no better
and yet he never cries about them and that night when we
  went down the stream there I thought his feet would hurt him
and he would cry but he never made a sound and when I
  asked him he told me they did not hurt and I thought maybe
the cold water helped him not to feel it—and she
  stopped and said nothing more and Ko'olau said
—It was true that his feet were not hurting him—and she looked up
  and he said—Mine are hurting me less and less now
though the sores seem to be getting worse the way they did
  on Kaleimanu's feet before we came to the valley—

33.

When they got back to Limamuku they found him
  out on the level ground across the stream lying
looking up along the cliffs and the cliff top and he said
  he was cold and they felt his hands and feet and he was
cold everywhere and Ko'olau brought a blanket
  and Pi'ilani said—do you think we could go
for part of the day down to where it is warmer—and Ko'olau said
  that they should look now for somewhere else and they gathered up
their few things and and he carried Kaleimanu in the blanket
  on top of the rolled bundle and they went down the stream
watching as carefully as ever and crossed a gorge
  where the cliffs almost met above them but opened out
just below there and taro was growing at the base of them
  by the rock face in the reflected sunlight and deep woods
covered the nearby slopes He told her the name of that place
  was Oheoheiki there were cave shelters in the rock
and there was food all around them and it was warmer
  below the gorge and Kaleimanu seemed better again
and they went on every day learning the valley again
  like some place that was new to them as it reappeared
out of what they remembered and what had happened there
  the whole of Kalalau seemed to be empty now
the echoes sounded as though no one else was there
  besides themselves but they knew the places from which

someone could watch from the heights or the side valleys
	or the turns on the trails and they took care not to
show themselves where they could be seen from any of those places
	they made their fires far back by the cliff faces or in caves
when it rained they stayed in caves far up in the gorge
	and in the sunlight they skirted old taro ponds where the weeds
were returning and looked out from bushes at the blackened
	rings and pointed out to each other where the houses had been
Ko'olau took Kaleimanu down into the clearings
	full of sunlight and they would gather food among trees
they had known before and they watched the light change from
	summer and the moon swell and the rains quickened
When Kaleimanu was left by himself he made up
	stories of his own which he told them as though they had happened
and he had seen them and after the chills he would tell them
	where he had been travelling all that time while they
held him and rocked him in the blanket and talked to him

34.

The months of autumn passed and they moved from one sheltered place
	to another sleeping in hollows among the cliffs
the rains were growing heavier toward the end of the year
	all the clothes they had were becoming the same color
the taro ponds were brimming and they worked together
	in the sunlight clearing some of the overflows
pulling weeds and piling them on the banks as they were
	pulling the taro to eat and they found stones for pounding it
wherever they went because there had been houses
	by the ponds for so long and banana groves and fruit trees
sugar cane tamarind and candlenut trees and the stones
	that had been used as tools for generations were lying
by the stone walls and steps and platforms of the houses
	where the grass was fringing the black clearings again
and the three of them had grown used to hearing the empty
	valley as an unbroken sound in which there were no
voices except their own and still they spoke softly
	and close and would hear the note of the valley recede
as they bent among the taro leaves and it was there
	around them again when they stood up One morning
Pi'ilani was down in the taro pond wearing
	the ragged dress and a pair of trousers she had made
out of some cloth they had found and over them Ko'olau's
	jacket and hat to keep the sun off it was a morning
when the sound of the valley was not clear sometimes the sick wind
	did that or rain somewhere or a mist and she stood up

among the leaves listening thinking that she had heard
    something different and then there was nothing and then
a man's cough and not Ko'olau and she crouched under
    the broad leaves and stopped breathing and heard men's voices
and she looked up to where the trail climbed the side of the valley
    and she saw that half-white Wili Kini the cane burner
looking down toward her and she drew back under the leaves
    but she was sure he had seen her and she heard him whistle
and looked out and saw Kelau and Keoki come up
    beside him and she slipped along in the mud under the leaves
and out to where Ko'olau was sitting with Kaleimanu
    she was breathless telling that there were men there
Wili Kini and others Kelau and Keoki up there
    and he asked—Did they see you—and she said—Yes
when Wili Kini saw me he whistled—and Ko'olau said
    —Come and hide—and he took his gun and they crawled under
the thicket and listened hearing the voices come closer
    and when the talking came to the thicket and stopped outside it
Ko'olau stood up facing them holding the rifle

35.

—Oh it is Ko'olau—Wili Kini said and the others
    came up and said—Ko'olau—and Wili Kini told him
—I am happy to see you we never knew where you were
    we saw somebody down in the taro and we were looking
for one Japanese who has been stealing from houses
    over Hanalei and Haena way and they caught him
but he got away and we thought that was who was down there—
    and all three came over to Ko'olau and held out
their hands and said—Ko'olau—and they embraced and he said
    —Now you all know we are here what does that mean for us—
and Wili Kini said—I am your friend Ko'olau
    I will help you if I can—and the others said the same thing
and Kelau who had long been Ko'olau's friend and whose house
    the soldiers had used for a guard post had tears in his eyes
and they asked how he was and Pi'ilani and Kaleimanu
    and Ko'olau called them to come out and they all sat down
and Pi'ilani brought food for them to eat together
    and Kelau said how glad they had been to see the soldiers go
and Kini told about the five lepers who had been caught
    and about the ones who had got away and were still hiding
in the cliffs over Hanalei side and they said
    that Ko'olau seemed to have driven the soldiers away
but no one knew what had become of the three of them
    at first people thought they had escaped from the valley

up the cliffs but then the time passed and no one saw them
        in Kekaha or Mānā or anywhere and they wondered
whether they could still be alive and Pi'ilani
        saw the men looking at Kaleimanu and at Ko'olau's
feet and Ko'olau said—We are well in spite of them—
        and they told him what had happened to the lepers
from the valley the steamer took them to Honolulu
        they had heard about it and it was in the papers
it took four men to carry the Judge down the gangplank
        in his city suit with his broad hat and the band
of peacock feathers around it and his blue sunglasses
        he told them that in his opinion they were all pirates
and their authority was pirates' authority
        he could not use his hands or his feet and they carted him
to the hospital along with Kaenaku and that
        little girl whose whole face was gone and Kamalinui
and he died there a few weeks later They sat in silence
        Tears ran down Pi'ilani's face and Wili Kini said
—If you see any cattle they might be mine you can shoot them
        and eat them if you want to—and Ko'olau thanked him
but he said—You know I could never repay you—

36.

The next day they were down there and they heard voices again
        and watched from hiding and saw Kelau and his wife
Keapoulu coming down the same trail and they went out
        and greeted each other in the old way this time
without suspicion crying and embracing each other
        and their friends had brought along clothes for all of them
and matches and a bag of fish caught that night and another
        of dried fish and some cooking pots and knives and gourds
and they cried together and ate together talking
        about friends they all knew and what had happened to each one
since the summer and Kelau and Keapoulu
        sat with them through the middle of the day talking
they were all trying to tell each other everything
        Kelau said that a few people of Kalalau
were talking about moving back and rebuilding their houses
        and Ko'olau nodded and said—You will remember
not to tell anyone that you have seen us here—and they
        promised and promised again as they were saying good-bye
and after they were gone months passed and became years
        in which they spoke with no one else though they saw people
they knew come back into the valley Wahinealoha
        came back with his wife and they built their house again

in the old place and cleaned out their taro ponds and they kept
    chickens a few at first and then there were many of them
and Pi'ilani or Ko'olau went every day
    and watched what they were doing but Ko'olau said
that Wahinealoha should not know that they were there
    He said—He is someone who says yes to everybody—
and they agreed that they must let no one in the valley
    know that they were there because then everyone would know
and Kelau had said he had heard that a reward
    had been offered to whoever could catch Ko'olau
so they moved more often than before taking more care
    to leave nothing behind them that would show that they had been there
they watched the Pā family come back and build their house again
    and then one neighbor after another but they never
showed themselves and they saw cattle from time to time
    that must have been Wili Kini's and Ko'olau's rifle
was never far but he said he would not use it again
    except to protect them and Kaleimanu grew weaker
month by month and his nose shrank away and his mouth puckered
    it was hard for him to hold anything and he shivered
more often and for longer and they carried him everywhere

37.

It was summer again and they were in the upper valley
    where it was safer to risk a fire and one morning
they looked down to the bay and saw a whaleboat coming in
    and Ko'olau made his way down the valley to learn
who had arrived and he managed to see from a hiding place
    Wahinealoha walking down to the beach
and loudly greeting twelve young men nine of them haoles
    the other three Hawaiians whom he knew from Kekaha
he thought the whaleboat was the one Knudsen kept at Kekaha
    and as the haoles came closer with Wahinealoha
he saw that Knudsen's sons had come with friends of theirs
    and Wahinealoha was telling them that he could have
chicken for them all to eat and yes he could show them
    where the battlefield had been and Ko'olau's stronghold
and the boy he recognized as Eric was telling his friends
    how this Ko'olau who had worked for his father and this
Louis Stolz had shot it out here a couple of years ago
    it sounded strange to hear it called a couple of years
and Wahinealoha said nobody knew what had happened
    to Ko'olau and whether he and his family
were dead or still living somewhere in the valley but no one
    had seen them and Ko'olau heard Eric tell them

that he had known Ko'olau since he had been a boy
        and they had ridden to Halemanu together and gone out
hunting together and Ko'olau was the best shot
        he had ever seen and he admired him and Ko'olau
as he listened was trying to think what reason Eric
        would have for speaking like that to Wahinealoha
and he watched them go up the trail to the temple platform
        where the soldiers had camped the first night and on up the valley
and he followed and watched them go part way up the stream
        and then go back down and sit eating along the beach
and later swim in the surf and then leave in the whaleboat
        heading toward Nualolo and that night they talked about
Knudsen and Halemanu and Waiawa and Kekaha
        and their friends and then the summer went on and they moved
through the valley like birds as Kaleimanu said once
        when a dark thrush flicked past them among the tree shadows
before evening in the upper valley and then autumn
        was there in the light and they saw how weak he was growing

38.

It had been three years since the night they set out from Kekaha
        and they nursed Kaleimanu into the end of the year
and though the upper valley was safer for lighting fires
        it was colder up there and the small clearings where the sun
shone but he could still remain hidden where almost all
        down in the lower valley and Ko'olau's own feet
were growing worse but he said to Pi'ilani that it was
        the chills shaking the child that frightened him most and he told her
one night that Knudsen had said about the leper house
        that it was seldom the sickness itself that they died of
but he had said that it weakened a person so deeply
        one way and another that something else at last
would take them down—But he was always thin like that—she said
        —and often cold and his lips would turn blue and he shivered—
—This may have been following him a long way—Ko'olau said
        The next day he climbed the cliffs away from the trail
high up to where he knew the petrels nested the 'uwa'u
        that Kaleimanu kept talking about in his story
and he waited and caught one in his hands which were beginning
        to grow numb and to curl and stiffen and as he caught it
he knew that he would not be able to do it again
        and he took it down finding it hard to cling to the rock
with his feet feeling almost nothing though he saw that the sores
        were torn and bleeding and his feet seemed to be shrinking
back into the heels and he thought how hard it would be

     to come up there again but he carried the bird
to Pi'ilani and they made a broth of it
     and gave it to Kaleimanu that night telling him
what it was and he drank it saying 'uwa'u
     over and over and then he seemed to be better
for a few days and then a few more but they could see
     that he was sinking away from them whatever they did
he was still with them when the year turned at the rising
     of the Pleiades and through the winter almost
to the days when the light changed to spring and one night then
     he grew cold and weak from shivering and he was
too far to hear them and his breathing grew hoarse and then stopped
     and they knew he was gone and they sat with him until morning
and then they took him up to a small cave hidden
     in a buttress at the base of the cliff and they dug
a grave for him inside it and lined it with ferns and buried him

39.

As they laid him in the ferns she began the chanting
     in a low voice patting her knee she chanted to the water
dripping down to them and past them and below them she chanted
     to Kane there on the cliff top to the altar of Kane
the water of Kane who listens and to Kane the sound of rain
     to Kane the light that comes back Kane the silence
Kane the silence of the stones Kane the silence
     of the face of the child we are waiting for you
for you at the place you know at the foot of the mountain
     to see whether you are coming back and then they sat there
until it was full daylight and they covered him with ferns
     and with the earth and set stones on the grave and sat there
all that day and it seemed to Pi'ilani that she had
     turned into a shadow with no weight and no senses
and when the light began to go from the air she longed
     to walk down to the shore and into the sea and lie there
floating with the waves moving her and she told Ko'olau
     that she wanted to go down to the water and let it hold her
but she knew it would be too dangerous someone would see her
     and he said he had the same wish to go down to the ocean
and walk into it and let it carry him and wash him new
     and he said that someone might see them but that it was the time
to go and they went carefully down through the safe places
     and on down the valley after dark and out over the stones
of the shore and out into the waves and rocked there
     she felt the tears burn on her face and the knowledge
that Kaleimanu had gone was rocking her and turning

into her and into knowing that she would lose Koʻolau
and that she was losing him as they rocked in the same waves there
    looking up at the same night clouds over the deep valley
she knew it that night as they went up through the darkness
    to the cliffs and the grave and after that night she knew it
as she had known that she was no longer afraid after that time
    on the ledge when she had agreed that they should all die
together if the moment came now a fear made of hope
    went out of her and a fear made of none took its place
they left the grave without offerings and went down
    toward the valley and slept that night in another place

40.

Without Kaleimanu to take care of any more
    and keep warm and carry with them it was easier to move
around the valley and to her it seemed too easy
    as though she had been cut adrift and was floating away
but Koʻolau's feet were much worse after the day
    when he climbed the cliff and after they buried Kaleimanu
the torn sores were deeper and they never stopped bleeding
    and rotten water came out of them and she saw
him walking on the open sores as his feet shrank back
    and when he walked he left prints of blood and fluid and rags
of flesh trailed behind his footsteps then she took pieces
    of clothes that were falling apart and she washed them in the stream
and wrapped them around his feet and he cut a stick to walk with
    —We do not have to travel very far or move very fast
the way we live—she said and it was a summer of plenty
    they watched friends of theirs come and rebuild their houses
and take care of the fruit trees beside their taro ponds
    and there were fruit trees wild or untended up through the valley
fern shoots and shellfish from the streams and he still carried
    the rifle from one sleeping place to the next and it lay
within reach at night but she saw the way he held it now
    distantly absently as though he had forgotten it
the kamani stick that he used for walking was nearer
    to his mind and grasp than the rifle seemed to be
and they had hidden the other guns months before that
    she saw that his hands were curling tighter the fingers
shrivelling until it was awkward for him to eat
    and he picked up more things with the heels of his hands
but he seemed almost well that summer although he was weaker
    than she had ever believed he could be and in
the evenings they would sit in the dark as the coals
    closed themselves in the ashes and they would say nothing

for a long time and then find that they had been thinking
    of the same thing and they would talk of what they remembered
without sadness or it seemed to be without sadness
    and then would be silent again and she would start to chant
under her breath patting a shell or her knee bringing the chant
    out of the darkness around them and offering it
to the darkness ahead of them and she thought of his face
    as it was crumbling into itself that summer and autumn
and winter and when they slept to the sound of the rain
    some nights she dreamed of white sand and voices along the shore

THE SHORE

I

The shore was what she had always known but could not see
     she saw nothing clearly except the sands and the footsteps
it was like Kekaha and Mānā and it seemed that it was
     Kekaha and Mānā but it was neither of them
and out to sea it was dark and the voices had just gone
     they had just been there and she was still hearing them but they
were silent again and there was only the breathing
     of the sea and she opened her eyes on the ghost dawn
and saw the owl in the hala root watching her
     where she was lying on his grave under the ferns in the thicket
as she stared at it she was thinking of Kawaluna
     and when she closed her eyes and opened them again the owl
was gone and she lay knowing where she was and she heard
     the trees dripping and the stream whispering below the rock wall
and she remembered the whole of it in a moment
     the last months together four years after they had come
into the valley the winter rains sweeping the cliffs
     the streams roaring at night and rocks crashing and lunging down
through the trees and day by day it was harder for him to move
     with his feet nearly gone and his hands almost useless
and his mouth twisted into itself so that it was hard
     to eat or drink and he talked about what she would do
after he was gone his fear that if they were to find her
     she would be punished for what he had done and for staying
with him and for their life together they saw footprints
     in the mud by the streams as they moved from one shelter
to another and as she went down over the rocks
     to get food for them and they talked of the footprints
whose they might be and who might be trying to find them
     one time as they were moving upstream in the water
they found a bundle tied like an offering sheltered by ferns
     beside the trail and he said they should not touch it
no one must know they were there and at other times
     during those months they found bundles like that by the trails
up near the cliffs and knew someone was looking for them
     either to trap them or try to help them but they never
touched them and she went on getting food from the stream
     and wild fruit from the valley and he talked about how long
it might be after he was gone before it would be safe
     for her to be seen and be recognized and go back
to Kekaha and her mother and her family again

2.

She remembered Kaleimanu saying that he was falling
       asleep before he died and his face was in front of her
all during the days when she could see Ko'olau
       sinking from beside her those months when he was going
the same way the child had gone it was more than seven months
       like that and at the beginning of that time he could
still talk to her as they had always talked and they stayed
       close in their words but later when he tried to talk to her
it sounded as though he were calling from a long way off
       in a hoarse voice though there was a day in one of those long spells
of green sunlight and fragrance and stillness that arrive sometimes
       in the winter with the drops shining at the ends of the leaves
when he spoke to her again from no distance and told her
       that after he was gone he wanted her to bury
his rifle with him because he said she had never been
       the one who had used it and it would stay in the ground with him
afterward and that then she should leave the valley
       and go back to Kekaha and their house and families
and when she was questioned she should tell them the truth
       that she had stayed with him and their child as she had always
said she would do and as she had promised to do
       when they were married and that she had killed no one
but had come with him and stayed with him until the end
       and when she had buried him in that ground where she was lying
and had left him there in the sleep of the seasons
       and gone down the stream through the trees and close to the houses
of people she knew who had come back and had passed by there
       down into the sea and out through the turning of the waves
and had lain there again looking up at the clouds and the stars
       that appeared and vanished between them she stepped out
onto the rocks and went around by the side of the valley
       to leave no trail and went to a spot near a side stream
where there was a thicket of lantana next to the water
       near a path that led along by the taro ponds
a place where she could be hidden from everyone
       but look out and see them and hear what they were saying
and she crawled into the deep thicket and made a bed there
       and slept alone for the first time in the valley
wanting to be near some of the people she knew
       but not wanting to show herself to them not yet not yet

3.

Then for a while she made her home in the thicket
  listening to the voices during the daytime
as they went by on the path and to those who were working
  in the taro ponds recognizing some of them trying
to hear what they said and learn what had been happening
  while she had been up in the cliffs however long that had been
syllables floated past out there like butterflies and she
  tried to catch the sounds of names even her own name
she kept watching for signs of soldiers of the Provisional
  Government or of the police and only after dark
would she come out of the thicket to gather fruit and fern shoots
  after the moon rose and she lived that way until the moon
had returned to where it had been when he died and then when it
  darkened again and before it grew full she crept
out of her hiding place toward the end of one day
  when she heard them all going home from the taro ponds
and she smelled the smoke rising from the evening cooking fires
  she stood up and watched the last sunlight out on the headland
and when it was gone she moved farther from the houses
  keeping off the trail as she started back toward the cliffs
she had wrapped tightly the few things she still had with her
  the knife the rope the can of matches in her one blanket
and as she climbed along by the stream she put wild fruit
  inside the front of her dress as she passed trees she knew
after dark she paused at one of the places where they had lived
  when there had been three of them and she sat with the moonlight
coming through the 'ohia leaves and the halas
  she looked back down through the valley where she had been
where she had known that pain was ahead of her and she looked
  for that pain as though she might see it but there was
only the moonlight in the valley now where she had stepped past
  the days and where she had lost and hidden and had known
what she was losing and had expected to die
  she looked through the moonlight and thought that perhaps she
had died and was seeing the valley from afterwards
  but she felt it still around her sheltering her
protecting her as it had done through all that time
  and a love for it welled up in her eyes and filled
with moonlight and she stood up and started along the trail
  and climbed to the mountain house where they had first stayed
when they came at the beginning the roof had fallen in
  the leaning timbers were deep in moss and she rested there
as the moon was setting and slept until the stars
  were growing faint and then she went on up the trail
with the darkness dropping away around her and came out
  into the cool of the cliffs and she climbed until dawn

and kept on climbing until she came to the cliff top
    as the rays of the sun were reaching down into the valley
and she stepped out on the level brink of Kalou
    and turned to see it all below her in the morning

4.

Time had vanished since she had stood at the top of the cliff
    looking down and out over the valley of Kalalau
seeing it from outside and above and then it had been
    somewhere she had not seen before and now it seemed
as she looked down into it that it was her own life
    out of which she had climbed and the whole valley with the clouds
and the cloud shadows passing over it was closer
    than the night's sleep that was behind her and she knew it
wherever she looked she knew what was under the trees
    what was in each hollow and she stood there seeing again
what had happened in each place then carefully she
    took her leave of a life that she felt was still with her
she spoke to it aloud out of the aching of her body
    calling by name to one part of the cliffs and the valley
after another You Kamaile guarding the darkness
    of Kane you that watch over the sleep of Koʻolau
You Kahalanui that hid us at the beginning
    under your wing You Waimakemake that kept us
safe from the soldiers' bullets I will remember you
    with love until I am nothing but bones in the ground
You Koheo that embraced us and Puneʻe
    where we were never hungry and Limamuku
green hollow above the waterfalls into you
    we had vanished when they could not find us and You curtained
cliffs of Kaʻalaneo with the ridge below
    that kept them from seeing us You rock face of Kalahau
that broke the flights of the bullets everywhere around us
    You Oheoheiki that welcomed us and fed us
and shaded us through the hot days and kept us dry in the winter
    you were like a parent to us and you Kaluamoi
that cradled us when we needed you and hid us from the hunters
    where we saw the clouds blow away and the stars shining
and the waterfalls white far above us you Kalalau
    where I am leaving hands and arms that I love eyes that I love
faces that I love you that hide them and keep them
    I am going away now I will not set eyes on you now
you will be hidden from me now I am cold with a coldness
    that was not there in the night not there until this moment
a coldness in me a coldness all around me spreading out
    the thickets are tangled in Kuhonua the flowers

have fallen onto each other in piles the sea is wild
    under the battering south wind the Waipao wind Kalalau
the wind at the edge shook her and she turned away

5.

She went slowly along the trail that followed the cliff
    from Kilohana to the path down the Kaunuahoa
and the valley of Halemanu and the mountain house
    of the elder Knudsen whom they used to call Father
the house where they had stopped when they were coming over
    those years before when all of them were together
the moment she turned from the cliffs a great weariness
    settled into her the weariness of the climb
caught up with her all at once and the weariness
    of uprooting herself at last from her life of hiding
and from the bare ground a great effort even though the thoughts
    of her mother and of Kekaha and her friends there
had been with her all that time and more closely than ever
    after she had buried Koʻolau and had gone down
to hide through the days so close to people she knew
    hearing their voices and as she lay there in the thicket
listening to their voices sometimes she thought of Kekaha
    and saw it more clearly than the day that she was watching
through the lantana leaves and now as she walked down the trail
    like a shadow in the forest it was not the forest
that she had come to know like a thought of her own
    in which every sound was something she recognized
During those years in the valley sometimes she saw faces
    and houses and moments from long before in Kekaha
and then among them places by the stream and moments
    of light in the valley and when she saw the house
at Halemanu she stopped as the place and her own
    memory of it came together not all at once
but hesitantly and then she walked down watching
    to see whether anyone was there but the house was empty
and she went nearer under the big trees through the running
    sound of the stream and saw the blind stare of the windows
the day was going and she climbed the front steps
    onto the lanai and sat looking down the green slope
as the light lengthened and she took out the last
    of the fruit she had brought with her from Kalalau
and the rain began whispering into the trees around her
    she unrolled the blanket on the lanai and lay down
and when she closed her eyes the stream she went on hearing
    was in Kalalau somewhere and she tried to think of its name

6.

In the first light she saw the mist travelling in silence
     under the dark trees and she thought she was in the night world
where there were no faces and she was not sure where she was
     until her hand moved on the cold blanket and she felt
the rough wool that had come with her so far from its first life
     stained and torn through years of hers and then she remembered
Halemanu the house of the birds and she heard them
     all around her beginning the day and she sat up
and rolled up the blanket and walked down with the bundle
     to the Brook of Tears below the house and put her face in it
she remembered where there were guavas along the trail
     and she started down through the mist moving stiffly
slowly after the climb of the day before and she heard
     the forest stirring around her as she had come to hear
the valley around her through the years of hiding
     Where the trail was joined by another she heard something
in dry leaves on the ground and at once she was gone
     among the bushes until she saw that it was a pair
of dark thrushes finding their food and now that she
     was on her way to being among people again
she found that she did not want to be seen by them
     she was not sure what she would do when she was back
in Kekaha before faces she knew or used to know
     but as she went back to the trail she listened as before
and as the mist thinned and wore away into the opal shade
     of the 'ohia trees it seemed to her that the forest
was exposed to the daylight and she moved cautiously
     down the mountain to the broken rim of the canyon
everywhere open and she moved away from there
     out of the sound of the wind through which she could hear
nothing else and she went on past the ghost place that smelled
     of dried fish still and came to the turn where the west slope
of the mountain all lay before her as far as the coast
     Waimea and Kekaha and the broad shore before Mānā
glittering in a crescent and the sea beyond them
     she stopped at each turn watching for signs of anyone
on the trail below her and she stopped at the spring thinking
     of where she was and trying to recall Kekaha
which all at once seemed to be like the other side of a door
     she stopped at a turn and stared over Waimea and where the trail
forked she turned toward Kekaha letting the day pass
     approaching it along the back trail past the small valleys
and at dusk she passed like a shadow among the houses
     to the tamarind tree and her mother's back door

7.

There was a fire burning between rocks and her mother
        and Kinoulu were bending over something they were cooking
and she walked toward them slowly until they stood up and saw her
        and burst out with those cries that were sounds both of love
and of grief and they stood with their arms around her
        wailing and crying and she cried with them and Ida
came out of the house so much taller that Pi'ilani
        was sure she must be someone else and then she knew her
and they stood there crying together auwe auwe auwe
        for all that was lost and the pain and the finding again
repeating each other's names and then Ida was gone
        and came back bringing Kepola's parents and went again
and came back with Ko'olau's parents Kukui
        and Kaleimanu and they all stood embracing and crying
by then it was dark and the fire shone on their wet faces
        showing grief and joy and bewilderment and it was long
even before the questions began and longer
        before anyone thought of eating but she told them
that she was thirsty and they brought her water and watched her
        hold it up and drink and they talked to her the whole time
and Kukui could be heard crying above all the rest
        and then they brought soft things and had Pi'ilani sit down
with something to lean back on and something for her feet
        and someone brought her cold sweet potatoes and someone else
fish and taro but before she could eat they wanted her
        to tell them something and then the crying began again
and she told them of the deaths and of the soldiers
        a little at a time and of the houses being burned
and the hiding and the time on the ledge and the bullets
        then someone came bringing Ko'olau's cousin Palila
the one they both called Sister and she cried louder
        than Kukui and told Pi'ilani how the soldiers
had come to her house at night and had taken her
        and her husband and ordered them to come with them
to Kalalau and told them that they had to go up
        and make Ko'olau surrender and said that if they did not
they would be killed and she cried and told them how frightened
        they had been with the soldiers' bayonets in their backs
making them go up onto the ledge and how happy they were
        when they found no one there and Pi'ilani said nothing

8.

She woke in the dark again believing that she was nowhere
        a tide without waves a night without leaves or streams
a wooden stillness then she followed the smell of wood
        to her mother's house and knew where she was and heard
her mother stirring in sleep and the next time she looked
        there was enough light for her to let her eyes roam
over the dark boards of the walls in the room where she
        had not slept since before she had gone with Koʻolau
it came back to her from that time through the way it was now
        fishing nets sagging from the pegs for clothes and sacks standing
in the corner then her mother woke on the other side
        and they began their morning together and Kinoulu
and Ida came bringing fruit and Piʻilani said—Now
        tell me while we are here by ourselves how you came back
after you left us that morning—and Kepola said
        —Kala led us along the loose rock into the ferns
where there was a pig tunnel and we crawled after him—
        —With those hooks on the uluhe ferns tearing us—Ida said
—But Kala told us not to widen the tunnel at first—
        Kepola said—or the soldiers might find it and try
to come after us——And then we came out on the other side
        of the rock wall—Ida said—And we started to go up
in a crack of the cliff and I was so frightened
        that I was trying not to shake——Then we heard the shooting—
Kepola said—But the soldiers were on the other side
        of that cliff where it runs out and we even heard bullets
but nowhere near us—And Ida said—Kala told us
        that the soldiers could not see us but I was afraid
that they would see us when we got higher and we would
        not be able to move there in the rock and when I looked down
it was a long way to fall but we kept on climbing
        after Kala hearing the shooting and the echoes
that went on and on around us and then we came up
        into bushes near the top of the rock and the ground
was steep and crumbly but there were places to step and he
        waited for us at every step and then there was a ridge
where he told us the goats ran and we went up that way
        that was steep too but there were aʻaliʻi bushes
but some places it was like walking on top of a wall
        and I never looked down the sides—And Kepola said
—At the top we were in the woods with only the goat track
        but we went along and then we were on a trail
and all at once we met Kua up there watching the cliff top—

9.

Kepola said—He had come up from Halemanu
        he told us he had been up there every day since they heard
that Koʻolau had shot Stolz he had watched along the trail
        from Waimea and had seen the boats come into the bay
and he had watched the soldiers come up from Waimea
        and set up their sentry post in the trees above the trail
he went and talked with them none of them friendly at first
        the haoles suspicious asking him who he was
and what he was doing there but the Hawaiians knew him
        and they all knew who Mr Knudsen was and then Kua
went by every day and talked with them and saw the mirrors
        and heard what the soldiers were doing down in the valley
and what they were planning and he saw who the soldiers
        caught at the top of the trail and took away
to Waimea he rode with them part way he warned
        friends bringing things to the valley and told them about
the sentry post he could hear the big gun booming
        from far down in the valley and he kept watching then
to see whether any of us might be coming up
        and he told Kala not to let the soldiers see him
and then Kala left us and it was Kua who brought us down—
        Kepola said it with sadness and disbelief
—It was Kua who brought us to Halemanu and down here
        all the way down but we never told everybody
only family you know and to all the others
        we just said we made it back and what a long way it was
and you know that is true but nothing about Kala
        or Kua and of course we knew nothing about you
what had become of you and that was true it was true—
        Then Kepola cried with her arms around Piʻilani
and Koʻolau's father Kaleimanu came and Kukui
        and Kawaluna and all the grandparents and they
went over the stories and the questions and Kaleimanu
        said that Palila and others were talking of having
a big feast for Piʻilani with everyone there
        but Kaleimanu said he thought that would not be wise
and Piʻilani said that she wanted her homecoming
        to be as quiet as possible with as little talk
as possible and she said she hoped it would be a long time
        before the government people heard that she had come home

10.

Pi'ilani's father Ho'ona came home later from the mill
        and said that he had heard down there that she had come back
and then they went over the whole story again and when
        they stopped for a while Pi'ilani asked her father
who had told him that she was home and he said—You know
        how news travels—and he told her who had told him
then she said—That is why I do not want everybody
        coming now that I am back and asking and asking
going away talking there is too much talk already—
        And they all considered that and agreed with her
and Kepola said—It is not only government
        you know there were always some who said Ko'olau
was too stubborn he went his own way he spoke out—
        —I suppose so—Pi'ilani said and Ho'ona went on—When he told them
he would not go to Moloka'i if they ordered him to go
        even then some said he was a trouble-maker
and they called it a shame—and Pi'ilani said
        —I know some of those—and Kepola said—It is worse now—
And then one day Ho'ona brought news that would make it still worse
        —Dr Smith—he said—But not old Dr Smith in Koloa
whom you remember—and Pi'ilani said—The one
        who sent Niuli away——Not him—Ho'ona said—His son
young Dr Smith everyone liked him he was a kind man
        and he has been killed he was shot in his own house
and by a Hawaiian at night there in Koloa
        his sister was living with him and she had gone to bed
he was writing a letter at a table and there were horses
        in the street and feet on the steps and a knock at the door
and when he opened it this man Kapea shot him
        full in the chest and then rode off but they caught him
he did it because the doctor had seen that Kapea's
        sister and another woman in the family
had leprosy and he had told them that he would
        have to report it and he was a friend of the family
he had taken care of them he had them live in his house
        when the father was sick and everyone knew that he
took care of Hawaiians for nothing when they needed him—
        —When did it happen—Pi'ilani asked—Just now—
Ho'ona said—It was Friday night he was shot—

II.

She learned that all the lepers had been taken away
         from the house in Kekaha where Valdemar Knudsen
had arranged for them to be cared for and that Knudsen
         had been sick recently and seldom left Makaweli
she stayed at home with her family and with Kawaluna
         and she could talk with Kawaluna about the valley
the days and nights in hiding the cold the sickness the dying
         the darkness the sounds in the night the burying
the valley at night when the soldiers had all gone
         the sound of the empty valley it was only to
Kawaluna that she could talk about those things
         and Kawaluna would sit without moving and listen
and when Pi'ilani stopped she would say—Yes—but if
         someone else came they seemed to be talking about nothing
and to those outside the family Pi'ilani
         said little and waited for the questions to stop and she thought
that some day the government would hear that she was back
         and someone would come asking but the months passed and the winter
and Ho'ona came back from the mill one evening and told her
         in a low voice that there was a rumor of someone
from Hanalei finding Ko'olau's grave in Kalalau
         and showing people things that he had taken out of it
and Pi'ilani felt a cold hand tighten around her
         that would not let go of her and she asked Ho'ona
what he knew about the man and the things from the grave
         and who had told him and that night she said nothing
and lay awake and then got up and went out and made her way
         behind the houses to the house of Ko'olau's family
she saw Kawaluna sitting outside and sat beside her
         and after a while told her in a hushed voice all
that she had heard and Kawaluna said that Ho'ona
         had told them and that others had told them the way everyone
tells secrets and Pi'ilani heard that she said it
         with her own laugh and Kawaluna said—And so you
stayed awake—and when Pi'ilani said nothing
         Kawaluna asked her—Are you afraid to know
whether you think the grave this man found was Ko'olau's—
         And Pi'ilani said—I have to see—and Kawaluna
said—Then you have to see—and after a while she said
         his name—You have to see Kalua i Ko'olau—

12.

The next day Piʻilani said to Koʻolau's father
    —It was not Koʻolau's grave that the man broke into
I am sure of that but now someone claims to have found it
    I want to go back to the place where I buried him
and visit his grave—He said—You should have someone with you—
    —Not to the grave—she said—But maybe part of the way—
Kaleimanu said—I would go myself but my legs
    I think are too old for the climb down so maybe I will ask
Kuala at Waiawa when I go up there tomorrow
    he was a good friend of Koʻolau's they used to hunt
together up at Kokeʻe with Kua and he spoke
    to Koʻolau as to an elder brother and I know
he went with Kua along the edge there while you were
    in the valley he used to take things from the ranch
for the lepers in Kalalau he does not talk much
    and if a stranger asks him questions he says nothing
he has come here with Koʻolau——I remember him—she said
    and it was Kuala who was waiting for her
in the early light a few mornings later and she
    mounted the horse that Kaleimanu had saddled for her
and rode up the trail behind Kuala and there were
    friends of his from the ranch staying at Halemanu
one of them rode with them up to the cliff and the trail head
    below Kilohana to take back the horses
and she saw Kalalau open again before her
    with the clouds coming over it telling nothing
and again she started down the trail under Na Iwi
    stepping into her own memory into the same light
and the air and the rock smells and the cries of white birds
    wheeling and flashing below her as she went down
and the shadows climbing around her the goats calling
    on a cliff far away in the white sun and she let Kuala
get ahead of her at the turns until she was
    going down alone into all of it and when they came
to the stream she told him to go on by himself
    and told him she would meet him some time later at the house
of Kelau and Keapoulu who were friends of his
    from the days when he used to come over into Kalalau
with Kua and Koʻolau and hunt in the valley
    and she watched him go down the trail and stood listening

13.

Then she crept silently down the trail behind him
    and stood again listening and again and stood listening
and waited to be sure that he was not hiding and coming back
    she thought that even he might be turned around by
curiosity and try to see where she was going
    she waited hearing the sounds of the valley the stream
there below her the trees in the late afternoon the birds
    then she stepped back hearing her own footsteps and watching
the forest as she went up the trail and aside
    carefully to the left through the ferns under the trees
breaking nothing and drawing the fronds back together
    behind her and then stopping still as a thrush stops
in the fallen leaves to look around without moving
    she climbed slowly into the long hollow between
the rock walls at the foot of the cliffs and came silently
    through the green shade at each step drawing it shut again
until she stood before the ferns where she had buried him
    and once more she stood listening and heard the whisper
of that place as she knew it in her mind a breath
    a rustling lighter than water and she bent in the ferns
and looked and saw that nothing had been touched and that moss
    had grown back over the stones she had set on his grave
she knelt and the tears came and shook her and when she closed
    her eyes she was there in the time when they were all
still together cold and wet a time with dread running through it
    like an echo at night but it was a time that she
tried to touch in the darkness with her head on her knees
    crying silently and then she stopped and whispered
into the moss—Koʻolau Koʻolau Here I am—
    and then she was still and stood up and looked around her
it was the same place that she knew and had kept in her mind
    when she was not there but it seemed that she had not seen it
before in its own light and age in which she was
    a stranger like a dream that had vanished upon waking
and now the grave was part of the place and its light and age
    it was looking past her at something she could not see
that must be all around her in the daylight and the shadows
    She drew the ferns back and made her way down through the rocks
the way she had come and when she reached the trail again
    the sun had already gone from the top of the cliffs
and she went on to the house of Kelau and Keapoulu

14.

Their house was set in a lap of rock with the cliff behind it
        they were standing outside watching for Pi'ilani
as she climbed toward them and they ran down the path to meet her
        greeting her as at her homecoming in Kekaha
crying and wailing and drawing her back up the slope
        then the questions and fragments of stories tumbling over
each other all that had happened since they had last seen her
        down there by the taro pond with the things they had brought
for all three of them when there had been three of them
        and then nothing and they had not known and no one had heard
and they brought things at other times food and clothing
        cooking pots and knives and tools other friends had sent for them
to bring over but they never knew where to leave them
        where the three of them might be or whether they were alive
but all that winter they left bundles by the upper trail
        hoping some of them would be found and Pi'ilani
sat with her arm around Keapoulu and told her
        —We found some of them and knew they might be from you
but we never knew who might be watching for us
        looking to see whether those things had been taken
and coming to think that we were up there somewhere and hunting
        for us so we never touched them we left them there
to make it seem that we were not here in the valley—
        Then they started telling her which friends had come back
into Kalalau and of their learning that she had
        returned alone to Kekaha and they cried and she said
—Now they tell me that someone is saying he has found
        Ko'olau's grave—and they said to her—Some men came by here
from Hanalei side and said they were hunting goats
        and went down to talk with the Pā family whom one of them
said he knew and they met Wahinealoha
        you know the way he is when any stranger is coming
so they asked about Ko'olau and he said that he could
        show them places they wanted to go and then they went on
by themselves he says and must have been looking for the grave
        and they came down saying they had found it—And Pi'ilani
said nothing at first and then she said—Whatever they
        found it was not Ko'olau—and Kelau said he never
thought it was Ko'olau—We never believed that they
        had found our friend there were always graves up there and we
can guess sometimes whose they were and sometimes nobody can say—

15.

Half waking again knowing that she was in the valley
        but under a roof once more she lay still in the darkness
it seemed to her that she felt nothing and knew no names
        no stories and that she was flying without moving
in a night without stars without end without morning
        or memory and then she thought This is the grave
that is not a grave this is the wind that is not air
        this is where they will never find us and even as
she thought it she knew that she was Pi'ilani
        in the house of their friends Kelau and Keapoulu
her hand was touching the black grass of the wall and she knew
        why she was there with Kuala sleeping outside
and then she slept and woke knowing that it was near day
        and she got up and went out to watch the clouds trailing
their long arms across the sky showing a fragment
        with its stars in their places fading as she looked
and then closing over them again and the dark valley
        under them seemed to her like the sleep of a child
closed in itself then she heard the grass rustle in the door
        and Keapoulu whisper behind her—Sister—
and they stood together at the edge of the rock platform
        with their arms around each other and then sat down
and Keapoulu began to tell her who they should visit
        and Pi'ilani spoke of friends she had seen in the valley
when she was alone and living in the lantana thicket
        listening to them and Keapoulu told her
which taro ponds they were working now and which families
        had rebuilt their houses and had babies and who was fishing
down in the caves and out in the bay and she said
        they were dancing again up on the temple platforms
three of the teachers were back and the children went up there
        almost every day and danced the way they used to
and Kelau came out and joined them and told Pi'ilani
        who was planting new fruit trees beside the ponds there would be
more oranges than before and papayas on the banks
        and mangos in the lower places and tamarinds near the shore
—It is beginning over again—he said as the first
        daylight revealed the valley below them under the trees
and she thought of all of them waking there and of going
        down there herself and them seeing her as she was now

16.

She tried to say something about that to Kawaluna
    later when Kuala had been to see Wili Kini
and whoever else he had wanted to see over there
    and she had guessed that in any case he had come mainly
as a way of paying respect to his friend Koʻolau
    and after she had said her good-byes in the valley
as she had never done before and they had climbed together
    to the top of the cliff one morning starting before daybreak
and then on along the trail down from Kilohana
    to Halemanu and friends and horses and they had ridden
down the far side of the mountain with the light in their eyes
    as the day was sinking and she had seen Kekaha below her
with something of the same strangeness the same stillness
    and distance the same light of disbelief welling
out of a place so familiar that she had known
    on that morning when she walked down into the valley
which she had watched for so long like a face the face of her days
    and when she closed her eyes at any hour could see it rock
by rock tree by tree shadow and water and there it was
    again and her eyes were open and it looked to her
like the other side of itself and out of reach even when
    she touched the cold stream or the moss by the waterfall
and before she came to hear voices and the surprise of friends
    one after another welcoming her back to them
from far away far away and all day as they talked
    and friends joined them and they cried and ate and began
again and brought her the children to see and asked
    the same things over and over and kept telling her
that this was her home too now and they they would build
    a house for her in the valley if she would stay there
they said that to her on the first day and they asked her
    where she would like it to be and she smiled and talked to them
about her mother and she felt like a cloud in no wind
    but she told them that she would come back to the valley
and Kawaluna nodded—You will go there again—
    Piʻilani said—When I saw it in the other time
we were together and we were going to be together
    as long as we were alive and that was the way I saw
Kalalau then but now it looks like another place
    since I am no longer the one who was hiding there—

17.

But now she felt that she was hiding in Kekaha
          she lived in the back of Kepola's house and she listened
to find out who was coming and what was in their voices
          she seldom went far from the house and then she followed
the back lane but she walked as she had always walked
          and she told Kepola that she was not hiding
though she never knew what the officers would do
          if they found her now that she had come back after
what had happened and she did not want people asking
          about Kalalau and Kepola said—They stop asking
after a while but you know they will start again
          if they hear anything—So Pi'ilani stayed at home
and kept house with Kepola and talked with Kawaluna
          who listened to her but never seemed to ask questions
waiting for whatever Pi'ilani wanted to tell her
          and it was still that same summer when Naea came up
from a whaleboat to say to Kepola that someone else
          was saying he had found Ko'olau's grave and his rifle
Pi'ilani thought they will always say they found his rifle
          and she listened to Naea and all she said
was—Thank you—but a few days later Penekila
          the same Penekila from the old days disturbed the dogs
to tell them the same thing and Pi'ilani asked him
          what he had found out and who had told him and he answered
so that she was startled to see that he had not changed at all
          he was always on the other foot it was like trying
to pick up a roach with two fingers and she watched him
          while he was talking and thought that she would never
be able to tell the truth of it by listening
          to Penekila and then he said he was going
into Kalalau the day after next and he told her
          that if she wanted to go he would bring a horse for her
and she said yes she would go and as he was leaving
          she saw the way Kepola was staring after him
and she said to her mother—Do you want to come too—
          and Kepola shook her head slowly and Pi'ilani
told Kawaluna that she was going again
          and with Penekila this time and Kawaluna said
—Why do you think Penekila came to tell you—

18.

He said nothing as they rode up out of Kekaha
    and then when the trail narrowed toward the ridge and the brink
of the canyon and they went one behind the other
    they could not talk and she looked ahead at his shoulders
that seemed to her to tell everything about him
    and it occurred to her that he could never see them himself
she was looking at something about him that he
    could never see and she felt a touch of embarrassment
and kept her eyes from his back and when they stopped at the spring
    she asked him again what he had learned and he told her
about meeting a man in Waimea a haole name
    she had never heard and this man said that he travelled
to dig up things to sell and he told Penekila
    who he had dug up and what he had found in the graves
and where he had sold things and to whom and for how much
    —He must be rich—Pi'ilani said—He did not seem rich—
Penekila said—But maybe he has all the money
    buried away somewhere———Did he ask you to help him—
Pi'ilani asked—He said he had been told that I might
    know things that would be of interest to him—Penekila said
—And did you—Pi'ilani asked and she listened
    to the way he did not answer her and began
to tell her how he had come to be working for Stolz
    who had said he needed a native able to talk
to the natives and Penekila laughed—How did he know
    you could do that—Pi'ilani asked—After I was
working for him and he got to know me I heard how he
    talked about natives nothing new only the way
he said it he told me that if they betrayed him he would
    skin them alive and things like that and he told me
over in Kalalau that if I did not do
    as he ordered he would shoot me he would shoot anyone
who betrayed him and he told me to tell Ko'olau
    that he had gone to Hanalei that afternoon
when he went looking for Paoa and what could I do—
    Pi'ilani said—We thought it was like that—and she stood up
and they rode on to a camp at Kilohana
    where they left the horses with friends but in Kalalau
after they parted she followed him a long way
    down the trail watching him before she turned back to the grave

19.

No one had been there since she had left it months before
    she stood listening to the place in its own sound
with the grave part of it now and she heard only
    the hour at the end of summer as she remembered it
at last she lay down on the moss listening to the ground
    under the ferns but this time she did not stay long
with Penekila in the valley and she sat up
    with the old caution and listened and when she slipped out
did not go back to the trail but down to the stream
    and to the way they had come that night when they left the ledge
at Waimakemake and she climbed out at the old camp
    below the ledge all overgrown now with guava
and the creeping barbed uluhe ferns and she could see
    that someone had been there but not for months and ferns
were closing in over what she remembered there
    as though she had never been there and she skirted the clearing
and went down through the trees to the fork in the stream
    and on to the house of Kelau and Keapoulu
and their greetings and the evening of talking together
    and she told them why she had come and with whom and said
that the grave had not been found and they told her that this time
    they had seen the man who came asking questions and Kelau
had listened to him and had gone after them when
    Wahinealoha led the haole up the trail
and had watched when the man went on alone and had followed him
    —He never found anything up there—Kelau said
—except in Naoheiki's old mountain house all fallen down now
    he fished out one old rifle only part of it
you remember it was always there never worked
    he picked that up and took it away and a few more things
I never saw little things that was all the grave he found—
    Then they talked about Penekila and what they thought
he had come over for and Pi'ilani said
    that he was staying down with Wahinealoha
and the next morning they all went visiting and her friends
    begged her again to stay in Kalalau and she did stay
longer than before waiting to see what Penekila
    was doing over there and he said he was going
to Hanalei and was gone for days but it was Kelau
    who said—When Penekila tells me he is going
to Hanalei I begin to ask myself where he might be—

20.

Friends down near the bay said they had seen Penekila
    on the trail to Hanalei and some who had family there
and went there often said they had noticed him going
    into the old sheriff's house and there were those who wondered
whether Penekila might still be working for the police
    in one way or another but no one knew for certain
and they talked about the new sheriff named John Coney
    whom they had heard was not so bad and Keapoulu
urged Pi'ilani to stay on with them and friends there
    talked again about building a house for her and she stayed
to watch for Penekila though she was wary
    about going back to the grave again for fear
of making a trail and being followed but she climbed
    toward the cliffs every few days and followed the paths
in the upper valley looking for signs that someone
    had been through there and she told Kelau and Keapoulu
that she would not leave the valley as long as Penekila
    was on that side of the mountain and Kelau told that
to Wahinealoha who told everyone
    that she was waiting for Penekila and they talked about that
until one afternoon when she was down at the shore
    watching the fishing in the deep cave and the children
at the edge of the water and helping to load taro
    into the whaleboat for Ni'ihau her friend Keke
next to her turned and said—There he is—and they stood up
    and watched Penekila come down the trail and Pi'ilani
could tell from the way they were looking that some of them
    must have thought that Penekila was her lover
and her shoulders burned with shame as she turned back to the taro
    and that evening when Kelau told her that Penekila
was back she asked whether he had talked about leaving
    for Waimea and Kelau said he would ask him
but the next morning Penekila came up to the house
    to tell them that he was going and when and to ask
whether Pi'ilani wanted to go with him
    then the next day were the good-byes and the stepping back
and the morning after that the climb before daybreak
    there was a turn in the trail where he had gone ahead
and she stopped and looked back at the valley she had left
    it looked new and shining in an age that never changed
and farther away than she had ever seen it

21.

Even Kepola had heard that she had been waiting
        for Penekila this time and that she had stayed so long
because of Penekila and had come back part of the way
        with Penekila and Pi'ilani said—Nobody
has found the grave—and for a while that was all she said
        but she stayed at home as before and she told Kawaluna
and Kepola of her suspicions of Penekila
        and Kawaluna nodded and then laughed and Pi'ilani
looked at her and then began to laugh and Kepola laughed
        they all laughed all the women in the family
thinking of Penekila and what some people thought
        That winter they learned of the death of Valdemar Knudsen
and Ho'ona and Kaleimanu went to the funeral
        and they mourned him in Kekaha and said he was a good haole
and wondered what would come after him and then in the spring
        two men came to the house asking for Pi'ilani
one of them was the new High Sheriff John Coney
        and the other his assistant named Kaumeheiwa
and Kepola said she would try to find Pi'ilani
        and went and whispered to her but Pi'ilani said
—It is time to talk to them—and she walked into the house
        and greeted them and asked them to sit down and she looked
closely at Kaumeheiwa whom she had not seen
        since he had gone off with the soldiers in the whaleboat
she sat facing them both and the sheriff said—I was
        going to tell you not to be frightened but I think
that is not necessary—and Pi'ilani said nothing
        —Will you tell me what happened as you remember it
after you left here with your husband and son and went
        into Kalalau until you came back here alone—
and Pi'ilani said—My mother was with me
        part of that time and she can sit here and listen—
and she reached her hand to Kepola who sat down next to her
        —Yes I will tell you—Pi'ilani said and she answered
his questions and told him about it all from the night
        they left until she climbed back out of the valley
Kepola was crying but Pi'ilani's voice
        was steady as she stared past them and when she had stopped
they could hear the children playing down along the beach
        dogs barking and the evening cries of the stilts and the sheriff
told her he believed her and that she would not be blamed
        or made to suffer for anything that had been done

22.

So it seemed to have come to a kind of resting place
        at least in the government records but after the summer
one day Kaumeheiwa rode up to the house with a paper
        for Pi'ilani it was a note from the sheriff
enclosing a report that he had made of finding
        a grave in upper Kalalau that he believed
to be that of the leper Ko'olau he told of the rocks
        on top and the rotting boards and the raincoat and the rifle
and the note said the report had gone to the papers
        but he was sending this copy in case she had
anything of her own to say and she thanked Kaumeheiwa
        and told him she would send a message to the sheriff
and when he was out of sight she took the report and note
        to Kawaluna and read them to her and they sat
in silence and then Kawaluna asked—What will you do—
        Pi'ilani said—You know it is not Ko'olau's grave—
Kawaluna said—Yes I know—and Pi'ilani
        said—This time I know too and maybe the next time
I will know it the way you do but this time there were no boards
        there was no raincoat and it is the wrong rifle
I can even guess whose grave it might be but it cannot
        be Ko'olau's——Is that the message you will send
to the sheriff—Kawaluna asked her—Yes but I must
        go back to his grave myself before I send it
and tell him that I have been there and no one has found it
        I want to be able to say to him that I have seen it—
—Maybe after this time you will know—Kawaluna said
        —This time I will go by myself—Pi'ilani said
—I will tell only you and Kepola that I am going—
        and she put her head down in Kawaluna's lap
and felt Kawaluna's hand on her head and the tears ran
        and she forgot how long she stayed there but she remembered it
when she opened her eyes and saw the owl watching her
        from the hala root close to the foot of the grave
all of it came back at once and she could still feel
        Kawaluna's hand on her head though the tears on her face
were cold and she closed her eyes feeling the hand there
        and when she opened them again the owl was gone
she put her face down onto the moss of the grave
        —Ko'olau—she said—Kalua i Ko'olau
It is Pi'ilani I am here Kawaluna was here—

23.

The stream was swollen and loud as she picked her way
        down through the first gray light to the trail and then climbed
the path to the house of Kelau and Keapoulu
        and they greeted her and she told them why she had come
told of the sheriff's visit and what he had said to her
        —And this time—she said—I will stay only today
and rest and start back tomorrow—and as she said it
        she felt a sinking coldness in her breast at the thought
of Kawaluna feeling that Kawaluna might be gone
        Keapoulu was pregnant and they sat talking
while the sun rose and Kelau went down to the taro pond
        and after a while Keapoulu and Piʻilani
walked down the valley meeting friends and they asked her
        the same questions and she told the story over
and over and then went back with Keapoulu
        and Kelau came up from the taro and they spent the day
together and friends came in the evening and she said
        good-bye to them all that night and before daybreak
she was on the trail up out of the valley and it seemed
        that she was still asleep and was climbing in endless
silence then a stone turned under her foot and the fright
        woke through her and she went carefully to the summit
it was late morning and she had been climbing for hours
        and she turned at the top and in her weariness
looked back one more time over Kalalau and saw it
        moving away from her like a vessel without a sound
toward the horizon and then she was walking under the trees
        on the trail to Halemanu and no one was there now
and she slept again and slept the whole of that day
        and that night and in the morning went on to Kekaha
Kawaluna had died and had wanted to be buried
        in the old way she had kept to but Kukui had wanted
a Christian service and Hoʻona had taken her part
        and by that time there was a young Hawaiian minister
there in Kekaha who had come and read from his book
        the grave was behind the house on the side toward the mountain
Kepola showed her the wilted flowers in the moonlight
        and Piʻilani stared down and saw only the moonlight

24.

The life with her mother the old life of Kekaha
        closed around her the months passed over her like clouds
she lived as before like anyone in the families

hers and Koʻolau's she was no different no different
but the life she had thought of as her own was past
    it was gone and she woke into what was not there
even the dread in the valley the nearness of death
    day after day the pain and helplessness and the anguish
of losing and of watching the light fade in those faces
    it had been there with her and awake in her even
the age alone in the lantana grove after they
    were in the ground they were there in the valley with her
it was part of what had drawn her back when she heard
    those first claims that someone had found his grave it was
what she still knew of that time and what she had had to touch
    and see and have around her again just as it had been
but she saw now that when she went back it was already gone
    and now she had come into Kawaluna's certainty
that no one would find Koʻolau's grave and with that she knew
    that her life there was gone and that it had been her life
and here she was in a before and after that she had
    always known and could never have foreseen and she knew
that she was older she was the same but older
    it seemed to have happened while she was somewhere else
and to keep happening when she was somewhere that she
    could not remember and she saw how the others were growing
old around her her mother and Koʻolau's family
    as though they did not notice it happening and it
was already past but when they would draw the nets in
    at daybreak she would go down to the shore with them
and haul on the rope and as the net crawled through the shallows
    with the fish flashing and shining in the clench of death
wrung in their lives and shuddering against her there
    in the same waves there was nothing else and then it would
be afterward and years had passed and she was sure
    that it all must have been forgotten now and they must think
that it was somebody else they had heard about somebody
    they used to see and she thought that now there was only
what she remembered of that life that had been there with her

25.

Hoʻona had been living much of the time in Waimea
    for years and everyone knew of his other family there
and his grown daughter but he came back to Kekaha
    almost every week for a night or two and one day
several years after Kawaluna died he told
    Piʻilani that the Hon William Sheldon in Waimea
had left a message for him and when Hoʻona

had called at the Sheldons' house he had been shown in
by Mrs Sheldon who was Hawaiian and they had
    gone into the parlor and she had asked him to sit down
and they talked for a while about the church in Waimea
    and the work of Pastor Rowell and then Mr Sheldon
had come in and said that his brother John had asked him
    to find out whether Pi'ilani would be willing
to meet him and talk with him about what had happened
    in Kalalau and Mr Sheldon said—Our father
as perhaps you know was a newspaper editor
    who founded one of the first newspapers on the island
of Hawai'i over a half a century ago
    our mother was Hawaiian and my brother has suffered
at the hands of the Provisional Government
    because of his loyalty to the deposed Queen
Liliuokalani and no doubt because of his
    writings in defense of Hawaiian causes for John too
is a newspaper man like our father and in both
    languages and he is a man of deep Christian zeal
which I know matters to you and if your daughter
    would consent to talk with him about her own life
so that he could write it down in Hawaiian and publish it
    for Hawaiians to read my wife and I would be happy
to have her stay with us here as our guest for as long
    as it takes her to recall the events and for him
to write them down and prepare the story for publication—
    and Ho'ona said to her—I think Mr Sheldon
is a fine man and you know he is in the legislature—
    but Pi'ilani said nothing at first and went and sat
on the doorstep and Ho'ona talked to Kepola
    about the Sheldon house and how he had known Mr Sheldon
in the church and Pi'ilani sat looking toward the mountain
    and then she stood up and said—I can talk with him—

26.

Ho'ona came back two days later and told her
    when to be ready and Pi'ilani and Kepola
washed and packed her best clothes in a box and made three
    new dresses and Kukui gave her a new straw hat
with a band of feathers and Ho'ona was anxious
    for her to take shoes they got her shoes out of their wrapping
and cleaned them up and Pi'ilani asked him where
    she would have to wear shoes and he did not answer at first
but he said she should have them with her and he told her
    to be sure to take the Bible that Reverend Rowell

had given her when she finished going to his school
    and they got that out and put a new cloth around it
—Do you remember your Bible—he asked her and she could hear
    that he was trying to sound like Reverend Rowell
—I remember it—she said—Because in the Sheldon house
    I am sure they read the Bible every day—he told her
and on the day before she was to go she and Kepola
    made leis for her to wear and the Sheldon carriage came
driven by a young man who had worked at Waiawa
    with Kaleimanu and he and Ho'ona put the box
of Pi'ilani's belongings into the carriage
    and she said good-bye to Kepola and all the friends
who had gathered like a flock of birds to stand watching
    and Pi'ilani said—Waimea Waimea
you would think it was the moon and I used to walk there to school
    every day and back—and she laughed and said—I will be home
before the moon is new—and then they drove off and her face
    darkened as Ho'ona began talking to her as though
she were at school and she watched the road where she used to walk
    but she had not been to Waimea since Kaleimanu
was a child and the last time she had come with Ko'olau
    they had been on horses and Kaleimanu was riding with him
and now that she was in the carriage she felt naked
    without him and as they came closer to Waimea
it was all familiar but it looked strange like someone
    who has been waked up suddenly and there were new houses
in place of some of the old ones there were many of them
    that she did not recognize and many were painted
and there were many people whom she did not know and they came
    to a big new house painted gray and stopped at the door

27.

Ho'ona got down and reached back to take her hand
    but he was in her way and she stepped down without him
and when she looked up she saw them coming out of the door
    onto the lanai at the top of the steps first there was
a Hawaiian woman maybe as old as Kepola
    and then two haole men with white hair and moustaches
and as Ho'ona raised a hand toward Pi'ilani
    and was about to say something the woman said
—You must be Pi'ilani come in come in I am
    Becky Keaonaueole Sheldon and this is my husband
William Sheldon and his brother John Sheldon and you
    are welcome to our house and are among friends here
and she held out both hands to Pi'ilani and drew her

up the stairs and kissed her on both cheeks in the Hawaiian manner
and then turned to her husband and he and his brother
        repeated the greeting and Pi'ilani saw with relief
that they were not wearing shoes but when they led her
        into the cool house she saw shoes lined up in pairs
inside the front door and Pi'ilani looked at the stairs
        and the hatstand where she saw herself in the mirror
looking like a stranger with her hat on—I will show you
        your room—Mrs Sheldon said—And then you must be thirsty—
and she led Pi'ilani up the stairs saying—Nalu
        will bring your trunk up for you and you will meet Mele
who helps in the house—and she showed Pi'ilani
        the washstand and the chamber pot in its cupboard
and then she straightened in the middle of the room and said
        —John has talked about you for a long time wanting to meet you
he has prayed that you would come we all pray in the evenings
        together I hope you will pray with us—and Pi'ilani
nodded slowly—Come down and join us when you are ready—
        Mrs Sheldon said and she left Pi'ilani
looking at the walls painted sky blue and the picture
        of Jesus over the table the pegs for clothes
the open window with white curtains blowing and she
        could look down to a white fence and a garden plot
with a barn beyond it and then the dry pasture
        along the beach and suddenly to her surprise
she heard someone behind her and turned to see a boy
        holding the old box with all of the things from Kekaha

28.

Mrs Sheldon came and helped her to do the right things
        and it was true what Ho'ona had told her about
the Bible because when they came down to supper
        they prayed and when they were standing at the table
Mr Sheldon prayed for them and then John Sheldon prayed for them
        and thanked the Lord for bringing them Pi'ilani
to show them that He did not forsake his children
        and when they sat down to supper and Mele came in
with the soup John asked Pi'ilani whether she had
        brought her Bible with her and when she said—Yes—Mr Sheldon
told her that they read the Bible every morning
        before breakfast and would be happy if she would join them
it was like being back at school at Reverend Rowell's
        but was easier in a way because they all spoke
Hawaiian in the house and prayed in Hawaiian
        and read from the Hawaiian Bible though Mr Sheldon

spoke of the government's plan to get rid of the language
        and of Thurston boasting every year about how many
schools there were now in which not a word of Hawaiian
        was ever heard—A pity—Mr Sheldon said
in English—But we will tell your story in Hawaiian—
        John Sheldon reassured Pi'ilani—And can we begin
tomorrow morning——Yes—Pi'ilani answered
        and the passage of the Bible that they read before breakfast
was from the Book of Exodus and they each read in turn
        about the deliverance of the people of Israel
the crossing of the Red Sea and the Lord holding back
        the waters and drowning the army of Pharaoh
and when they finished reading Pi'ilani saw
        that they were all looking at her as they said Amen
and after breakfast she went into the parlor
        with John Sheldon and he opened a notebook on the table
and said—From what I have read and heard I believe
        that the cliff below Kilohana which I must confess
I have never seen is the place from which warriors
        used to hurl torches far out over the valley
and watched them sink like stars falling have you heard of that—
        —I have heard about it—Pi'ilani answered
—Because I think that might be part of our title—he said
        —The Firebrands Flung from The Heights of Kamaile and The Hero
of the Cliffs of Kalalau or something like that—

                                29.

He asked her about things that happened before she was born
        and he asked her about Ko'olau and when they were children
and about times that she had forgotten and she answered him
        as well as she could and when she told him about
Ko'olau's baptism she could see that he was pleased
        and he said he was sure that their faith and baptism
had sustained them in the trials they had endured
        but when he read back to her what he had written about them
it sounded like a story about somebody else
        more than like what she remembered of what happened
but she could not think how to tell him that it had been
        not like that and would never have belonged in those words
that came from church but she could see that he wanted it
        to be true and down under all those words it was true
and he thought the words made it true but she kept thinking
        of the time when Sheriff Coney asked her about
what happened in Kalalau and all he had wanted
        was for her to say what she remembered about it

and she thought how much easier that had been and how
    Mr Sheldon always seemed to be hoping to hear
something better but she thought he was a kind man and she liked him
    and his sister-in-law Mrs Sheldon told her
that his wife too was Hawaiian and that he spoke often
    of his Hawaiian mother and she said that he was
a real scholar and talked of Abraham Fornander
    who had befriended their father and of Fornander's
collection of the stories of the Hawaiians
    and his comparison of their customs and beliefs
with those of peoples who had lived in other places
    a long time ago and he told her that Fornander
had believed that the Hawaiians were the lost tribes
    of Israel and Mr Sheldon had said that
it might be true but he said that too was a story
    and he said that Fornander's wife was also Hawaiian
and Mrs Sheldon said I love to hear him talk
    about his mother and father and Mr Fornander
and their newspapers and Mr Fornander said
    that the story is all that we have when things are over
the story begins as an echo of what went before
    but then it is only the story we are listening to

30.

In the afternoon Ho‘ona came to the house
    to ask whether Pi‘ilani would like to go out
for a walk through Waimea with him and he had brought her
    a parasol and a lei to wear and they went
past the courthouse and the churches and he said he could show her
    the Kauai family house but before they went so far
he asked whether she would like to stop at a friend's
    for a glass of juice and a piece of watermelon
and he led her behind the Rowells' house and along the lane
    by the river bank to a house under a mango tree
in the doorway stood a woman about her own age
    and Ho‘ona said—Pi‘ilani this is Kealia—
and for a moment the two women stared at each other
    then Ho‘ona said to Pi‘ilani—This is your half sister—
—Come in come in Pi‘ilani—Kealia said
    and Pi‘ilani went up the steps slowly and stood
looking at Kealia and then she kissed her
    on both cheeks and Kealia kissed her in return
and then they embraced and Kealia began to cry
    —I have wanted to meet you for a long time—she said
—and ever since I was small I have been afraid of you

I heard everything about you I saw you when you came
to church I heard how beautiful you were and I thought
    when I saw you how beautiful you looked and all the time
when you were gone and we heard what was happening
    I kept praying for you—and she stopped and covered her face
and took Pi'ilani's hand and Pi'ilani said
    —A long time ago when we were small I saw you once
in church I remember and I tried to see what you looked like—
    and they both laughed and a child appeared in the doorway
—This is my daughter—Kealia said—This is Shirley
    Come and meet your Aunt Pi'ilani—she said to the child
who inched forward and Pi'ilani knelt and said
    —How are you Shirley—and the child said—I am very well—
and they kissed—Come in—Kealia said—and meet—
    but an older woman had appeared behind her
and when Pi'ilani turned to her she said—I am her
    mother Malukauai Kaiwi welcome Pi'ilani—
and she led her into a room where a table was set
    with plates and melons and a pair of candlesticks

31.

Most afternoons after that while Pi'ilani
    was staying at the Sheldons' she would meet Kealia
and they would walk around Waimea or sit in the shade
    and talk while Shirley and her friends played nearby
they sat talking for hours and Pi'ilani said
    that she had never talked so much in her whole life
they talked about Ho'ona and about when they were children
    and about everyone they knew and Waimea and the mill
and Kekaha and Makaweli but they did not talk
    about Kalalau at first nor about Ko'olau
and all that she was telling John Sheldon about
    in the mornings and hearing him read back to her
but they talked about the Sheldons and Kealia said
    how different from each other the brothers seemed to be
and both of them married to Hawaiian women
    and she said—In their family they have no trouble with that
but some haoles do I can tell you my aunt my mother's
    sister used to work for Charles Gay a few years ago
before he moved to Lanai you know Mr Gay
    he was Mr Knudsen's brother-in-law one of the grandsons
of Eliza Sinclair who bought Ni'ihau and died
    at Makaweli in the time when you were away
Mr Gay took care of the ranch and people liked him I hear
    but when he married a Hawaiian woman my aunt says

his mother disowned him and cut him out of her will
  and that was when he took what was his and went over
to the island of Lanai and they never spoke after that
  she told me his daughter went once to see her grandmother
just so they could have met one time before the old woman
  died and my aunt says her grandmother sat up straight
in her chair and would not say one word to the girl
  so many families with people not speaking
to each other haole families Hawaiian families
  do you think I would ever be able to meet your mother—
And Pi'ilani said—It might happen some day
  after she hears about you—and it seemed a strange thing
to be saying as though both of them were children
  but then everything in those days seemed as though it had
come out of hiding and strangest of all was the Sheldons'
  parlor in the mornings and telling John Sheldon
about the years in Kalalau and whether she had prayed
  on the ledge at Waimakemake and trying to say
the words she had chanted that day when she left the valley

32.

One evening Mrs Sheldon led Pi'ilani
  into the parlor after dinner and showed her
an album of old pictures of the family
  and of the islands years before and portraits of people
from still earlier times and to Pi'ilani
  they were familiar and untouchable as dreams
or as the story about herself as Mr Sheldon
  read back to her the parts that he had written down
then he and his brother came into the parlor and joined
  in the conversation over the photographs
and John Sheldon said to Pi'ilani—I hope that you
  will agree to have your picture taken to be published
along with the story of Kalalau I have taken
  the liberty of speaking with a photographer
here in Waimea who makes studio portraits
  and would be happy to oblige us—and Mrs Sheldon
said—I would love to have a picture of you for the album—
  and Pi'ilani agreed to it but she said—I look
more angry in pictures—and they laughed and Mrs Sheldon said
  —That is because they tell you to hold still and you become
very serious—And Mr Sheldon asked—are there
  other pictures of you—And Pi'ilani said
—A few—And then he asked about pictures of Ko'olau
  and the house and she said there were a few of those

—Bad ones—she said—Some you can hardly see anything—
 —I would like to look at them—Mr Sheldon said—And perhaps
publish them too—and when he said it she did not
 want anyone but her family to see them
but then she thought that if she was telling the story
 showing the pictures was part of it and they seemed
as far away from the faces and days she remembered
 or almost as far as pictures in the album
of places she had never seen and so one afternoon
 Mrs Sheldon and Mele came and helped her to dress
and hung a lei around her neck and they took a big Bible
 and bouquet of flowers from the garden and Mrs Sheldon
and John and Pi'ilani went down to the studio
 where Pi'ilani sat in a straight chair clutching
the flowers by the neck in her right hand and the Bible
 in her left and held still looking angry for her picture

33.

Mr Sheldon said that his story was complete
 except for what he called finishing touches and he wrote it
all over again and when that was done he read it
 to all of them that evening and Mrs Sheldon cried
and the next day they took a lunch out toward Koloa
 and Mr Sheldon said he would like to see Kekaha
and asked Pi'ilani whether she would show it to him
 and she looked at them all and then nodded and he said
that there might be those who would challenge the facts of their story
 and so he had decided to swear to the truth of it
before a notary public and he asked her
 whether she would add her name to his and she looked
at Mrs Sheldon and the others and she nodded
 and later he told her that he and the photographer
would like a picture of her standing high among rocks
 holding a rifle and he said they could find a place
at the mouth of Waimea canyon that would provide
 a setting that would look like Kalalau and she said
they must not say it was Kalalau and he told her
 it was the picture of her that mattered and they went
the next day and rode up the canyon and the photographer
 kept her standing up in the rocks with an old rifle
while he crouched under his black sheet behind the camera
 and she looked down at him with the sun in her eyes
and none of it seemed to have anything to do
 with Kalalau and then they were saying good-bye
in front of the Sheldon house as though she were going away

forever and thanking each other and John Sheldon
and Ho‘ona were with her in the Sheldon carriage
        on the way back to Kekaha and Kepola
got out the pictures for them to look at and Ho‘ona led
        Mr Sheldon around Kekaha and they came back
and sat talking and eating watermelon and then
        Mr Sheldon stood up and promised to bring back the pictures
and was gone and Kepola and Pi‘ilani sat talking
        about Kealia and Malukauai and the house
by the Waimea river and when Ho‘ona
        was out of the house Kepola said she thought
it was time for all of them to know each other

34.

One day a man and a boy rode up to the house
        at Kekaha and the man leaned over the pommel
and said—Pi‘ilani—and she looked up and it was Kala
        and he jumped down and embraced her and—This is my son
Iwa—he said and the child bent for her to kiss him
        —Is your mother at home—Kala asked and Kepola came out
and kissed him and he said—It has been ten years ten years
        and I wanted to see you and Ida I have
thought of you many times after that day when we went
        up like smoke into the cliff in Kalalau—and he laughed
They went into the house and the family gathered
        to celebrate and he told them that he had hidden
in the cliffs for weeks and then gone down to his friends
        at Wili Kini's ranch and worked there for a while
and then along the coast toward Kilauea and there
        he had started a family—And Kua is married too—
he said—A few years back after I heard that you
        were home in Kekaha he married a widow
over near Hanalei and I go to see him
        he has a few horses and a garden out that way—
and he said he remembered how brave Ida had been
        when they were climbing out that morning and now she was
grown up and beautiful and as he talked Pi‘ilani
        felt how far away Kalalau seemed to have become
and how her telling about it at the Sheldons' house
        seemed to have drawn a shadow across it blurring
and fading it like the pictures and Kala looked
        so much older that she would scarcely have recognized him
but when he spoke of Kalalau it seemed as fresh and clear
        in his words as ever and she saw then that it was
the terrible moments there that she did not want to forget

the time on the ledge with the sound of the bullets
and the cannon echoing and that night when they went down
        through the stream with Kaleimanu and the voices
of the soldiers were so close that she had been sure
        they could hear her and she could still smell the smoke of their
cigarettes through the smoke of their campfire and then
        the sickness of Kaleimanu day by day she did not
want it to slip through her fingers now and be gone
        or his dying and their burying him she wanted
to keep even the pain of it and she felt that it was
        slipping away from her and what she saw in her mind
was the long sand at Mānā when the tide had gone out

35.

When Mr Sheldon's book was published Nalu came from Waimea
        to invite Pi'ilani and Kepola and Ho'ona
and Ko'olau's parents Kukui and Kaleimanu
        to Waimea to celebrate it and he said
he would be back the next day with the carriage for them
        At the Sheldon house there was food on a long table
in the back garden and they all prayed and gave thanks
        for the Lord's mercy and this work well done and Mr Sheldon
read from the psalms He that dwelleth in the secret place
        of the Most High shall abide under the shadow
of the Almighty and he read it first in Hawaiian
        and then in English while Kukui cried and Mrs Sheldon
cried but Pi'ilani seemed to be looking at something
        out past them and they said Amen and began to talk
as though they had wanted to know each other for years
        Mr Sheldon's other brother Henry was there with his wife
and they started to talk of their brother John all the places
        where he had lived and his newspapers and the time
when he was a fisherman and his loyalty to the Queen
        which had led the government to seize his possessions
and to put out a warrant for his arrest—He should
        have been here to read that psalm—his brother William said
And then they were all eating shellfish and Kepola
        said to Pi'ilani—Do you think this would be
a good day to meet Malukauai and Kealia
        since we are here in Waimea and it is a kind
of family time only how could we do it
        without Ho'ona because he cannot be there
when we meet—and Pi'ilani looked at Ho'ona
        talking with Henry Sheldon and she said—The Sheldons
have arranged to have Nalu take us home in the carriage
        but I will tell Mrs Sheldon that we have friends

here in Waimea to whom we want to show the book
        and let Nalu take Kukui and Kaleimanu
you can tell Ho'ona that I am going to see Kealia
        and that you want to meet her but not with him there
and I will ask them whether they want to see us today
        and will come to the church and tell you—and both of them laughed
behind their hands like children making up a new game

36.

Malukauai said she wanted to meet Kepola
        but she was embarrassed to have her see the house as it was
and she wanted to be sure that Ho'ona was not
        anywhere around and she thought about it and they agreed
to meet under the mango tree beside the Rowells' house
        and Pi'ilani went to the church and found her mother
standing out in front of it in the shade and Ho'ona
        had gone—When I told him he looked frightened—she said
—I wonder who he could be afraid of—and she walked
        with Pi'ilani past the Rowells' big house and they all
met shyly with small voices under the old tree
        and stood talking about nothing with those same voices
and then Kealia said to Pi'ilani—
        —Do you have the book—and Pi'ilani showed it to them
and said—That copy is for you—and Kealia
        showed it to Malukauai and they opened it
to Pi'ilani's picture and they all stood looking at it
        and Pi'ilani put her hands to her face and suddenly
Malukauai was crying and Kepola embraced her
        and then they all embraced and Malukauai said
—It is silly for us to be standing out here
        as though we had no place of our own to go to
but you must promise not to pay attention to the house
        I never thought we would have somebody coming today—
and she led them along the river lane to her house
        and Kealia brought Shirley back from the neighbors
for them to meet and kept finding things for them to eat
        as they sat talking and in a moment when they were
silent Malukauai looked at Pi'ilani
        and said—Are you glad he wrote the book—and Pi'ilani
did not answer for a long time they waited
        and finally she said—Yes—and Kealia
picked it up and looked at the title page—She will
        read it to me—Malukauai said—And we will
keep it there with the Bible on that table—
        —And will you come to see us in Kekaha—Kepola asked

37.

So they arranged for a visit to Kekaha
          —Maybe only women—Kepola said and Malukauai
said—I think he would be ashamed but you know how families
          crowd in and get curious it will be all right—
And Kepola Kukui Kinau Ida and Pi'ilani
          started getting food ready days before and then
Kaleimanu and his friends saw that they were making
          a banquet and they brought more fish and they took it
for granted that the whole family would be there
          and they asked which day it would be and that morning
they brought crabs and sea urchins shellfish and seaweed
          reef fish and eels and mangos papayas and melons
it was all piled up before Kaleimanu asked
          Kepola what the occasion was that they were
celebrating and when she told him he told his old father
          and they all began laughing and Kaleimanu said
Ho'ona has to be here even if we have to bring him
          tied hand and foot like a sacrifice and we will go
and get him and say—Ho'ona are you not coming
          to the feast——What feast is that—he will ask——You never
heard—we will ask—Everybody in Kekaha will be there—
          —Malukauai would be embarrassed—Kepola said—
—We will bring him later—Kaleimanu said—And you can
          warn her after she knows everybody and this time
the laugh will be on Ho'ona—And Kepola
          and the rest of the family made the first visit
of Malukauai and Kealia and Shirley
          a great feast and Kinau played the ukelele
as she had not done for years and the chants and dancing
          began and were well under way when the men came back
with Ho'ona and he stood speechless and they told him
          to eat and make himself at home and went on singing
all the neighbors were there and when the dancing was over
          and they were standing and sitting in twos and threes
eating and talking Ho'ona went over to where
          Kepola and Malukauai were sitting and he stood
looking at them not knowing what to say and Kepola
          put up her hand and said—Not one word not one word
go have something to eat and pay no attention to us
          as you see we are able to entertain ourselves—

38.

By the time the neighbors had left and the fire had died down
     and the talk had sunk to low voices from under the trees
Kepola looked up and said to Malukauai
     —It is too late for you to go back to Waimea
please stay here with us tonight if you do not mind
     not much room there will be plenty to eat in the morning—
Malukauai said—You are inviting me now
     to sleep in this house—and Kepola said—Yes I am—
and they went on clearing up after the banquet
     while there was still daylight they put away the food
and Pi'ilani fed the dogs as the sun went down
     Shirley was falling asleep and Ida put her to bed
and at last there were only Kepola and Pi'ilani
     and Malukauai and Kealia sitting
on the front steps looking out at the sea rustling
     along the sand and the stars over the black shell
of Ni'ihau and for a while no one said anything
     and then Malukauai said—I told you I have a sister
she used to work out at Makaweli and she knew
     the Knudsens and now for years she has been working
for a family on the other side of the island
     up near Kilauea by the name of Ewart they have
a big farm and pastures up that way and dairy cattle
     up on the hills she says it is very beautiful
and they are good to her and she likes it there and keeps
     telling me to come and see her but it is a long trip
and she does not get to Waimea very often
     but she came to see me last week and Kealia
showed her your book and my sister was trying to read it
     and Kealia read some parts of it to her and later
she told us something that had happened up the coast there
     she used to say that one of the things she liked there
was the way the Ewarts played music she said they all
     had their houses near each other and the families
and their children would all get together in the evening
     several times a week and every one of them played
some instrument and so after the milking and dinner
     they would sit and play music for hours with the candles
burning she says they have a piano and they have
     violins and even a harp and one night when they stopped
they heard a flute playing all by itself out in the dark—

39.

—They listened and then the flute stopped and they waited
    and then they went back to playing but listening
and did not hear it again but a few nights later
    when they stopped what they were playing to play it over
they heard the flute again and it went on playing
    where they had stopped and Mr Ewart put down his violin
and opened the door onto the long lanai and the flute
    stopped right there and they all sat listening and one
of the Ewart girls who had been to college said
    that it must be a ghost but they sat there with the door open
and after a while went back to playing the same music
    and listening and then Mr Ewart said I know
that flute playing and they looked at him when he said it
    but then he went back to playing and a few nights later
they heard the flute music coming from the pastures again
    when they had finished playing and Mr Ewart opened the door
and picked up a lantern that he had ready there
    and they followed him out toward where the sound seemed to be
coming from but the playing had stopped when the door
    opened and they were frightened and held up lanterns
staying close behind Mr Ewart that night they found
    nothing and then the next day Mr Ewart found hoofprints
under a tree and hoofprints leading toward the farm
    of a neighbor who had been there longer than they had
a family from Germany named Bertelmann
    with a dairy farm like their own and they all remembered
Christian Bertelmann who had been a child when they came there
    and had grown up into a tall young man who loved
music and sang and who used to come for a time
    and play the flute with them in the evenings and he had
represented Kauai in the legislature but that
    had been years before and then they had not seen him
for a long time and the family said he was sick
    and then that he was away in a hospital
but only last month Mr Ewart had heard that the sickness
    was leprosy and that they had dressed up Christian
as somebody else and sent him away to Japan
    where there was supposed to be a cure for that now
but they never cured him and to get him back this time
    they had him dressed up as a tall woman in mourning
who had come from Germany in response to a bid
    for a German wife that one of the Bertelmanns
was said to have published in a German newspaper—

40.

—Their house is built around a courtyard she told me
　　which nobody can see from outside and they built him
a room of his own inside the courtyard and in there
　　he could take off those clothes and only the family
ever saw him and to console himself he would play
　　the flute or he would go out at night and ride his horse
across the pastures and then he would go and listen
　　to the music from the Ewarts' where he used to play
and then he began to take his flute out with him
　　and play when he heard them and then they heard him and he
stopped doing that and they thought the ghost had gone but he
　　still played farther out where they could not hear him or could not
be sure they were hearing anything and then he
　　died my sister told me and she said that happened
not long ago and she said that only the family
　　knows where he is buried—And she stopped and they sat
hearing the long low wave ending on the shore—A flute—
　　Pi'ilani said—There was a man in Kalalau
down by the stream who played the flute and when I heard it
　　I would go on thinking I heard it all the next day—
Later that summer at Hofgaard's store in Waimea
　　some of them who had seen Sheldon's book were talking
about Ko'olau and some remembered him and Judge Kauai
　　and the shooting of Stolz and what Coney had said
after he talked with Pi'ilani and they spoke of those
　　pictures of her somebody had heard she was beautiful
but said you would never think so from those photographs
　　they agreed she looked plain and they talked about the lepers
still being shipped off to Moloka'i in the same way
　　Hofgaard was an old man by then and he said to them
—Those things happened a long time ago but I went to see her
　　she told me that she does not regret anything
she said Stolz came to kill her husband and the soldiers came
　　to kill her husband and that if her life came to her
again the way it did the first time she would live it
　　all the same way—And when Hofgaard had left Pi'ilani
had said to her mother—Why do you think that man came
　　to see me Did he think I would tell him something else
after all of the others he has listened to
　　what does he know now about what I remember
maybe he only wanted to see for himself
　　whether I was the one in the book he had been reading
where he told me that some of the words were too crooked for him—

THE RIVER SOUND

(1999)

For Paula

Ceremony After an Amputation

Spirits of the place who were here before I saw it
     to whom I have made such offerings as I have known how to make
     wanting from the first to approach you with recognition
     bringing for your swept ridge trees lining the wind with seedlings
     that have grown now to become these long wings in chorus
     where the birds assemble and settle their flying lives
     you have taught me without meaning and have lifted me up
     without talk or promise and again and again reappeared to me
     unmistakable and changing and unpronounceable as a face

dust of the time a day in late spring after the silk of rain
     had fallen softly through the night and after the green morning
     the afternoon floating brushed with gold and then the sounds
     of machines erupting across the valley and elbowing up the slopes
     pushing themselves forward to occupy you to be more of you
     who remain the untouched silence through which they are passing
     I try to hear you remembering that we are not separate
     to find you who cannot be lost or elsewhere or incomplete

nature of the solitary machine coming into the story
     from the minds that conceived you and the hands that first conjured up
     the phantom of you in fine lines on the drawing board
     you for whom function is all the good that exists
     you to whom I have come with nothing but purpose
     a purpose of my own as though it was something we shared
     you that were pried from the earth without anyone
     consulting you and were carried off burned beaten metamorphosed
     according to plans and lives to which you owed nothing

let us be at peace with each other let peace be what is between us
     and you now single vanished part of my left hand bit of bone finger-end index
     who began with me in the dark that was already my mother
     you who touched whatever I could touch of the beginning
     and were how I touched and who remembered the sense of it
     when I thought I had forgotten it you in whom it waited
     under your only map of one untrodden mountain
     you who did as well as we could through all the hours at the piano
     and who helped undo the bras and found our way to the treasure

and who held the fruit and the pages and knew how to button
     my right cuff and to wash my left ear and had taken in
     heart beats of birds and beloved faces and hair by day and by night
     fur of dogs ears of horses tongues and the latches of doors
     so that I still feel them clearly long after they are gone
     and lake water beside the boat one evening of an ancient summer
     and the vibration of a string over which a bow was moving

as though the sound of the note were still playing
and the hand of my wife found in the shallows of waking

you who in a flicker of my inattention
        signalled to me once only my error telling me
        of the sudden blow from the side so that I looked down
        to see not you any longer but instead a mouth
        full of blood calling after you who had already gone gone
        gone ahead into what I cannot know or reach or touch
        leaving in your place only the cloud of pain rising
        into the day filling the light possessing every sound
        becoming the single color and taste and direction

yet as the pain recedes and the moment of it
        you remain with me even in the missing of you
        small boat moving before me on the current under the daylight
        whatever you had touched and had known and took with you
        is with me now as you are when you are already there
        unseen part of me reminding me warning me
        pointing to what I cannot see never letting me forget
        you are my own speaking only to me going with me
        all the rest of the way telling me what is still here

The Stranger

(After a Guarani legend recorded by Ernesto Morales)

One day in the forest there was somebody
who had never been there before
it was somebody like the monkeys but taller
and without a tail and without so much hair
standing up and walking on only two feet
and as he went he heard a voice calling Save me

as the stranger looked he could see a snake
a very big snake with a circle of fire
that was dancing all around it
and the snake was trying to get out
but every way it turned the fire was there

so the stranger bent the trunk of a young tree
and climbed out over the fire until he
could hold a branch down to the snake

and the snake wrapped himself around the branch
and the stranger pulled the snake up out of the fire

and as soon as the snake saw that he was free
he twined himself around the stranger
and started to crush the life out of him
but the stranger shouted No No
I am the one who has just saved your life
and you pay me back by trying to kill me

but the snake said I am keeping the law
it is the law that whoever does good
receives evil in return
and he drew his coils tight around the stranger
but the stranger kept on saying No No
I do not believe that is the law

so the snake said I will show you
I will show you three times and you will see
and he kept his coils tight around the stranger's neck
and all around his arms and body
but he let go of the stranger's legs
Now walk he said to the stranger Keep going

so they started out that way and they came
to a river and the river said to them
I do good to everyone and look what they
do to me I save them from dying of thirst
and all they do is stir up the mud
and fill my water with dead things

the snake said One

the stranger said Let us go on and they did
and they came to a carandá-i palm
there were wounds running with sap on its trunk
and the palm tree was moaning I do good
to everyone and look what they do to me
I give them my fruit and my shade and they cut me
and drink from my body until I die

the snake said Two

the stranger said Let us go on and they did
and came to a place where they heard whimpering
and saw a dog with his paw in a basket
and the dog said I did a good thing
and this is what came of it
I found a jaguar who had been hurt
and I took care of him and he got better

and as soon as he had his strength again
he sprang at me wanting to eat me up
I managed to get away but he tore my paw
I hid in a cave until he was gone
and here in this basket I have
a calabash full of milk for my wound
but now I have pushed it too far down to reach

will you help me he said to the snake
and the snake liked milk better than anything
so he slid off the stranger and into the basket
and when he was inside the dog snapped it shut
and swung it against a tree with all his might
again and again until the snake was dead

and after the snake was dead in there
the dog said to the stranger Friend
I have saved your life
and the stranger took the dog home with him
and treated him the way the stranger would treat a dog

The Gardens of Versailles

At what moment can it be said to occur
the grand stillness of this symmetry
whose horizons become the horizon
and whose designer's name seems to be Ours

even when the designer has long since
vanished and the king his master whom
they called The Sun in his day is nobody again
here are the avenues of light reflected

and magnified and here the form's vast claim
to have been true forever as the law
of a universe in which nothing appears
to change and there was nothing before this

except defects of Nature and a waste of marshes
a lake a chaos of birds and wild things
a river making its undirected
way it was always the water that was

motion even while thirty six thousand men
and six thousand horses for more than three
decades diverted it into a thousand
fountains and when all those men and horses

had gone the water flowed on and the sound
of water falling echoes in the dream
the dream of water in which the avenues
all of them are the river on its own way

Chorus

The wet bamboo clacking in the night rain
crying in the darkness whimpering softly
as the hollow columns touch and slide
along each other swaying with the empty
air these are sounds from before there were voices
gestures older than grief from before there was
pain as we know it the impossibly tall
stems are reaching out groping and waving
before longing as we think of it or loss
as we are acquainted with it or feelings

able to recognize the syllables
that might be their own calling out to them
like names in the dark telling them nothing
about loss or about longing nothing
ever about all that has yet to answer

What Is a Garden

All day working happily down near the stream bed
    the light passing into the remote opalescence
it returns to as the year wakes toward winter
    a season of rain in a year already rich
in rain with masked light emerging on all sides
    in the new leaves of the palms quietly waving
time of mud and slipping and of overhearing
    the water under the sloped ground going on whispering
as it travels time of rain thundering at night
    and of rocks rolling and echoing in the torrent
and of looking up after noon through the high branches
    to see fine rain drifting across the sunlight
over the valley that was abused and at last left
    to fill with thickets of rampant aliens
bringing habits but no stories under the mango trees
    already vast as clouds there I keep discovering
beneath the tangle the ancient shaping of water
    to which the light of an hour comes back as to a secret
and there I planted young palms in places I had not pondered
    until then I imagined their roots setting out in the dark
knowing without knowledge I kept trying to see them standing
    in that bend of the valley in the light that would come

A Night Fragrance

Now I am old enough to remember
people speaking of immortality
as though it were something known to exist
a tangible substance that might be acquired
to be used perhaps in the kitchen
every day in whatever was made there
forever after and they applied the word
to literature and the names of things
names of persons and the naming of other
things for them and no doubt they repeated
that word with some element of belief
when they named a genus of somewhat more than
a hundred species of tropical trees and shrubs
some with flowers most fragrant at night
for James Theodore Tabernaemontanus
of Heidelberg physician and botanist
highly regarded in his day over
four centuries ago immortality
might be like that with the scattered species
continuing their various evolutions
the flowers opening by day or night
with no knowledge of bearing a name
of anyone and their fragrance if it
reminds at all not reminding of him

Night Turn

In late summer after the day's heat is over
I walk out after dark into the still garden
wet leaves fragrance of ginger and kamani
the feel of the path underfoot still recalling
a flow of water that found its way long ago
toads are rustling under the lemon trees
looking back I can see through the branches
the light in the kitchen where we were standing
a moment ago in our life together

Before a Departure in Spring

Once more it is April with the first light sifting
    through the young leaves heavy with dew making the colors
remember who they are the new pink of the cinnamon tree
    the gilded lichens of the bamboo the shadowed bronze
of the kamani and the blue day opening
    as the sunlight descends through it all like the return
of a spirit touching without touch and unable
    to believe it is here and here again and awake
reaching out in silence into the cool breath
    of the garden just risen from darkness and days of rain
it is only a moment the birds fly through it calling
    to each other and are gone with their few notes and the flash
of their flight that had vanished before we ever knew it
    we watch without touching any of it and we
can tell ourselves only that this is April this is the morning
    this never happened before and we both remember it

Remembering

    There are threads of old sound heard over and over
    phrases of Shakespeare or Mozart the slender
    wands of the auroras playing out from them
    into dark time the passing of a few
    migrants high in the night far from the ancient flocks
    far from the rest of the words far from the instruments

Another River

    The friends have gone home far up the valley
    of that river into whose estuary
    the man from England sailed in his own age
    in time to catch sight of the late forests
    furring in black the remotest edges

of the majestic water always it
appeared to me that he arrived just as
an evening was beginning and toward the end
of summer when the converging surface
lay as a single vast mirror gazing
upward into the pearl light that was
already stained with the first saffron
of sunset on which the high wavering trails
of migrant birds flowed southward as though there were
no end to them the wind had dropped and the tide
and the current for a moment seemed to hang
still in balance and the creaking and knocking
of wood stopped all at once and the known voices
died away and the smells and rocking
and starvation of the voyage had become
a sleep behind them as they lay becalmed
on the reflection of their Half Moon
while the sky blazed and then the time lifted them
up the dark passage they had no name for

Echoing Light

When I was beginning to read I imagined
that bridges had something to do with birds
and with what seemed to be cages but I knew
that they were not cages it must have been autumn
with the dusty light flashing from the streetcar wires
and those orange places on fire in the pictures
and now indeed it is autumn the clear
days not far from the sea with a small wind nosing
over dry grass that yesterday was green
the empty corn standing trembling and a down
of ghost flowers veiling the ignored fields
and everywhere the colors I cannot take
my eyes from all of them red even the wide streams
red it is the season of migrants
flying at night feeling the turning earth

beneath them and I woke in the city hearing
the call notes of the plover then again and
again before I slept and here far down river
flocking together echoing close to the shore
the longest bridges have opened their slender wings

Returns After Dark

Many by now must be
dead the taxi drivers
who sat up before me
twenty even thirty
could it be forty years
ago when no matter
where that time I had gone
if the day was over
and the lights had come on

by the time I could see
the Magellanic Clouds
rise from the black river
and the white circuitry
that ordered us over
the bridge into the crowds
and cliffs of the city
familiar as ever
my life unknown to me

I was beholding it
across another time
each dark facade I thought
looked as it had before
the shining was the same
coming from lives unknown
in other worlds those white
windows burning so far
from the birth of the light

227 *Waverly Place*

When I have left I imagine they will
repair the window onto the fire escape
that looks north up the avenue clear
to Columbus Circle long I have known
the lights of that valley at every hour
through that unwashed pane and have watched with no
conclusion its river flowing toward me
straight from the featureless distance coming
closer darkening swelling growing distinct
speeding up as it passed below me toward
the tunnel all that time through all that time
taking itself through its sound which became
part of my own before long the unrolling
rumble the iron solos and the sirens
all subsiding in the small hours to voices
echoing from the sidewalks a rustling
in the rushes along banks and the loose
glass vibrated like a remembering bee
as the north wind slipped under the winter sill
at the small table by the window until
my right arm ached and stiffened and I pushed
the chair back against the bed and got up
and went out into the other room that was
filled with the east sky and the day replayed
from the windows and roofs of the Village
the room where friends came and we sat talking
and where we ate and lived together while
the blue paint flurried down from the ceiling
and we listened late with lights out to music
hearing the intercom from the hospital
across the avenue through the Mozart
Dr Kaplan wanted on the tenth floor
while reflected lights flowed backward on the walls

Sixth Floor Walk-Up

Past four in the afternoon the last day here
the winter light is draining out of the sky
to the east over the grays of the roofs
over the tiered bricks and dark water tanks
clock towers aerials penthouse windows
rusted doors bare trees in terrace gardens
in the distance a plane is coming in
lit by the slow burn of the sun sinking
two weeks before the solstice and the lingering
perfect autumn still does not seem to be
gone the walls of the apartment and the long
mirrors are becoming shadows the latest
telephone already cut off is huddled
against the wall with its deaf predecessors
the movers have not showed up for what is left
bare bed bare tables and the sofa the piled
LP's the great chair from which at this hour
once I called up a friend on Morton Street
to tell him that all the windows facing
west down the avenue were reflecting
a red building flaming like a torch
somewhere over near the old post office
on Christopher Street the sirens were converging
all the bells clanging and the sky was clear
as it is now they are stacking Christmas trees
along the fence again down at the corner
to the music of the subway under
the avenue on its way to Brooklyn
twenty-five years

Legend

Our own city had the second highest
VD rate in the country yielding
only to Hagerstown Maryland
we boasted aged somewhere around eleven

taking credit for it thinking we might
even be first it was fundamental
knowledge closer to home than the famous
roller coaster down at Rocky Glen
which we agreed was one of the world's
most dangerous with its hairpin trestle
out over water and the whole thing
about to collapse a lady got on
back in the summer with a baby
and when they got off the baby was dead
but the steady aura of the unspeakable
emanated from figures like Jennie
Dee the reigning madam whom we had not seen
but we all knew she rode in a chauffeur-driven
black Cadillac with flags on the fenders
and was friends with the mayor the Chamber
of Commerce and the police it was a mile
exactly to the courthouse downtown
by the short cut over the embankment
and along the weedy right-of-way to the iron
truss across the already stove-black
Lackawanna drunks who fell in there
were known to be blown-up and all shades of blue
by the time they were fished out on the South Side
the paint was worn off the top of the truss
where we ran across it into the smell
of the gasworks which haunted us part way
up the steep cobbles past the one gray house
all by itself with its shades drawn tight
and lights on in the daytime we never
saw anyone go in or come out of there
two dollars to the best of our belief
on the far side of the street whispering
through the cold echoes under the railroad bridge

Clear Water

Once a child's poem began a pond of time
what followed must have flowed from what a child

remembered in time about a child
he had once been except that the poem

began in a time before the poem
and before the pond that the child remembered

once a child's pond began a remembered
time that a child followed until the pond

was the time a poem began with a pond
that a child thought he remembered once not flowing

but by the time the poem began it was flowing
once upon the memory of a child

whose poem began before he was a child
a murmur flowing from before he began

though what he remembered once began
with the poem on the pond of a child's time

a child began a poem once in a time
remembered with a pond that he had seen

flowing from a spring he had never seen
kept by an unseen giant who once was a child

whose name was Mimir before the child
began the poem once in remembered time

the giant keeps the beginning before time
in the spring of mourning under the pond of time

Harm's Way

How did someone come at last to the word for patience
and know that it was the right word or patience

the sounds had come such a distance from the will to give pain
which that person kept like a word for patience

the word came on in its own time like a star
at such a distance from either pain or patience

it echoed someone in a mirror who threatened with fire
an immortal with no bounds of hatred or patience

the syllables were uttered out of the sound of fire
but in silence they became the word for patience

it is not what the hawk hangs on or the hushed fox
waits with who do not need a word for patience

passing through the sound of another's pain
it brings with it something of that pain or patience

but how did whoever first came to it convey
to anyone else that it was the word for patience

they must have arrived at other words by then
to be able to use something from pain for patience

there is no such word in the ages of the leaves
in the days of the grass there is no name for patience

many must have travelled the whole way without knowing
that what they wanted was the word for patience

it is as far from patience as William is from me
and yet known to be patience the word for patience

Whoever You Are

By now when you say *I stop somewhere waiting for you*
who is the I and who come to that is you

there are those words that were written a long time ago
by someone I have read about who they assure me is you

the handwriting is still running over the pages
but the one who has disappeared from the script is you

I wonder what age you were when those words came to you
though I think it is not any age at all that is you

stopping and waiting under the soles of my feet
this morning this waking this looking up is you

but nothing has stopped in fact and I do not know
what is waiting and surely that also is you

every time you say it you seem to be speaking
through me to some me not yet there who I suppose is you

you said you were stopping and waiting before I was here
maybe the one I heard say it then is you

The Causeway

This is the bridge where at dusk they hear voices
far out in the meres and marshes or they say they hear voices

the bridge shakes and no one else is crossing at this hour
somewhere along here is where they hear voices

this is the only bridge though it keeps changing
from which some always say they hear voices

the sounds pronounce an older utterance out of the shadows
sometimes stifled sometimes carried from clear voices

what can be recognized in the archaic syllables
frightens many and tells others not to fear voices

travellers crossing the bridge have forgotten where they were
     going
in a passage between the remote and the near voices

there is a tale by now of a bridge a long time before this one
already old before the speech of our day and the mere voices

when the Goths were leaving their last kingdom in Scythia
they could feel the bridge shaking under their voices

the bank and the first spans are soon lost to sight
there seemed no end to the horses carts people and all their
     voices

in the mists at dusk the whole bridge sank under them
into the meres and marshes leaving nothing but their voices

they are still speaking the language of their last kingdom
that no one remembers who now hears their voices

whatever translates from those rags of sound
persuades some who hear them that they are familiar voices

grandparents never seen ancestors in their childhoods
now along the present bridge they sound like dear voices

some may have spoken in my own name in an earlier language
when last they drew breath in the kingdom of their voices

The Chinese Mountain Fox

Now we can tell that there
must once have been a time
when it was always there
and might at any time

appear out of nowhere
as they were wont to say
and probably to their
age it did look that way

though how are we to say
from the less than certain
evidence of our day
and they referred often

through the centuries when
it may have been a sight
they considered common
so that they mentioned it

as a presence they were
sure everyone had seen
and would think familiar
they alluded even

then until it became
their unquestioned habit
like a part of the name
to that element it

had of complete surprise
of being suddenly
the blaze in widened eyes
that had been turned only

at that moment upon
some place quite near that they
all through their lives had known
and passed by every day

perhaps at the same place
where they themselves had just
been standing that live face
looking as though it must

have been following them
would have appeared with no
warning they could fathom
or ever come to know

though they made studied use
of whatever system
logic calculus ruse
they trusted in their time

to tell them where they might
count on it next and when
if once they figured right
as though it travelled in

a pattern they could track
like the route of some far
light in the zodiac
comet or migrant star

but it was never where
they had thought it would be
and showed the best of their
beliefs successively

to be without substance
shadows they used to cast
old tales and illusions
out of some wishful past

each in turn was consigned
to the role of legend
while yet another kind
of legend had wakened

to play the animal
even while it was there
the unpredictable
still untaken creature

part lightning and part rust
the fiction was passed down
with undiminished trust
while the sightings began

to be unusual
second-hand dubious
unverifiable
turning to ghost stories

all the more easily
since when it had been seen
most times that was only
by someone all alone

and unlike its cousins
of the lowlands captive
all these generations
and kept that way alive

never had it been caught
poisoned or hunted down
by packs of dogs or shot
hung up mounted or worn

never even been seen
twice by the same person
in the place it had been
when they looked there again

and whatever they told
of it as long as they
still spoke of it revealed
always more of the way

they looked upon the light
while it was theirs to see
and what they thought it might
let them glimpse at any

moment than of the life
that they had rarely been
able to catch sight of
in an instant between

now and where it had been
at large before they came
when the mountains were green
before it had a name

The Old Year

I remember the light
at the end of one year
the gold mist is still bright
thousands of miles from here

and voices are calling
across the steep meadows
until the late falling
asleep of their echoes

less than a breath before
the silence where they are
the bare veined limbs are more
clear than ever but far

out of reach as always
lit by a new distance
and its beam that catches
the ring of last moments

I have stayed up to see
each time they are farther
than I thought they would be
one after another

those occasions that I
was to be happy in
while they were passing by
as I knew even then

they are farther away
once more the glimpses of
the sun one winter day
the eyes of early love

city after city
frozen in the night sky
each deafening party
spinning as the sparks fly

they appear in a new
perspective of absence
that each was led into
and the good rooms that once

upon a time have been
each in its turn the heart
of a whole horizon
have been taken apart

emptied and finally
left out in the cold air
to be recalled only
as dreams of what they were

what we dream now is here
the hours that we forget
in the garden the clear
leaf light after sunset

in the dream we believe
the house sails on the hill
it never means to leave
and the winter moon still

floats on its lucid bay
in the life where we met
and the year and the day
have not gone from us yet

Lament for the Makers

I that all through my early days
I remember well was always
    the youngest of the company
    save for one sister after me

from the time when I was able
to walk under the dinner table
    and be punished for that promptly
    because its leaves could fall on me

father and mother overhead
who they talked with and what they said
    were mostly clouds that knew already
    directions far too old for me

at school I skipped a grade so that
whatever I did after that
    each year everyone would be
    older and hold it up to me

at college many of my friends
were returning veterans
    equipped with an authority
    I admired and they treated me

as the kid some years below them
so I married half to show them
    and listened with new vanity
    when I heard it said of me

how young I was and what a shock
I was the youngest on the block
    I thought I had it coming to me
    and I believe it mattered to me

and seemed my own and there to stay
for a while then came the day
    I was in another country
    other older friends around me

my youth by then taken for granted
and found that it had been supplanted
    the notes in some anthology
    listed persons born after me

how long had that been going on
how could I be not quite so young
    and not notice and nobody
    even bother to inform me

though my fond hopes were taking longer
than I had hoped when I was younger
    a phrase that came more frequently
    to suggest itself to me

but the secret was still there
safe in the unprotected air
    that breath that in its own words only
    sang when I was a child to me

and caught me helpless to convey it
with nothing but the words to say it
    though it was those words completely
    and they rang it was clear to me

with a changeless overtone
I have listened for since then
    hearing that note endlessly
    vary every time beyond me

trying to find where it comes from
and to what words it may come
    and forever after be
    present for the thought kept at me

that my mother and every day
of our lives would slip away
    like the summer and suddenly
    all would have been taken from me

but that presence I had known
sometimes in words would not be gone
    and if it spoke even once for me
    it would stay there and be me

however few might choose those words
for listening to afterwards
    there I would be awake to see
    a world that looked unchanged to me

I suppose that was what I thought
young as I was then and that note
    sang from the words of somebody
    in my twenties I looked around me

to all the poets who were then
living and whose lines had been
    sustenance and company
    and a light for years to me

I found the portraits of their faces
first in the rows of oval spaces
    in Oscar Williams' *Treasury*
    so they were settled long before me

and they would always be the same
in that distance of their fame
        affixed in immortality
        during their lifetimes while around me

all was woods seen from a train
no sooner glimpsed than gone again
        but those immortals constantly
        in some measure reassured me

then first there was Dylan Thomas
from the White Horse taken from us
        to the brick wall I woke to see
        for years across the street from me

then word of the death of Stevens
brought a new knowledge of silence
        the nothing not there finally
        the sparrow saying Bethou me

how long his long auroras had
played on the darkness overhead
        since I looked up from my Shelley
        and Arrowsmith first showed him to me

and not long from his death until
Edwin Muir had fallen still
        that fine bell of the latter day
        not well heard yet it seems to me

Sylvia Plath then took her own
direction into the unknown
        from her last stars and poetry
        in the house a few blocks from me

Williams a little afterwards
was carried off by the black rapids
        that flowed through Paterson as he
        said and their rushing sound is in me

that was the time that gathered Frost
into the dark where he was lost
  to us but from too far to see
  his voice keeps coming back to me

then the sudden news that Ted
Roethke had been found floating dead
  in someone's pool at night but he
  still rises from his lines for me

MacNeice watched the cold light harden
when that day had left the garden
  stepped into the dark ground to see
  where it went but never told me

and on the rimless wheel in turn
Eliot spun and Jarrell was borne
  off by a car who had loved to see
  the racetrack then there came to me

one day the knocking at the garden
door and the news that Berryman
  from the bridge had leapt who twenty
  years before had quoted to me

the passage where *a jest* wrote Crane
falls from the speechless caravan
  with a wave to Bones and Henry
  and to all that he had told me

I dreamed that Auden sat up in bed
but I could not catch what he said
  by that time he was already
  dead someone next morning told me

and Marianne Moore entered the ark
Pound would say no more from the dark
  who once had helped to set me free
  I thought of the prose around me

and David Jones would rest until
the turn of time under the hill
    but from the sleep of Arthur he
    wakes an echo that follows me

Lowell thought the shadow skyline
coming toward him was Manhattan
    but it blacked out in the taxi
    once he read his *Notebook* to me

at the number he had uttered
to the driver a last word
    then that watchful and most lonely
    wanderer whose words went with me

everywhere Elizabeth
Bishop lay alone in death
    they were leaving the party early
    our elders it came home to me

but the needle moved among us
taking always by surprise
    flicking by too fast to see
    to touch a friend born after me

and James Wright by his darkened river
heard the night heron pass over
    took his candle down the frosty
    road and disappeared before me

Howard Moss had felt the gnawing
at his name and found that nothing
    made it better he was funny
    even so about it to me

Graves in his nineties lost the score
forgot that he had died before
    found his way back innocently
    who once had been a guide to me

Nemerov sadder than his verse
said a new year could not be worse
  then the black flukes of agony
  went down leaving the words with me

Stafford watched his hand catch the light
seeing that it was time to write
  a memento of their story
  signed and is a plain before me

now Jimmy Merrill's voice is heard
like an aria afterward
  and we know he will never be
  old after all who spoke to me

on the cold street that last evening
of his heart that leapt at finding
  some yet unknown poetry
  then waved through the window to me

in that city we were born in
one by one they have all gone
  out of the time and language we
  had in common which have brought me

to this season after them
the best words did not keep them from
  leaving themselves finally
  as this day is going from me

and the clear note they were hearing
never promised anything
  but the true sound of brevity
  that will go on after me

Suite in the Key of Forgetting

You remember surely
is the way it begins
in a time afterwards
far from the beginning
which no one remembers

remember that story
of Nerval's beginning
away on a journey
one year in Germany
in some river city
Cologne or Frankfurt if
I remember rightly
Frankfurt surely and he
gave the year precisely
as it occurs to me
though only its number
if indeed I am not
inventing after all

though that date must have been
fixed in his memory
like the year of a scar
loss or discovery
from his mid-century
which by now is only
a flutter in the words
for all that was flying then
through the echoing hall

but as you recall he
explored the boulevards
and offerings of that
brimming metropolis
and stood in the market
of furs staring at what
had been stripped from the lives

of the white bear that woke
in the kingdom of white
the blue fox that journeyed

like a day in daylight
I thought of them again
one evening in Paris
more than a century
later when a spotlit
furrier's shop flaunted
twelve infant sables ranged
with mouths locked on a gold
collar I remember
who was with me and what
year it was that summer
but not where we went then
after those skins were passed
it seems to me he came
to the racks of old books
dark backs closed on themselves
standing among strangers
no longer wanted by
part of their own story
some name on the flyleaf
with a date and an Ex
Libris in that city
well known for its freedom
to publish so that lives
histories and journals
memoirs from anywhere
might have ended up there

he had already bought
more than he should have but
still he could not resist
wandering through others
and came at last to one
written half in German
half in French recounting

so the title page claimed
the extraordinary
history of the Count
and Abbé of Bucquoy
with the remarkable
details of his escape
from the prisons of Fort
l'Évêque and the Bastille
along with several works
of his in verse and prose
and particularly
the *game* of women and
was that the English word
game some affectation
already out of date
or was it a misprint
for the French gamme or scale
like the English gamut
rooted in the lowest
note of the hexachord
chanted in Latin to
St John the Baptist one
tongue or the other came
to a like suggestion
and the uncertainty
in the language as he
read it might have warned him
of untrustworthy ground
and evasions to come
but that escaped me too
when I read in my turn
and even when it came
to mind long afterwards
the bookseller wanted
what sounded like too much
for that book or at least
more than he felt he should
spend by that time and he
told himself he would find
the volume easily

in Paris and took down
title and publisher
and where the opus had
first been offered for sale
a century and more
before though again he
might have noticed the light
insubstance of the names
Jean de la France vendor
at Good Faith an address
in Hope he copied it
all and in good faith left

do you remember as
he had asked Daphne once
thinking of Octavie
do you remember that
song that begins again
always begins again
under the sycamore
under the white laurels
or the trembling willows
that song of love do you
remember the temple
he was recalling her
face as she stood before
the great columns the marks
of her teeth in the skins
of the bitter lemons
the cave of the dragon's
seed and the quaking of
promise the promises
do you remember

how it went after he
woke in Paris again
and there set out to find
that same book in a time
much restricted of late
by the censor in all

fiction written to be
continued but he told
himself that his subject
was in fact history
and when asked for a name
he said the Abbé of
Bucquoy imagining
there in the capital
turning up in no time
the documentation
for this personage who
once had been flesh and blood
there was the book itself
more than once listed in
France though said to be rare
but surely somewhere in
a public library
private collection or
specialist's cabinet
he was sure he recalled
clearly what he had read
of the Abbé's story
from the volume that he
had not bought in Frankfurt
and he had found the same
details of the Abbé's
adventures in Madame
Dunoyer's witty and
curious letters though
they spoke at a remove
and under the new law
it would be ruinous
to recount those events
without the Abbé's own
words for confirmation
particularly in
a country where persons
who possessed power or
the pretense of power
were certain to use it

you would be wise a friend
told him not to rely
upon Madame's letters
for your authority
wait for the National
Library to open
on October the first
there on the day the name
of the book after some
time was discovered but
not the book and they said
come back in three days and
they had not found it then
it may be in among
the novels they told him

novels he cried but this
is history itself
it tells of the revolt
of the Camisards and
the Protestants going
into exile the league
of Lorraine and Mandrin
raising his army there
to take Beaune and Dijon
yes the librarian
said I know but the wrongs
of the past were made at
different times and they
can be put right only
one by one and upon
particular request
no one can help you here
but Monsieur Ravenal
and unfortunately
he is not in this week

came the Monday and yes
Monsieur Ravenal was
there in the reading room

and the person of whom
the inquiry was made
actually knew him
and offered to provide
an introduction which
could not have been received
with greater courtesy
I am enchanted he
said to meet you and I
ask you but to grant me
a few days before I
devote myself to your
interest for I am
this week at the bidding
of the public and now
we have been introduced
you have become you see
a private acquaintance

which could not be denied
he considered the room
and the public from whom
he had been set aside
watching distinguished but
impoverished scholars
providing six hundred
quotidian readers
with the usual fare
and those who had come there
to get out of the cold
and sleep safe in a chair
endangering such books
as fell into their hands
ordinary idlers
retired bourgeois salesmen
presently unemployed
widowers copyists
ancient lunatics such
as that poor Carnaval
who appeared every day

clad in red or sky blue
or apple green and crowned
with a wreath of flowers
he remembered them all
out of earlier times
other days of his own
he watched them tearing out
pages poring over
columns of addresses
none had given a name

and from this library
he knew that some volume
with no other of its
kind in the world vanished
almost daily and went
unmissed for a while that
single survivor that
sole testimony gone
he thought of the burning
of the library in
Alexandria and
not by Islam but by
his sainted ancestors
he was writing it all
to the Director of
the National and he
was remembering as
he wrote it another
visit to Frankfurt years
earlier and the lives
he was looking for then

that was the first letter
of twelve and whose was this
charmed hand writing it down
only from memory
was it our poor Gérard
whom the men of science
as his unfeeling friend

Dumas repeated it
had pronounced sick and in
need of treatment whereas
for us Alexandre
said his stories his dreams
are better than ever
at one time he will be
Sultain Ghera Gherai
Duke of Egypt or Count
of Abyssinia
Baron of Smyrna and
write a letter to my
supreme authority
requesting permission
to declare war upon
Emperor Nicolas
or did the hand belong
to someone whom Dumas
had never laid eyes on

whose efforts to summon
that memoir of Bucquoy
from the forest of shades
drew him from library
to library and on
to the ruins of stone
set upon stone to keep
some memory alive
the bones of a chateau
eyeless its library
gone the tomb of Rousseau
and a family tree
ancient vast unlikely
and part of another
journal or memoir by
a beautiful ill-starred
forbear of the Abbé
or so-called Abbé as
some reference put it
she must have been the one

he had been trying to
remember the whole way

what he found was perhaps
a hundred pages in
her own hand the paper
foxed the ink ghostly her
name had been Angélique
the Count's daughter who cared
neither for jewels nor
adornments longing for
death to still her longing
until love came to her
and misfortune seized her
following her until
she was alone and with
nothing to cover her
nakedness and no one
knew what became of her

what did become of her
she was not in her name
given to the story
not in whatever he
could remember of her
not in her own words
that enchanted melting
being impossible
to hold or to believe

Testimony

The year I will be seventy
who never could believe my age
still foolish it appears to me
as I have been at every stage
but not beyond the average
I trust nor yet arrived at such

wisdom as might view the damage
without regretting it too much

though I have sipped the rim by now
of trouble and should know the taste
I am not certain as to how
the pain of learning what is lost
is transformed into light at last
some it illumines from their birth
and some will hunger to the last
for the moment and hands of earth

while some apparently would give
the open unrepeatable
present in which they wake and live
to glimpse a place where they were small
or in love once and be able
to capture in that second sight
what in the plain original
they missed and this time get it right

they would know how to hold it there
a still life still alive and know
what to do with it now and where
to hang it and how not to go
from there again perhaps although
when they were living in its day
they could not wait for it to go
and were dying to get away

and at one time or another
some have tied themselves tight to cling
desperately as though they were
in white water and near drowning
onto in fact the very thing
they most wanted to be rid of
hanging on despite everything
to their anguish and only love

the shell games move around the block
one where a crowd is always drawn
promises a time off the clock
at any moment to the one
who is smart enough to put down
the present hour and calculate
what it will be worth later on
and meanwhile hold the breath and wait

hope lingers with its dear advice
that gets to each in different ways
growing up means you sacrifice
what you like now knowing it pays
with champagne in the holidays
and comforts that are meant to stay
and come to that as the man says
what is the present anyway

and I of course am taken in
by each of them repeatedly
whatever words I may have been
using since I have used any
reached me out of a memory
on the way to some plan or promise
not yet there and after many
notices I have come to this

what is it then I hear the same
linnet notes in the morning air
that I heard playing when I came
now the new light has reached to
where
the pleated leaves are holding their
hands out to it without moving
and as the young day fills them there
I am the child still listening

who from a farmhouse once in spring
walked out in the long day alone
through old apple orchards climbing

to a hilltop where he looked down
into a green valley that shone
with such light all the words were poor
later to tell what he had known
they said that was the night pasture

I am the child who plans the Ark
back of the house while there is still
time and rides bareback on the dark
horse through the summer night until
day finds us on the leafless hill
who stands at evening by the lake
looking out on it as I will
as long as I am here awake

to see the coming of the day
here once more that comes once only
I am new to it the same way
I was when it first dawned on me
no one else has turned into me
under the clothes that I have worn
I know that I am the same me
that I have been since I was born

the boats do not appear to be
any farther on the river
they shine passing as silently
through the bright sunlight as ever
I am at the window over
the Palisades where I look down
the back wall of the church over
the viaduct and Hoboken

never suspecting that this may
be the one time it will happen
my father asking me today
whatever his thought may have been
if I will promise that I can
be quiet if I go along

and stay with him while he works on
his sermon and my promising

the keys ring at the heavy door
the old skin of varnish opens
our feet echo on the sloped floor
down dark aisles to the green curtains
of the chancel and our outlines
flicker along the sunbeams through
the deep underwater silence
of this sleep we have waked into

stairs circle to the high window
where as I kneel to watch the bright
river I hear behind me Thou
fool and then the typewriter write
and stop and him repeat This night
under his breath with certainty
again Thou fool again This night
shall thy soul be required of thee

but I pretend I do not hear
I know that he is speaking to
somebody who is never here
I keep looking out the window
the boats that I can see there no
longer ply the living water
the room his words are spoken to
long ago vanished into air

how many years since we lived there
we were told after we had gone
the church was sold in bad repair
to stand empty and be torn down
soon and the place where it had been
and the long grass knew it no more
no stone was left upon a stone
trees climbed out of the ruined floor

stretching their shadows up the wall
of the long brick apartment house
next door until they entered all
the stories of the south windows
children were brought up inside those
frames with the branches always there
families behind those shadows
have grown and moved away somewhere

after whole lives at that address
during which they have never seen
the place without its squatter trees
poplars and the scorned common one
that some call the tree of heaven
wars have dragged on and faded since
the last neighbors have forgotten
that anything else stood there once

and in a few months it will be
since the night my father died
a quarter of a century
as time is numbered on this side
the rain then sluicing down outside
past midnight and the hour of one
I came in from the street and dried
and never heard the telephone

and after I had gone to bed
to lie listening while the rain
beat on the roof above my head
and watch the lights reflected on
the blue ceiling turning again
backward I heard the door open
my closest friend had braved the rain
with the message that he was gone

only a little while before
maybe an hour or so since they
had tried to call me and not more
than a few minutes either way

from where the clocks had stood they say
when I was born perhaps we passed
that close and missed in the same way
it used to happen in the past

whoever was he talking to
back when he spoke to me and when
I heard his voice as I still do
though now the words are almost gone
who do I hear that I heard then
as in those moments when he would
tell something about Rimerton
in the train smoke of his childhood

looking onto the Erie tracks
in front and from the rear windows
down the steep bank below the backs
of the jacked houses and their rows
of cabbages and potatoes
in summer to the ragged line
past which the later river flows
on after all of them have gone

he made it sound as though it was
a garden since it had been lost
some glow of a distant promise
colored the words he favored most
for the age when they were poorest
his mother with seven children
who had survived he was the last
she kept them upright on her own

after the man who married her
and fathered them had taken off
working his way down the river
to Pittsburgh and the city life
they said he drank which was enough
for most of them to tell of him
nobody played Hail To The Chief
when my grandfather made it home

hers were the threads in which they all
were sewn and they had made of her
an ancient on a pedestal
before I can remember her
established in her rocking chair
with her Bible by the window
her needle pausing in the air
little more would I ever know

except in remnants handed down
as patchwork through the family
none of them telling how her own
life unfurled but for one early
glimpse of the time she waved good-bye
too small to know what it was for
as the young men went marching by
on their way to the Civil War

they could repeat it back to her
didn't you Mumma they would say
wave good-bye to them remember
for company get her to say
what she could tell about that day
being held up high at the gate
and she would laugh and look away
with nothing further to relate

the very way my father and
the rest of them persistently
told no more of what had happened
than their old favorites and he
never went on with a story
he began and any question
would extinguish it completely
so what was past was past and gone

that cold summer after he died
my mother each time anyone
asked what she would do now replied
that she would live on there alone

all of the garden beds were sown
she liked to be out in the air
taking care of them on her own
some told her she would die out there

fall over and be found some day
and she would nod and say that she
could not think of a better way
to go and laugh at that but she
meant what she said as they could see
some remembered then her saying
when the subject came up that she
never was afraid of dying

when had she first felt that was so
her father died when she was four
from then on she would never know
what she knew of him any more
was it he she had seen before
and his eyes with the day inside
going away already or
was all that after he had died

out of the remnants in her head
made up of what she had been told
after that minute by the bed
and her closed eyes close to the cold
forehead with nothing she could hold
tight and believe that it was him
all the pictures of him looked old
and not one of them looked like him

but things were there instead of him
papers he had once written on
clothes he had worn turned into him
in the days when the shades were down
and the black butterfly hung on
the door to tell the street to mourn
and the box was lying open
under the room where she was born

in the house in Colorado
Denver the glint of promise where
the doctors told him he should go
repeating that the mountain air
perhaps and their words trailed off there
he might go on inspecting for
the railroads just as well out there
hope had been what they came out for

the train was carrying the night
back it kept beating in her mind
keeping time with the thread of light
around what the man called the blind
one of the strangers being kind
she felt her mother lying warm
beside her and reached out to find
the wrapped bird of her brother's arm

they were already far away
in a place they would never know
rolling a darkness through its day
all of it would be long ago
when she woke up in Ohio
which she had never seen but where
everyone spoke to her as though
she had always been living there

and known the bedroom and the bed
that her mother had always known
and the house that her mother said
had been hers until she had grown
and married it still seemed her own
my mother thought that it must be
familiar from the names alone
all that she had just come to see

there were no mountains any more
it seemed they had been forgotten
her brother Morris said they were
still there over the horizon

and the gods too through whose garden
she had heard that they had wheeled her
in her carriage in the hidden
time before she could remember

when next she woke there was the black
city Pittsburgh tight around her
she prayed they might be taken back
to the house above the river
in Ohio where her father
was born it was called Cheshire there
they had stayed with her grandfather
why could they not be living there

some day they might her mother said
but for now they would have to be
here she spoke of their daily bread
since all the insurance money
had been lost and it was only
here that she could earn a living
for them and her own family
was their home for the time being

and they visited Ohio
sometimes through that next summer when
her mother did not seem to know
how sick she had become by then
there in the foreground of the brown
photographs she is the shadow
taking pictures of her children
the sun hats and the wide hair bow

the white horse and the garden swing
the summer was not even done
and the heat when she lay dying
all the shades drawn and everyone
whispering in the corner on
the landing passing the word pain
back and forth then the bending down
to kiss her and she too was gone

and everyone in black again
the shaken veils still whispering
what will happen to the children
how could she bear such suffering
a few of them remembering
how beautiful she used to be
and remained so through everything
until this marked her finally

and it was Pittsburgh after that
brought up by her mother's mother
assured that they were fortunate
to be fed clothed and together
in one house after another
with no one in the family
uncles aunts or her grandmother
able to hang onto money

maybe her mother would have been
able to keep things in order
the work that she had found had been
with figures as a bookkeeper
at the Woman's Exchange and her
hand was elegant and even
with a clear grace that my mother
kept in mind when she held a pen

she loathed it from the day she went
to Shakespeare School Morris did too
she hated every day she spent
in the house on Penn Avenue
doubly so from the time she knew
one aunt her mother's sister Ride
baptized Marie had moved in too
shortly after her mother died

Ride then was getting a divorce
from Uncle Jack and they heard Ride
insist it was his fault of course
but they were making him provide

at least after the way he lied
and ran around behind her back
as she talked they could hear his side
everyone had liked Uncle Jack

my mother young as she was then
considered Ride haughty and vain
later she thought she might have been
unjust to her but it was plain
she felt Ride had been blessed in vain
with that life they had together
and had thrown it away again
a gift not good enough for her

while my mother kept thinking of
what she had known of her parents
who she was sure had been in love
how they had clung to every chance
so that even in their absence
she felt what they had tried to hold
as it was slipping through their hands
and none of that could have been told

not that she ever would have said
a word about it anyway
she would carry it in her head
like a number that knew its way
to the next column of the day
making a shorthand as she went
that none could read and she would say
no one would know what she had meant

she was determined that she would
leave no loose end whatever she
might have to do she would be good
at school quiet and orderly
all the homework done perfectly
piano lessons practised long
and the fine seams finished neatly
so that there would be nothing wrong

but if only her mother lived
she liked to think that maybe they
by some miracle might have moved
to Ohio again one day
before too long and they could stay
near Aunt Susan she could recall
sometimes hearing her mother say
that that would be congenial

there were the cousins whom she knew
Sam and Minerva and she ran
down the list of the others who
lived near there she could see each one
and remember when she had gone
to visit them and play beside
the river in the summer sun
then one day her grandmother died

that was death in a different place
it burned to tell her she had been
wanting in gratitude and grace
toward the shade of this short woman
who had taken all of them in
by turns until they said her door
never could keep out anyone
so she took boarders and stayed poor

Morris had moved out and found work
still nursing dreams of college but
from his salary as a clerk
at the railroad office he brought
my mother an allowance that
he paid until he had made sure
her own wages were adequate
though scarcely to take care of her

she was the star secretary
at North Church and awakened there
the ardor of that seminary
student who drove the preacher's car

anyone would have noticed her
beautiful as she was by then
you can still see in a picture
a shadowy reproduction

her mother's beauty there again
some agreed who remembered that
Morris did not deny it when
they would say that and he heard it
he could see what made them say it
but did not believe either one
looked like the other no he thought
neither resembled anyone

she and the optimistic young
man driving toward the ministry
stepped out together before long
theater and boating party
outings in someone's Model T
and then the ring and planning for
the wedding Morris would just see
when he died she was twenty-four

her mother's will in pencil had
not half filled a folded paper
so small that it might have drifted
out of one world through another
unnoticed saying she would rather
one had her broach and one a ring
after those were taken from her
to leave her without anything

Morris had a way of reading
lost to everything around him
one valve in his heart was bleeding
they had known of that for some time
before long he could scarcely climb
the front steps without breathing hard
then there was nothing left of him
his blanket his library card

and of her father there was this
imitation alligator
case clasping the full deck of his
passes as railroad inspector
none good for transit any more
none anyway transferable
no one she knew had set out for
most stations on the timetable

all three had seen while they were young
blankness arriving through the day
it followed as they moved among
others it never went away
there was nothing they knew to say
but the same words the others said
in church closing their eyes to pray
and seeing nothing just ahead

and she had seen them watching it
known its reflection in their eyes
every time recognizing what
was not there every time it was
the same unaltering surprise
while each in turn had told her they
believed in that which never dies
and will be there again one day

and she believed it in the words
so familiar they must be true
she said them over afterwards
in those days as she used to do
when she was small before she knew
why they were said time after time
or what they were referring to
she would understand that in time

the same words in other voices
were all waiting in the country
when they moved to the first churches
Yatesborough and Rural Valley

to stand in the cemetery
and hear the praying as before
and to sing of the day when we
shall meet on that beautiful shore

by and by but it seemed to be
a truth without a face like air
while she saw her own dead plainly
they appeared in her mind somewhere
close to her always waiting there
outside what the words were saying
in the third year of marriage their
first child signalled it was coming

it was hard for her to believe
that a new life was on the way
to her who had grown up to grieve
for lives in turn taken away
as one after another they
had left her for that absent place
might a life come to her and stay
she could see nothing of its face

but with the year turning in her
she wrote a letter out ahead
to the unseen in case she were
not to stay with you as she said
so you might be sure she wanted
you from the moment that she knew
you were there she had not needed
to know more than that about you

the illusion of testaments
so careful and so shrewdly planned
so finely tuned their instruments
so often reconsidered and
words and characters realigned
to determine a future where
the here and now will understand
what they have coming to them there

cards change before they can be played
at times only the words stay on
long after everything they said
and had provided for is gone
while the mansions like bread upon
the waters become history
whole writings come to light again
saying what was supposed to be

when the cold year was dark and young
their child was born who she would say
whenever that bell had been rung
had been perfect in every way
it was a boy and she said they
informed her he was beautiful
but they had taken him away
before she had seen him at all

and then it never would be clear
why within minutes he was dead
when he had scarcely wakened here
a rush of blood into the head
was the cause of it so they said
but was that from some injury
at birth or mishap afterward
nobody would tell that story

if it turned out to be a son
she meant to name him for her father
and so they did when he was gone
and then both were gone together
by the same name and years later
I was to be the son who read
the clipped notice and her letter
but only after she was dead

those were her deaths before my day
by that time she could turn to hear
outside the voices on her way
a stillness only partly here

and whatever she would hold dear
giving herself up to its care
she looked beyond it without fear
toward what she felt was waiting there

with my father I could not tell
what after all death meant for him
I heard him at one funeral
after another on that theme
preaching of heaven from the time
the smell of flowers frightened me
in a school friend's living room
as they drew me past the body

I knew the words he always said
which others had taught him to say
in that voice he put on to read
from scripture and said Let us pray
he told me that death came the way
sleep brought quiet to our bodies
we could not see what went away
but what was buried fed the trees

it did not sound as good to me
as he was telling me it was
I hoped that it would never be
and I would not get to that place
myself but would be me always
he told me that we all grow tired
at last and will be glad for peace
that waits for us as a reward

how much of that did he believe
where were those answers coming from
were they what he was certain of
in his own body all the time
alone travelling sick with some
nameless humiliating ill
when he kept asking to go home
out of the veterans' hospital

these nights that we see the comet
in the northwest as the stars come
saying the name we have for it
now which is nothing like its name
in lost languages the last time
it could be seen from where we are
thousands of years ago our name
of which it remains unaware

as it will be when next it swims
into what eye may then be here
after our knowledge and our hymns
draw the tail of their vanished sphere
on through an unremembered year
I think of how I thought of him
then in myself and tried to hear
his sounding of what was to come

after the words of ringing text
youthful hopes and dawns of promise
the sleepless gnawing that came next
in a row of empty churches
marriage heading in separate ways
children growing into distance
and such money as there was
used for buying more insurance

years ago it came to me
how cold his white feet must have been
in the new shoes shined perfectly
to step out where the ice was thin
mind made up against drink and sin
smoking swearing cards and dancing
the bad boys who liked playing in
streets and the threat in everything

and then a big church of his own
when he had never finished school
that looming Presbyterian
flawed yellow brick tabernacle

that they told him used to be full
behind it passers-by could see
across the river to the still
skyline of the shining city

on the eve of the Depression
there he stayed marking time for years
before he turned and started down
through latter-day architectures
largely maintained by faith and prayers
pinched salaries lame in coming
decades later he said in tears
that he had failed at everything

but I had seen him with the old
the sick and dying and alone
sometimes all they may need he told
me one time is to have someone
listen to them and he had known
by then the voices growing small
the smells of beds the waiting bone
the pictures far off on the wall

and screams out of the wells of pain
shaking the curtains in the night
the breath starting its climb again
the eyes rolling away in fright
liquids glittering through the light
colors opening on the bed
the hands still hoping as the white
shadows tightened around the head

Aunt Sue so shrunk inside her skin
that toward the last they could not find
a vein to put a needle in
he had heard what they had in mind
as they lay staring at the end
it was still something he was told
he prayed with them and he was kind
and then he wanted to be old

helpless and taken care of by
somebody else he always said
he had something wrong with him they
had never found though they had tried
until the night one sat beside
him reading psalms and as he read
Therefore will not we fear he died
saying that he was not afraid

which I do hope and trust was so
a thing to save and put away
by then maybe they did not know
and surely neither one could say
what had stayed with them all the way
apart from any names for it
three times she bowed her head to say
good-night to the closing casket

alone then as she chose to be
she set her own house in order
even neater than formerly
from the glassed back porch table where
she had her meals and opened her
mail she looked out on the garden
and the rain of that cold summer
not good weather to be out in

she wrote her letters there when she
had washed and dried the dishes her
dread as she put it was to be
a burden to someone ever
not to be able to take care
of herself eventually
that was one thing she had never
wished to live long enough to see

she had examples close to hand
the old friends whom she visited
who could no longer understand
her name or anything she said

but stared up at her from the bed
when they recognized in her place
someone she knew had long been dead
she felt a cloud across her face

then nursing homes and hospitals
walkers and wheel chairs and IV's
letters with medical details
tolling losses of faculties
tumors and incapacities
strokes attacks vistas of the ward
and the vacant paralysis
no one could alter or afford

friends wrote of places she might go
communities planned for the old
she sat writing by the window
while the gray days went on she told
how high the weeds had grown this cold
had made the berries late again
and to pick them she had to hold
the big umbrella in the rain

and yet she had no wish to move
the winter was the only thing
that worried her she would not leave
her neighbor who came that evening
when her number went on ringing
had trouble opening the door
tripped over the body lying
where it had been left just before

when I am gone she used to say
get the Salvation Army in
have them take everything away
but when the time came I moved in
turned in rooms where their lives had been
and emptied out cupboards and shelves
drawers cabinets cellar kitchen
of things not worth much in themselves

then all at once it was autumn
the leaves turning and the light clear
and I was watching the day come
into the branches floating near
the window where year after year
I woke up looking into them
shots in the woods told of a deer
somewhere and crows called after them

my parents gone I met their friends
over again someone each day
gave them whatever odds and ends
they were inclined to take away
listened to what they had to say
of what appealed to them and why
cut glass or dolls or dinner tray
lives were to be remembered by

clothes went to be passed on to some
murmured names whom I never knew
after most of those who had come
whose sayings I had listened to
I was left wordless with a new
rear-view figure I had been shown
another aspect of those two
whom I was certain I had known

my brother-in-law finally
came with a rental van one day
my sister and her family
carried the furniture away
we stood outside trying to say
what might remain still to be said
then they got going all the way
to Michigan taking the bed

I stayed there among the echoes
planning to finish up a few
last things a clear day toward the close
of autumn I still had to do

one the instructions urged me to
Burn these it said in my mother's
hand on the bundle and I knew
who had written her those letters

and all of my father's sermons
his note consigned now to the fire
even the one in which I once
in childhood had heard him inquire
What have we lost and listened for
the answer but was never sure
it would be somewhere in the pyre
and would escape me as before

I took them out into the garden
past the fence to the iron drum
they had kept there to burn things in
lit the first page saw the flame climb
into the others fed it some
later years and then the letters
set the grill safely over them
as the fire rose to burn for hours

morning flowed over the bare floor
after everything had been done
nothing was left to come back for
I could not tell then what had gone
or whether or all of us had known
that daylight in the empty room
that I had not seen until then
that had no story and no name

I had given those things away
that never had belonged to me
and by that time whose life were they
whose ornaments and memory
even those days that seemed to be
mine went off somewhere on their own
disappearing in front of me
before I saw that they were gone

years earlier when I was young
I sat up with Old French to read
Villon in his unbroken tongue
knowing by then that I would need
his own words if I was indeed
to hear what their rough accent tells
playing across a kind of deed
that left things to somebody else

his voice gone from it long ago
a shadow on an empty lake
those names drifting through its echo
pronounced now only for the sake
of the turns he contrived to make
at their expense who in their time
sat on everything they could take
and let the rest gaze up at them

and they had blown away in dust
and the gross volumes of their fame
had shrunk to footnotes at the last
which the readers of a poem
looked up only because some name
had stopped them in a passage there
but that was not what they had come
to be reading the poem for

even the language of their day
had grown foreign not just to me
no one had spoken it that way
lo this many a century
some of those words remained only
because his pen had set them down
one night before he was thirty
as the bell tolled at the Sorbonne

hard as it was to catch the wave
of song running those syllables
from a voice in an unknown grave
that could have been nobody else

a note out of the ground that calls
unaltered from the start I heard
and its own moment without bells
that went on ringing afterward

I walked out in the summer night
under the silent canopy
of sycamores along the street
and his words made it seem to me
how easy in his century
writing a poem must have been
I was some years short of twenty
and saw the ease was plain Villon

cat burglar's ninth life wanted for
assorted acts of robbery
including churches also for
murder caught tortured ripe to die
freed in a round of amnesty
to his underworld haunts and whores
used up gone missing at thirty
with no suggestion of remorse

who could believe a thing he said
though he swore on one testicle
that it was love alone that had
brought him to this deplorable
state and to drawing up his will
in verse giving it all away
which was more true than probable
like someone dying in a play

at twenty what first stayed with me
were his long slow notes and the snows
then in a few years I would be
the age he was when he wrote those
first parting words while the ink froze
that was youth of which he would say
so soon how suddenly it goes
and all at once has flown away

no one would write that way again
forever after as I knew
but in a dream that I had then
more than once I climbed up into
the attic and went over to
that trunk forbidden as the Ark
which no eye ever looked into
under the rafters in the dark

once when my father opened it
he said how long it had been since
those boots went hunting coon at night
and when my mother looked in once
she unwrapped a dress and ribbons
laughing at what had come to light
garments and relics of her parents
ghostly gloves and lace veils still white

when I opened it in the dream
besides what I remembered there
I found hidden along with them
bundles of writing paper where
poems I had forgotten were
formed in a hand that was my own
as I read they seemed familiar
and they all sounded like Villon

and there I left them as I thought
but then as I was coming near
the rapids and had almost shot
into my own thirtieth year
I thought I should set down before
its end a farewell reckoning
of what was bound to disappear
with that youth which I was leaving

and with the clock face looking on
I wrote out a few notes in some
manner that seemed right to me then
but finding how far I was from

settling yet with the time to come
put the half-hearted things away
where I might get to them some time
possibly on a later day

and now already it is May
one of these nights the plovers flew
north they had vanished on their way
when the stars rose that told them to
and it was days before we knew
while they had reached the northern lights
and white days and were coming to
where first they rose into their flights

and in our turn we felt the roar
loose us once more down the runway
and we were flung far out before
ourselves lifting above the day
the coast of shadows fell away
a time of clouds walking in sleep
carried us on its turning way
another light crossing the deep

into a late age sinking toward
that gray light where the ghosts go home
a time before long afterward
its halls through which the echoes come
with their sounds trailing after them
swirling down the shadowy air
then the way south another time
resurfaced but still going there

turn after turn appearing as
leaves floating just under water
each the newest in a series
and at evening arriving here
at the ridge above the river
garden and house in the long light
that fades from them as we appear
in time to see them before night

all of their seasons shut away
the garden not remembering
but the hand older in the way
the key turns in the opening
smell of wood and the house waking
here and there out of its shadows
through the blackbird's evening warning
from the trees under the windows

naming the twilight from before
with the first stars there already
and from outside the terrace door
over the village roofs we see
this year the comet steadily
lighting the sky it has come through
while points kindle in the valley
the constellation Bretenoux

the dark comes slowly in late spring
still cold in the first nights of May
I woke through it imagining
the bright path of a single ray
from that house we left far away
then I remembered where we were
and those were lights down on the way
that we had taken to come here

later the singing wakened me
those long notes again beginning
out of the dark crown of a tree
in the oak wood their slow rising
tumbling down into a rushing
stream while from farther along
the ridge another listening
nightingale begins its own song

under this roof I listened to
the singing of their ancestors
forbears these voices never knew
now it is more than forty years

since I first peered through the shutters
into an empty house along
wrecked walls and rubble on the floors
where no one had lived for that long

and almost that long since the night
I first set up the folding bed
carried in through the evening light
while the swallows brushed past my head
to the beams where they had nested
it was this season and I heard
later the sounds the dark house made
and then that singing afterward

I slept into another time
and the sayings of a country
that before summer had become
more recognizable to me
than strands of my own memory
though it was not where I was from
and my own words would never be
the common speech where I had come

I could believe only in part
what my own days had led me to
belonging elsewhere from the start
or so I thought *I expect you*
had not wanted the garden too
he said before he signed the deed
I answered at once that I knew
it was the garden I would need

Mentiere's potatoes for one year
then digging through the overgrown
docks and nettles in late autumn
to put a patch of lettuce in
and turning up bits of iron
broken forks square nails made by hand
cow shoes shell buttons that had been
gone for a long time in that ground

then hearing when the trees were still
naked in spring some cold morning
the garden door scrape on its sill
and it was old Delsol coming
with the cows and again threading
them through the doorway one by one
to plow the garden following
his voice as they had always done

his voice reaching back to them then
seems to come from no farther now
than when their breaths were braided in
the rows and as they turned the plow
rose over the finished furrow
then the bowed heads came back again
to where I watch until they go
out through the door above the lane

sound of that door crossing the stone
words calling to silent creatures
close behind that is the garden
that has vanished and reappears
surfacing behind the others
as the new leaves and loved faces
unfold out of a fan of years
and it lives among their shadows

and if ever I am to make
a rough draft of a reckoning
along the lines it was to take
at the moment youth was heading
out into the darkness flying
toward its own north and to this day
the one place that it was going
so far to find no one can say

I suppose I could start it here
at the house that one time I knew
maybe as well as anywhere
it was in youth that I came to

that door and by now there are few
ways left into those painted caves
that a light might still wander through
and find footprints of former lives

though indeed I have never known
much of note about those who were
here in the days before my own
met one woman who was born here
but whatever I might ask her
she had little enough to tell
of what she had left behind her
when she married out of it all

I wonder through what window she
first saw that time and from what room
and where the beds were in which they
woke and died and now not a name
remains from any family
then there were nuns who taught school here
at the turn of the century
in the years growing toward the war

only what now is left to me
can I hope to guide as it goes
looking north over the valley
from this room where the oven is
that baked their bread in the old days
for this place I too left behind
often and in so many ways
and set the feather in the wind

in deadly half-earnest Villon
launching into a legacy
found before he had well begun
that the form allowed him every
kind of digression and delay
that would put off the bitter list
which I confess appeals to me
who would rather leave that for last

my life was never so precious
to me as now James Wright once wrote
and then looked at his words and was
he said taken aback by what
he saw there but some thought like that
lives in my mind these years these days
through which the speed that is the light
brings me to see it as it goes

a bright cloud on a spring morning
lit with more than I remember
the first rays of sunrise turning
from the ridge across the river
along the valley and over
the young leaves and Paula waking
and I am still on the way here
seeing long before believing

how can this be the moment for
pointing all of it on its way
and putting out next to the door
those parting words that never say
much of what they were meant to say
although I know it would be wise
since none of this has long to stay
to learn to kiss it as it flies

and try to put in order some
provision or at least pretense
of that and with good grace in time
in spite of the way documents
have of making another sense
quite unforeseen when they were signed
to suit a later circumstance
and the bent of a different mind

did Villon's heirs ever collect
anything that he meant for them
yet in fact what could he expect
when some items he left for them

varied in quality and some
were not registered in his name
and never had belonged to him
which would have made them hard to claim

but when it comes to that there are
things that I take to be my own
that I would like a good home for
and would be happy to pass on
only I see I do not own
even the present worth of them
for numbering and handing down
so nothing will be lost of them

and though whatever I may leave
is clear to me how can I say
what an heir will in fact receive
when even now the words I say
sometimes are heard another way
as nothing is dependable
while I still have the chance I may
as well bestow things as I will

I leave to Paula this late spring
with its evenings in the garden
all the years of it beginning
from the moment I met her in
Fran's living room and the veiled green
leaves were young that we walked under
that night it was still April then
as we started home together

and to Paula besides the rest
that my mother called tangibles
whatever singing I have missed
from the darkness beyond the walls
the long notes of those nightingales
that began before I listened
first to their unrepeated calls
that song that never seems to end

and wakes the wren in the deep night
and the blackbird before morning
as we lie watching the moonlight
that has remembered everything
the stones of the old house shining
the cloud of light veiling the hill
and the river below shining
upwards as though it were still

there will be other things of course
as with Paula there always are
early light seen from later years
every vanishing reminder
of the way our days together
suddenly are there behind us
ours still but somewhere else before
we believed they were leaving us

or understood how they could go
like that faster than we can see
in spite of everything we know
and would have done to make them stay
they were already on their way
and their speed quickened when we came
to meet and there ignorantly
began these years in love with time

this year when the wild strawberries
only now begin to ripen
along the wall above the house
as I set foot in the garden
early this morning from my own
shadow there floats up as lightly
as the shadow if it had flown
a black redstart there before me

alighting a few feet away
the rust tail feathers quivering
as weightless as its flight the way
a hand trembles above a string

and the eye a black pearl holding
me and the new daylight on each
leaf around us in the morning
in that moment just out of reach

where I stood in other seasons
in the same garden long ago
and heard the clack of those small stones
under water letting me know
that a forbear of this shadow
with the same song and charactery
but far from either of us now
was nearby with an eye on me

and down the long rows of those days
observed what I was doing then
from the house roof or young pear trees
diving and appearing again
on the fork I left standing in
the ground out there and turned away
a moment the bird was there when
I turned back as it is today

as close as once it would appear
to those who in their time have stood
on this ground before I was here
that song was here before they made
their way up into the oak wood
and first herded stones around them
there was always something they did
that made this shadow follow them

and something that I came to do
later that it would recognize
at once and keep returning to
taking me each time by surprise
though how I figured in its eyes
I cannot say but as one who
brought the dark up to the surface
showing this ancient what was new

some would never heed anything
so small and as they thought of no
use to them but some kept finding
names for how it came to follow
and would vanish in the furrow
turning up just in front of them
and gone before they saw it go
a trick of shadow on a stream

coming so close and never held
seeming to have no weight at all
a pausing flourish whose wings fold
black as a cloak above the tail
that color that will not be still
which I have seen in the first light
fade out and return after all
with the sun setting into it

what could we know of each other
by the light of the same morning
in the moment that we were there
I could see that its mate was waiting
in a bush nearby repeating
those fine notes over and over
which the first one was echoing
something like I am here I am here

I leave what makes them reappear
out of my shadow once again
in a May morning of this year
and what in me they may have seen
without more fright than they have shown
and safe distance and whatever
between us never will be known
to them and to their heirs forever

and I leave to Jannah Arnoux
on this day when she turns eighty
the old house that she came back to
all those years out of each city

affair or eminence that she
had managed or been brought to in
the long story of her beauty
where she always began again

since the first day that she stared in
across the sill as a strange child
too small for school and old women
kissed her face that had just travelled
from the other side of the world
which she had seen sink in the sea
Indochina then it was called
they said they were her family

unlike the others she had lost
the Chinese mother scarcely known
French father whose brother a priest
could not bring her up on his own
so sent her home and would have gone
himself if only God had willed
all of them shrank and darkened then
in the memory of a child

who grew up to the haute couture
one black braid almost to the floor
for Ricci then the Prefecture
as the wife smiling at the door
to diplomats before the war
then a cell in the Resistance
the Gestapo were dying for
on a side street in Vichy France

still in her twenties when the bells
kept ringing that the war was done
with its fathomless burials
and still looking no older than
when first she stepped down from that train
to Paris and her student days
she turned toward the turns of fashion
a shrewdness she claimed was Chinese

years in the capital and yet
all of her youth seemed still with her
in full assurance when she met
Serge painting frescoes in a bar
and they started designing their
fabric that reached from an antique
house in a nearby market square
Paris Corsica Martinique

stores and houses in all of them
seasons spent in far-off places
this was still where they lived and came
in at the door of the same house
and heard the rooms hear their voices
as though they never had been gone
they keep planning to leave it less
they agree as the years go on

I leave her all the orchards on
the south hill and the road climbing
up through the tilled vineyards of Glanes
with the peach blossoms opening
and the moments of homecoming
grown into one to reappear
as it seemed something was being
given back in the spring this year

and to Serge good and gentle friend
painter musician cook so graced
with talents that some have opened
all by themselves and run to waste
gardener startled by how fast
even the long summer twilight
starts to go and straightens at last
to gaze out on the rest of it

I leave the tiered ridges beyond
Cornac with the mist deepening
in the valleys and the darkened
grapes across the bronze slope waiting

with the autumn light ripening
the time of harvest like a pear
then the hushed snow he loves along
the terraces of Quarante Peires

beyond the far end of the year
and I leave to Fernande Delsol
while the spring is still with us here
that echoes from outside the wall
the clack of her hoe in the cool
morning before the dew is dry
with her grandchildren off to school
and her kitchen standing empty

and her hat above the row
of young green at that hour casting
on the ancient wall its shadow
her back clenched from years of lying
awake coughing scarcely breathing
one daughter dead the other gone
saying now she is profiting
while the day has not yet begun

what can I leave her after all
that I know would give her pleasure
when it was always hard to tell
what would be right to bring to her
if it was something she might wear
with her plain tastes anything too
obvious would embarrass her
shy as she is of what is new

and never one for wasting time
wishing for things that were not hers
though I hear her from time to time
wish for health hers or another's
and for rain in the dry summers
and for the grandchildren to stay
out of trouble a few more years
and then get married properly

and wish for coming days to be
spared evils that still lie in wait
and I nod each time and agree
wishing kind health weather and fate
upon us both and beyond that
though it is hazardous to give
somebody else a present that
the one who gives would like to have

leave her the morning as it is
clear and still with the bell from down
across the valley reaching us
to say the hour over again
so that we can pay attention
to what time it may be this time
looking up at the one between
the ones told and the next to come

and seeing what was always there
the furrows traced across the field
in the same places where they were
when she looked at them as a child
the new leaves glowing on the old
trees in the time before her eyes
and a day she had not beheld
until then take her by surprise

I leave the house itself again
and close the door remembering
Ruhe sanft mein holdes Leben
heard on another day in spring
the shimmer of those notes floating
through the open door years ago
some of them are still echoing
through us northward as we go

down from the ridge under the high
cries of kites wheeling while the sun
climbs past them into the clear sky
all the wheels are turning by then

too fast to see and we fly on
and as the lights come on return
across the humming bridge again
to the nova where I was born

and evening on Washington Square
Margaret home her door opening
and John and Aleksandra there
dinner all together talking
over last plans for their wedding
guests flowers music clothes with less
than two days to spend rehearsing
the program and its promises

besides that to be practical
I leave them now for future use
something that both of them know well
the long light on the avenues
Fifth or Seventh or they may choose
when the moment occurs to them
early or late a day like this
in spring or a day in autumn

and I leave Matthew and Karen
who flew in from San Francisco
on the eve of this occasion
carrying Luke the baby to
the wedding with months still to go
before his first light year has flown
I leave a message for him now
for them to give him later on

and for themselves to take back west
flashes from another island
signalling farther up the coast
the salt wind racing from beyond
the whetted shadow where the land
vanishes under the wide glare
summer and its lingering sound
through the days they remember there

as others do who have for years
returned there thanks to Margaret
her auspices in what is hers
that whole shoreline of Nantucket
that she sees as first she saw it
a Coast Guard station on the dune
where an age put out the whaleboat
praying they would get back again

hers and for her also remain
the fresh snow outside the windows
when she has stayed to read alone
and the moment the fox passes
and she does not know what he sees
while the winter sun flashes on
the wings of swans gathered across
the long pond at Little Compton

I wake now in her house again
in that part of the galaxy
where my view of this round began
in the stone cloud in the city
and the sparks flying around me
were the moments of all the days
that I had come so far to see
some of them I would recognize

and some I thought burned a long time
in the same section of the sky
and my way came so close to them
they were the worlds that I saw by
so when their light was gone if I
closed my eyes there appeared to be
a day still present in the eye
that made the dark harder to see

the Manhattan for which I had
no name the moment I was born
bit after bit had orbited
into place and was being torn

down and I would see it return
as glittering reflections cast
in clusters high adrift in turn
through their towers of blowing dust

so that already it was late
when first it burned before my eyes
and they opened into the light
and gazed out upon a surface
where features without faces rose
revolved and went away again
that was the only way it was
and the way it had always been

it turned out that the world was old
I stood up to see it was so
all the stories that I was told
happened such a long time ago
there was nobody left to know
at what time they had once been true
and after that where did they go
only my hearing them was new

and the light as it came to me
and for a moment was the day
in appearance was new to me
though it had travelled a long way
the whole night had fallen away
behind it since it had begun
that sole occurrence of its way
through the dark before anyone

the city moving on the screen
now is the latest in a line
and the others that I have seen
here in the years that have been mine
turning into each other shine
through the fresh colors everywhere
and I see where I am again
knowing what is no longer there

that age just beneath the surface
where I lived at the high windows
north and east on Waverly Place
and woke to watch as the sun rose
over the stacks and roofs across
the Village and all day and night
the long mirrors the panes of glass
the walls wheeled with the passing light

before I left for anywhere
even if it was not for long
I climbed the last stairs to the door
onto the roof and turned among
the compass points to look along
the dark line across the river
where at one time when I was young
I tried to see what might be here

as the cars on the avenue
rushed in one current under me
red lights bobbing on their way to
the tunnel I hoped I would be
back before long to that city
and find everything still the same
as I was leaving it and we
would wake up there in the next time

how did it vanish even as
I stood watching at the window
I heard after dark the horses
at eleven when they would go
passing in double file below
the trembling panes and take the day
under all its blue helmets to
the barn down there a little way

when they had passed I thought I heard
a hush follow them for a while
in the avenue afterward
lasting perhaps only until

the lights changed by the hospital
and the late taxis thinning out
at that hour lunged ahead to sail
their double tracers down the street

and as the days themselves have gone
friends have not been there suddenly
so many leaving one by one
each of them taking a city
we knew that will not again be
seen until last night's barn gives back
once more into the coming day
the sons of laughing Gruagach

so many gone and there it burns
the stone flames climbing as they did
flashing again while the day turns
colors not caught or recorded
not recalled never repeated
fire of this time my one city
of what the light remembers made
bright present turn to ash slowly

now there remain out of those days
fewer friends than there used to be
there is more left than we can use
of this still unfinished city
running its old film Mercury
poised at corners over the pulse
that pounds as the living hurry
already late for somewhere else

as a child I came on a bridge
we rose over the white river
I saw all down the farther edge
shadows standing by the water
shining one behind another
the cables ran past one by one
then there were none and we were there
but the place I had seen was gone

in time I learned they were the same
though I could not say what they are
out of which these scant heirlooms come
that I must set in order for
friends still residing here and there
between the rivers though it is
a while since I have noted their
true condition in some cases

to Mike Keeley since I believe
we have been friends since both of us
were beginning to shave I leave
for his free uncontested use
what stretch of Morton Street may please
him best and his own choice of neighbors
and a magic wand to ease
his vacuum cleaner up the stairs

and for his guests who come to town
his own family or Mary's
or Jacqueline and Clarence Brown
I leave him the old Getty place
to remind them a bit of Greece
those white though flaking capitals
that facade out of other days
the severe lines of the old walls

Getty I suspect had not stayed
there for some time and it may be
no one after him had loved it
so the great plantations empty
and with the house naturally
goes the walled ailanthus garden
behind it for Mike and Mary
on spring evenings to wander in

and I leave to Galway Kinnell
friend I think for about as long
since those days in the dining hall
as waiters when we were too young

for the war and later coming
from Europe after years away
meeting again half believing
to compare notes in the city

the whole of Greenwich Street that runs
along the Hudson where the piers
stagger and groan when the tide turns
complaining idly by the waters
their tones drowned by the truck motors
tires on cobbles shouts unloading
carcasses into warehouse doors
and the racks of iron ringing

I leave him in particular
out of the high wall of facades
that look west across the river
toward Jersey and the Palisades
one where the wooden staircase leads
above a sausage factory
redolent echoing splintered treads
reaching the top floor finally

dusty machines and black pulleys
in the ceiling and a transom
ajar over the door that was
the way the burglar must have come
as he saw once when he got home
but had not taken anything
I hope he finds it all this time
just the same with nothing missing

to Jay Laughlin so he will have
somewhere to lay his head when he
stays in the city now I leave
at the west end of Waverly
on Bank Street the brick house where he
once learned the true height of the doors
so that wherever he may be
he knows it after all these years

and I leave to James Baker Hall
circling as the white pigeons do
above those roofs as though he still
were attached to a loft he knew
up over Seventh Avenue
his feet again in that high place
and for his coming to and fro
by the blue door his parking space

I leave Ben Sonnenberg the whole
of Eighth Street west of Fifth although
the fire keeps taking such a toll
it is scarcely the Rialto
that I expect he used to know
parts of a different parade
show up for dress rehearsals now
guessing what games are being played

to Richard Howard who has been
a perpetual prodigy
from the first phoneme he took in
I leave that end of Waverly
above the university
where the Villages east and west
echo each other endlessly
below the books that line his nest

and at moments to come when he
turns from words or from whatever
art sense discourse or faculty
held his attention I leave for
him to glance up and recover
the flash of that late salmon light
before sunset off the river
that glows along Eleventh Street

and to his gentle neighbor Grace
Schulman at that corner they share
already where Waverly Place
runs west into Washington Square

musicians jugglers the street fair
the sounds of an invisible
river rushing around her there
that she hears now when she stands still

to Bill Matthews to hear again
every note as he pleases though
he seems at home now far uptown
I leave the music that for so
long rose from under my window
that Vanguard where a few of his
late heroes used to come and go
with the sun in the black cases

to Harry Ford so he will have
somewhere disposed to keep body
and soul agreeable I leave
at the moment the Gramercy
Tavern and Union Square Café
both for variety an art
demands devotion constantly
though the taste of it may be short

to Alastair Reid born nomad
child of one island moving on
island by island satisfied
with what he could pack neatly in
a suitcase I leave on this stone
as it changes in the water
all the islands that he has known
turning up out of each other

to Francesco Pellizzi for
wherever he wants it to be
I leave the stillness of the water
toward the end of a winter day
at South Street by the Battery
the rivers gathered into one
that turns the color of the sky
and the lights starting to come on

I leave Gerald Stern the window
into his old apartment on
106th Street although
just the outside looking in
to see himself as he was then
and the faces still there in stone
before the five flights on Van Dam
and the windows that gaze uptown

over the low roofs toward that gray
tower cut out of another
plane part shadow making the day
in whose sky it appears appear
hard to believe shaped of mid-air
a specter named for some remote
image of another empire
that high beams color now at night

I stood beside that building one
summer before I started school
my mother took me that time when
she was getting me dressed for fall
we took the ferry to Canal
in those days and the street cars had
the sides open to keep them cool
a breeze came to us as we rode

the escalators of that day
Macy's I think and probably
Best's bird cages she used to say
that she never liked that city
but there were times it seemed when she
was happy to be there standing
beside a fountain telling me
who that was in gold and flying

we were walking down Lexington
and she said we were going to
pass the highest building in
the world the one she said I knew

that we always looked over to
across the river but today
I would stand and be able to
see up to the top all the way

after I had done that she said
if I would think of all that height
as the time the earth existed
before life had begun on it
yes with the spire on top of it
and the lightning rod then the time
since life began would lie on that
like a book she read to us from

and the whole age when there had been
life of the kind we knew which we
came to call human and our own
on top of that closed book would be
to the time underneath it only
as thick as one stamp that might be
on a post card but we would see
none of that where we were today

we walked along the avenue
over the stamp I had not seen
where would the card be going to
that the stamp was to be put on
would I see what was written down
on it whenever it was sent
and the few words what would they mean
that we took with us as we went

Inauguration

Whose was the hand then
around the bolted door
that first night in the house
empty for decades

beyond the dark floor piled with rubble
while outside the broken panes only the long
unseen cold grass of spring was stirring

one hand like a gray rag fluttering
unmistakable in the black doorway
inching toward the bolt as though
a wind were pushing it from behind
and a dim light going before it
leading this way this way

the swallows in the beams
never stirred in their own furled sleep
no sound came from the cracks in the walls
Even if it went away
I would have seen it
even if it did nothing
it would know I had come

A Claim

Even through the days as a believer
doubt would shadow the distant light
over the valley deep in itself
the voices that rang clear of it
never lingered
and long before I left
I had already gone

each time I turned away
it all stepped into that water
where it would seem to be the same
almost the same
and the heart would sink at the sight of it
without knowing why
the same heart come again
once more expecting nothing
and caught by what was never there

That Music

By the time I came to hear about it
I was assured that there was no such thing
no it was one more in the long trailing
troupe of figures that had been believed but
had never existed no it had not
resounded in the dark at the beginning
no among the stars there was no singing
then or later no ringing single note
threaded the great absences no echoing
of space in space no there was no calling
along the lights anywhere no it was not
in the choiring of water in the saying
of a name it was not living or warning
through the thrush of dusk or the wren of morning

The Wren

Paper clips are rusted to the pages
before I have come back to hear a bell
I recognize out of another age
echo from the cold mist of one morning
in white May and then a wren still singing
from the thicket at the foot of the wall

that is one of the voices without question
and without answer like the beam of some
star familiar but in no sense known threading
time upon time on its solitary way
once more I hear it without understanding
and without division in the new day

Syllables

Mornings of fog with the voices of birds
flicking through it names rising to whisper
after them like the mist closing behind
I have brought my life here where it must have been once
whitethroat chaffinch who see everything once
I have brought it back remembering them
so there must be something of it here now
in the fog flying once without a name

Wanting to See

Some moss might be the color of the book
in which all the feathers were black and white
it was better that way they assured her
turning the pages never trust colors
of birds on paper in life they are not
like that the true ones flying in a day
that has since been removed they have been seen
looking out through their names in those black trees
the river turned white before you were born

Orioles

The song of the oriole began as an echo
but this year it was not heard afterward
or before or at all and only later
would anyone notice what had not been there
when the cuckoo had been heard again
a calling shadow but not the goldfinch
with its gold and not that voice through the waterfall
the oriole flashing under the window
among the trees now at the end of the hall
of the palace one of the palaces
St Augustine told about Here he said

you enter into the great palaces
of memory and whose palaces were they
I wondered at first knowing that he
must have been speaking from memory
of his own of palaces of his own
with his own days echoing in the halls

Jeanne Duval

There are those he said
who would not be at all surprised
that it seemed to you
familiar as you have named it
though remember that
we who have been here all the time
seeing it as our
own are less likely to have it
emerge before us
for the first time ancient as light
and know it at once
out of all we have forgotten

now that you tell us
how it appeared to you he said
we catch sight of it
ourselves as you may have seen it
in this deep forest
the valley curtained with shadows
of oaks the mossed roofs
where the tracks come out of the woods
the hamlet of Jeanne
Duval and rising from the lane
this one plain building
its pink stone glowing like a lamp

arches at the base
of the walls none like the others
across wide porches

opened at different times into
the main manor of
Jeanne Duval perhaps it was this
which you thought you were
seeing years ago beside those
oaks and that fountain
that empty village those arches
that tower and one
old man trying to remember

it would not be true
to say we knew you were coming
any more than we
can think that the ancestors knew
that we would be here
but just as your sight of the house
the sound of its name
from the line of mothers the door
where you came into
the swirl of dogs children faces
of different ages
to stand in a large family

set your blood beating
suddenly faster as though you
had been there before
so each of us seems to know you
and will tell you that
after you have gone in to meet
Jeanne Duval herself
she will be happy to see you
how long it has been
some of it will come back something
that you recognize
you will know her when you see her

Sheep Passing

Mayflies hover through the long evening
of their light and in the winding lane
the stream of sheep runs among shadows calling
the old throats gargling again uphill
along known places once more and from the bells
borne by their predecessors the notes
dull as wood clonk to the flutter of all
the small hooves over the worn stone
with the voices of the lambs rising through them
over and over telling and asking
their one question into the day they have
none will know midsummer the walls of the lane
are older than anyone can understand
and the lane must have been a path a long time
before the first stones were raised beside it
and must have been a trail from the river
up through the trees for an age before that
one hoof one paw one foot before another
the way they went is all that is still there

Moissac

Now I see it after years of holding
reflections of parts of it in my mind
children have been born here and have grown up
married gone off to war divorced and died
since the last time I stood on these same stones
whose white is the color I remember
but I see the colors of all of them
on walls and here and there on the carved stones
had fallen away from me as they had
been falling before I had ever seen them
from the walls and the figures carved in stone
it is quieter than I remember

smaller of course and closer and the smile
of Eve harder than ever to see there
is it a smile after all the hollow
in the stone face by the doorway looking
down at the serpent climbing onto her
in silence neither one hearing ages
behind them from which they have come nor those
before them in the colors of the days

Seed Time

The old photographs the prints that survived
made their way into the days of August
into the backs of the deep glaring noons
August came and already they were in place
old in arrival and knowing the ways
of settlers though not of the first ones they
recall no colors nor what those were good for
initials have become dust and shadows
water is wrapped in sheets and glass is blank
but here and there faces go on staring
from paper without moving or noticing
that August has come that this is August
here is the bird of August and the dry breeze
stirring the leaves in the dust of morning
here is the white sky that has come at last
here is the bright day the prints have led to

Frame

But look this is not yet
the other age
this is the only one
between the brown
pictures and the blank film

there was even
a sign saying Today
in a window
but what it was announcing
was days ago

I forget now
what it was there to say
it was something
else whatever
is announced is over

whether or not
it has been seen at dusk
when it is time
to grow up and too late
to take pictures

Shore Birds

While I think of them they are growing rare
after the distances they have followed
all the way to the end for the first time
tracing a memory they did not have
until they set out to remember it
at an hour when all at once it was late
and newly silent and the white had turned
white around them then they rose in their choir
on a single note each of them alone
between the pull of the moon and the hummed
undertone of the earth below them
the glass curtains kept falling around them
as they flew in search of their place before
they were anywhere and storms winnowed them
they flew among the places with towers
and passed the tower lights where some vanished
with their long legs for wading in shadow
others were caught and stayed in the countries

of the nets and in the lands of the lime twigs
some fastened and after the countries of
guns at first light fewer of them than I
remember would be here to recognize
the light of late summer when they found it
playing with darkness along the wet sand

Waves in August

There is a war in the distance
with the distance growing smaller
the field glasses lying at hand
are for keeping it far away

I thought I was getting better
about that returning childish
wish to be living somewhere else
that I knew was impossible
and now I find myself wishing
to be here to be alive here
it is impossible enough
to still be the wish of a child

in youth I hid a boat under
the bushes beside the water
knowing I would want it later
and come back and would find it there
someone else took it and left me
instead the sound of the water
with its whisper of vertigo

terror reassurance an old
old sadness it would seem we knew
enough always about parting
but we have to go on learning
as long as there is anything

Travelling West at Night

I remember waking at the rivers
to see girders of gray sleepless bridges
appearing from sleep out of a current
of cold night air velvet with the secret
coal smoke of those small hours and nobody
on night roads the few words of toll-keepers
old complaints of gates and cables the bark
of bridge floors leaping up from under us
and the swelling hiss of a surface just
beneath us not loud but while it was there
nothing else could be heard except as calls
far off in some distance meaning that we
were already there in the dark country
before in the land beyond the rivers
one by one past the clutched hunches of sleep
the black country where we were expected
was waiting ahead of us on the far
shore unchanged remembering us even
when we had forgotten and then we went
on into the wordless dark beyond each
river thinking that we were going back

This Time

Many things I seem to have done backward
as a child I wanted to be older
now I am trying to remember why
and what it was like to have to pretend
day after day I saw places that I
did not recognize until later on
when nothing was left of them any more
there were meetings and partings that passed me
at the time like train windows with the days
slipping across them and long afterward
the moment and sense of them came to me
burning there were faces I knew for years

and the nearness of them began only
when they were missing and there were seasons
of anguish I recalled with affection
joys lost unnoticed and searched for later
with no sign to show where they had last been
there with me and there was love which is thought
to be a thing of youth and I found it
I was sure that was what it was as I
came to it again and again sometimes
without knowing it sometimes insisting
vainly upon the name but I came to
the best of it last and though it may be
shorter this way I am glad it is so
it would have been too brief at any time
and so much of what I had found early
had been lost as I made my way to this
which is what I was to know afterward

The Notes

I was not the right age to begin
to be taught to play the violin
Dr Perpetuo told my father
when I was four with these very hands
were we too young in his opinion
or were we already too old by then
I come now with no real preparation
to finger the extinct instruments
that I know only by reputation
after these years of trying to listen
to learn what I was listening for
what it is that I am trying to hear
it is something I had begun
giving ear to all unknown
before that day with its explanation
about the strings and how before you can
play the notes you have to make each one
I never even learned how to listen

Left Hand

One morning I look at it with surprise
that gives off a known but fathomless sound
what is it that I recognize with such
unappeased gratitude this is what I
have taken to be my own all my life
my own left hand that had nothing to do
but what I wanted as well as it could
that grew up with me as a part of me
with no mind of its own that I know of
and no existence apart from my own
its scars its habits are my own story
it does not hear what I say about it
or know what I know of its long journey
before it was mine the little finger
reaching to touch the thumb the first time
startled speechless finding the way to it
again kindling a brightness beyond it
to which it belonged and with which it was
going what can I say to it even
now when it has helped me on to the words
that have been picked up before I had learned
what they might be for and when the time comes
to use them what can they hold and carry
how far can they reach what sense will they touch

Late Glimpse

They were years younger than I am
centuries ago
when they spoke of themselves as old
looking at the empty sky

end of November as we call it now
winter light no age over the gray sea
a petrel flies in at evening
trailing its feet in the sunset

Accompaniment

Day alone first of December with rain
falling lightly again in the garden
and the dogs sleeping on the dark floorboards
day between journeys unpacking from one

then packing for another and reading
poems as I go words from a time past
light migrants coming from so long ago
through the sound of this quiet rain falling

Field Note

Its marbled fields remember spring
dew in the bare light shimmering
and the surprise of beginning
when there was only the morning
with its unknown high clouds passing
neither pausing nor listening
while its branches were opening
white flowers to their day shining
that one time and a bell ringing
in the north and no one counting

The String

Night the black bead
a string running through it
with the sound of a breath

lights are still there from
long ago when
they were not seen

in the morning
it was explained
to me that the one

we call the morning star
and the evening
star are the same

THE PUPIL

(2001)

For Paula

Prophecy

At the end of the year the stars go out
the air stops breathing and the Sibyl sings
first she sings of the darkness she can see
she sings on until she comes to the age
without time and the dark she cannot see

no one hears then as she goes on singing
of all the white days that were brought to us one
by one that turned to colors around us

a light coming from far out in the eye
where it begins before she can see it

burns through the words that no one has believed

The Comet Museum

So the feeling comes afterward
some of it may reach us only
long afterward when the moment
itself is beyond reckoning

beyond time beyond memory
as though it were not moving in
heaven neither burning farther
through any past nor ever to
arrive again in time to be
when it has gone the senses wake

all through the day they wait for it
here are pictures that someone took
of what escaped us at the time
only now can we remember

Sonnet

Where it begins will remain a question
for the time being at least which is to
say for this lifetime and there is no
other life that can be this one again
and where it goes after that only one
at a time is ever about to know
though we have it by heart as one and though
we remind each other on occasion

How often may the clarinet rehearse
alone the one solo before the one
time that is heard after all the others
telling the one thing that they all tell of
it is the sole performance of a life
come back I say to it over the waters

The Time of Shadow

This is the hour Marais told us about
some time in the days before we were born
while the sun went down over Africa
in the youth of the century and age
gathered upon him with the returning
black ceiling of morphine   Eugène Marais
watching our ancestors in the evening
our contemporaries in the strange world
their descendants had made as shadows reached
toward them he recognized in their shadow
a shadow of his own it was the time
for boasting before the end of the day
strutting and playing having decided
upon the sleeping place near the water
the time of the children playing swinging
by a rock pool and then the sun went down
and the voices fell silent and the games
were still and the old were overcome with

a great sadness and then the sounds of mourning
began for the whole loss without a name
he called it the hour of Hesperean
Melancholy but as he knew it could
visit at its own moment here it is
the choir loft in the church burned long ago
childhood in a blue robe and suddenly
no sound but the depth of loss unknown loss
irreparable and nameless and tears
with no word for them although there may be
playing again later in the darkness
even for a long time in the moonlight
and singing again out of the dark trees

The Hours of Darkness

When there are words
waiting in line once more
I find myself looking
into the eyes of an old
man I have seen before
who is holding a long white cane
as he stares past my head
talking of poems and youth

after him a shadow
where I thought to see a face
asks have you considered
how often you return
to the subject of not seeing
to the state of blindness
whether you name it or not
do you intend to speak of that
as often as you do
do you mean anything by it

I look up into the year
that the black queen could still see

the year of the alien lights
appearing to her and then going
away with the others
the year of the well of darkness
overflowing with no
moon and no stars

it was there all the time
behind the eye of day
Rumphius saw it before
he had words for anything
long before he wrote
of the hermit crab *These*
wanderers live in the houses
of strangers wondering
where they had come from
Vermeij in our time
never saw any creature
living or as a fossil
but can summon by touch
the story of a cowrie
four hundred million years old
scars ancestry and what
it knew in the dark sea

there Borges is talking
about Milton's sonnet
and Milton hears the words
of Samson to someone else
and Homer is telling
of a landscape without horizons
and the blind knight whom no one
ever could touch with a sword
says in my head there is
only darkness
so they never find me
but I know where they are

it is the light
that appears to change and be many
to be today
to flutter as leaves
to recognize the rings of the trees
to come again
one of the stars is from
the day of the cowrie
one is from a time in the garden
we see the youth of the light
in all its ages
we see it as bright
points of animals
made long ago out of night

how small the day is
the time of colors
the rush of brightness

Flights in the Dark

After nights of rain
the great moths of December
drift through green fronds
into the end of the year

I watch their eyes
on the door near midnight
memories of the sun
near the solstice

and their wings made of darkness
the memory of darkness
flying in time
remembering this night

The Marfa Lights

Are they there in the daytime
east of town on the way to Paisano Pass
rising unseen by anyone
climbing in long arcs over Mitchell Flat
candles at noon being carried
by hands never named never caught on film
never believed as they go up the long stairs
of the light to glide in secret or dance
along the dazzling halls out of sight
above where the air shimmers like a sea

only when the curtain of light
is fading thin above the black Glass Mountains
and the first stars are glittering
do the claims of sightings begin
they may occur from anywhere facing
the removes of those broken horizons
though most of them nowadays
are likely to come from somewhere on Route 90
looking south toward the Chinatis
a marker has been set up by the road there

and cars begin to stop before
sundown pulling over into the lay-by
designated with rimrocks folding chairs
are unlimbered while there is still light
and positioned among the piled stones at spots
expecting them as niches along
sea cliffs expect their old fishermen
tripods are set up and telescopes
they all seem to know what they are waiting for

then buses with lines of faces
peering over each other at the windows
at one time out there was the place to take
a date it used to mean something different
if you said you had been out to see
the lights but almost everybody

had seen them whether or not they had
seen just the same things and all were shadowed by
the same explanations there were reports
of those lights before there were cars or ranches

they were seen over wagon trains
on their way up from the valley and seen shining
above the bare moving forests
of cattle horns in the pass sometimes a light
would drift and swell and suddenly
shudder and fly up bursting apart from one
color to another some say
they will turn out to be something simple
a trick of the atmosphere
and some do not think they are anything

insisting that people will believe
whatever they want to in the same way
that herdsmen and cowhands in the Chinatis
for a hundred years would whisper
that the lights were the ghost of the war chief
Alsate who had been captured
and dragged off to his death and his followers
sold into slavery of course
by now there have been investigations

inconclusive until the present
telling us in our turn what we do not know
what the evidence amounts to
perhaps and how far the theories have gone
to suggest what these bright appearances
portend in the eye of the mind where we know
from the beginning that the darkness
is beyond us there is no explaining
the dark it is only the light
that we keep feeling a need to account for

Migrants by Night

Weeks after the solstice
now in the winter night
the roar of surf thunders
from the foot of the sea cliffs
the heavy swells crashing
after their voyages
out of the deep north
the roar lifts from them
to roll on without them
as they break in the foam
of the ones before them
with that sound under them
carrying the mountain
into the midst of the sea

which they have always been
since the first motion
that was in no place then
out of no place began
gathering itself in turn
to become a direction
under the clear wind
from the place of origin
that now lifts the thin
swift cries of the plovers
over the dark ocean
each one calling alone
unseen to hear again
another in the wind

in a season between
journeys with no horizon
they fly in the night
as though it could be known
from season to season
as though it were their own
to hear each other in
while it turns around them

and the waves of light flow in
from the first motion
bringing it with them
all the way to the moment
when the cry comes again
again before it flies on

In the Open

Those summer nights when the planes came over
it seemed it was every night that summer
after the still days of perfect weather
I kept telling myself what it was not
that I was feeling as the afternoon
light deepened into the lingering
radiance that colored its leaving us
that was the light through which I would come home
again and again with the day over
picking my way from Whitehall through the new
rubble in the known streets the broken glass
signaling from among the crevices
fallen facades hoses among the mounds
figures in rubber coming and going
at the ruins or gathered with lowered
voices they all spoke in lowered voices
as I recall now so that all I heard
was the murmured current I can still hear
how many in that building I might hear
something like that how many in that one
then a quiet street the shop doors open
figures waiting in lines without a word
with the night ahead no it was not fear
I said to myself that was not the word
for whatever I heard as the door closed
as we talked of the day as we listened
as the fork touched the plate like a greeting
as the curtains were drawn as the cat stretched
as the news came on with word of losses

warning of the night as we picked up the ground sheet
and the folded blankets as I bent down
to remember the fur of Tim the cat
as the door closed and the stairs in the dark
led us back down to the street and the night
swung wide before us once more in the park
Often after the all-clear it would be
very cold suddenly a reminder
hardly more than that as I understood
of the great cold of the dark everywhere
around us deeper than I could believe
usually she was asleep by then
warm and breathing softly I could picture
how she must look the long curve of her lips
the high white forehead I wondered about
her eyelids and what calm they had come to
while the ice reached me much of the night was
in pieces by then behind me piled up
like rubble all fallen into the same
disorder the guns shouting from the hill
the drones and the broad roar of planes the screams
of sirens the pumping of bombs coming
closer the beams groping over the smoke
they all seemed to have ended somewhere without
saying this is the last one you seldom
hear the dog stop barking there were people
on all sides of us in the park asleep
awake the sky was clear I lay looking
up into it through the cold to the lights
the white moments that had traveled so long
each one of them to become visible
to us then only for that time and then
where did they go in the dark afterward
the invisible dark the cold never
felt or ever to be felt where was it
then as I lay looking up into all
that had been coming to pass and was still
coming to pass some of the stars by then
were nothing but the light that had left them
before there was life on earth and nothing

would be seen after them and the light from
one of them would have set out exactly
when the first stir of life recognized death
and began its delays that light had been
on its way from there all through what happened
afterward through the beginning of pain
the return of pain into the senses
into feelings without words and then words
traveling toward us even in our sleep
words for the feelings of those who are not
there now and words we say are for ourselves
then sounds of feet went by in the damp grass
dark figures slipping away toward morning

Overtone

Some listening were certain they could hear
through the notes summoned from the strings one more
following at a distance low but clear
a resonance never part of the score
not noticed during the rehearsals nor
prayed into the performance and yet here
with the first note it had been waiting for
holding silent the iced minors of fear
the key of grief the mourning from before
the names were read of those no longer there
that sound of what made no sound any more
made up the chords that in a later year
some still believed that they could overhear
echoing music played during a war

Fires in Childhood

That Sunday we drove home through the mountains
it was gray spring Easter the trees still bare
by the river my father was somewhere

in England the radio on for once
each fading station crackling the same news
through paper far off the bombs coming down
behind the voices all night on London
the city burning and the searchlight rays
groping up through the smoke St. Paul's was still
untouched though waves of bombs went on falling
I kept seeing Alice roller skating
and close to me on the piano stool
whom my fat cousin claimed he found sitting
on the floor once so he saw everything

Glassy Sea

As you see each of the stars has a voice
and at least one long syllable before
words as we know them and can recall them
later one by one with their company
around them after the sound of them has
gone from its moment even though we may
say it again and again it is gone
again far into our knowledge there are
words as we know for whatever does not
die with us but the sound of those words lasts
no longer than the others it is heard
only for part of the length of a breath
among those clear syllables never heard
from which the words were made in another
time and the syllables themselves are not
there forever some may go all the way
to the beginning but not beyond it

The Moment

In the country in which I was a child
in an age some time before mine they found
a black river sleeping deep in the ground
stream of black glass veined current of night stone
old to the touch and they believed it was
for them to burn though the ones who woke it
died of it in the sunlight by their doors
breath sifting the blackened days still it was
broken like glass and gleamed like the surface
of a river older than the river
and was polished as an eye but an eye
from the sleep this side of the diamond
taking from the light of the present
nothing that we can tell or that we see
not noticing everything that has gone
but staring at what has yet to happen

Any Time

How long ago the day is
when at last I look at it
with the time it has taken
to be there still in it
now in the transparent light
with the flight in the voices
the beginning in the leaves
everything I remember
and before it before me
present at the speed of light
in the distance that I am
who keep reaching out to it
seeing all the time faster
where it has never stirred from
before there is anything
the darkness thinking the light

Far Company

At times now from some margin of the day
I can hear birds of another country
not the whole song but a brief phrase of it
out of a music that I may have heard
once in a moment I appear to have
forgotten for the most part that full day
no sight of which I can remember now
though it must have been where my eyes were then
that knew it as the present while I thought
of somewhere else without noticing that
singing when it was there and still went on
whether or not I noticed now it falls
silent when I listen and leaves the day
and flies before it to be heard again
somewhere ahead when I have forgotten

Aliens

When they appeared on the terrace soon after daybreak
high above the sea with the tide far out I thought at first
they were sparrows which by now seem to have found their
    way everywhere
following us at their own small distances arguing over
pieces of our shadows to take up into their brief flights
eluding our attention by seeming unremarkable
quick instantaneous beyond our grasp as they are in
    themselves
complete lives flashing from the beginning each eye bearing
the beginning in its dusty head and even their voices
seemed at first to be the chatter of sparrows half small talk
    half bickering
but no when I looked more closely they were linnets the
    brilliant
relatives the wanderers out of another part of the story

with their heads the colors of the ends of days and that
    unsoundable
gift for high delicate headlong singing that has rung
even out of vendors' cages when the morning light has
    touched them

Mid-Air Mirror

When I looked across the river
to where we are sitting talking
quietly in the high white room
through the late winter afternoon
old friends found after a long time

what I saw from that end of time
was only the light reflected
on all the buildings facing west
the Metropolitan Tower
white and the brick cliffs glittering
high beyond the green ferry barns
and untouched day where we are now

the ferry barns have disappeared
and ferries passing back and forth
on the loom of fine river light
while we have pursued a notion
that we were learning as we turned

among the galaxies learning
we called it as we recognized
some place we were and the known light
sometimes voices of friends again
but not ourselves the dark of space
not ourselves yet the farthest light

A Term

At the last minute a word is waiting
not heard that way before and not to be
repeated or ever be remembered
one that always had been a household word
used in speaking of the ordinary
everyday recurrences of living
not newly chosen or long considered
or a matter for comment afterward
who would ever have thought it was the one
saying itself from the beginning through
all its uses and circumstances to
utter at last that meaning of its own
for which it had long been the only word
though it seems now that any word would do

Unspoken Greeting

Morning without number not yet knowing of such things
coming out before anything to the eyes of birds
hushed light before the sun brings back the reflections of
    syllables
cool instant when the colors lie deep in a breath before
    meaning
presence never identified given back now altogether
out of the unbroken dark and the beams of stars that were
    not there
behind the whole of night out of their light you appear once
rising through yourself in stillness at the speed of starlight
while the dragonfly hovers above the glassy pond
on its wings of veined sky before occurrence or mention
boundless morning not ever to be approached or believed or
    seen again

The Open Land

Mist iridescent over the rice fields
mountains far away those gray fish running
so that they scarcely seem to be moving
rolled hay camped nearby in shaven meadows
sleeping into winter as the roads sleep
into themselves into their unseen age
leading the whole of their lives while the light
appears always to come from just before
so that all of it seems to be familiar
known in passing like clouds but the only
words for it are ways to tell of distance

Before the Flood

Why did he promise me
that we would build ourselves
an ark all by ourselves
out in back of the house
on New York Avenue
in Union City New Jersey
to the singing of the streetcars
after the story
of Noah whom nobody
believed about the waters
that would rise over everything
when I told my father
I wanted us to build
an ark of our own there
in the backyard under
the kitchen could we do that
he told me that we could
I want to I said and will we
he promised me that we would
why did he promise that
I wanted us to start then
nobody will believe us

I said that we are building
an ark because the rains
are coming and that was true
nobody ever believed
we would build an ark there
nobody would believe
that the waters were coming

A Calling

My father is telling me the story of Samuel
not for the first time and yet he is not quite repeating
nor rehearsing nor insisting he goes on telling me
in the empty green church smelling of carpet and late dust
where he calls to mind words of the prophets to mumble in a
    remote language
and the prophets are quoting the Lord who is someone they
    know
who has been talking to them my father tells what the Lord
said to them and Samuel listened and heard someone calling
    someone
and Samuel answered Here I am and my father is saying
that is the answer that should be given he is telling me
that someone is calling and that is the right answer
he is telling me a story he wants me to believe
telling me the right answer and the way it was spoken
in that story he wants to believe in which someone is calling

Remembering the Signs

My father took me to Coney Island
that one time because it was closed or on
the point of closing a day past the end
of summer and the hot busy season
so we could see the place it had happened
up until then where the rides had begun

into that silence gates had shut behind
he told me how dangerous they had been
even if we had come when they opened
there was not one on which we would have gone
nor paid for tickets into the darkened
side shows to look at what should not be seen
it was enough he said to walk around
getting to see it just as it was then

Lit in Passing

In the first sound of their own feet
on the steps outside the empty
house they might have heard it under
the talk that day as it told them
in a language they pretended
not to understand a word of

here begins the hollow to come

presenting itself as a small
triumph before he turned forty
the big house twelve echoing rooms
thirty-six windows that would need
curtains my mother said at once
and the huge church across the street

everything to be done over
fresh and new at the beginning
in those first milk and honey days
even new stained glass windows made
downstairs on the long tables of
the church kitchen the webs of lead
and gray glass waiting for the light

they even made one at that time
for the house the manse a window
over the landing on the stairs

halfway up my mother never
liked it she did not explain why
there was a shield with a ruby
at the center a red point climbed
up the stairs through the afternoon
marked us as we went up and down

those last years we were together

At Night Before Spring

Two nights before the equinox that will
turn into spring in the dark the next time
before the last spring in a thousand years
as we count them I find myself looking
at the transparent indigo humor
that we called the night back in the daytime
and I see beyond acceleration
each of the lights complete in its own time
in the stillness of motion the stillness
with no beginning all in one moment
a friend beside me whom I do not see
without words making it come clear to me
the youth of heaven the ages of light
each of them whole in the unmoving blue
each with its number known in the unknown
each with its only self in the one eye
even as I watch it we are passing
the numbers are rising as I am told
they will rise and it will be spring again
it seems that I have forgotten nothing
I believe I have not lost anyone

One Night in April

Tonight no sound
of any bird
second night after
the full moon
only the wind now
I think the plovers
must have flown
I see the silver
clouds crossing the moon
out of the east
northeast
moving fast
a day ago
I heard them
fly over calling
and a night ago
they were still here
I heard them overhead
but by now they are
maybe a thousand
miles on their way
northward over
the dark of the ocean
as they fly they are
calling those two
notes now too far
tonight to hear

Unknown Bird

Out of the dry days
through the dusty leaves
far across the valley
those few notes never
heard here before

one fluted phrase
floating over its
wandering secret
all at once wells up
somewhere else

and is gone before it
goes on fallen into
its own echo leaving
a hollow through the air
that is dry as before

where is it from
hardly anyone
seems to have noticed it
so far but who now
would have been listening

it is not native here
that may be the one
thing we are sure of
it came from somewhere
else perhaps alone

so keeps on calling for
no one who is here
hoping to be heard
by another of its own
unlikely origin

trying once more the same few
notes that began the song
of an oriole last heard
years ago in another
existence there

it goes again tell
no one it is here
foreign as we are
who are filling the days
with a sound of our own

Daylight

It is said that after he was seventy
Ingres returned to the self-portrait
he had painted at twenty-four and he
went on with it from that far off though
there was no model and in the mirror
only the empty window and gray sky
and the light in which his hand was lifted
a hand which the eyes in the painting would not
have recognized at first raised in a way
they would never see whatever he might
bring to them nor would they ever see him
as he had come to be then watching them
there where he had left them and while he looked
into them from no distance as he thought
holding the brush in the day between them

Worn

Then what I come back to now is
an age that I could not have seen
until this time and as others
I knew did not live to see it
but where is it at this moment
in spring when the morning shows me
again what I thought I had known
for so long the river taking
its time the stones lifted out
of the ground and set into walls
for a while waiting to return
the tools passed from hand to hand
keeping the shine of the handles
the hollows of the stone doorsills
polished as though they were daylight
so that I step over them to
turn into the time I go through

Downstream

Those two for whom two rivers had been named
how could it be that nobody knew them
nobody had seen them nobody seemed
to have anything to say about them
or maybe even to believe in them
if I asked who was Juniata who
was Marietta finding their names on
the map again feeling my throat tighten
and a day growing warmer in my chest
if I heard their names so I knew they were
secret and I was silent when we traveled
when we came close to them and caught sight
of the skin of water under the bending
trees the curves where they came out of hiding
and every time always they were different
always in secret they were beautiful
they had been waiting for me before I
heard they were there and they knew everything
Juniata was older sometimes and
sometimes a girl a late day in summer
a longed-for homecoming Marietta
was a little ahead of me waiting
and shy about nothing taking my hand
showing me and what has become of them
who would believe now what they were like once
nobody can remember the rivers

Before the May Fair

Last night with our minds still in cold April
in the late evening we watched the river
heavy with the hard rains of the recent spring
as it wheeled past wrapped in its lowered note
by the gray walls at the foot of the streets
through the gray twilight of this season
the cars vanished one by one unnoticed

folded away like animals and last
figures walking dogs went in and shutters
closed gray along gray houses leaving
the streets empty under the cries of swifts
turning above the chimneys the trailers
parked under the trees by the riverbank
stood as though they were animals asleep
while the animals standing in the trucks
were awake stirring and the animals
waiting in the slaughterhouse were awake
the geese being fattened with their feet nailed
to the boards were awake as the small lights
went out over doorways and the river
slipped through the dark time under the arches
of the stone bridge restored once more after
the last war the bells counted the passing
hours one sparrow all night by a window
kept saying This This This until the streets
were the color of dark clouds and under
the trees in the cold down by the river
the first planks were laid out across the trestles
and cold hands piled them for the coming day

Once in Spring

A sentence continues after thirty years
it wakes in the silence of the same room
the words that come to it after the long comma
existed all that time wandering in space
as points of light travel unseen through ages
of which they alone are the measure and arrive
at last to tell of something that came to pass
before they ever began or meant anything

longer ago than that Pierre let himself in
through the gate under the cherry tree and said
Jacques is dead and his feet rustled the bronze leaves
of the cherry tree the October leaves fallen

before he set out to walk on their curled summer
then as suddenly Pierre was gone without warning
and the others all the others who were announced
after they had gone with what they had of their summer
and the cherry tree was done and went the way of its leaves

as they wake in the sentence the words remember
but each time only a remnant and it may be
that they say little and there is the unspoken
morning late in spring the early light passing
and the cuckoo hiding beyond its voice and once more
the oriole that was silent from age to age
voices heard once only and then long listened for

The Veil of May

No more than a week and the leaves
have all come out on the ash trees
now they are more than half open
on the ancient walnuts standing
alone in the field reaching up
through the mute amazement of age
they have uncurled on the oaks from
hands small as the eyelids of birds
and the morning light shines through them
and waits while the hawthorn gleams white
against the green in the shadow
in a moment the river has
disappeared down in the valley
the curve of sky gliding slowly
from before not seeming to move
it will not be seen again now
a while from this place on the ridge
but over it the summer will
flow and not seem to be moving

The Youth of Animals

They start by learning to listen
for the approach of the first time
ages before their eyes open
upon the night that holds them
younger than the night they had known
which was always whole and unseen
and then they see the first light come
to find them and when it knows them
they call out for it is the one
that they knew before they began

then what happens is the first time
and they see it all around them
as they know the song of hunger
repeating the notes of its climb
out of them and hear the answer
coming back to its only name
the way one after the other
the days come back to the same
faces where they have lived before
and find them again the first time

there was never a time before
but each day the eyes are wider
and the horizon tempts them more
whenever they see it again
one morning they wander farther
out toward it than ever before
not sure what they have come for
and then they come to the first time
and before they know it are gone
that one time and the time after

The Hollow in the Stone

Not every kind of water will do
to make the pool under the rock face
that afterward will be clear forever

not the loud current of great event
already far downstream in its moment
heavy with the dark waste of cities
not the water of falling
with its voice far away from it
not the water that ran with the days
and runs with them now

only the still water
that we can see through all the way
whatever we remember
the clear water from before
that was there under the reflections
of the leaves in spring and beyond
and under the clouds passing below them

Late Song

Long evening at the end of spring
with soft rain falling and flowing
from the eaves into the broken
stone basin outside the window
a blackbird warning of nightfall
coming and I hear it again
announcing that it will happen
darkness and the day will be gone
as I heard it all years ago
knowing no more than I know now
but once more I sit and listen
in the same still room to the rain
at the end of spring and again
hear the blackbird in the evening

The Source

There in the fringe of trees between
the upper field and the edge of the one
below it that runs above the valley
one time I heard in the early
days of summer the clear ringing
six notes that I knew were the opening
of the Fingal's Cave Overture
I heard them again and again that year
and the next summer and the year
afterward those six descending
notes the same for all the changing
in my own life since the last time
I had heard them fall past me from
the bright air in the morning of a bird
and I believed that what I had heard
would always be there if I came again
to be overtaken by that season
in that place after the winter
and I would wonder again whether
Mendelssohn really had heard them somewhere
far to the north that many years ago
looking up from his youth to listen to
those six notes of an ancestor
spilling over from a presence neither
water nor human that led to the cave
in his mind the fluted cliffs and the wave
going out and the falling water
he thought those notes could be the music for
Mendelssohn is gone and Fingal is gone
all but his name for a cave and for one
piece of music and the black-capped warbler
as we called that bird that I remember
singing there those notes descending
from the age of the ice dripping
I have not heard again this year can it
be gone then will I not hear it
from now on will the overture begin

for a time and all those who listen
feel that falling in them but as always
without knowing what they recognize

First Sight

There once more the new moon in spring
above the roofs of the village
in the clear sky the cold twilight
under the evening star the thin
shell sinking so lightly it seems
not to be moving and no sound
from the village at this moment
nor from the valley below it
with its still river nor even
from any of the birds and I
have been standing here in this light
seeing this moon and its one star
while the cows went home with their bells
and the sheep were folded and gone
and the elders fell silent one
after another and loved souls
were no longer seen and my hair
turned white and I was looking up
out of a time of late blessings

First of June

Night when the south wind wakes the owl
and the owl says it is summer
now it is time to be summer
it is time for that departure
though the blanket dates from childhood
it is time whoever you are
to be going they are older
every one of them there is spring
no longer this is the south wind

you have heard about that brings rain
taking away roofs with a breath
and a season of grapes in one
blind unpredictable moment
of hail this is the white wind that
you cannot believe here it is
and the owl sails out to see whose
turn it is tonight to be changed

Unseen Touch

Surprised again in the dark by the sound of rain
falling slowly steadily a reassurance
after all with no need to say anything
in spite of the memories of dust and the parched waiting
the green lost and the slow bleaching out of the hills
here is the known hand again knowing remembering
at night after the doubting and the news of age

The Summer

After we come to see it and
know we scarcely live without it
we begin trying to describe
what art is and it seems to be
something we believe is human
whatever that is something that
says what we are but then the same
beam of recognition stops at
one penguin choosing a pebble
to offer to the penguin he
hopes to love and later the dance
of awkwardness holding an egg
on one foot away from the snow
of summer the balancing on
one foot in the flash of summer

The Black Virgin

You are not part of knowing are you
at the top of the stairs in the white cliff
in the deep valley smelling of summer
you are not part of vanity although
it may have climbed up on its knees to you
and paid to be a name cut on the way
you do not need the candles before you
you would not see them I suppose if you
were to open your eyelids you are not
seen in what is visible it appears
and the crown is not part of you whatever
it is made of nor the robe of days
with its colors glittering you are not
part of pride or owning or understanding
and the questions that have been carried to you
life after life lie there unseen at your feet
oh presence in silence while the dark swifts
flash past with one cry out in the sunlight

To the Spiders of This Room

You who waited here before me
in silence mothers of silence
I always knew you were present
whether or not I could see you
in your gray clouds your high corners
spinners of the depths of shadows

who recur without memory
rising from beneath the moment
as it breathes trembles and is gone
bearers of a message not known
heirs of an unseen lineage

this is the moment to thank you
for ever appearing to me

through these years keepers of no word
attentive in this mute room while
the bird sang and the rain murmured
and the voice echoed from the road

patient guardians who revealed
in each sound the hour of the fly

Above the Long Field

Those lives of which I know nothing
though I stand at the same window
watching a day in the old tree
the constellations in daylight
and hear one bird with the short song

those are things they too must have known
so they have been gone a long time
and by the time I come to them
already they are far away
notes of sheep bells on the last day
those sheep wore them threading the lane
without knowing that there would be
no more of those days and I heard
them go but did not know that then

it was a quiet day like this
clear and still as I recall it
with a few voices carrying
from a long way a day in spring
I think it was although I know
that it happened too in autumn

an hour like this before the white
sky of summer or the white hill
of winter a day in color
but in unremembered colors

Under the Day

To come back like autumn
to the moss on the stones
after many seasons
to recur as a face
backlit on the surface
of a dark pool one day
after the year has turned
from the summer it saw
while the first yellow leaves
stare from their forgetting
and the branches grow spare

is to waken backward
down through the still water
knowing without touching
all that was ever there
and has been forgotten
and recognize without
name or understanding
without believing or
holding or direction
in the way that we see
at each moment the air

Simon's Vision

After his youth Simon went south
in search of it thinking of bees
in September and hills of thyme
gray and shining and the winter
light under glass on long tables
in the damp of a nursery
wild geraniums cyclamens
the still bells of campanulas
and a beautiful witch and he
found all of them and now I wish

I had gone to see them in their
house up in the cliff according
to his directions at the time
for in a while the world Simon
had come to began to show through
so that he saw the other side
and this one where the colors are
and the flowers rise and we know
the same words he said all his life
looks to him like the stars at noon
though all is what it was before
blood of trees sugar in the dark
the idea of leaves in sleep
birds flying over an airport
finally turning into clouds
before we can really see them

Wings

Among my friends here is an old man named
for the first glimpse of light before daybreak
he teaches flying that is to say he
is able to fly himself and has taught
others to fly and for them it is their
only treasure but he has not taught me
though I dream of flying I fly in dreams
but when I see him he tells me of plants
he has saved for me and where they came from
a new one each time they have leaves like wings
like many wings some with wings like whole flocks
but they never fly he says or almost
never though there are some that can and do
but when they fly it is their only treasure
he says that if he taught me now to fly
it would be one treasure among others
just one among others is what he says
and he will wait he tells me and he speaks
of his old friends instead and their meetings

at intervals at a place where they fought
a battle long ago when they were young
and won and the ancient forest there was
destroyed as they fought but when they return
it rises again to greet them as though
no harm had ever come to it and while
they are there it spreads its wings over them

A Morning in Autumn

Here late into September
I can sit with the windows
of the stone room swung open
to the plum branches still green
above the two fields bare now
fresh-plowed under the walnuts
and watch the screen of ash trees
and the river below them

and listen to the hawk's cry
over the misted valley
beyond the shoulder of woods
and to lambs in a pasture
on the slope and a chaffinch
somewhere down in the sloe hedge
and silence from the village
behind me and from the years

and can hear the light rain come
the note of each drop playing
into the stone by the sill
I come slowly to hearing
then all at once too quickly
for surprise I hear something
and think I remember it
and will know it afterward

in a few days I will be
a year older one more year
a year farther and nearer
and with no sound from there on
mute as the native country
that was never there again
now I hear walnuts falling
in the country I came to

The Night Plums

Years afterward in the dark
in the middle of winter I saw them again
the sloes on the terraces
flowering in the small hours
after a season of hard cold and the turning
of the night and of the year and of years
when almost all whom I had known there
in other days had gone
and the stones of the barnyard were buried
in sleep and the animals were no more
I watched the white blossoms open
in their own hour naked and luminous
greeting the darkness in silence
with their ancient fragrance

In the Old Vineyard

That was a winter of last times
waking upstairs in the cold
empty house of the master
of San Beltran with its new floors
of imitation marble
its bare rooms living with echoes
though the window had been open
all night to another cold

that came down from the mountains
bringing the sound of sheep bells
from somewhere among the clouds
and before the sun was up
I would open the front door
as the fishermen my neighbors
were bringing the night catch
up the stairs to spread out
on the gray stones of the hour
then as the first rays kindled
the upper terraces
across the valley I heard
every morning the same
voice of a girl singing
her flight of notes that rose
along the tiers of stone
to touch the whole morning
with their hovering song
older than I could know

Just Now

In the morning as the storm begins to blow away
the clear sky appears for a moment and it seems to me
that there has been something simpler than I could ever believe
simpler than I could have begun to find words for
not patient not even waiting no more hidden
than the air itself that became part of me for a while
with every breath and remained with me unnoticed
something that was here unnamed unknown in the days
and the nights not separate from them
not separate from them as they came and were gone
it must have been here neither early nor late then
by what name can I address it now holding out my thanks

To a Friend Who Keeps Telling Me
That He Has Lost His Memory

And yet you know that you remember me
whoever I am and it is to me
you speak as you used to and we are sure of it

and you remember the child being saved
by some kind of mother from whatever
she insists he will never be able
to do when he has done it easily
the light has not changed at all on that one
falling in front of you as you look through it

and decades of explaining are a fan
that opens against the light here and there
proving something that then darkens again
they are at hand but even closer than they are
is the grandmother who entrusted you
with her old Baedecker to take along
on the Normandy landing where it turned out
to have powers and a time of its own

but the names fade out leaving the faces
weddings and processions anonymous
where is it that the sudden tears well up from
as you see faces turning in silence
though if they were here now it would still be
hard for you to hear what they said to you

and you lean forward and confide in me
as when you arrived once at some finely
wrought conclusion in the old days
that what interests you most of all now is birdsong
you have a plan to take some birds with you

Planh for the Death of Ted Hughes

There were so many streets then in London
they were always going to be there
there were more than enough to go all the way
there were so many days to walk through them
we would be back with the time of year
just as we were in the open day

there were so many words as we went on walking
sometimes three of us sometimes two
half the sentences flying unfinished
as we turned up the collars that had been through the wars
autumn in the park spring on the hill
winter on the bridges under what we started to say

there was so much dew even in Boston
even in the bright fall so many planets poised
on the sills of transparent houses it was coming to pass
around us the whole time before it happened
before the hearts stopped one after the other
and the silent wailing began that would not end

we were going to catch up with some of the sentences
in France or Idaho we were going
to shake them out again and listen
to what had not been caught by history or geography
or touched at all by the venomous weather
it was only a question of where and when

A Collection

After you were gone we found the garden
asking our way they all knew about it
we climbed out of town along the ravine
crossed the small bridge in the winter sunlight
came to the high wall and the parched gray door
knocked and heard nothing nothing knocked again

louder and heard the dripping of water
and nothing but knocked one more time and then
rubber boots on cement and the old man
your gardener coming from watering
the orchids motionless in their shelters
on their walls as he does every morning
though most of them are dormant at this time
but your green *Laelia digbyana*
was blooming reigning over a kingdom
in exile and by the house door I saw
two dogs shepherds staying where you left them

A Death in the Desert
for Bruce McGrew

You left just as the stars were beginning to go
the colors came back without you
you left us the colors
sand and rocks and the shades of late summer

Calling Late

Oh white lemurs who invented the dance
this is the time afterward
can you hear me
who invented the story

part of the story

oh blind lemurs who invented the morning
who touched the day
who held it aloft when it was early
who taught it to fly
can you hear the story

can you see now

oh shining lemurs who invented the beginning
who brought it along with you all the way
throwing it high up catching it never letting it fall
throwing it ahead throwing it far overhead
leaping up to it climbing into it

going to sleep in it shutting your eyes
with it safe inside them
are you listening

to the story
it has no beginning

One of the Laws

So it cannot be done to live
without being the cause of death
we know it in our blood running
unacknowledged even by us
we know it in each of our dreams
and in the new day's rising we
recognize it one more time
address it by another name

it is the need to tell ourselves
how it is not our fault that makes
it more terrible the hunger
to pardon ourselves because of
who we are the earnest belief
that we have a right to it from
somewhere because we deserve one

that brings up the pain of birth to
become cruelty and raises
story upon story cities
to indifference denying

existence to most suffering
while living off it kept alive
by it called by it from moment
to moment and by the right name

Star

All the way north on the train the sun
followed me followed me without moving
still the sun of that other morning
when we had gone over Come on over
men at the screen door said to my father
You have to see this it's an ape bring
the little boy bring the boy along

so he brought me along to the field
of dry grass hissing behind the houses
in the heat that morning and there was
nothing else back there but the empty day
above the grass waving as far away
as I could see and the sight burned my eyes
white birds were flying off beyond us

and a raised floor of boards like a house
with no house on it part way out there
was shining by itself a color
of shadow and the voices of the men
were smaller in the field as we walked on
something was standing out there on the floor
the men kept saying Come on over

it's on a chain and my father said
to me Don't get too close I saw it was
staring down at each of our faces
one after the other as though it might
catch sight of something in one of them
that it remembered I stood watching its eyes
as they turned away from each of us

in the burning day See it has its
bucket of water one of the men said
and that's higher than the dogs can get
but you wouldn't want to go up near it
I have to be careful bringing its food
keep out of reach sometimes it will swing that
chain and take to shrieking so it would

scare you unless you knew what it was
no way of telling how old it would be
but they don't live too long anyway
the heat was shimmering over the grass
as we left and it stood up straight watching us
until we were too far for it to see
and were gone already on our journey

Feast Day

Almost at the end of the century
this is the time of the pain of the bears
their agony goes on at this moment
for the amusement of the wedding guests
though the bears are harder to find by now
in the mountain forests of Pakistan
they cost more than they used to which makes it
all the more lavish and once they are caught
their teeth are pulled out and their claws pulled out
and among the entertainments after
the wedding one of them is hauled in now
and chained to a post and the dogs let loose
to hang on its nose so that the guests laugh
at the way it waves and dances and those
old enough to have watched this many times
compare it with other performances
saying they can tell from the way the bear
screams something about the children to be
born of the couple sitting there smiling
you may not believe it but the bear does

Good People

From the kindness of my parents
I suppose it was that I held
that belief about suffering

imagining that if only
it could come to the attention
of any person with normal
feelings certainly anyone
literate who might have gone

to college they would comprehend
pain when it went on before them
and would do something about it
whenever they saw it happen
in the time of pain the present
they would try to stop the bleeding
for example with their hands

but it escapes their attention
or there may be reasons for it
the victims under the blankets
the meat counters the maimed children
the animals the animals
staring from the end of the world

The Fence

for Matthew Shepard

This was what the west was won for
and this was the way it was won
but things were not like the old days
no Indians left to shoot at
a long time since the last bounties
on their kind no more wolves to hang
and stand next to for the picture
nothing left by the time they had

their first guns but the little things
running in front of them maybe
a hawk for the barn door if they
were lucky or a coyote
to string up on the barbed wire fence
which was what the fences were for
but they were growing up thinking
there had to be something better
it was time to find somebody
like themselves but different
in a way they could give a name to
point at make fun of and frighten
somebody who would understand
why it was happening to him
when he was tied to the barbed wire
which was what the fence was there for
and when he was beaten until
they thought it was time to leave him
and they drove away growing up

The Sleeper

On one of the last days of the installation in darkness
of the unlit procession that would continue its motionless
     march
to the end of the world and beyond it staring at nothing
after a ceremony during which mouths were opened
repeatedly but no words were shouted sung or spoken
the dog was carried into the tomb between two lines of bearers
followed by an orchestra holding silent instruments
and was lowered slowly into its far corner of that day's light
a sleeping dog not a guardian not a living dog
not a dog that had lived until then or had ever been born
a dog known from some life that would not be known again
the sculptor was the first in one file of bearers
and the sculptor's hand was the last to touch the figure
asleep in clay before they left it to its own sleep

and were blindfolded and turned around like planets and they
    groped
along the procession of horses chariots armor
to the light they remembered and the smells of smoke and
    cooking
then voices dogs barking dogs running among houses the
    sculptor
watched dogs searching and knowing what they were looking
    for
dogs asleep seeing somewhere else while his eye was on them

In Time

The night the world was going to end
when we heard those explosions not far away
and the loudspeakers telling us
about the vast fires on the backwater
consuming undisclosed remnants
and warning us over and over
to stay indoors and make no signals
you stood at the open window
the light of one candle back in the room
we put on high boots to be ready
for wherever we might have to go
and we got out the oysters and sat
at the small table feeding them
to each other first with the fork
then from our mouths to each other
until there were none and we stood up
and started to dance without music
slowly we danced around and around
in circles and after a while we hummed
when the world was about to end
all those years all those nights ago

Through a Glass

My face in the train window no color
years later taking me by surprise
when remembered looking older of course
behind it the fields I had known that long
flashing through it once again before I could
catch them the afternoon light the small lane
swinging by where an old man was walking
with a dog and their shadows while the face
raced past without moving and was neither
the daylight going nor the sight of it
once a snake left its whole skin by my door
still rustling without breath without a sound
all of a piece a shade out in the air
the silent rings in which a life had journeyed

Before Morning

A name in the dark a tissue of echoes

a breath repeated on the arch of my foot
the mute messenger
last one to have heard the music

I remember them saying
that I used to wake up laughing
into the cold so that the carriage shook
and never told why
it was always said that I was a happy child

the window over the street
the song of the trolley wires
from before

light singing along them
as I listened

it was the morning and it knew me
how did it find me

I was awake and watching and I remember

later when there were names it passed
all the way through them
coming going never turning
never in doubt though I grew older
and thought of differences
and moved away

and left the easel standing in the grass
at the top of the bank
facing the street
as though it were a mirror

the picture of bare day

the portrait of the light scarcely begun
as it would look when it found me

Earlier

Came from far up in the cool hour
from under the bridges the light
that was the river at that time
not a bird do I recall now
maybe never heard their voices
except the geese of the streetcars
stopping at the corner hissing
then the numb bell and the cello
rocking away into itself

one street east ran the avenue
on the cliffs facing the river
where I could see the light rising
from beyond the songs of the white tires
the teeth of roofs and the thin trees

and down there the harbor waited
in its tracks under messages
that shuffled across viaducts
between worlds never touched or smelled
their distant sounds motes in an eye

east of them flowed that hushed shining
recognizable yet unknown

Memorandum

Save these words for a while because
of something they remind you of
although you cannot remember
what that is a sense that is part
dust and part the light of morning

you were about to say a name
and it is not there I forget
them too I am learning to pray
to Perdita to whom I said
nothing at the time and now she
cannot hear me as far as I
know but the day goes on looking

the names often change more slowly
than the meanings whole families
grow up in them and then are gone
into the anonymous sky
oh Perdita does the hope go on
after the names are forgotten

and is the pain of the past done
when the calling has stopped and those
betrayals so long repeated
that they are taken for granted
as the shepherd does with the sheep

To Echo

What could they know of you
to be so sure of
that it frightened them
into passing judgment upon you
later from a distance

elusive wanderer *speaking*
when sound carries
over a river

or across a lake
recognized without being seen

beauty too far
beyond the human

then where did you go
do you go
to answer

often with voices
that once spoke for
the listeners

though only the last things

they called
ends of names greetings
the question Who

The Wild

First sight of water through trees
glimpsed as a child
and the smell of the lake then
on the mountain

how long it has lasted
whole and unmoved and without words
the sound native to a great bell
never leaving it

paw in the air
guide
ancient curlew not recorded
flying at night into
the age of night
sail sailing in the dark

so the tone of it
still crosses the years
through death after death
and the burnings the departures
the absences
carrying its own
song inside it

of bright water

Transit

Wyatt was on the way home
on a mission
trusted again more or less
but in a strange bed he died
Dante had gone the same way
never getting home with his breath

and with faces not known
clouding over them
what are you doing here
at the end of the world
words far from the tree
and the green season
of hearing

and not dying this time
or not planning to
but staying on with things to do

and eyes that can do nothing for you
by the tuned shore of dust
all of it lit from behind after singing

so soon

Usage

Do the words get old too
like all the things they are used for
which they follow trying
to keep in step with
to be the names of
to say what they are

shadows of wheat
in the waving wheat
a note waiting to be played
the small figure
appearing at last in the eyes
of statues
light moving over one face
words grow old without
speaking of such things
as long as they are there

only later
when the words are older
they start after
in another time

and what can they tell of age
itself
they that grow older

they that were always
older beyond knowing
when they say youth
youth
where is it every time

Home Tundra

It may be that the hour is snow
seeming never to settle not
even to be cold now slipping
away from underneath into
the past from which no sounds follow
what I hear is the dogs breathing
ahead of me in the shadow

two of them have already gone
far on into the dark of closed
pages out of sight and hearing
two of them old already
one cannot hear one cannot see

even in sleep they are running
drawing me with them on their way
wrapped in a day I found today
we know where we are because we
are together here together
leaving no footprints in the hour

whatever the diaries say
nobody ever found the pole

Monologue

Heart
as we say
meaning it literally
and you do

hear it when
we speak
for the voice addressing you
is your own

though we know now
that the you
we are speaking to
is not the person
we imagine
yet we go on telling you

day after day of the person
we imagine
ourselves to be

forgetting as we tell you
learning even from joy
but forgetting
and you hear

who is speaking
you hear it all
though you do not listen

The Name of the Air

It could be like that then the beloved
old dog finding it harder and harder
to breathe and understanding but coming

to ask whether there is something that can
be done about it coming again to
ask and then standing there without asking

To Maoli as the Year Ends

Now that I think you no longer hear me
you go on listening to me
as you used to listen to music
old friend what are you hearing
that I do not hear though I listen
through the light of thirty thousand days
you still hear something that escapes me

The Flight of Language

Some of the leaves stay on all winter
and spring comes without knowing
whether there is suffering in them
or ever was
and what it is in the tongue they speak
that cannot be remembered by listening
for the whole time that they are on the tree
and then as they fly off with the air
that always through their lives was there

Heights

The dark morning says See how you forget

mountains camped by a stream
the chipped lake
gold strokes on the high
clawed hollows
where you never set foot

what would you see from there

not the past
which is fiction
nor the present which is the past

you would stand there shaken
in the presence of vertigo the god
clutching the air

hearing that one
note

you keep forgetting

This January

So after weeks of rain
at night the winter stars
that much farther in heaven
without our having seen them
in far light are still forming
the heavy elements
that when the stars are gone
fly up as dust finer
by many times than a hair
and recognize each other
in the dark traveling
at great speed and becoming
our bodies in our time
looking up after rain
in the cold night together

PRESENT COMPANY

(2005)

To
Matt and Karen
and to
John and Aleksandra
beloved present company

To This May

They know so much more now about
the heart we are told but the world
still seems to come one at a time
one day one year one season and here
it is spring once more with its birds
nesting in the holes in the walls
its morning finding the first time
its light pretending not to move
always beginning as it goes

To the Soul

Is anyone there
if so
are you real
either way are you
one or several
if the latter
are you all at once
or do you
take turns not answering

is your answer
the question itself
surviving the asking
without end
whose question is it
how does it begin
where does it come from
how did it ever
find out about you
over the sound
of itself
with nothing but its own
ignorance to go by

To a Reflection

You are what we believe
even if we know better
seeing is believing
though you write backwards
your left our right
so that we never can read you
if there is any message
directed toward us from

the other side which we
cannot touch cannot reach
and can see only from here
where there is something you seem
to be showing us over
and over again without
a sound as though you were
the light itself returning

apparently to the same place

To the Face in the Mirror

Because you keep turning toward me
what I suppose must be
my own features only
backward it seems to me
that you are able to see
me only by
looking back from somewhere
that is a picture of here
at this moment but
reversed and already
not anywhere

so how far
away are you

after all who seem to be
so near and eternally
out of reach
you with the white hair
now who still surprise me
day after day
staring back at me
out of nowhere
past present or future
you with no weight or name
no will of your own
and the sight of me
shining in your eye

how do you
know it is me

To Waiting

You spend so much of your time
expecting to become
someone else
always someone
who will be different
someone to whom a moment
whatever moment it may be
at last has come
and who has been
met and transformed
into no longer being you
and so has forgotten you

meanwhile in your life
you hardly notice
the world around you
lights changing
sirens dying along the buildings
your eyes intent

on a sight you do not see yet
not yet there
as long as you
are only yourself

with whom as you
recall you were
never happy
to be left alone for long

To Impatience

Don't wish your life away
my mother said and I saw
past her words that same day
suddenly not there
nor the days after
even the ones I remember

and though hands held back the hounds
on the way to the hunt
now the fleet deer are gone
that bounded before them
all too soon overtaken
as she knew they would be

and well as she warned me
always calling me home
to the moment around me
that was taking its good time
and willingly though I
heeded her words to me
once again waking me
to the breath that was there

you too kept whispering
up close to my ear
the secrets of hunger

for some prize not yet there
sight of face touch of skin
light in another valley
labor triumphant or
last word of a story
without which you insisted
the world would not be complete
soon soon you repeated
it cannot be too soon

yet you know it can
and you know it would be
the end of you too only
if ever it arrives
you find something else missing
and I know I must thank you
for your faithful discontent
and what it has led me to
yes yes you have guided me
but what is hard now to see
is the mortal hurry

To Age

It is time to tell you
what you may have guessed
along the way without
letting it deter you
do you remember how
once you liked to kneel looking
out of the back window
while your father was driving
and the thread then of pleasure
as you watched the world appear
on both sides and from under
you coming together
into place out of nowhere
growing steadily longer

and you would hum to it
not from contentment but
to keep time with no time
floating out along it
seeing the world grow
smaller as it went from you
farther becoming longer
and longer but still there
well it was not like that
but once it was out of sight
it was not anywhere
with the dreams of that night
whether remembered or not
and wherever it was
arriving from on its way
through you must have been growing
shorter even as you
watched it appear and go
you still cannot say how
but you cannot even tell
whether the subway coming
in time out of the tunnel
is emerging from
the past or the future

To Lingering Regrets

Without wanting to
I have come slowly
to admit that I know
who you are one by one
O lovely and mournful
with downcast eyes
appearing to me as
you are turning away
to stand silent and late
in a remembered light
touched with amber

as the sun is going
from a day that it brought
you come to me again
and again to wait
as beautiful as ever
at the edge of the light
you have not changed at all
as far as I can tell
and you learn nothing from me
who do not talk with you
but see you waiting there
without once moving toward you
O forever hopeful
and forever young
you are the foolish virgins
with no oil for your lamps
and no one else to lead you
where you want to go

To My Teeth

So the companions
of Ulysses those that were
still with him after
the nights in the horse the sea-lanes
the other islands the friends
lost one by one in pain
and the coming home one
bare day to a later
age that was their own
but with their scars now upon them
and now darkened and worn and some
broken beyond recognition
and still missing the ones
taken away from beside them
who had grown up with them
and served long without question
wanting nothing else

sat around in the old places
across from the hollows
reminding themselves
that they were the lucky ones
together where they belonged

but would he stay there

To the Ancient Order of Legs

Barefoot all the way
from the embryo
and the drifting sands
where the prints washed away
untold lives ago
you were born to be
one of a number
upholding a larger
company on one
side or the other
always in the infantry
and singular though
at first you were many
balancing alternately
unable to see
where you were going
climbing along yourself
by the numbers in
a pace of your own
and stepping into
new talents positions
memberships bringing
the count down to
eight and four and two
coming in turn to be
less dispensable
half solitary painful
surviving ancestor
heir to the distances

sustain the limbs of friends
you that have borne the world
this far in us all walk on
light on your feet as
the days walk through the days

To My Legs

Tonight I look at you
as of course I never could
and think of the old horses
the little I was told about them

out of gratitude
comes a recognition
of being too late
standing on the empty
platform in the wrong
clothes or none at all
whatever may have been said
before during or afterward

all at once the old horses
were nowhere to be seen
after they had brought us
so far without a word
and I know what happens
to them however
I may pretend not to
a last step into the air
and out of gratitude comes
a picture of nothing

the speechless
obedient journeys
the running in battles
as the fields fall silent
the full veins of youth
gone without a sound

To the Tongue

Whatever we say
we know there is another
language under this one

a word of it is always
there on the tip of you
unsayable and early
O you for whom
all the languages have been named
who have none of your own

naked sleeper in the cave
where you were born
dreamer without words
who first tasted
a verb of the world
you who speak as though
you could see

you have not forgotten
the serpent your ancestor
its fluttering inarticulate flame
of expectation
on the way to you

To the Gift of Sight

What has happened to my eyes
I ask the distances
these days when the light is here
disclosing the late pages
the first leaves of spring
the gray river again
holding the still sky
that shines through it
down in the valley

it is not long ago
that I believed what I saw
without a shadow of doubt
clear contours letters
sharp figures standing for
themselves in my eyes

yet I could see then
how the time kept hiding
moments behind themselves
one after the other
a day at a time
behind the present
and the years were seen only through
each other with their outlines
melting into each other
until they were no longer
immediate or distinct

now those seasons and meanings
inside each other
as one cast a floating
penumbra around themselves
they wear a veil in the light
that makes me prize the glimpse
of them I have
the naked skin of the world
whatever of it can be seen

it uncurls in the cold light
and faces surface
and folded wings
in the water of morning

To the Corner of the Eye

Even now if I
were to call you
you would not come one step closer

though I might
call you my own

attentive companion
never far and never
domesticated
glimpse of the wilderness
in every light
on all sides
nameless familiar

in you a moment
appears before I
can recognize it
yet when I turn to face you
you have stepped aside
leaving me only
the look of things
I once thought I knew

while you are no farther
than you ever were

beginning where I am
with your unseen land
stretching away beyond you
to no horizon

To the Shadow

Only as long as there is light
as long as there is something
a cloud or mountain or wing
or body reflecting the light
you are there on
the other side
twin shape formed of
nothing but absence
made of what you are not
and we recognize you
when we wave
a part of the darkness
waves at the same moment
not answering though
nor mocking us
no
no you are not the self we know
from night to night

To Another William

After most of nine hundred years your words
born of a language that has not been spoken
through more lifetimes than I can imagine
cling to my breath even with its accent
of knowing nothing in a time and place
where anyone who heard you pronounce them
yourself now would not understand what they
were saying all this time as the year turned
new again as the white flower opened
in the cold night as the hands remembered
what they wanted once more as the days grew
few as the one song rose out of nothing

To History

You with a muse of your own
in the old gallery
that profile of grave beauty
still countenance of no
discernible age eyes somewhere

else alighting
afterwards through someone
of whom now we know
nothing but the words from later
indicating a presence
to be wooed bowed to attended
never ignored
                    but she makes

no promises arbiter
of what the speechless
living moment would be
remembered by

she knows you

and knows you are never
the way it was
                    aspect
all in the telling
you were not there at the time
but only in phrases
following each
other looking back

while she says nothing but waits

To the Unlikely Event

You have been evoked so often
like some relative in office
whom we have heard of by name
all these years but have never met

you inhabit a kind of fame
a voice without time or senses
beyond anything said of you
so that doubtless you do not hear
the recurring inadequate
references to you which rise
from another age rehearsing
wrong images or none at all

and whenever you may arrive
at last for a visit you come
in pure innocence and too late
to be recognized once you are
here sudden drop in the dials
in the light or the affections
windfall or surprise legacy

but once you come you do not go

how can we ever address you
in your unlikelihood boundless
indifference abroad in your
uncharted self to which only
random syllables find the way
and to what words can we entrust
our groundless hope saying *there there*
to them *how unlikely you sound*

already as though this might be
the mission you were conceived for
it could be what you always meant

and the hope itself when we turn
at the last minute to put it
into words what is there to say
that seems even possible
                              may

it go on just as it is may
that day never come may it be

spring in the morning together
and without end
                    how unlikely
it sounds when we come to say it

it does not help much to recall
how unlikely it is that we
turned up here with the beginning
strewn around us of which we know
nothing hear nothing remember
only the moment before us
which we believe as it happens
when it appears to be likely

oh be unlikely forever

To a Departing Companion

Only now
I see that you
are the end of spring
cloud passing
across the hollow
of the empty bowl
not making a sound
and the dew is still here

To Lili's Walk

Strange that now there should be no sign of you
visible on the dusty way between
the shadows where the morning light comes through
to lie across those places we have been
time and again though at the other end
of the day when the sun was nearly gone
and from the other side the beams lengthened
under the trees where you kept setting one
foot down carefully before the other
weaving upstream along with me to where
we would go no farther then together
and I said you know the way back from there
I will wait and you can follow alone
and between us the night has come and gone

To a Friend Travelling

The harsh cry of a partridge
echoes along the valley
through the misty rain
two months after you left
you would recognize it
though you no longer noticed the sound
except in your dreams

once again I do not know
where you may be
where to think of you
how to send you anything
whether you need it or not

you may be far away by now
yet I keep hearing your footsteps
all day in the house
in another room
this is like one of those letters

written on a mountain
in China more than
a thousand years ago

by someone staring
at the miles of white clouds
after a friend's departure
there were so many of those
unsigned and never sent
as far as we know

To the Sorrow String

You invisible one
resounding on your own
whatever the others
happen to be playing
source of a note
not there in the score
under whatever key
unphrased continuo
gut stretched between
the beginning and the end
what would the music
be without you
since even through
the chorus of pure joy
the tears hear you
and nothing can restrain them

To _____

There is no reason
for me to keep counting
how long it has been

since you were here
alive one morning

as though I were
letting out the string
of a kite one day at a time
over my finger
when there is no string

To the Consolations of Philosophy

Thank you but
not just at the moment

I know you will say
I have said that before
I know you have been
there all along somewhere
in another time zone

I studied once
those beautiful instructions
when I was young and
far from here
they seemed distant then
they seem distant now
from everything I remember

I hope they stayed with you
when the noose started to tighten
and you could say no more
and after wisdom
and the days in iron
the eyes started from your head

I know the words
must have been set down

partly for yourself
unjustly condemned after
a good life

I know the design
of the world is beyond
our comprehension
thank you
but grief is selfish and in
the present when
the stars do not seem to move
I was not listening

I know it is not
sensible to expect
fortune to grant her
gifts forever
I know

To Grief

O other country
which we never left
rich in anniversaries
each in turn wearing your crown
how many of them are there
like stars returning every one alone
from where they have been all the time
each one the only one
and to whom do you belong
incomparable one

recurring never to be touched again
whether by hand or understanding
familiar presence suddenly approaching
already turned away
reminder hidden
in the names

back of the same sky
that lights the days as we watch them
what do you want it for
this endless longing that is only ours
orbiting even in our syllables
why do you keep calling us as you do
from the beginning without a sound
like a shadow

To Absence

Raw shore of paradise
which the long waves reach
just as they fail
one after the other
bare strand beyond which
at times I believe I see
as in a glass darkly
what I know here
and now cannot be
a face I can never touch
a gaze that cannot stay
which I catch sight of
still turned upon me
following me
from under the sky
of your groundless country
that has no syllable of its own
what good to you
are the treasures beyond
words or number
that you seize forever
unmapped imperium
when only here
in the present
which has lost them
only now
in the moment you

have not yet taken
does anyone know them
or how rare they are

To the Knife

You were what made us cry
in the light to start with
we could see you were there
and we saw what you were
we were hiding from you
and would have been happy
to go on with the dream
that you could not find us
cold flame sight without eyes
line where both shores the seen
and the unseen come down
into nothing to pass
between to separate
to open to divide
what had been once from what
once it had been to tell
apart bringing always
the touch of the present
though the dread of you flares
up far ahead of you
and the memory of
you lingers and goes on
burning ahead of you
we plead with you who have
no ears for us we beg
in private and in vain
do not see us at all
ever we are not here
or if you see us do
not touch us wherever you
were going to touch us

or if you do touch us
divide us from something
it would be good to lose
and save us for ourselves

To Prose

Whatever you may say
whatever you pretend
you do not begin or end
when the stories do
the ones that you repeat
later starting again
or when the days that you tell
all those that never
themselves said a word
have long been utterly still
and yet you were there
when they were
you were heard
commenting in the unmetered
service of understanding
your description
remains current for some time
after the face has gone
even if not written down
but you are different
from what you recount
and although we know
only scattered fragments of you
glimpses of birds in bushes
gestures in car windows
of which we forget
at once almost everything
you define us
we are the ones who need you
we can no longer tell

whether we believe
anything without you
or whether we can hear
all that you are not
O web of answer
sea of forgetting is it true
that you remember

To Duty

Oh dear

where do you keep yourself
whose least footstep wakens
all those sentences
that begin *I thought*

what makes you so sure
as you lay claim
to the cloudless sky of morning

assuming the grammar of the hours
and whatever they
are supposed to be saying
even if we try
to imagine what life
would be like without you

you who do not
seem to listen
you who insist
without a sound
you who know better

even better you say
than nature herself

you who tell us
over and over
who we are

To Billy's Car

You were not going anywhere
any more

with your nose to the wall
and your cracked tires
but it seems you went just the same
and nobody noticed

by then we ourselves had gone
from the smell of your mildewed velvets
and the mica hue of the world
through your windows after supper
and the touch of your numb controls

by then the model airplanes
I suppose were no longer turning
on their strings under the ceiling
of the silent room kept
the way Billy's dead brother had left it
and his grandmother had stopped
baking cakes and crying
at all the dying
she kept mumbling over

and by that time no doubt
the girl we talked about
with whom we were both in love
who went to a different school
so that we never saw her
except in the choir on Sunday
had married somebody else

with a lot of money
looking through your old windshield
that had been there all winter
we could see the grass
that was growing on the wall that year
as we went on talking
into the spring evening

To the Present Visitors

Now we come to the famous classroom
where every year a fortunate few
in the days of their youth study
autumn forgetting the numbers beforehand
as they have been doing since the words
were all in Latin no cameras
allowed in here notice the slight breeze
from the windows here among the trees
and the fragrance at the end of spring
notice the leaves outside the window frames
the new grass in the light of morning
notice the charts of colors on the walls
set in order and the moons in the calendars
the constellations the dark dials
the portraits of flowers still as the tables
here they study what is too far away
ever to grasp and too near to recognize
notice the leaves changing as we watch
then it will be summer and these studies
will be over and then it will be autumn
and most of them will be forgotten
notice the bell in place outside the door
and the dog lying near the foot of the stairs
waiting for a time that she remembers

To the Present Tense

By the time you are
by the time you come to be
by the time you read this
by the time you are written
by the time you forget
by the time you are water through fingers
by the time you are taken for granted
by the time it hurts
by the time it goes on hurting
by the time there are no words for you
by the time you remember
but without the names
by the time you are in the papers
and on the telephone
passing unnoticed there too

who is it
to whom you come
before whose very eyes
you are disappearing
without making yourself known

To the Air

Just when I needed you
there you were
I cannot say
how long you had been
present all at once
color of the day
as it comes to be seen
color of before
face of forgetting
color of heaven
out of sight within
myself leaving me

all the time only
to return without
question never
could I live without you
never have you
belonged to me
never do I want
you not to be with me
you who have been
the breath of everyone
and of each word spoken
without needing to know
the meaning of any of them
or who was speaking
when you are the wind
where do you start from
when you are still
where do you go
you who became
all the names I have known
and the lives in which
they came and went
invisible friend
go on telling me
again again

To Muku Dreaming

There in that place
where you are running
are you alone now

you who always know
who is there

there in the place your feet
are touching
are you far from home

you who always know where you are
sleeping and waking

there in the place
where you can see
I see nothing at all
though this day is still here
in which I see you asleep

there where you can hear
I hear nothing
not that the sky is silent

how far do you know
our way
the first time

there when you see
us walking

you who have known all along
that we were there
you see that we

do not have to get anywhere

To the Dust of the Road

And in the morning you are up again
with the way leading through you for a while
longer if the wind is motionless when
the cars reach where the asphalt ends a mile
or so below the main road and the wave
you rise into is different every time
and you are one with it until you have
made your way up to the top of your climb
and brightened in that moment of that day
and then you turn as when you rose before

in fire or wind from the ends of the earth
to pause here and you seem to drift away
on into nothing to lie down once more
until another breath brings you to birth

To That Stretch of Canal

Spring is here dearie I seen a robin up
the canal this morning froze to death
CANAL NEIGHBOR

By now the towpath leads on without you
who were the only reason it was there
in the days that went on barges when you
were young and they vanished on the long sky where
you carried them and when I first saw you
nothing was left of them except that sky
in your later life when I would know you
on summer evenings watching swallows fly
low to your surface and when ice held you
all winter though you were slipping away
even then and what now remains of you
but this long dry grave a shallow valley
and shreds of marsh in the last tracks of you
with things still waving that were thrown away

To the Blue Stork

How strange to have flown so far
beyond seasons and continents
through all those generations
and the stories about you
not one of them ever true
since there was no one who knew you
or the blue you remembered

to find yourself with one eye
looking out at a city
from a picture of you standing
on the side of a black truck
with the other eye invisible
keeping watch on the darkness

and over you those letters
pretending to be yours
nothing to do with you
saying *Blue Coal* although
it was the night's own color
and only its flame was blue
other letters under you

called you *The Smokeless Fuel*
one more story about you
then in quotes as though you
had said it *You Scratch My Back
I'll Scratch Yours* but I knew
that never came from you

O smokeless hue it was you
alone I believed and not
anything said about you
it was your eye that I watched
as it watched the shining day
turning to sky it was you
who could see it was burning

To the Sound of the Gate

Hinge squeak and the small groan
of the spring turning in sleep
both wakened by the cluck
of the latch tongue
and the gate opening

long after the gate is gone
and the fence down
all the square pickets each one
and the shadows in between
painted green over brown
through the summer afternoon

vanished in midair
at Fourth Street by the corner
and inside the gate
that is not there
the flight of steps to the front door
gone and the door they climbed to
and the garden etched on its window
sealed up and shingled over

only the sound of you opening
is still there

To the Stone Paddock by the Far Barn

There where you
had been set down as deep
as a large room into the ridge
like a squared step
rimmed on the low sides
with remnants of walls
lined up on the ledge
high above the river
in another time
and with age the veteran faces
of limestone had lichened
and weathered in their places

I came upon you
many lives further on
when the hands that had heaved
the stones onto each other

and the feet that had stepped
over the sills
set in your west and north walls
the heads that had turned there
and the syllables they had raised
into their weather
had been forgotten
and wars had passed
into clouds on the far ridges
and no one had come back
and brambles had buried you

I was a child when I found you
it seems to me now
in ignorance I came
to the summer blackberries
ripening before me
that were hiding beneath them
your breathless phrase
of a lost language
and as I let
the late daylight in
I was held where I stood
and started to listen

days seasons and years
I have sat in the shade
of your south wall
while the light rolled
over the valley
quince petals still float
across the spring morning there
and the weasel ripples
along the ivy
on your east wall
and in the woods beyond it
birds sing in the hawthorns
in the oaks and bird cherries
autumn brings the scent
of earth and black currants

and the quick bark of the fox
frost creaks in your winter grass

I have imagined staying
there while the walls fell
around me
cradled in the sound of you

To a Few Cherries

Peter and I are up where the branches
sink and swing out underfoot as though they
were not anchored and with the lightest breeze
the limb one hand is holding pulls away
like someone being called but we go on
reaching higher into the leaves where they
shimmer against the light toward a dark one
set among them for the sweetest they say
are those highest up and now the season
is over the last are the best and we
are eating more as we climb drunk on you
laughing but old Delsol warns us from down
below *Don't trust that tree* until we leave you
untasted for all the rest of the story

To My Mother

This very evening I reach
the age you were when you died
I look through the decades
down past the layers of cloud
you had been watching the dark
autumn sky over the garden
and had told me months before
with a grace note of surprise
that you were an old woman

and you laughed at the sound of it
all my life you had told me
that dying did not frighten you
yours was the voice that told me
that I was not afraid
you stood up to go in
knowing it would rain that night

you had seen death many times
before I ever knew you
I am watching the rain now
fall on another garden
I hear your words in my head
it was the winter solstice
before I was thirty
that I was the age you had been
on the day I was born
to slip between numbers
through the measureless days

To My Grandfathers

You who never laid eyes on each other
only one of whom I met only once
and he was the one whose wife could never
forgive him neither would most of their sons
and daughters for the red list of his sins
mainly drink and slipping off downriver
to leave them and live to be a nuisance
out in a shed that time I was brought over
to meet him before they took him away
and you who died when my mother was four
with your fond hopes your wing collar and your
Bessie there was nothing you had to say
to each other to form an influence
soundless as that of planets in their distance

To My Aunt Margie

How could we tell what neither of us knew
that summer morning long ago when I
was a child dressed and combed for meeting you
whose name had floated like part of the sky
over me since before I heard it my
mother's one revered older cousin who
never had married but taught school and by
that time had retired to the hotel you
had for your palace snowcapped majesty
before the fall you came to stay with us
and we took walks in the cemetery
with our dog and when you died you left me
all you had and it bought me the old house
that claimed me on first sight as it still does

To My Father's Houses

Each of you must have looked like hope to him
once at least however long it lasted
he who claimed he saw hope in every grim
eyeless gray farmhouse uninhabited
on a back road and hope surely was needed
every time they were shown into the bare
resonant rooms of the manse provided
by his next church and looked around to where
their lives would wake and they would never own
where they woke and he managed to buy you
never to live in though he thought he might
and projected you onto his days one
by one in the borrowed house they came to
for the last years until the sheet went white

To My Brother

Our mother wrote to you
before you were born
a note you might open
at some later date
in case she should not
be there to tell you
what was in her mind
about wanting you
when she had not seen you

that was before
my time and it
never turned out like that
you never saw the letter
and she never saw you
who were perfect they said
and dead within minutes
that far ahead
of me and always
looking the other way
and I would be the one
to open the letter
after she was gone

and you had answered it
without a word
before I was there
to find out about you
unseen elder
you perfect one
firstborn

To Micky

Since you have come now
to remember nothing
tell me at any rate
what you have forgotten
however it may have gone
for you are the only one
left who still had
all of it in your head
whatever it all
may have amounted to
and you looked after it
there I suppose the way
you took care of everything
and of everybody in turn
without a word about it
for you seemed to be able
to lay hands on anything
I happened to ask you about
when I had the sense to ask
Harry building dance platforms
along the river some time
back before Admiral Dewey
and what drove your sister
during another war
to jump from the Ford City bridge
and Dutch withered in age
with crayons melted in her hair
from sleeping against the steam pipe
the year the boiler froze
was that all it came down to
those bits you found for me
I may as well ask you
only you would know

To Doris

If I had seen this silk
when it mattered to you
in the way that the long
parade of that nature

caught your eye and held you
coaxing you to covet
one after the other
for years those flowers of

no season which enticed
you to imagine their
still petals that recur
in these profuse patterns

of finished artifice
as a veil hovering
about some figure of
yourself suggesting you

behind flowers of silk
on a black ground I would
have found these peonies
of a distant time these

colors motionless on
black less clear than they are
now that you are not here
who wanted to wear them

To the Old

By now you could almost
be anyone and by now
it seems that is who you are

when did it happen
when did it
come to pass
unperceived in spite
of the warnings of a lifetime

surely it was not so
that summer day arched
above the shallow
stream over your shadow
to see the transparent fish
flash beneath your face
they are still flying there
silent in the same sky
where no one else sees them

surely it was not so
when first your fingers
listened under clothing
to the skin calling to you
over the hills
as you still hear it
far away only you

where now
are the questions
that you alone can answer
are they old enough yet
to know who you are
have they heard that you
are still here
do they have the words
would they recognize you

you who could almost be no one

To the Dog Stars

But there is only one of you
they say as though they knew
and it may even be true
one moment at a time
along the journey of light
yet they keep finding you
farther and farther shining
from before they believed you
or ever could have seen you
burning before and after
anything they could have known
each one the only direction
and they have no names for you

although we cannot see through
the transparent days
we go on following you
out of the flash of childhood
out of the blaze of youth
out of the lights we knew
we have been following you

after father and mother
and all the faces we came to
and the eyes that we saw through
our breath the beat of our blood
the soles of our feet our hair
go on following you

To the Tray Dancers

None of the words drifting
across the upturned faces
down in the packed street
was meant for your ears
all the way up there

too high to believe
on that June morning
in the strange city
the year I was nine
all the words were saying hush
whatever they were saying
as we stood watching you
up on the roof of the hotel
that seemed even taller
than it looked in the post cards
could you be real at all
so high and small and far
from who we thought we were
you seemed to move more slowly
than we did down here
you in the shining gown
you in the black suit and top hat
raising your hands once
then turning to the ladder
that rose from behind you
and spidering all the way
up the high pole to the round
tea tray there on top
while a drum rolled until
first one then both of you
stood on the tray up there
in the clouds and daylight
and you raised your hands again
then the music began
and you started to dance
revolving together
turning around and
around on the tray
arms out over air
heads thrown back as you whirled
and where were we all that time
what were we standing on
with our terrors spinning
on top of the pole
while the music went on

and when it stopped
we knew we were falling
until we saw you climb down
toward the lives waiting
at the foot of the air
where a whisper began
that it was all an act
to sell some brand of shoes
but you bowed and were gone
and left us as we had been

To the Mistakes

You are the ones who
were not recognized
in time although you
may have been waiting
in full sight in broad
day from the first step
that set out toward you
and although you may
have been prophesied
hung round with warnings
had your big pictures
in all the papers
yet in the flesh you
did not look like that
each of you in turn
seemed like no one else
you are the ones
who are really my own
never will leave me
forever after
or ever belong
to anyone else
you are the ones I
must have needed
the ones who led me

in spite of all
that was said about you
you placed my footsteps
on the only way

To Luck

In the cards and at the bend in the road
we never saw you
in the womb and in the cross fire
in the numbers
whatever you had your hand in
which was everything
we were told never
to put our faith in you
but to bow to you humbly after all
because in the end there was nothing
else we could do

but we were not to believe in you

and though we might coax you with pebbles
kept warm in the hand
or coins or relics
of vanished animals
observances rituals
none of them binding upon you
who make no promises
we might do such things only
not to neglect you
and risk your disfavor
O you who are never the same
who are secret as the day when it comes
you whom we explain
whenever we can
without understanding

To the Blank Spaces

For longer than by now I can believe
I assumed that you had nothing to do
with one another I thought you had arrived
        whenever that had been

more solitary than single snowflakes
with no acquaintance or understanding
running among you guiding your footsteps
        somewhere ahead of me

in your own time O white lakes on the maps
that I copied and gaps on the paper
for the names that were to appear in them
        sometimes a doorway or

window sometimes an eye sometimes waking
without knowing the place in the whole night
I might have guessed from the order in which
        you turned up before me

and from the way I kept looking at you
as though I recognized something in you
that you were all words out of one language
        tracks of the same creature

To the Morning (1)

Was there once a day when I knew what to ask
looking into the bright hour while it was arrayed before me
were there actual words of the only language
native to that hour and to me that rose unbidden by thought
gone at once taken by the moment as it heard them
while the shadow moved unperceived and the breath
went with its sails and the faces turned and were
there no longer though the love was still talking to them
as it is still talking to them while the rooms fade and dissolve

and the houses turn into seasons and now when so much has
vanished is it possible that in some other time
I knew how to speak of you early light
breeze in the garden toward the end of a year together
in which we wake remembering
or did you come by yourself without anyone knowing your
    name

To Monday

Once you arrive it is plain
that you do not remember
the last time

you are always
like that
insisting upon
beginning
upon it all beginning
over again
as though nothing had really happened
as though beginning
went on and on
as though it were everything
until it had begun

you never know who you are
the hands of the clock find you
and keep going
without recognition
though what your light
reveals when it rises
wakes from another time
which you appear to have forgotten

travelling all that way
blank and nowhere
before you came to be

with the demands
that you bring with you
from the beginning

each time it is
as though you were the same
or almost
O unrepeatable one
needing nothing yourself
and not waiting

To the Long Table

The sun was touching the wet black shoulders of olives
in a chipped dish descended from another century
on that day I remember more than half my life ago
and you had been covered with a tablecloth of worn damask
for lunch out on the balcony overhanging the stream
with the grapes still small among the vine leaves above us
and near the olives a pitcher of thin black acrid wine
from the cellar just below and an omelette on a cracked white
    platter
a wheel of bread goat cheeses salad I forget what else
the ducks were asleep down on the far side of the green pond
Jacques came and went babbling fussing making his bad jokes
boasting about the old days that nobody else remembered
the lacquered carriages the plumes on the horses and what his
    mother
had replied to the admiral whose attentions amused her
all the castles they had lost before he had grown up
and when the meal was over he said you too were for sale
he had discovered you in a carpenter's shop
where you had been used as a workbench without regard
for your true worth and the scars on you came from there
your history without words upon which words have gathered

To the Margin

Following the black
footprints the tracks
of words that have passed that way
before me I come
again and again to
your blank shore

not the end yet
but there is nothing more
to be seen there
to be read to be followed
to be understood
and each time I turn
back to go on
in the same way
that I draw the next breath

the wider you are
the emptier and the more
innocent of any
signal the more
precious the text
feels to me as I make
my way through it reminding
myself listening
for any sound from you

To the Middle

O you who pass like a day and never
a soul that sees you guesses who you are
as you go until the rest is over
if someone happens to look back that far
how could you have been known when once you came
unannounced and transparent as the air

at different times for each one yet the same
each one must think as you slip by them there
as the moment before and the next one
which makes no sign that you have come and gone
you upon whom all time and battles turn
so it appears that you are here always
a stillness in the passage of the days
around which the ages of heaven burn

To the Next Time

Knowing as I do
that you will not be there
whenever it may be
that I imagine you
I go on even so
day after day as though
I might believe in you

with your unseen stars again
back at home in the places
they had moved away from
already by the time
I could remember them
and my age what it was
whenever it may have been
that I looked forward from
to you as though that time
when it was there were less
believable less true
and less present than you

so that even if you
occurred and were the same
you could not help but be
different in your way
while any temporary

moment I live through
may still seem to be
a passing sketch of you
as you were meant to be
this time this time

To the Light of September

When you are already here
you appear to be only
a name that tells of you
whether you are present or not

and for now it seems as though
you are still summer
still the high familiar
endless summer
yet with a glint
of bronze in the chill mornings
and the late yellow petals
of the mullein fluttering
on the stalks that lean
over their broken
shadows across the cracked ground

but they all know
that you have come
the seed heads of the sage
the whispering birds
with nowhere to hide you
to keep you for later

you
who fly with them

you who are neither
before nor after
you who arrive

with blue plums
that have fallen through the night

perfect in the dew

September 10, 2001

To the Words

When it happens you are not there

O you beyond numbers
beyond recollection
passed on from breath to breath
given again
from day to day from age
to age
charged with knowledge
knowing nothing

indifferent elders
indispensable and sleepless

keepers of our names
before ever we came
to be called by them

you that were
formed to begin with
you that were cried out
you that were spoken
to begin with
to say what could not be said

ancient precious
and helpless ones

say it

September 17, 2001

To the Grass of Autumn

You could never believe
it would come to this
one still morning
when before you noticed
the birds already
were all but gone

even though year upon year
the rehearsal of it
must have surprised
your speechless parents
and unknown antecedents
long ago gathered to dust
and though even the children
have been taught how to say
the word *withereth*

no you were known to be
cool and countless
the bright vision on all
the green hills
rippling in unmeasured waves
through the days in flower

now you are as the fog
that sifts among you
gray in the chill daybreak
the voles scratch the dry earth
around your roots
hoping to find something
before winter
and when the white air stirs
you whisper to yourselves
without expectation
or the need to know

September 18, 2001

To Ashes

All the green trees bring
their rings to you
the widening
circles of their years to you
late and soon casting
down their crowns into
you at once they are gone
not to appear
as themselves again

O season of your own

from whom now even
the fire has moved on
out of the green voices
and the days of summer
out of the spoken
names and the words between them
the mingled nights the hands
the hope the faces
those circling ages dancing
in flames as we see now
afterward
here before you

O you with no
beginning that we can conceive of
no end that we can foresee
you of whom once we were made
before we knew ourselves

in this season of our own

September 19, 2001

To Zbigniew Herbert's Bicycle

Since he never
really possessed you
however he may have longed to
in secret

so that in dreams he knew
each surface and detail of you
gleam of spokes and chrome
smells of grease and rubber
the chain's black knuckles

day by day you
remained out of sight
so that he never had to
lock you up or hide you
because nobody could see you

and though he never
in fact learned how to ride you
keeping his round
toppling weight upright
on the two small toes
of water slipping
out from under

once he was well away
hands on the grips feet off the ground
you could take him
anywhere

at last like the rain
through the rain

invisible as you were

September 21, 2001

To the Coming Winter

Sometime after eleven the fireworks
of the last fête of this autumn begin
popping down in the valley a few sparks
here and there climbing slowly through thin rain
into the darkness until they are gone
above the carnival din and the caught
faces lit by wheeling rides in that one
moment looking up still and shining what
are they celebrating now that the fine
days are finished and the old leaves falling
and fields empty this year when a season
has ended and we stand again watching
those brief flares in the silence of heaven
without knowing what they are signalling

September 23, 2001

To the Smell of Water

But is it really you
behind the pretenses
beyond dust and distances
beneath the salt and the siren
announcements and ancient
impurities and decays
that claim to be you

we have thought we knew you
emerging around us
as we came to the lake
and racing by us
as we listened to the river
and reminding us
from the ends of the streets
and waving across the boardwalk
and along the sand
and hovering above the clear glass

as a child I ran to you
with a pounding heart
and out in the desert
the camel turns to you
and the rain at night
falls through you

yet it is said that none
of the breaths that we
believe to be you
is really your own
for you have none
that is yours alone

and what we take to be
you is only
what is told about you
while you remain
apart from it like our days
our nights our years

To the Beginning of Rain

You never guessed
that anyone was watching

I knew you were on the way
I wondered how long it would be
until you appeared
falling before there was
any knowledge of falling
falling with no way of knowing

without why or where
pure falling
what is it
like

even from here
I can tell for an instant
it is not like anything

the color of air
but not air
nor like air
the color of leaves and their shadows
passing through them as though
they were not there
color of the sight of an eye
moving across the eye but
not remembering it

color of light at this moment
but not light
color of going
as it goes
color of not knowing
as it went

To a Mosquito

Listen to you
me me me
nothing but *me*
even without a voice
and rash though it may be

to sing out anyway
here I am this is me
out for your blood

do you mean to tell me
we are some kind of kin
blood relatives
your many offspring
something to me

by blood presumably
but with the gift of flight

on wings as fine
as light glinting across water
and with the deaths they carry

you need not tell me
that you are here
because of me
you follow me everywhere
by my breath you find me
by the life of my body
you hunger to be close to me
whatever I am doing

though we do not take
each other personally
you recognize me
I make the world right for you
it is as though you
believe I owe you something

To Glass

Which of you was first
you or the days

at pretending not
to be visible
to be there but not visible

by fire out of sand

which of you first
started to look
like the other

and to look like
the air
and the hour
and the colored light
that you allow us
to see through you
to recognize the day
turning out of reach

while you appear to be
stillness itself
no one at all
holding in place

the promise
of the known world
on the other side

which the birds fly into
the last time

To Purity

I have heard so much about you

if you claim to be you
I will know it is not true

if you say nothing I will listen
as I do
with my own
old mixed feelings
of hope and reservation

hearing through them
whatever might be you

the way I see
the white light from
the beginning
through the colors of the garden
through a face an eye

To Salt

Taste of taste

you that know without saying

you that also began somewhere in the light
as a dust
in the light
long before anything could have tasted you
before anything could have recognized you
traveller through the dark through the earth through the sea
finding your way in time into sweat and blood
and into tears that we know as our own
or another's

O great silent teacher whose scripture we fulfill
you that made us able to taste you

you lead us to the light and to the darkness
you teach us the coming and going of each other
you wake us with joy and pain and terror
one at a time or all together
as long as we recognize you

as long as we know
the touch of you on our lips

To the Lightning

Now I can believe
that you never left

that always you
were there outside time
thinking in the dark
a moment of the world
waking it
to its only instant
changing it
even before it knew

ancestor

whom your children
have never remembered
not one of them
and whose illumination
they could not hope to survive

beginning

around us all that time
unchanged as we travelled
from whom our eyes are descended
and the things we say

whenever we see you
there is a question
we do not dare to remember
and you disappear
before there are words for it

is that from you too

To the Escape of Light

How late
was it
could you tell

by the time
rhyme came
to occur as though
it might be your shadow
in flight
your echo

O you
who began far
beyond what you
knew

all at once
out of the utter
darkness that no one
could be said to know

showing
yourself where
you would go
as you
appeared there

for the only time
how long can you
go on guiding
yourself through

darkness into
darkness as though
you knew

To a Leaf Falling in Winter

At sundown when a day's words
have gathered at the feet of the trees
lining up in silence
to enter the long corridors
of the roots into which they
pass one by one thinking
that they remember the place
as they feel themselves climbing
away from their only sound
while they are being forgotten
by their bright circumstances
they rise through all of the rings
listening again
afterward as they
listened once and they come
to where the leaves used to live
during their lives but have gone now
and they too take the next step
beyond the reach of meaning

To the Fire

How long I have been
looking into you
staring through you into
the other side
there is no way of telling

it appears to have continued
from an age of its own
this scrutiny of the bright
veil rising and the lit
corridors of the embers
in which I see the days

beyond touch beyond reach
beyond all understanding
beyond their faces
beneath your dangerous wings
you at whose touch
everything changes
you who never change

there in you one at a time
are days unknown
turning the corners
and the unseen past
the unrecognized present
familiar but already
beyond identity

expressions without selves
appearing finally within you
of whom the light is made

To Smoke

Even now when we
can no longer remember
how much of the scent
of the world we gave up
life after life in the hope
of being able to hold
something in our hands

we recognize you at once
every time without fail
day or night wherever
you may be coming from
across the hill or
under the door
and we imagine you
even when you are not there

we can never be sure
you reach all the way to us
out of somewhere we have forgotten
we wake into dreams of you
as the bees do
hoping it is not true

the world is burning
you have always been warning
us too late and only
as you were leaving
ghost of what we have known
something reminds us of you
in the fragrance of morning
in the opening flowers
in a breath at the moment
when it seems to be ours

To Forgetting

Queen of the night
whose reign began
before
always before
mother of how
the story goes
song older than singing

you sweep up my footsteps
how did I find my way here
now there is no way back
you blow my words away
without my hearing you

you erase the faces
even of the living
you travel backward
wherever you are going

taking the days with you
all of them
even the ones I imagined
were safe forever

sovereign of terrible freedom
O you without feature
and without end
whose face I never see
or never remember
how can I love you

except when you appear
for a moment wearing
the veils and the long train
of memory

disguised as memory
the queen of the day

To the Wires Overhead

This is the year
when the swallows did not come back

you have not noticed

now all spring
the evening messages
are no longer passing through
the feet of swallows
lined up in a row
holding you
under the high
strung sparks of their voices

with the notes of that
music changing

as once more they would go
sailing out and once more
singly or in pairs or
several together
across the long light they would
skim low over the gardens
and down the steep pastures
and over the river
and would come back to their places
to go on telling
what was there while it was there

you do not hear
what is missing

To a Tortoiseshell Lyre

Do you know how beautiful you are
did you ever know such a thing

O hollow cradle of light
large as an empty embrace
shape of old waves
and of supplication and offering
fashioned out of all
the ambers of memory

here at the center
at the deepest part
where your heart has been
the notes were plucked
once according to
a time of music
to accompany the singing
that someone claimed
would be here forever

here your heart began
as an echo
in answer to the sea
here once you heard
how the light came through it

To the Gods

When did you stop
telling us what we could believe

when did you take that one step
only one
above
all that

as once you stepped
out of each of the stories
about you one after the other
and out of whatever
we imagined we knew
of you

who were the light
to begin with
and all of the darkness
at the same time
and the voice in them
calling crying
and the enormous answer
neither coming nor going
but too fast to hear

you let us believe
the names for you
whenever we heard them
you let us believe the stories

how death came to be
how the light happened
how the beginning began
you let us believe
all that

then you let us believe
that we had invented you
and that we no longer
believed in you
and that you were only stories
that we did not believe

you with no
moment for beginning
no place to end
one step above
all that

listen to us
wait
believe in us

To the Veil

Small mist
suddenly on the windshield
reflection of an unseen field
of lavender in the air
not flowering there

patch of translucent
uncolored twilight
after the day of color

dazzling shadow
how
have I come to know you

as when a forgotten
dream returns
to stand in the daylight

neither appearing nor
disappearing
in front of the day
like the day itself

constantly unforeseen
and yet recognized
as though it had long been known

To the Way Back

If you can be said
to remember

and by that I mean
if you
can be said to remember

anything

if you
can be
said to be
anything

remember how
you came to be
how you came
to pass

remember who it was
in whose feet
you took the first steps

that was me
not watching
to see whether
you were there

not waiting for you
don't forget
the way back my
mother said

not forgetting you
forgetting you
in the dark of the shoes
in the sounds of the stairs
in the opening door

now that you
have not been there
for so long
do you remember
where you were
before I turned
to look for you

To the Thief at the Airport

Disciple of not knowing
your face keeps reappearing
out of its shady morning
among the cars and saying
that used phrase about looking
for where you were not going

thin smoke for your vanishing

in the moment revealing
suddenly what was missing
the clasped tender of being

someone all the cards telling
the dates and places giving
numbers pictures everything

without even mentioning

those worn familiars each thing
beyond price and worth nothing
from their new absence mocking
any thought of replacing
by then they had no meaning
wherever you were hiding

where your prayers had been leading

to that moment not knowing
what it was you were holding
under your sweater breathing
to the night of not knowing
to contain you like nothing
so you could go on living

To the Afterlife

The way we talk

before those who we tell ourselves
do not hear us

is that really the way
we talk the rest of the time
how can we ever be sure of it
once we start listening
to ourselves as we do
when we talk in front of you

and when are you not there

how old you must be
who do not sleep
and never meet our eyes
though you are never out of them
you who were not born

if you do not hear us
we can ask anything of you

listen

now in the still night
the sound of breathing
remember it
whether you hear it or not

To Finding Again

Everything else must have changed
must be different
by the time you appear
more than ever the same

taking me by surprise
in my difference
my age
long after I had come
to the end
of believing in you
to the end of hope

which was not even
the first of the changes

when I imagined
that I was forgetting you
you did not even need memory

to remain there
letting the years vanish
the miles depart

nothing surprising in that

even longing
does not need memory
to know what to reach for

and nothing surprises you
who were always there
wherever it was

beyond belief

To the Surgeon Kevin Lin

Besides these words that are made of
breath and memory with features
of both and are only mine as
   I address them to you

what do I owe to that steady
fire I watched burning behind your
glasses through the dire spelling-out
   when we met that first day

and to the passion of the boy
from Taiwan and the sharp knowledge
it burned a way to until it
   stood before the open

red cavern and between pulses
was sure how to do what came next
had it not been for that would I
   have been here this morning

at home after a night's rain as
the first sunlight touches the drops
at the tips of the leaves I owe
            you the sight of morning

To Days of Winter

Not enough has been said
ever in your praise
hushed mornings
before the year turns new
and for a while afterward
passing behind the sounds

Oh light worn thin
until the eye can
almost see through you
still words continuing
to bloom out of yourselves
in the way of the older stars
your ancestors

season from before knowledge
reappearing
days when the sun is loved most

To a Friend Turning Fifty

Peter we talk as though
we knew what the years were
that seem to slip from us
            even before

they arrive where have they
gone where were they heading
from the beginning where
            did they start from

before there were numbers
in the hollow with no
circumference that we
　　　　　still feel turning

and keep counting the turns
inventing numerals
to call them by but they
　　　　　leave us the names

which are nothing to them
and what they bring us for
a present is without
　　　　　name or number

unseizable as this
daylight in which the life
you have come to appears
　　　　　to you all at

once congratulations
let the day welcome you
as its guest the way you
　　　　　welcome your friends

To Being Late

Again again you are
the right time after all

not according to
however we planned it

unforeseen and yet
only too well known
mislaid horizon
where we come to ourselves
as though we had been expected

you are where it appears now
and will stay from now on
in its own good time
it was you we came to
in the first place
hearing voices around us
before we knew what they said

but you always surprise us
it is you that we
hurry to
while you go on waiting
to the end of space

and when we get to you
we stop and listen
trying to hear whether
you are still there

To the Morning (2)

It does not matter to you
what I fail to understand
as the light enters the sky

you arrive for the first time
knowing everything at once
and offer the beginning
again whether anyone
can see what it is or not
while it is here before us

as though it had always been
here as it is with nothing
forgotten even while you

are turning away again

To the Moss

How you came to know all that you are sure of
how you discovered the darkness of green
uncurling into the daylight out of
its origins unsounded as your own
how you learned to fashion shapes of water
into softness itself that stayed in place
and kept some secret of caves wherever
you were but with such welcome seemed to rise
that in time you became as some believe
a model for the cheek and then the breast
the wren felt she knew most of that before
there were breasts or cheeks and she made out of
living bits of you the globe of her nest
as though that was what you had grown there for

To an Old Acacia

Into the morning fine white rain
keeps drifting along the valley
taking it away already
though it is still spring
with the brief blue flights flashing
to the nest above the kitchen window

and you appear to me again
where you have not stood for so long
wherever we may have been

I see it is evening where you are
though you seem as near
as a figure in the room
all day you have held
a single note of darkness
one rough hollow column
the sound of a breath

neither knowing nor not knowing
through the glare of high summer
and the incandescent cicadas

is the note I remember now
the one that I heard
in those days
when your gnarled branches might still
hold out white flowers
over the dead limbs

when it is night
do you still echo the owl

To the Story

Even now I suppose you are hiding
in the daylight the way you always do
            granting only

the most cursory kind of attention
or none at all like a self off in some
            other country

other time other life as though you knew
better than the moment while the moment
            is quietly

there unproclaimed with its occasions its
events signalling from their distances
            you fail to see

as it passes before you what you will
never manage to remember later
            the missing key

to the present and its unrepeated
life and so you will have to make it up
            as plausibly

as you can out of odds and ends of what
someone wrote down or you may remember
      if memory

serves you or you will conjure from those same
elements and selves summoned out of some
      other country

other time other life some other tale
that never happened to be the truth of
      what could not be

told as it lived and breathed and eluded
our attention as though in itself it
      had no story

To a Dormouse

You never knew how you came by your names
in any language because none was yours
Muscardinus avellanarius
      whom your mother

did not call that nor refer to you as
one of the *Gliridae* it was somewhere
in the north that the word for you first told
      only of your

fondness for sleeping through the world's winter
how did they learn that did anyone come
upon you once before you woke and want
      to remember

something of that time glimpsed from far away
it happens to us too words that pretend
to represent us may at this moment
      be making their

transits from one stranger to another
as though they were uttered during our sleep
and did Buffon himself ever meet you
        who said you were

smaller than squirrels but fatter and not
to be tamed as squirrels might be but with
your teeth would defend yourself to the last
        and he never

said anything of your color like that
of a fawn in the shade nor of your tail
the grace in it the small tuft at the end
        nothing of your

elegant mask nor of the curious
quiet of your eyes their steady lights
awake in their distances over us as
        they would appear

above the curtain rod in the evening
and watch us through dinner and then vanish
but this time when I find you it seems that
        you stayed on there

looking down into the room all winter
empty table plates put away no one
there and you fell asleep into the sleep
        of the future

To the Parting Year

So you are leaving everything
the way it is
taking only your day with you

already you are out of reach
you do not know us or hear us

you scarcely remember us
already we cannot imagine
where you are

what we remember of love is starlight

To the New Year

With what stillness at last
you appear in the valley
your first sunlight reaching down
to touch the tips of a few
high leaves that do not stir
as though they had not noticed
and did not know you at all
then the voice of a dove calls
from far away in itself
to the hush of the morning

so this is the sound of you
here and now whether or not
anyone hears it this is
where we have come with our age
our knowledge such as it is
and our hopes such as they are
invisible before us
untouched and still possible

To the Unfinished

Clear eminence without whom I would be
nothing O great provision never seen
barely acknowledged even wished away
          without thinking

you in whose immeasurable presence
the darkness itself comes to be itself
and light recalls its colors and each sound
            comes echoing

your undertone I have forgotten when
I first woke into knowing you were there
before words ever reached me but that time
            under your wing

is still with me you have carried it all
the way along with faces that surface
appearing almost as they were before
            and with the spring

that returns through its leaves never the same
you have brought me once more to the old house
after all these years of remembering
            without knowing

it was you who kept opening the way
offering me what I had to choose it is
you who come bringing me the only day
            in the morning

To Paula

We keep asking where they have gone
those years we remember and we
reach for them like hands in the night
knowing they must be as close as
that those twenty years that were
just here we did not set them down
no not that first night talking at
Il Monello what did we say
and then the joy of that summer
that became the joy of the years
after it yes that is where they

are they turned into each other
love and all and have turned into
us now the way a journey turns
into the traveller even
as its sequence is forgotten
they turned into this later joy
one day on another island
near the end of another year
wondering what became of them

To Myself

Even when I forget you
I go on looking for you
I believe I would know you
I keep remembering you
sometimes long ago but then
other times I am sure you
were here a moment before
and the air is still alive
around where you were and I
think then I can recognize
you who are always the same
who pretend to be time but
you are not time and who speak
in the words but you are not
what they say you who are not
lost when I do not find you

To the Happy Few

Do you know who you are

O you forever listed
under some other heading
when you are listed at all

you whose addresses
when you have them
are never sold except
for another reason
something else that is
supposed to identify you

who carry no card
stating that you are—
what would it say you were
to someone turning it over
looking perhaps for
a date or for
anything to go by

you with no secret handshake
no proof of membership
no way to prove such a thing
even to yourselves

you without a word
of explanation
and only yourselves
as evidence

To the Book

Go on then
in your own time
this is as far
as I will take you
I am leaving your words with you
as though they had been yours
all the time

of course you are not finished
how can you be finished
when the morning begins again

or the moon rises
even the words are not finished
though they may claim to be

never mind
I will not be
listening when they say
how you should be
different in some way
you will be able to tell them
that the fault was all mine

whoever I was
when I made you up

THE SHADOW OF SIRIUS

(2008)

to Paula

The Nomad Flute

You that sang to me once sing to me now
let me hear your long lifted note
survive with me
the star is fading
I can think farther than that but I forget
do you hear me

do you still hear me
does your air
remember you
o breath of morning
night song morning song
I have with me
all that I do not know
I have lost none of it

but I know better now
than to ask you
where you learned that music
where any of it came from
once there were lions in China

I will listen until the flute stops
and the light is old again

Blueberries After Dark

So this is the way the night tastes
one at a time
not early or late

my mother told me
that I was not afraid of the dark
and when I looked it was true

how did she know
so long ago

with her father dead
almost before she could remember
and her mother following him
not long after
and then her grandmother
who had brought her up
and a little later
her only brother
and then her firstborn
gone as soon
as he was born
she knew

Still Morning

It appears now that there is only one
age and it knows
nothing of age as the flying birds know
nothing of the air they are flying through
or of the day that bears them up
through themselves
and I am a child before there are words
arms are holding me up in a shadow
voices murmur in a shadow
as I watch one patch of sunlight moving
across the green carpet
in a building
gone long ago and all the voices
silent and each word they said in that time
silent now
while I go on seeing that patch of sunlight

By the Avenue

Through the trees and across the river
with its surface the color of steel
on a rainy morning late in spring
the splintered skyline of the city
glitters in a silence we all know
but cannot touch or reach for with words
and I am the only one who can
remember now over there among
the young leaves brighter than the daylight
another light through the tall windows
a sunbeam sloping like a staircase
and from beyond it my father's voice
telling about a mote in an eye
that was like a mote in a sunbeam

Note

Remember how the naked soul
comes to language and at once knows
loss and distance and believing

then for a time it will not run
with its old freedom
like a light innocent of measure
but will hearken to how
one story becomes another
and will try to tell where
they have emerged from
and where they are heading
as though they were its own legend
running before the words and beyond them
naked and never looking back

through the noise of questions

Accompaniment

The wall in front of me is all one black
mirror in which I see my hands
washing themselves all by themselves
knowing what they are doing
as though they belong to someone
I do not see there and have never seen
who must be older than I am
since he knows what he is doing
above the basin of bright metal
in the black wall where the water looks
still as a frozen lake at night
though the bright ripples on it
are trembling and under me the floor
and my feet on it are trembling
it is late it was late when we started
over my shoulder my mother's voice
is telling me what we do next
on the way and how the train is made
that is taking us away and in a while
I will be asleep and I will
wake up far away
we are going south
where I know that my father
is going to die
but I will grow up before he does that
the hands go on washing by themselves

Without Knowing

If we could fly would there be numbers
apart from the seasons
in sleep I was flying south
so it was autumn
numberless autumn with its leaves
already far below me
some were falling into

the river of day
the invisible surface
that remembers and whispers
but does not tell even in sleep
not this time

The Song of the Trolleys

It was one of the carols
of summer and I knew that
even when all the leaves
were falling through it as it passed
and when frost crusted the tracks
as soon as they had stopped ringing
summer stayed on in that song
going again the whole way
out of sight to the river
under the hill and hissing
when it had to stop
then humming to itself
while it waited until
it could start again
out of an echo warning
once more with a clang of its bell
I could hear it coming
from far summers that I
had never known
long before I could see it
swinging its head
to its own tune on its way
and hardly arrived before it
was going and its singing
receding with its growing
smaller until it was gone
into sounds that resound
only when they have come to silence
the voices of morning stars
and the notes that once rose

out of the throats of women
from cold mountain villages
at the fringe of the forest
calling over the melting
snow to the spirits asleep
in the green heart of the woods
Wake now it is time again

From the Start

Who did I think was listening
when I wrote down the words
in pencil at the beginning
words for singing
to music I did not know
and people I did not know
would read them and stand to sing them
already knowing them
while they sing they have no names

Far Along in the Story

The boy walked on with a flock of cranes
following him calling as they came
from the horizon behind him
sometimes he thought he could recognize
a voice in all that calling but he
could not hear what they were calling
and when he looked back he could not tell
one of them from another in their
rising and falling but he went on
trying to remember something in
their calls until he stumbled and came
to himself with the day before him
wide open and the stones of the path
lying still and each tree in its own leaves

the cranes were gone from the sky and at
that moment he remembered who he was
only he had forgotten his name

The Pinnacle

Both of us understood
what a privilege it was
to be out for a walk
with each other
we could tell from our different
heights that this
kind of thing happened
so rarely that it might
not come around again
for me to be allowed
even before I
had started school
to go out for a walk
with Miss Giles
who had just retired
from being a teacher all her life

she was beautiful
in her camel hair coat
that seemed like the autumn leaves
our walk was her idea
we liked listening to each other
her voice was soft and sure
and we went our favorite way
the first time just in case
it was the only time
even though it might be too far
we went all the way
up the Palisades to the place
we called the pinnacle
with its park at the cliff's edge
overlooking the river

it was already a secret
the pinnacle
as we were walking back
when the time was later
than we had realized
and in fact no one
seemed to know where we had been
even when she told them
no one had heard of the pinnacle

and then where did she go

Child Light

On through the darkening of the seeds and the bronze
    equinox
I remember the brightness of days in summer
too many years ago now to be counted
the cotton-white glare floating over the leaves
I see that it was only the dust in one sunbeam
but I was a child at the time

I hear our feet crossing the porch
and then the glass door opening
before we are conducted through the empty rooms of the
    house
where we are to live

that was on a day before I was nine
before the lake and the water sloshing in the boat
and what we heard about refugees
and before Billy Green explained to me about sex
and I saw my first strip mine
and before the war
and before the sound of the train wheels under me
when the leaves were still green
before the word for autumn

that was before Ching and Gypsy
and the sun on the kitchen table
with the window open
before the deaths by bombing
and by sickness and age and by fire and by gas
and by torture
and before the scratched varnish of the study hall
and before the camps
and coming to Conrad and Tolstoy

it was before the deaths of schoolchildren
whom I had known and whom I heard of

and before looking out into the trees after dark
from the window of the splintery unlit chemistry lab
into the scent of the first fallen leaves

Empty Lot

There was only the narrow alley between us
and we lived beside the long dusty patch
of high ragweed that first parched summer
and then the heart leaves of the old poplar cradled
down to the dust in the fall when the men gathered there
of an evening to toss quoits into the sky
toward the clay pits facing them and in winter
the drifted snow showed where the wind whirled
between the houses and I watched the sun go down
out beyond there behind the mountain
and the moon sailing over the lot late at night
when I woke out of a dream of flying
and yet there was no way to imagine that place
as it had been for so long
with the world to itself before there were houses
when bears took their time there under trees they knew
now we were told that it belonged to
the D&H Coal Company and they
would do nothing with it but keep it

in case they ever should need to sink
an emergency shaft to miners
in trouble below there nobody could say
how far down but sometimes when the night
was utterly still we knew we had just heard
the muffled thump of a blast under us
and the house knew it the windows trembled
we listened for picks ticking in the dark

No

Out at the end of the street in the cemetery
the tombstones stared across the wheeling shadows
of tombstones while the names and dates wept on
in full daylight and behind them where the hill
sheared off two rusted tracks under a black
iron gate led up out of pure darkness
and the unbroken sound of pure darkness
that went on all the time under everything
not breathing beneath the sounds of breathing
but no they said it was not the entrance
to the underworld or anything like that
in fact all the houses along the street
had been paid for by what had come from there
in the days of the negatives of the pictures

The Piano

It may have survived to this day somewhere
in another life
where they speak of its age as a measure of unimportance
not realizing that it was always as old as it is now
something I understand from its sound which has not changed
coming from the slender valleys under the keys
never explored and not expecting to be noticed

each valley waking a different echo
out of the narrow vibrant shadow
between the piano and the wall that emerges above it
papered to be wheat fields without wind
with no horizon and with a smell of walls and night

through the notes my mother's hand appears
above my own and hovers over the keys
waiting to turn the pages of Czerny
whose composition has completely dissolved

from her hand a scent of almonds rises
which she had put on after whatever she had been doing
it survives with the sound into another life

some time ago a few inches of beaded molding
fell from the panel behind the music rack
to lie at the foot of it waiting to be put back

her fingers remember the right notes and keep listening for
    them
the veins on the backs of her hands are the color
of the clear morning sky beginning to haze over

Secrets

Time unseen time our continuing fiction
however we tell it eludes our dear hope and our reason

that is a pure condition of the story
and wherever our parents came from is another century

an age which they themselves could barely remember
but carried with them as their own year after year

hidden away hardly looked at until the secret
without their noticing had faded all the details white

for my mother it came to be the lace veil covering
the front of the baby carriage where she was being

wheeled through the Garden of the Gods when her parents
        were
still alive as she told about it later

and for my father it was the glare bleaching the surface
of the river as he sat under the white blaze

of summer in the rowboat tied above the waterline
where he was allowed to hold the oars and imagine

leaving did he see any farther when he was
dying in summer after midnight and before the solstice

coughing saying he was not afraid and was the veil still there
when my mother turned from her own garden one evening
        that same year

telling a friend on the telephone that she was going
to get some rest now and her glasses were lying

apart from her on the floor not more than an hour
later when a neighbor pushed the door open and found her

A Likeness

Almost to your birthday and as I
am getting dressed alone in the house
a button comes off and once I find
a needle with an eye big enough
for me to try to thread it
and at last have sewed the button on
I open an old picture of you
who always did such things by magic
one photograph found after you died
of you at twenty

beautiful in a way
I would never see
for that was nine years
before I was born
but the picture has
faded suddenly
spots have marred it
maybe it is past repair
I have only what I remember

Raiment

Believing comes after
there were coverings
who can believe
that we were born without them
he she or it wailing
back the first breath
from a stark reflection
raw and upside-down
early but already
not original

into the last days
and then some way past them
the body that we
are assured is more
than what covers it
is kept covered
out of habit which
is a word for dress
out of custom
which is an alteration
of the older word *costume*
out of decency
which is handed down
from a word for what
is fitting

apparently we believe
in the words
and through them
but we long beyond them
for what is unseen
what remains out of reach
what is kept covered
with colors and sizes
we hunger
for what is undoubted yet dubious
known to be different
and our fabrics tell
of difference
we dress in difference
calling it ours

Europe

After days untold the word
comes You will see it
tomorrow you will
see what you have only heard of
ever since you were too small
to understand And that night
which I would scarcely remember
I lay looking up through
the throb of iron at sea
trying again to remember
how I believed it would look
and in the morning light
from the bow of the freighter
that I know must have gone by now
to the breaker's decades ago
I could make out the shadow
on the horizon before us
that was the coast of Spain
and as we came closer another
low shape passing before it

like a hand on a dial
a warship I recognized
from a model of it I had made
when I was a child
and beyond it
there was a road down the cliff
that I would descend some years later
and recognize it
there we were all together
one time

Photographer

Later in the day
after he had died and the long box
full of shadow had turned the corner
and perhaps he no longer was watching
what the light was doing
as its white blaze climbed higher
bleaching the street and drying the depths
to a blank surface

when they started to excavate the burrow
under the roof where he had garnered his life
and to drag it all out into the raw moment
and carry it down the stairs
armload by armload to the waiting dumpcart
nests of bedding clothes from their own days
shards of the kitchen there were a few bundled papers
and stacks of glass plates heavy and sliding
easily broken before they could be got down
to the tumbril and mule
pieces grinding underfoot
all over the floor and down the stairs
as they would remember

fortunately someone who understood
what was on the panes bought everything in the studio

almost no letters were there but on the glass
they turned up face after face
of the light before anyone had beheld it
there were its cobbled lanes leading far into themselves
apple trees flowering in another century
lilies open in sunlight against former house walls
worn flights of stone stairs before the war
in days not seen except by the bent figure
invisible under the hood
who had just disappeared

Traces

Papers already darkened
deckled because of the many years
bear signs of a sole moment
of someone's passage
that surely was mine
not a sound of it now
coming from its land
that was all there was
in its time
with all its leaves
and the barking not noticed
in the distance
and the silence in the books then

now the machine that does that
is taking the world away
just across the streambed
at the foot of the garden
what can abide as we
follow among those
who have forgotten
and what do we remember
eyes but not the seeing
often we did not know
that we were happy

even when we were not
how could we have known that
at no distance

Inheritance

At my elbow on the table
it lies open as it has done
for a good part of these thirty
years ever since my father died
and it passed into my hands
this *Webster's New International
Dictionary of the English
Language* of 1922
on India paper which I
was always forbidden to touch
for fear I would tear or somehow
damage its delicate pages
heavy in their binding
this color of wet sand
on which thin waves hover
when it was printed he was twenty-six
they had not been married four years
he was a country preacher
in a one-store town and I suppose
a man came to the door one day
peddling this new dictionary
of fine paper like the Bible
at an unrepeatable price
and it seemed it would represent
a distinction just to own it
confirming something about him
that he could not even name
now its cover is worn as though
it had been carried on journeys
across the mountains and deserts
of the earth but it has been here
beside me the whole time

what has frayed it like that
loosening it gnawing at it
all through these years
I know I must have used it
much more than he did but always
with care and indeed affection
turning the pages patiently
in search of meanings

A Broken Glass

Gold rim worn bare here and there

gold ring below it
broken after more than two centuries
nine facets under it tapering inward
suddenly splintered with a new light
irrevocable as light is
while the stem on which they converge
with six facets flowing down it
remains untouched
and the base onto which they run out
like streams frozen below their waterfalls
has noticed nothing heard nothing
and it is only when the glass has been broken
after holding so many days and nights
that I see clearly on the pieces the whole flower
the tall gold iris that has been growing there
longer than I know

out of the gold ground

Lament for a Stone

The bay where I found you faced the long light
of the west glowing under the cold sky

there Columba as the story goes looked
back and could not see Ireland any more

therefore he could stay he made up his mind
in that slur of the sea on the shingle

shaped in a fan around the broad crescent
formed all of green pebbles found nowhere else

flecked with red held in blue depths and polished
smooth as water by rolling like water

along each other rocking as they were
rocking at his feet it is said that they

are proof against drowning and I saw you
had the shape of the long heart of a bird

and when I took you in my palm we flew
through the years hearing them rush under us

where have you flown now leaving me to hear
that sound alone without you in my hand

A Note from the Cimmerians

By the time it gets to us
we can make nothing of it
but questions or else it makes
us turn out to be only
questions that we are helpless
not to ask
in the first place

is it real which is to say
is it authentic which is
to say is it from someone
not one of us and if so
how do we know that and where
has it come from what petal
of our compass or from what
age of the orbiting phrase
before us as we say it
in the language we speak now
and for whom was it set down
or to whom is it addressed
now or will it speak later
in another meaning and
is it a question itself
or the back of a question
advancing or receding
from our point of view and are
we to believe they exist
in truth those shapes of antique
hearsay whom no one has seen
by day the Cimmerians
who dwell in utter darkness
it is said or perhaps live
on the other side of it

A Codex

It was a late book given up for lost
again and again with its sentences

bare at last and phrases that seemed transparent
revealing what had been there the whole way

the poems of daylight after the day
lying open at last on the table

without explanation or emphasis
like sounds left when the syllables have gone

clarifying the whole grammar of waiting
not removing one question from the air

or closing the story although single lights
were beginning by then above and below

while the long twilight deepened its silence
from sapphire through opal to Athena's iris

until shadow covered the gray pages
the comet words the book of presences

after which there was little left to say
but then it was night and everything was known

Beyond Question

What is it then
that Kent said he could see
in Lear's countenance
he called it authority
to give it a name
though it is recognized
whenever seen or heard
whether it is staring
from the pupil
of the dead animal
or blocking the road
when the brakes have gone
or irreversible
in the doctor's syllables
or in the headline or the fine
print or the waiting envelope
or surfacing in the mirror
it is there

whole untouched never
answering it is in
the sound of breathing
and in a voice
bird or human calling calling
it burns in the single
instant of pain
flashing its colors
it runs in the mind
of water and in
the dumbness of touch
in the only light
in the pace of nightfall

Youth

Through all of youth I was looking for you
without knowing what I was looking for

or what to call you I think I did not
even know I was looking how would I

have known you when I saw you as I did
time after time when you appeared to me

as you did naked offering yourself
entirely at that moment and you let

me breathe you touch you taste you knowing
no more than I did and only when I

began to think of losing you did I
recognize you when you were already

part memory part distance remaining
mine in the ways that I learn to miss you

from what we cannot hold the stars are made

II

in memory of Muku, Makana, Koa

By Dark

When it is time I follow the black dog
into the darkness that is the mind of day

I can see nothing there but the black dog
the dog I know going ahead of me

not looking back oh it is the black dog
I trust now in my turn after the years

when I had all the trust of the black dog
through an age of brightness and through shadow

on into the blindness of the black dog
where the rooms of the dark were already known

and had no fear in them for the black dog
leading me carefully up the blind stairs

Calling a Distant Animal

Here it is once again this one note
from a string of longing

tightened suddenly from both ends
and held for plucking

tone torn out of one birdsong
though that bird

by now may be
where a call cannot

follow it
the same note goes on calling

across space and is heard now
in the old night and known there

a silence recognized
by the silence it calls to

Night with No Moon

Now you are darker than I can believe
it is not wisdom that I have come to

with its denials and pure promises
but this absence that I cannot set down

still hearing when there is nothing to hear
reaching into the blindness that was there

thinking to walk in the dark together

Good Night

Sleep softly my old love
my beauty in the dark
night is a dream we have
as you know as you know

night is a dream you know
an old love in the dark
around you as you go
without end as you know

in the night where you go
sleep softly my old love
without end in the dark
in the love that you know

At the Bend

I look for you my curl of sleep
my breathing wave on the night shore
my star in the fog of morning
I think you can always find me

I call to you under my breath
I whisper to you through the hours
all your names my ear of shadow
I think you can always hear me

I wait for you my promised day
my time again my homecoming
my being where you wait for me
I think always of you waiting

Into the Cloud

What do you have with you
now my small traveller
suddenly on the way
and all at once so far

on legs that never were
up to the life that you
led them and breathing with
the shortness breath comes to

my endless company
when you could come to me
you would stay close to me
until the day was done

o closest to my breath
if you are able to
please wait a while longer
on that side of the cloud

Another Dream of Burial

Sometimes it is a walled garden
with the stone over the entrance
broken and inside it a few
silent dried-up weeds or it may
be a long pool perfectly still
with the clear water revealing
no color but that of the gray
stone around it and once there was
in a painting of a landscape
one torn place imperfectly mended
that showed the darkness under it
but still I have set nothing down
and turned and walked away from it
into the whole world

A Ring

At this moment
this earth which for all we know

is the only place in the vault of darkness
with life on it is wound in a fine veil

of whispered voices groping the frayed waves
of absence they keep flaring up

out of hope entwined with its opposite
to wander in ignorance as we do

when we look for what we have lost
one moment touching the earth and the next

straying far out past the orbits and webs
and the static of knowledge they go on

without being able to tell whether
they are addressing the past or the future

or knowing where they are heard these words
of the living talking to the dead

Little Soul
after Hadrian

Little soul little stray
little drifter
now where will you stay
all pale and all alone
after the way
you used to make fun of things

Trail Marker

One white tern sails calling
across the evening sky
under the few high clouds touched
with the first flush of sunset
while the tide keeps going out
going out to the south
all day it has been six months
that you have been gone
and then the tern is gone
and only the clouds are there
and the sounds of the late tide

Dream of Koa Returning

Sitting on the steps of that cabin
that I had always known
with its porch and gray-painted floorboards
I looked out to the river
flowing beyond the big trees
and all at once you
were just behind me
lying watching me
as you did years ago
and not stirring at all
when I reached back slowly
hoping to touch
your long amber fur
and there we stayed without moving
listening to the river
and I wondered whether
it might be a dream
whether you might be a dream
whether we both were a dream
in which neither of us moved

III

Cargo

The moment at evening
when the pictures set sail from the walls
with their lights out
unmooring without hesitation or stars
they carry no questions
as their unseen sails
the beginning and the end
wing and wing
bear them out beyond
the faces each set in its instant
and beyond the landscapes of other times
and the tables piled with fruit
just picked and with motionless
animals all together known
in the light as still lives
they sail on the sound of night
bearing with them that life
they have been trying to show
from dawn until dark

Going

Only humans believe
there is a word for goodbye
we have one in every language
one of the first words we learn
it is made out of greeting
but they are going away
the raised hand waving
the face the person the place
the animal the day
leaving the word behind
and what it was meant to say

The Curlew

When the moon has gone I fly on alone
into this night where I have never been

the eggshell of dark before and after
in its height I am older and younger

than all that I have come to and beheld
and carry still untouched across the cold

Nocturne

The stars emerge one
by one into the names
that were last found for them
far back in other
darkness no one remembers
by watchers whose own
names were forgotten
later in the dark
and as the night deepens
other lumens begin
to appear around them
as though they were shining
through the same instant
from a single depth of age
though the time between
each one of them
and its nearest neighbor
contains in its span
the whole moment of the earth
turning in a light
that is not its own
with the complete course
of life upon it
born to brief reflection

recognition and anguish
from one cell evolving
to remember daylight
laughter and distant music

Day Without a Name

Not today then
will it be here after all
the word for this time
the name its age
today nothing is missing
except the word for it
the morning is too
beautiful to be anything else
too brief for waiting
and behind its pellucid passage
another light that does not
appear to be moving
fills the horizon
there the word
waited for
like a wild creature
not glimpsed this season
not seen by anyone
must be watching

Recognitions

Stories come to us like new senses

a wave and an ash tree were sisters
they had been separated since they were children
but they went on believing in each other
though each was sure that the other must be lost
they cherished traits of themselves that they thought of

as family resemblances features they held in common
the sheen of the waves fluttered in remembrance
of the undersides of the leaves of the ash tree
in summer air and the limbs of the ash tree
recalled the wave as the breeze lifted it
and they wrote to each other every day
without knowing where to send the letters
some of which have come to light only now
revealing in their old but familiar language
a view of the world we could not have guessed at

but that we always wanted to believe

Escape Artist

When they arrange the cages
for experiments
they have long known
that there is no magic
in foxes at any time
singly or by species
color region gender
whether in the wild
or after generations
bred in captivity
for some grade of fur
or trait of character
for the benefit
of a distant
inquiring relative
living in ambush and hope
clothes and mourning

but what after all
was magic and where
could it have come from
as the experts considered this
wordless descendant

of countless visions
apparitions tales
that vanished in the telling
this heir of conjurers
of disappearing acts
caged now in numbers
lost in plain sight

The Mole

Here is yet one
more life that we see only from outside
from the outside

not in itself but later
in signs of its going
a reminder
in the spring daylight

it happened when we were not noticing
and so close to us
that we might not have been here
disregarded as we were

see where we have walked
the earth has risen again
out of its darkness
where it has been recognized
without being seen
known by touch
of the blind velvet fingers
the wise nails
descendants of roots and water

we have seen them
only in death and in pictures
opened from darkness afterward

but here the earth
has been touched and raised
eye has not seen it come
ear has not heard
the famous fur
the moment that finds its way
in the dark without us

Eye of Shadow

Sentry of the other side
it may have watched the beginning
without being noticed in all
that blossoming radiance
the beggar in dark rags
down on the dark threshold
a shadow waiting

in its own fair time
all in its rags it rises
revealing its prime claim
upon the latter day
that fades around it
while the sky is turning
with the whole prophecy

o lengthening dark vision
reaching across faces
across colors and mountains
and all that is known
or appears to be known
herald without a sound
leave-taking without a word
guide beyond time and knowledge
o patience
beyond patience

I touch the day
I taste the light
I remember

A Letter to Ruth Stone

Now that you have caught sight
of the other side of darkness
the invisible side
so that you can tell
it is rising
first thing in the morning
and know it is there
all through the day

another sky
clear and unseen
has begun to loom
in your words
and another light is growing
out of their shadows
you can hear it

now you will be able
to envisage beyond
any words of mine
the color of these leaves
that you never saw
awake above the still valley
in the small hours
under the moon
three nights past the full

you know there was never
a name for that color

Worn Words

The late poems are the ones
I turn to first now
following a hope that keeps
beckoning me
waiting somewhere in the lines
almost in plain sight

it is the late poems
that are made of words
that have come the whole way
they have been there

A Letter to Su Tung-p'o

Almost a thousand years later
I am asking the same questions
you did the ones you kept finding
yourself returning to as though
nothing had changed except the tone
of their echo growing deeper
and what you knew of the coming
of age before you had grown old
I do not know any more now
than you did then about what you
were asking as I sit at night
above the hushed valley thinking
of you on your river that one
bright sheet of moonlight in the dream
of the waterbirds and I hear
the silence after your questions
how old are the questions tonight

Bashō's Child

Beside the Fuji River
there is a lost child crying
dead for three hundred years
and who knows how many more
since the evening in autumn
when her mother carried her
out to the water noise
that would cover the sound of her crying
and then walked back into the silence
and the child cried all night
and into the frosty daylight
when the men who discovered her
stood over her like shadows
their hands talking but only
to each other until one of them
at last bent to put something
on the leaves beside her
before they all went away
with the sound of her crying
following him and following
the words he would write about her
wherever the words might go

The Odds

His first winter in that city
after years in the north a friend
wrote to me of how people there
were dealing with the cold
he told me that crews
were digging up the avenue
down at the corner all day
the men keeping a fire going
in an oil drum with holes
down the sides and feeding it whatever
turned up and he had been watching

two men by the barrel with three
gloves between them passing one
glove back and forth
while they stamped their feet
and he had tried to tell whether
it was a right or a left glove

The Long and the Short of It

As long as we can believe anything
we believe in measure
we do it with the first breath we take
and the first sound we make
it is in each word we learn
and in each of them it means
what will come again and when
it is there in *meal* and in *moon*
and in *meaning* it is the meaning
it is the firmament and the furrow
turning at the end of the field
and the verse turning with its breath
it is in memory that keeps telling us
some of the old story about us

Unknown Age

For all the features it hoards and displays
age seems to be without substance at any time

whether morning or evening it is a moment of air
held between the hands like a stunned bird

while I stand remembering light in the trees
of another century on a continent long submerged

with no way of telling whether the leaves at that time
felt memory as they were touching the day

and no knowledge of what happened to the reflections
on the pond's surface that never were seen again

the bird lies still while the light goes on flying

My Hand

See how the past is not finished
here in the present
it is awake the whole time
never waiting
it is my hand now but not what I held
it is not my hand but what I held
it is what I remember
but it never seems quite the same
no one else remembers it
a house long gone into air
the flutter of tires over a brick road
cool light in a vanished bedroom
the flash of the oriole
between one life and another
the river a child watched

What the Bridges Hear

Even the right words if ever
we come to them tell of something
the words never knew
celestia for starlight
or *starlight* for starlight
so at this moment there may be words
somewhere among the nebulae
for the two bridges across the wide

rock-strewn river
part way around the bend from each other
in the winter sunlight
late in the afternoon more than half
a century ago with the sound
of the water rushing under them
and passing between them unvarying
and inaudible it is still there
so is the late sunlight
of that winter afternoon
although the winter has vanished
and the bridges are still reaching across
the wide sound of being there

The First Days

As I come from a continent
that I saw closing behind me
like a lost element
day after day before
I believed I was leaving it

here surfacing through the long
backlight of my recollection
is this other world veiled
in its illusion of being known
at the moment of daybreak
when the dreams all at once are gone
into shadow leaving only
in their place the familiar
once-familiar landscape

with its road open to the south
the roofs emerging on the way
from their own orbits according
to an order as certain
as the seasons
the fields emerald and mustard

and beyond them the precession
of hills with red cows on the slopes
and then the edging clouds of sheep

and the house door at evening
one old verb in the lock turning
and the fragrance of cold stone as once more
the door cedes in a dark hush
that neither answers nor forgets
and an unchanged astonishment

that has never been tamed nor named
nor held in the hand
nor ever fully seen
but it is still the same
a vision before news a gift
of flight in a dream
of clear depths where I glimpse
far out of reach the lucent days
from which now I am made

Heartland

From the beginning it belonged to distance
as the blue color of the mountain does

and though it existed on a map somewhere
and might be discovered by chance
and even be recognized perhaps
at an odd moment

it survived beyond
what could be known at the time
in its archaic
untaught language
that brings the bees to the rosemary

many years after it had been found
its true name remained
on the other side of knowledge

yet it was still there
like a season that has changed
but appears in the light

in the unspoken morning

Long Afternoon Light

Small roads written in sleep in the foothills
how long ago and I believed you were lost
with the bronze then deepening in the light
and the shy moss turning to itself holding
its own brightness above the badger's path
while a single crow sailed west without a sound
we trust without giving it a thought
that we will always see it as we see it
once and that what we know is only
a moment of what is ours and will stay
we believe it as the moment slips away
as lengthening shadows merge in the valley
and a window kindles there like a first star
what we see again comes to us in secret

Cave

Stone room dug into the brow of the ridge
one corner of it the rose-gray living rock
that covers the dark halls of the underworld
great maned green water-dog on the south wall
where the whitewash is mottled to a map of time
casement windows to the north facing
the quilt of small fields and the bend of river

far below them and set into the hillside
in the east wall the ancient oven mouth
a dark shape like the backs of sunrise and moonrise
and the black arches of the woodstove with its scrolls
of iron leaves and love goddess and rainbow
I have come back through the years to this
stone hollow encrypted in its own stillness
I hear it without listening

The Morning Hills

As those who are gone now
keep wandering through our words
sounds of paper following them
at untold distances
so I wake again in the old house
where at times I have believed
that I was waiting for myself
and many years have gone
taking with them the semblance of youth
reason after reason ranges of blue hills
who did I think was missing
those days neither here nor there
my own dog waiting
to be known

Cold Spring Morning

At times it has seemed that when
I first came here it was an old self
I recognized in the silent walls
and the river far below
but the self has no age
as I knew even then and had known
for longer than I could remember

as the sky has no sky
except itself this white morning in May
with fog hiding the barns
that are empty now and hiding the mossed
limbs of gnarled walnut trees and the green
pastures unfurled along the slope
I know where they are and the birds
that are hidden in their own calls
in the cold morning
I was not born here I come and go

Near Field

This is not something new or kept secret
the tilled ground unsown in late spring
the dead are not separate from the living
each has one foot in the unknown
and cannot speak for the other
the field tells none of its turned story
it lies under its low cloud like a waiting river
the dead made this out of their hunger
out of what they had been told
out of the pains and shadows
and bowels of animals
out of turning and
coming back singing
about another time

To Paula in Late Spring

Let me imagine that we will come again
when we want to and it will be spring
we will be no older than we ever were
the worn griefs will have eased like the early cloud
through which the morning slowly comes to itself
and the ancient defenses against the dead

will be done with and left to the dead at last
the light will be as it is now in the garden
that we have made here these years together
of our long evenings and astonishment

Youth of Grass

Yesterday in the hushed white sunlight
down along the meadows by the river
through all the bright hours they cut the first hay
of this year to leave it tossed in long rows
leading into the twilight and long evening
while thunderheads grumbled from the horizon
and now the whole valley and the slopes around it
that look down to the sky in the river
are fragrant with hay as this night comes in
and the owl cries across the new spaces
to the mice suddenly missing their sky
and so the youth of this spring all at once is over
it has come upon us again taking us
once more by surprise just as we began
to believe that those fields would always be green

The Silence of the Mine Canaries

The bats have not flowered
for years now in the crevice
of the tower wall when the long twilight
of spring has seeped across it
as the west light brought back
the colors of parting
the furred buds have not hung there
waking among their dark petals
before sailing out blind along their own echoes
whose high infallible cadenzas only
they could hear completely and could ride

to take over at that hour
from the swallows gliding
ever since daybreak over the garden
from their nests under the eaves
skimming above the house and the hillside pastures
their voices glittering in their exalted tongue
who knows how long now since they have been seen
and the robins have gone from the barn
where the cows spent the summer days
though they stayed long after the cows were gone
the flocks of five kinds of tits have not come again
the blue tits that nested each year
in the wall where their young
could be heard deep in the stones by the window
calling *Here Here* have not returned
the marks of their feet are still there on the stone
of their doorsill that does not know
what it is missing
the cuckoo has not been heard
again this May
nor for many a year the nightjar
nor the mistle thrush song thrush whitethroat
the blackcap that instructed Mendelssohn
I have seen them
I have stood and listened
I was young
they were singing of youth
not knowing that they were singing for us

Walled Place Above the River

There are fields smaller than this
I have seen them tilled and harvested
by the old who still labored by hand
down the lane and out on the upland
where they are forgotten now
their own names do not believe in them

and there are rooms bigger than this
in houses I have visited
finding myself in occasions
full of voices or sometimes silence
but not the silence here

the lid of earth inside the walls
in Dublin where Hopkins' bones were left
among those of fellow Jesuits
as I recall it is of a size
roughly comparable to this
which years ago I thought might be
where my own remains should lie

over there in the northeast corner
under the oak with the whole valley
beyond it blue at noon and the voice
of the oriole tumbling
from the woods to the east again
after years of absence
and three black-and-orange butterflies
cruising the white glare of the grass
is the only grave I know here

that of the donkey abandoned
by his mother and carried to the barn
cold nose out of the brambles
into which he had rolled and he followed
us and the warm bottle for a week
this is not a place made for knowledge

I do not know what the enclosure was built for
dug out facing north
toward the far side of the river
and levelled like a terrace
and why the walls were raised
stone on stone to form a square
with the two narrow passages
one toward the barn one toward the fields below
nor who made it nor how long ago

but I have been listening to it
since I was young and its voice is the same
though the leaves have changed and the seasons
and some of the longings
now a soft breath stirs the trees as morning ends
in a few days it will be summer

A Horse Heaven

The fence is new and the gate in it
of the same thin green wire that is there
just to remind them that they are home
in the long pasture below the woods
the tall gray horses all slender mares
moving lightly as clouds before me
close to me curious none of them
can remember me I tell myself
all of them must have been born since I
was here last and some of the young ones
watch me over their shoulders taking
no chances but some of the elders
move near to me with the same small wave
nudging them on and they look at me
as though maybe they had once known me

One of the Butterflies

The trouble with pleasure is the timing
it can overtake me without warning
and be gone before I know it is here
it can stand facing me unrecognized
while I am remembering somewhere else
in another age or someone not seen
for years and never to be seen again
in this world and it seems that I cherish
only now a joy I was not aware of

when it was here although it remains
out of reach and will not be caught or named
or called back and if I could make it stay
as I want to it would turn into pain

Parts of a Tune

One old man keeps humming the same few notes
of some song he thought he had forgotten
back in the days when as he knows there was
no word for *life* in the language
and if they wanted to say *eyes* or *heart*
they would hold up a leaf and he remembers
the big tree where it rose from the dry ground
and the way the birds carried water in their voices
they were all the color of their fear of the dark
and as he sits there humming he remembers
some of the words they come back to him now
he smiles hearing them come and go

Nocturne II

August arrives in the dark

we are not even asleep and it is here
with a gust of rain rustling before it
how can it be so late all at once
somewhere the Perseids are falling
toward us already at a speed that would
burn us alive if we could believe it
but in the stillness after the rain ends
nothing is to be heard but the drops falling
one at a time from the tips of the leaves
into the night and I lie in the dark
listening to what I remember
while the night flies on with us into itself

White Note

Autumn comes early this year
the last morning of August
fog fills the valley clouding
the late roses and the scent
of wet leaves floats in the light
one day after the full moon
it is the time of going
small flocks of migrant birds catch
like strands of wool in the trees
west of the village and wait
for something to remind them
of the journey and their own
way and when the fog lifts
they have gone and with them the days
of summer have vanished
and the leaves here and there begin
taking to themselves
the colors of sunlight
to keep them

Gray Herons in the Field Above the River

Now that the nights turn longer than the days
we are standing in the still light after dawn

in the high grass of autumn that is green again
hushed in its own place after the burn of summer

each of us stationed alone without moving
at a perfect distance from all the others

like shadows of ourselves risen out of our shadows
each eye without turning continues to behold

what is moving
each of us is one of seven now

we have come a long way sailing our opened clouds
remembering all night where the world would be

the clear shallow stream the leaves floating along it
the dew in the hushed field the only morning

No Shadow

Dog grief and the love of coffee
lengthen like a shadow of mine

and now that my eyes no longer
swear to anything I look out

through the cloud light of this autumn
and see the valley where I came

first more than half my life ago
oh more than half with its river

a sky in the palm of a hand
never unknown and never known

never mine and never not mine
beyond it into the distance

the ridges reflect the clouds now
through a morning without shadows

the river still seems not to move
as though it were the same river

The Making of Amber

The September flocks form crying
gathering southward
even small birds knowing
for the first time
how to fly all the way as one

at daybreak the split fig
is filled with dew
the finch finds it
like something it remembers

then across the afternoon
the grape vine hangs low in the doorway
and grapes one by one
taste warm to the tongue
transparent and soundless
rich with late daylight

September's Child

September light gray and rose touches the ridge above the
    valley
seeps upward at daybreak through its own silence
without beginning without stages with white clouds still
    cloaking the river
and a great ship of towers anchored on the one hill that rises
    through them
then amber morning and the markets unfolding
smiles of veteran vendors assembled once more in bright day
old hands holding honey jars sunlight on weathered faces
knowing summer and winter well but bound to neither of
    them
in the cool fragrance of wild strawberries raspberries spice
    bread
a morning when the first green figs are ripening
and single birds come bringing their late hopes as the light
    warms

recognizing through the remaining leaves a moment they
   have never seen
as I do waking again here after many lifetimes
to the sight of a morning before I was born

Remembering the Wings

What became of all the pigeons
along the ridge of the barn roof
the crest on the dark red tiled slope
those black Mondains broad as barges
the pheasant wings of the Cauchoises
the brilliant buffed copper Bouvreuils
the Carneauxs forever fighting
both Montaubans trailing their grace
elegant and amiable
two long indolent innocents
easy-come Bertie and Midnight
crown princes born for fair weather
Édouard said the fox would get them
Verdun still not far in his mind
out there watching in the long grass
it would climb up like a shadow
then what became of the children
who had gone to school with him
in the house just beyond the barn
even then the war was lying
out in the summer fields waiting
and then what became of Édouard
when I look and the roof is bare

Shadow Hand

Duporte the roofer that calm voice
those sure hands gentling weathered tiles
into new generations or
half of him rising through a roof

like some sea spirit from a wave
to turn shaped slates into fish scales
that would swim in the rain Duporte
who seemed to smooth arguments by
listening and whom they sent for
when a bone was broken or when
they had a pig to kill because
of the way he did it only
yesterday after all these years
I learned that he had suddenly
gone blind while still in his sixties
and died soon after that while I
was away and I never knew
and it seemed as though it had just
happened and it had not been long
since we stood in the road talking
about owls nesting in chimneys
in the dark in empty houses

Barrade

The stone tower on the barrens
alone there for five hundred years
grew back into night when night came
at its feet the walls around it
the dry pool the raised threshing floor
the ancient hollow acacia
the walnut trees by the pasture
were back in the dark they came from
the invisible sheep sifted
through sere grass with the circling sound
of a soft breath in the distance
later the owl the white lady
shrieked close across the darkened fields
to the mice waiting for her there
visible to no one but her
as she sailed up onto the stone
top of the tower and from it sang

Me Me to her moment and then
maybe silence until the hour
when a far-off echo began
from the earth and down under it
coming nearer an iron note
the night train through the cut before
the long turn down to the valley
and for only an instant through
a gap at the end of a dark field
the strip of yellow windows passed
like the days on a calendar
the long rays of their reflections
reaching across the naked earth
a moment and then never gone

Into October

These must be the colors of returning
the leaves darkened now but staying on
into the bronzed morning among the seed heads
and the dry stems and the umbers of October
the secret season that appears on its own
a recognition without a sound
long after the day when I stood in its light
out on the parched barrens beside a spring
all but hidden in a tangle of eglantine
and picked the bright berries made of that summer

Lights Out

The old grieving autumn goes on calling to its summer
the valley is calling to other valleys beyond the ridge
each star is roaring alone into darkness
there is not a sound in the whole night

Falling

Long before daybreak
none of the birds yet awake
rain comes down with the sound
of a huge wind rushing
through the valley trees
it comes down around us
all at the same time
and beyond it there is nothing
it falls without hearing itself
without knowing
there is anyone here
without seeing where it is
or where it is going
like a moment of great
happiness of our own
that we cannot remember
coasting with the lights off

Grace Note

It is at last any morning
not answering to a name
I wake before there is light
hearing once more that same
music without repetition
or beginning playing
away into itself
in silence like a wave
a unison in its own
key that I seem
to have heard before I
was listening but by the time
I hear it now it is gone
as when on a morning
alive with sunlight
almost at the year's end

a feathered breath a bird
flies in at the open window
then vanishes leaving me
believing what I do not see

One Valley

Once I thought I could find
where it began
but that never happened
though I went looking for it
time and again
cutting my way past
empty pools and dry waterfalls
where my dog ran straight up the stone
like an unmoored flame

it seemed that the beginning
could not be far then
as I went on through the trees
over the rocks toward the mountain
until I came out in the open
and saw no sign of it

where the roaring torrent
raced at one time
to carve farther down
those high walls in the stone
for the silence that I hear now
day and night on its way to the sea

The Old Trees on the Hill

When you were living
and it was later than we knew
there was an old orchard

far up on the hill behind the house
dark apple trees wrapped in moss
standing deep in thorn bushes and wild grape
cobwebs breathing between the branches
memory lingering in silence
the spring earth fragrant with other seasons
crows conferred in those boughs and sailed on
chickadees talked of the place as their own
there were still kinglets and bluebirds
and the nuthatch following the folded bark
the churr of one wren a dark shooting star
with all that each of them knew then
but whoever had planted those trees
straightening now and again over the spade
to stand looking out across the curled
gleaming valley to the far gray ridges
one autumn after the leaves had fallen
while the morning frost still slept in the hollows
had been buried somewhere far from there
and those who had known him and his family
were completely forgotten you told me
and you said you had never been up there
though it was a place where you
loved to watch the daylight changing
and we looked up and watched the daylight there

A Single Autumn

The year my parents died
one that summer one that fall
three months and three days apart
I moved into the house
where they had lived their last years
it had never been theirs
and was still theirs in that way
for a while

echoes in every room
without a sound
all the things that we
had never been able to say
I could not remember

doll collection
in a china cabinet
plates stacked on shelves
lace on drop-leaf tables
a dried branch of bittersweet
before a hall mirror
were all planning to wait

the glass doors of the house
remained closed
the days had turned cold
and out in the tall hickories
the blaze of autumn had begun
on its own

I could do anything

Lake Shore in Half Light

There is a question I want to ask
and I can't remember it
I keep trying to
I know it is the same question
it has always been
in fact I seem to know
almost everything about it
all that reminds me of it
leading me to the lake shore
at daybreak or twilight
and to whatever is standing
next to the question

as a body stands next to its shadow
but the question is not a shadow
if I knew who discovered
zero I might ask
what there was before

A Momentary Creed

I believe in the ordinary day
that is here at this moment and is me

I do not see it going its own way
but I never saw how it came to me

it extends beyond whatever I may
think I know and all that is real to me

it is the present that it bears away
where has it gone when it has gone from me

there is no place I know outside today
except for the unknown all around me

the only presence that appears to stay
everything that I call mine it lent me

even the way that I believe the day
for as long as it is here and is me

Rain Light

All day the stars watch from long ago
my mother said I am going now
when you are alone you will be all right
whether or not you know you will know
look at the old house in the dawn rain

all the flowers are forms of water
the sun reminds them through a white cloud
touches the patchwork spread on the hill
the washed colors of the afterlife
that lived there long before you were born
see how they wake without a question
even though the whole world is burning

Just This

When I think of the patience I have had
back in the dark before I remember
or knew it was night until the light came
all at once at the speed it was born to
with all the time in the world to fly through
not concerned about ever arriving
and then the gathering of the first stars
unhurried in their flowering spaces
and far into the story the planets
cooling slowly and the ages of rain
then the seas starting to bear memory
the gaze of the first cell at its waking
how did this haste begin this little time
at any time this reading by lightning
scarcely a word this nothing this heaven

The Laughing Thrush

O nameless joy of the morning

tumbling upward note by note out of the night
and the hush of the dark valley
and out of whatever has not been there

song unquestioning and unbounded
yes this is the place and the one time

in the whole of before and after
with all of memory waking into it

and the lost visages that hover
around the edge of sleep
constant and clear
and the words that lately have fallen silent
to surface among the phrases of some future
if there is a future

here is where they all sing the first daylight
whether or not there is anyone listening

NEW AND UNCOLLECTED
POEMS 1993–2011

The Stone

These junipers growing out from the yellow rocks
   now in the sunlight near the top of the steep slope
under its split cliff face and these dwarf oaks returning
   in silence not yet believing after so long
out of life and this hawthorn with its white light in flower
   this tangle of hazel and eglantine drawing
tight below the cliff where the hidden water slips out
   from its green lips darkening the stone in every
season and nursing a trailing shadow of horsetail
   and osiers below it these fresh holes clawed in the ocher
clay these traces of fox and badger these invaders
   have come back from before there were names for this place
before my friend Herault planted the pear trees here
   that have gone back to be quinces flowering with
the wild things and planted the peaches and the rest
   of the late orchard that is dry wood covered with moss
and before the Cavannes harvested their grapes here
   for generations when the whole village tilled the slopes
by hand and before the road from the valley was a cart lane
   and before the Romans and before it was understood
that the source in the cliff and the vipers living
   in the rocks were the same woman and that when they rolled
back into one brain they made from their breath a stone
   that would float in the air like a forgotten day

1993

Tide Line Garden
To Stanley Kunitz

With what you know now about a garden by the sea
I wish you had seen the one I walked in
one evening at the end of summer when I was young

I did not know then that it was a season
from which I would number the years that were to come
my eyes were still full of the south

the bleached slopes and hayfields
midday shimmering over the gray stones
lichen on parched plum bark
it had been the time of finding the ruined farmhouse half
    buried
under brambles on the ridge
where I would be living before long
it was that year and we were travelling north
up along the coast in the early days of September

the second war was still fresh in people's minds there
less than a decade after the Normandy landings
there was the quiet couple with the farm above the dunes
its old doors and windows recently painted sky blue
who talked of the nights before the invasion
the panzers waiting out under their apple trees
the blond young men shouldering into the cellar
walking out with their calvados talking loudly calling to the
    orchard
and the couple thinking Drink up Drink up young men
a little sorry for them
sitting up listening after the singing was over
for the sound of the RAF
that had known where to find those young men at daybreak
before they were even awake

the coastal cities were still mostly rubble
cobbles piled in the streets
Bayeux the stones darkened with rain
water running down the broken walls still trickling mortar
and the tapestry hanging in the long hall
the colors peering through shadows
that nobody could do anything about

the sound of feet edging beside that landing in silence
like the shuffling of a small wave
past Harold standing with the arrow in his eye
after most of a thousand years

sun along that coast and the sea wind had fallen late in the day
I can remember no other guests at the old house
its stones catching the west light off the salt meadows
which appeared to reach almost to the horizon
with the tide all the way out and flocks of sheep and white
    geese
drifting rimmed in light with their long shadows floating
    beside them

the house had become an inn some time after the war
the man in charge must have remembered those years
and he was pleased to show the place but scarcely open to
    questions
he said that much had been forgotten
and that often that was for the best
for a moment the smell of the occupation
seeped through the air of the meadows

beside the house a stream ran out to the salt flats
walls beyond a courtyard rose to a millpond
and a mill with a water wheel still turning
in beards of moss that dripped long strands of light

the family always kept it up he said
it was still being used even after the war

the family he said
was his wife's family
and evidently he preferred to say no more

the house must have been a place of substance for centuries
perhaps when the Sun King was building Versailles
part of an estate or the seat of a functionary
and the plain facade the stones of the windows and doorways
recalled reigns after that
inside it must all have been redone
in the years after the Revolution and Napoleon
ancient wallpaper upstairs
faded by the rays from the meadows

When you come down he said there is something
that might interest you

in front of the house he pointed along to his right
the color of the sunlight on one side of his face
the shadow of his arm draped along the hydrangeas
under the gray shutters

Down there through the garden he said
That used to be the park he said

the wall followed the small road outside
that ran above the salt meadows

he had pointed
to a broad drive that disappeared under trees
planes from the days of the armies of the Emperor
something to do with someone in the family then
the inevitable cypresses
in their dark time

stone edges from later days tumbling into shadows
under dusty ferns and piled branches
hydrangeas rusty azaleas
a few old rose bushes sinking into the shade
strap leaves of lilies darkened and drying
along one side
buried forms of forgotten gardens scarcely detectable
making the garden as it was

the drive curved under the low boughs
and I could see light at the far end through an iron gate
wide enough
as the old garden book I had just bought
recommended
for two carriages to be able to pass each other

the low light came over the wall under the trees
and along the drive near the far end
I saw a series of dark shapes

solid shadows casting solid shadow
extinction appeared to have come that far

as I approached I saw the headlights
the windshields
armored cars half-tracks gun carriers British
undamaged and looking almost new
except for the thick colorless film of nescience

I climbed into the first driver's seat
everything was there the gauges the instruments
the odometer registered fifty-three miles
before the garden

where the gates had been open
into a place long planned and never foreseen

1999

Ogres

          All night waking to the sound
          of light rain falling softly
          through the leaves in the quiet
          valley below the window
          and to Paula lying here
          asleep beside me and to
          the murmur beside the bed
          of the dogs' snoring like small
          waves coming ashore I
          am amazed at the fortune
          of this moment in the whole
          of the dark this unspoken
          favor while it is with us
          this breathing peace and then I
          think of the frauds in office
          at this instant devising
          their massacres in my name
          what part of me could they have

come from were they made of my
loathing itself and dredged from
the bitter depths of my shame

2003

The Swallows

The earth turns through its anniversaries
uncounted among all the galaxies

now ten weeks of its days and nights since she
last breathed and today half a century

since the morning when the papers were signed
that gave me the key to the half ruined

house here where nobody had been living
for most of the lifetime of the one ageing

woman who had been born here and swallows
knew their way in and out through the windows

in spring as they had always and as their
parents had before they could remember

and there were no words for their returning
no numbers for their days and their going

2006

Known Sound

After I can no longer see her
she says to me For a while there is all
that asking about how the body becomes
itself as it goes and what it is becoming
what is happening to it where it is going

step by step one moment at a time
and then all that falls aside like a curtain
and the body is gone with its worn questions
hollow joints marrow and breath and instead there is
the way whatever lived in it goes on as itself
neither before nor after neither moving nor still
and while the body was going somewhere
the way was there to begin with in the feet themselves
wherever they went and you know the sound

2006

Why Some People Do Not Read Poetry

Because they already know that it means
stopping and without stopping they know that
beyond stopping it will mean listening
listening without hearing and maybe
then hearing without hearing and what would
they hear then what good would it be to them
like some small animal crossing the road
suddenly there but not seeming to move
at night and they are late and may be on
the wrong road over the mountain with all
the others asleep and not hitting it
that time as though forgetting it again

2009

Young Man Picking Flowers

All at once he is no longer
young with his handful of flowers
in the bright morning their fragrance
rising from them as though they were
still on the stalk where they opened
only this morning to the light
in which somewhere unseen the thrush

goes on singing its perfect song
into the day of the flowers
and while he stands there holding them
the cool dew runs from them onto
his hand at this hour of their lives
is it the hand of the young man
who found them only this morning

2009

A Message to Po Chu-i

In that tenth winter of your exile
the cold never letting go of you
and your hunger aching inside you
day and night while you heard the voices
out of the starving mouths around you
old ones and infants and animals
those curtains of bones swaying on stilts
and you heard the faint cries of the birds
searching in the frozen mud for something
to swallow and you watched the migrants
trapped in the cold the great geese growing
weaker by the day until their wings
could barely lift them above the ground
so that a gang of boys could catch one
in a net and drag him to market
to be cooked and it was then that you
saw him in his own exile and you
paid for him and kept him until he
could fly again and you let him go
but then where could he go in the world
of your time with its wars everywhere
and the soldiers hungry the fires lit
the knives out twelve hundred years ago

I have been wanting to let you know
the goose is well he is here with me
you would recognize the old migrant

he has been with me for a long time
and is in no hurry to leave here
the wars are bigger now than ever
greed has reached numbers that you would not
believe and I will not tell you what
is done to geese before they kill them
now we are melting the very poles
of the earth but I have never known
where he would go after he leaves me

2010

By the Front Door

Rain through the morning
and in the long pool an old toad singing
happiness old as water

2010

Beginners

As though it had always been forbidden to remember
each of us grew up
knowing nothing about the beginning

but in time there came from that forgetting
names representing a truth of their own
and we went on repeating them
until they too began not to be remembered
then from that forgetting
came later stories like the days themselves
there seemed to be no end to them
and we told what we could remember of them

though we always forgot where they came from
and forgot what had been forbidden
whether or not it had been forbidden

but from forgotten pain we recognize
sometimes the truth when it is told to us
and from forgotten happiness we know
that the day we wake to is our own

2010

The Name of the Morning

Those first years that were not even years
and that I never knew were the first
of anything because I knew nothing else
I knew the light flashing on pigeon wings
and brightness shuttling back and forth along
telephone wires and meeting and racing on
and the silent flight of stairs at the front door
up and down and the sounds of the gate
of the streetcar and a horse under trees
the smell of paint blisters in the wakened light
those were the years when I knew nothing
before I went to school to learn everything

then I hurried to keep up with the morning
that ran beside me and I scarcely saw it
before it got away from me and I learned
time early and late and the words that waited
for telling time but the morning by then
was somewhere on the other side of the street

and I went on to learn names for the years
which they themselves did not use or know
and names for times now and then here and gone
names for losing finding and recognizing
afterward and even at the moment
before I knew that I loved the morning
and had never known a name for it
while it was there in its single light

2010

The Green Fence

My poor father
the French would say
meaning he is dead
as the newspaper said
almost forty years ago

but I find myself now
calling him that
for other reasons
I believe he was
afraid his whole life
the youngest child the last hope
trying to satisfy
his dour disappointed mother
talking his way into
one set of expectations
after another
that he knew he was not up to
neither his smiles nor
his outburst of temper
altogether sound

and my mother
with an orphan's caution
feeling that she was a stranger
wanting to do the best thing
walking to school with us
to keep us out of trouble
in the rough neighborhood
standing with us in the schoolyard
at recess to keep me
out of rough games
which were the only games
so I made no friends there

and of course I was not allowed
to play in the street
if anyone called me out

you have a big yard my father said
you can play in there with them
if I know who they are
but who wanted to come in there
I watched through the picket fence
that my sister and I
had helped to paint green that summer
over the old blistered brown
that I liked better
because of what it remembered

one day Salvatore
the fat Italian boy
who never played in their games
came and stood outside the fence
looking in between pickets
he had nothing to say
I told him I would tell
my father and he could come in
but he shook his head and sat down
on the sidewalk and looked in
and stayed there for a while
at supper I asked my father
about Salvatore coming in
and he thought and said maybe
is he Italian

another time there was May
who was black
I had never been close to a black girl
she did not play with anyone
she came slowly past the fence
and looked in and stopped
I asked her whether
she would like to come in
and she said nothing
holding onto one picket
I was curious to know
whether her color would rub off

and I touched the backs of her fingers
and for a moment we stood there

dear almost friends what happened
to you after
you wandered on down the street
and disappeared
I have been back
to where the fence used to be
and there is no one who remembers it

2010

Variation on a Theme

Thank you my life long afternoon
late in this spring that has no age
my window above the river
for the woman you led me to
when it was time at last the words
coming to me out of mid-air
that carried me through the clear day
and come even now to find me
for old friends and echoes of them
those mistakes only I could make
homesickness that guides the plovers
from somewhere they had loved before
they knew they loved it to somewhere
they had loved before they saw it
thank you good body hand and eye
and the places and moments known
only to me revisiting
once more complete just as they are
and the morning stars I have seen
and the dogs who are guiding me

2010

Turning

Going too fast for myself I missed
more than I think I can remember

almost everything it seems sometimes
and yet there are chances that come back

that I did not notice when they stood
where I could have reached out and touched them

this morning the black shepherd dog
still young looking up and saying

Are you ready this time

2011

Urticophilia

Oh let me wake where nettles are growing
in the cool first light of a spring morning
the young leaves shining after a night's rain
a green radiance glistening through them
as their roots rise into their day's color
a hue of sunlight out of the black earth
they made of their lives in the underworld
touching the darkness of their whole story
from which their leaves open to the morning
into a world they know and a season
they inherit let me wake where nettles
were always familiar and come and go
in the conversation their growth this year
compared with other years in the same places
the way they sting if barely brushed but not
if grasped firmly without hesitation
the best recipe for nettle soup with
new potatoes oh let the world's sense
come to me from the spring leaves of nettles

my true elders and not from the voices
with something to sell nor from the spreading
scar tissue of pavement numbing the flayed earth
not from the last words of the fast talkers
to whom the nettle leaves never listen

2011

The New Song

For some time I thought there was time
and that there would always be time
for what I had a mind to do
and what I could imagine
going back to and finding it
as I had found it the first time
but by this time I do not know
what I thought when I thought back then

there is no time yet it grows less
there is the sound of rain at night
arriving unknown in the leaves
once without before or after
then I hear the thrush waking
at daybreak singing the new song

2011

CHRONOLOGY

NOTE ON THE TEXTS

NOTES

INDEX OF TITLES & FIRST LINES

Chronology

1927   William Stanley Merwin born September 30, in New York City, the second son of William Stage Merwin (1896–1972), a Presbyterian minister, and Anna Jaynes (1898–1972). (Ancestors were Scottish, Welsh, and English, and the family name is Welsh; according to family legend, the first Merwin came to America in 1635 from Wales. Father was born in Rimerton, Pennsylvania, a village on the Allegheny River, the youngest of seven surviving children. Largely self-taught, he was awarded a scholarship at the age of sixteen to Maryville College in Tennessee, and after serving in the U.S. Navy during World War I, he attended the University of Pittsburgh and graduated from the Western Theological Seminary, now part of Pittsburgh Theological Seminary. Mother, born in Denver, Colorado, was orphaned at the age of six. Her great-grandfather fought in the Civil War, and rumors have linked her family to the Morris family of Revolutionary War fame. Her father, Hanson Hoadley Jaynes, of Danish and English extraction, worked as an inspector with the Pennsylvania Railroad, but was sent to Colorado after he was diagnosed with tuberculosis. After his death, her mother Bessie took her to live in Chester, Ohio, and eventually to Pittsburgh. While working as the secretary for the First Presbyterian Church, she met William Merwin, who was the pastor's chauffeur; they married in 1920. William Merwin was ordained in his first church, in Rural Valley, Pennsylvania, in 1924, and the following year the couple's first child, Hanson Jaynes Merwin, was born but died soon after birth. Shortly before William's birth they moved to Union City, New Jersey, where the Reverend Merwin was called to be pastor of the First Presbyterian Church.)

1929   Sister Ruth Ann born.

1931–35   Merwin hears his father, in the empty First Presbyterian Church, read from the sixth chapter of the book of Isaiah in the King James Version, and is mesmerized by the sound of words: "I wanted to hear that sound again, and to hear more of the life in the words, though I had only a remote sense of what the words meant, as I did sometimes when my mother read fairy tales to us. As we walked home I kept trying to remember phrases, mumbling them to myself under my breath." From the palisades at the back of the church, he often gazes across the Hoboken harbor and the busy Hudson at the skyline of Manhattan, and is fascinated by the river and its traffic. Teaches himself to read at age four. The earliest book he will remember is a tale about Indians living in the woods, an idea that intrigued him. *East o' the Sun and West o' the Moon*, translation of Norwegian folktales collected by Peter Christen Asbjørnsen and Jørgen Moe in the mid-nineteenth century, is a favorite book. Among the poems his mother reads to him are those of Robert Louis Stevenson's *A Child's Garden of Verses* and Tennyson's "The Brook"; as a child he reads *Robinson Crusoe* "four or five times," *The Swiss Family Robinson*, and all of Stevenson. Skips a grade at elementary school, then another, but is then moved back a grade because of the age difference between him and his classmates.

1936–42   Moves with family in 1936 to Scranton, Pennsylvania, where his father serves as pastor at the Washburn Street Presbyterian Church and the family lives in the twelve-room frame manse across the street, eking out a lean existence in the midst of the Depression. Wants to write words for the hymns he has heard in church, and begins to write and illustrate religious poems. Spends time in summers at a cottage at Fiddle Lake, an hour north of Scranton: "For a month or so the days there seemed like a complete time, with an age all its own." Attends local schools in Scranton, including West Scranton Junior High School, where he chooses to follow what was called "the classical curriculum" and embarks on a study of Latin. For his thirteenth birthday, his mother gives him *A Conrad Argosy*: "The first page of *Heart of Darkness* seized me in a spell, and as I read I longed to be able to write, and I began to try."

1942–43   Father enlists as a chaplain in the U.S. Army. With his sister, Merwin helps tend his mother's Victory Garden, an experience that instills a lifelong love of gardening. Attends school at Wyoming Seminary (known as "Sem") in Kingston, Pennsylvania, near Wilkes-Barre, a Methodist preparatory school. To help pay his tuition he waits on table in the dining hall and cleans the science labs. Having been forbidden by his parents to participate in school activities as a youngster, he tries everything at Sem, and joins the wrestling team, but he dislikes the school's restrictive regulations, particularly its strict segregation of boys and girls. His ambition is to attend the U.S. Naval Academy—"that ambition," he later wrote, "seems to me to have been, above all, an image of an underlying determination to get away."

1944–46   Too young to qualify for admission to the Naval Academy, he takes his college entrance exams and, having only heard the name "Princeton," adds it to his list of preferred colleges, and wins a scholarship there. Matriculates at Princeton in fall 1944; majors in English, and studies with critic R. P. Blackmur and poet John Berryman, who tells him, "I think you should get down in a corner on your knees and pray to the Muse, and I mean it literally." Befriends fellow students William Arrowsmith, Galway Kinnell, and Charles Rosen. Begins to translate plays of Federico García Lorca with the help of his Spanish professor, then goes on to Lorca poems. Devotes free time to horseback riding at night and haunting the Parnassus Bookshop on Nassau Street, where he spends what money he has on books by Thomas Wyatt and Fulke Greville, by Wallace Stevens and Ezra Pound. Spinoza, Beethoven, Milton, and Shelley are his passions; Pound becomes a literary model for him. Joins the Naval Air Corps in 1945. Vows not to follow orders to do violence to others and, regretting enlisting, asks his commanding officer to put him in the brig. Instead he is placed under psychiatric evaluation for seven months at the Chelsea Naval Hospital in Boston. Father visits him and tells him, "You must have the courage of your convictions," one of the few good things Merwin will remember about their relationship. Is moved to Bethesda Naval Hospital near Washington, D.C. Given a discharge as "psychologically unfit for military service," he returns to Princeton, where he spends as much time riding horses as in the classroom. In September 1946, writes Ezra Pound at St. Elizabeths mental hospital in Washington, D.C., where Pound had been remanded after his trial for treason; expresses sympathy for the older poet's situation and asks to correspond with him. Pound advises: "Try to write seventy-five lines a day. Now, at your age, you don't have anything to write seventy-five lines about, even if you think you do. So the thing to do is to get languages and translate." Merwin marries Dorothy Jeanne Ferry (b. 1923), a secretary for the Physics Department at Princeton, from nearby Morrisville, Pennsylvania, after they have been dating for a few months; Merwin's father officiates at the ceremony.

1947 Visits Pound at St. Elizabeths in April, and their correspondence continues. In a letter of September 27, Merwin writes that he has "written something every day—try to take two or three hours in the afternoon. Technique keeps at a steady lift, I believe"; in same letter, expresses admiration for Robert Lowell: "I believe Lowell's achievement to date to be of astonishingly large proportions, am continuously elated to find poetry of this sort and caliber possible, whether or not it is in my own direction." Graduates from Princeton; is named class poet and at graduation ceremony reads his poem "Graduation: Princeton 1947," dedicated "To those who are not graduating with our classes, because they are dead." In a note to the graduation committee, he explains, "if the requisite sentiments and unqualified optimism are nowhere to be found in this poem, that is so merely because I could not find them in myself, looking upon the occasion as I do with little optimism for the future." Takes intensive French course at McGill University in Montreal during the summer, and enrolls in Princeton graduate program to study Romance languages. Continues to correspond with Pound; one postcard instructs him to "Read seeds not twigs. EP." Grows a beard in honor of his mentor. Immerses himself in the work of William Carlos Williams.

1948 Publishes poem "Variation on the Gothic Spiral" in *Poetry*'s March issue. In summer, takes job tutoring his older friend Alan Stuyvesant's nephew, Peter Stuyvesant, at Alan's family estate, the Deer Park, in Hackettstown, New Jersey. Accepts offers for him and Dorothy to accompany Peter Stuyvesant and one of the boy's friends to Europe the following summer and, after that, to tutor the two sons of Maria Antonia da Braganza, sister of the pretender to the Portuguese throne.

1949 Sails aboard the Norwegian freighter *Nyhorn* with the two boys and Dorothy to Genoa, where they are met by Alan Stuyvesant. Spends the summer on the Côte d'Azur, based at Stuyvesant's villa at St. Jean Cap-Ferrat. For a salary of one *conto* (roughly forty dollars) a month, he and Dorothy tutor Maria Antónia's boys at a run-down Braganza family estate near Coimbra, Portugal, in the fall before moving with the family in early winter to a villa in Estoril, near Lisbon. Publishes poems and translations from the French of Joachim de Bellay, Jean Antoine de Baïf, and Richard I of England in the *Hudson Review*.

1950–51 In summer, travels through Spain and visits English poet Robert Graves on Mallorca: "I was determined to meet [him], so I just went and knocked on his door." Graves asks him to edit the addendum on birds in a new edition of his *White Goddess: A Historical Grammar of Poetic Myth* (1948), and then to tutor Graves's son William, which he does for a year, though his relationship with Graves becomes strained. At Graves's house, meets aspiring English playwright Dido Milroy (born Diana Whalley, c. 1912, in Gloucestershire), whom he will become involved with and eventually marry. After the tutoring job ends, he stays on Mallorca and rents a house in Deyá, writing a play, a verse masque, and the poems of *A Mask for Janus*, which he finishes and submits to the annual Yale Series of Younger Poets competition; W. H. Auden selects it as the winning submission in July 1951 and asks for cuts from Merwin. Begins visiting London. Through Ezra Pound's son Omar, meets and befriends T. S. Eliot. Meets Samuel Beckett in Paris. Writes verse play for children, *Rumpelstiltskin*, that is produced for BBC television in 1951.

1952–53 *A Mask for Janus* is published by Yale University Press in May 1952. Merwin supports himself largely by writing and translating for the BBC's Third Programme division, which broadcasts his verse play *The Pageant of Cain* (with music by composer John Hotchkis) on the radio in 1952; over the next four years, adaptations and translations for the BBC include a six-part television serial of *Huckleberry Finn* and radio versions of the anonymous fourteenth-century French play *Robert the Devil*, Lope de Vega's play *The Dog in the Manger*, Marivaux's play *The False Confessions*, and the *Poem of the Cid*. His marriage to Dorothy dissolves; he lives in London on Primrose Hill with Dido at 11 St. George's Terrace, once the residence of Lord Byron's widow.

1954–55 Publishes second poetry collection, *The Dancing Bears* (Yale University Press). Receives a *Kenyon Review* Fellowship for Poetry. In summer 1954, while driving with Dido through southwestern France in a beloved 1935 Daimler, discovers an old ruined farmhouse in Lacan de Loubressac, near Bretenoux in the department of the Lot, on a ridge overlooking the upper valley of the Dordogne River. "The view of the ridges beyond the valley," he later wrote, "reminded me of the ridges and the landscape of western Pennsylvania that I had loved as a child." Buys it for $1,200, his entire savings and the exact amount of the principal and interest on a small legacy earlier left to him by his aunt Margaret, known as Margie, a maiden schoolteacher cousin of his mother. "My life there, for large parts of the year over many years, was a lifetime education to me and was formative in my feelings about living, if not exactly in the woods, in a completely rural place that was rooted in tradition, and to live there as someone who belonged there." From September to December 1954, writes three hundred pages of an unfinished autobiography, then abandons it because, as he explains to an editor at Knopf, of "Constant Autobiographobia always, from the time the scheme was first bruited, Hatred of prose and narcissism—feeling that it was wrong, that I should be *making* something." Marries Dido in 1955.

1956 *Green with Beasts* is published by Knopf in the United States and by Rupert Hart-Davis in England, the first of Merwin's books to be published in England. *Darkling Child*, a play written in collaboration with Dido, is produced at the Arts Theatre, London. Merwin moves to Boston after he is appointed the Rockefeller Foundation's playwright-in-residence for one year at the Poets' Theatre in Cambridge. "Let me find," he writes in his journal about his return to America for the first time in seven years, "a hard eye, proud of having no mercy, needing none, for the thing it loves." Lives at 76 West Cedar Street in Boston. Meets George Kirstein, owner of *The Nation*, who becomes a life-long friend and surrogate father. They spend time sailing together, and Merwin later recalls he absorbed "some of the great lessons of my life" learning the world of sailing. Through Jack Sweeney, the librarian of the Lamont Poetry Room at Harvard, meets Ted Hughes and Sylvia Plath, both of whom become his close friends, in Boston and then in London. Meets Robert Lowell in Boston, and later sees him in Castine, Maine, where Lowell responds with admiration for the poems in Merwin's work-in-progress *The Drunk in the Furnace* after asking to read them. Socializes with Peter Davison, Philip Booth, and Adrienne Rich, among other poets.

1957   Merwin's play *Favor Island*, about a group of shipwrecked
           sailors who resort to cannibalism, is produced at the Poets'
           Theatre in May, and its first act is published in *New World
           Writing*; during his Cambridge residency he also works on
           the plays *The Gilded West*, about Buffalo Bill, and *A Peacock
           at the Door*, about a nineteenth-century murder in a small
           Pennsylvania town. Receives an award from the National
           Institute and Academy of Arts and Letters. The Academy's
           president, Malcolm Cowley, cites Merwin's "fertility of in-
           vention, range of effect, and willingness to take risks in the
           practice of an art which has, of late, been more and more
           characterized by timidity." When Poets' Theatre residency
           ends, Merwin returns to London. Receives a Bursary for
           Playwrights by the Arts Council of Great Britain. Spends
           evenings drinking at the pub with Louis MacNeice and
           Dylan Thomas; sees English poet Henry Reed and actor
           John Whiting.

1958–59   *Favor Island* broadcast on the BBC in 1958. Completes
           translation of *Eufemia* (1567) by the Spanish playwright
           Lope de Rueda. Begins publishing book reviews in *The Na-
           tion*. Spends winter of 1958–59 in Deyá on Mallorca to finish
           his translation, begun in 1952, of the Spanish epic *Poem of
           the Cid*, which is published by J. M. Dent in London in
           1959. In this period he writes few poems of his own: "In
           the late fifties," he recalled, "I had the feeling I had simply
           come to the end of a way of writing. . . . So there was a
           period of close to two years when I wrote very little poetry."
           The Merwins see Hughes and Plath frequently after the
           couple's return to England late in 1959, with Dido helping
           them to find a flat; both poets will use Merwin's study while
           he is away.

1960–61   On Easter weekend 1960, takes part in mass protest march
           from the Atomic Weapons Research Establishment at Alder-
           maston in Berkshire to Trafalgar Square in London, fifty-
           two miles away, the third and largest of several such demon-
           strations organized annually by the Direct Action Commit-
           tee Against Nuclear War; his account of the demonstration,
           "Letter from Aldermaston," appears in *The Nation*. Pub-
           lishes third collection of poetry, *The Drunk in the Furnace*
           (Macmillan, 1960), and translations of *Some Spanish Bal-
           lads* (Abelard-Schuman, 1961), *The Satires of Persius* (Indi-
           ana University Press, 1961), and Alain-René Lesage's play

Turcaret (in vol. 4 of *The Classic Theatre*, ed. Eric Bentley, Anchor/Doubleday 1961). Researches Coxey's Army protest march of the unemployed to Washington, D.C., in 1894, planning to write a long narrative poem about it that never comes to fruition. While still occasionally visiting London, he moves to New York City: "In the early sixties I had an apartment in New York on the Lower East Side, east of Tompkins Square, on the top floor of a building on East 6th Street that has since been torn down. The rent was very low. The front rooms looked out over a school and the old roofscapes of lower Manhattan to the Brooklyn Bridge. . . . Sometimes taxi drivers asked guests whether they really wanted to come to that neighborhood, and occasionally they even refused to drive there, but I loved living there and I walked endlessly through that section of the city and along the river to the end of the island. Much of the latter part of *The Moving Target* and the first part of *The Lice* were written there." Drives across the States, giving readings in St. Louis (with Mona Van Duyn) and Seattle (at the invitation of Theodore Roethke). His play *The Gilded West* is produced at the Belgrade Theatre in Coventry, England, in 1961.

1962   Is appointed poetry editor of *The Nation*, a post he holds for six months. Publishes his translation of the anonymous 1554 Spanish picaresque novel, *Lazarillo de Tormes* (Anchor/Doubleday). Writes essay "Act of Conscience," about antinuclear sit-in in San Francisco in May–June 1962 to support the three crew members of the trimaran *Everyman*, who had been arrested for attempting to sail to Christmas Island in the Pacific, where the United States was conducting a series of atmospheric nuclear tests; essay is withdrawn from slated publication by *The New Yorker* because of the Cuban Missile Crisis, then published by *The Nation* in December. During the Missile Crisis, writes a Swiftian satire against conscription and nuclear testing about a standing army of atomic mutants, "A New Right Arm," which is published the following year in *Kulchur* magazine.

1963   Sylvia Plath commits suicide in London on February 11; in the months preceding her death she had frequently written letters (now apparently lost) to Merwin, enclosing drafts of her *Ariel* poems and discussing her breakup with Ted Hughes. In spring, feeling an increasing alienation from the

United States, he leaves New York City to spend the next few years in his half-ruined farmhouse in France. Publishes translation from the French of *The Song of Roland* in Modern Library edition *Medieval Epics* (which also includes his translation of *Poem of the Cid*), and his fifth poetry collection, *The Moving Target* (Atheneum), which represents a new stage of his poetic method: "By the end of the poems in *The Moving Target* I had relinquished punctuation along with several other structural conventions, a move that evolved from my growing sense that punctuation alluded to and assumed an allegiance to the rational protocol of written language, and of prose in particular. I had come to feel that it stapled the poems to the page. Whereas I wanted the poems to evoke the spoken language, and wanted the hearing of them to be essential to taking them in."

1964–66   Living in France, Merwin works on poems of *The Lice*. "Certainly, most of *The Lice* was written at a point when I really felt there was no point in writing," he recalled in 1984. "I got to the point where I thought the future was so bleak that there was no point in writing anything at all. And so the poems kind of pushed their way upon me when I wasn't thinking of writing. I would be out growing vegetables and walking around the countryside when all of a sudden I'd find myself writing a poem, and I'd write it, and that was the way most of *The Lice* was written." For ten months in 1964–65, he is an associate with Roger Planchon's Théâtre de la Cité, in Villeurbanne, France. In fall 1966, resumes dividing his time between Manhattan and France when he comes to New York City for rehearsals of a production of his translation of Lorca's *Yerma*, which premieres at Lincoln Center on December 8, 1966; it is directed by John Hirsch, and members of the cast include Nancy Marchand, Frank Langella, and Maria Tucci.

1967   *The Lice* is published by Atheneum. Critics respond with both astonished praise and scorn to the cryptic new style this book announces, a swerve away from an earlier luxuriance toward a starker, apocalyptic tone.

1968   *Selected Translations 1948–1968* is published by Atheneum, with work brought over from poems in French, German, Russian, Spanish, Catalan, Portuguese, Italian, Chinese, Vietnamese, Romanian, Latin, Greek, Irish, Welsh, Quechuan, Caxinua, Eskimo, and Kabylia. In the fall, Merwin separates from Dido (an arrangement "which indeed did not represent a marked change over the actual situation of the preceding few years, but simply rendered it more or less formal").

1969   Rents an apartment at 227 Waverly Place, across the street from St. Vincent's Hospital, which he will keep as a pied-à-terre for several years; continues to travel to France during the summer but spends less time there because Dido uses the primary farmhouse at Lacan, and during his visits he stays elsewhere on the property or in a house nearby. Receives the P.E.N. Translation Prize for *Selected Translations 1948–1968*. Publishes several books of translations: *Transparence of the World* (Atheneum), from the French of poet Jean Follain; *Voices* (Big Table), from the Spanish of Italian-born Argentine poet Antonio Porchia; *Twenty Love Poems and a Song of Despair* (Jonathan Cape), from the Spanish of Chilean poet Pablo Neruda; and *Products of the Perfected Civilization* (Macmillan), selected writings by Sébastien Roch Nicolas de Chamfort, eighteenth-century French author and aphorist.

1970   Publishes poetry collection *The Carrier of Ladders* and prose book *The Miner's Pale Children*, both with Atheneum. To an interviewer, he says, "I have sometimes puzzled over the possibility of being an American poet (but what else could I be—I've never wanted to be anything else), and certainly the search for a way of writing about what America *is*, in my lifetime, is a perennial siren. But not, I think, in any way that's obviously Whitmanesque." At the State University of New York at Buffalo in October to give a reading and spend a few days as visiting lecturer, having been asked to sign a state-mandated pledge "to support the Constitution of the United States and the Constitution of the State of New York," he publicly refuses, denounces the loyalty oath as "humiliating," and takes up a collection for draft resisters: "I am not what is sometimes called 'politically minded.' Politics in themselves bore me profoundly, and the assumption of the final reality of the power to manipulate other men's lives merely depresses me. But injustice, official brutality, and the destruction on a vast scale of private liberties are all around me and I cannot pretend that it's not so, nor that I can accept such things, when I have a chance to say no to them." Later that autumn, with his companion

Moira Hodgson, travels to San Cristóbal de Las Casas in the Mexican state of Chiapas, where he buys a ruined convent, and spends winters there for the next four years.

1971   Refuses to accept the Pulitzer Prize that is awarded to *The Carrier of Ladders*, and writes from Montana a letter printed in *The New York Review of Books* on June 3: "I am pleased to know of the judges' regard for my work, and I want to thank them for their wish to make their opinion public. But after years of news from Southeast Asia, and the commentary from Washington, I am too conscious of being an American to accept public congratulation with good grace, or to welcome it except as an occasion for expressing openly a shame which many Americans feel, day after day, helplessly and in silence. I want the prize money to be equally divided between Alan Blanchard (Cinema Repertory Theater, Telegraph Avenue, Berkeley, California)—a painter who was blinded by a police weapon in California while he was watching American events from a roof, at a distance—and the Draft Resistance." W. H. Auden writes to the *Review* saying that, while he shares Merwin's political views, he protests Merwin's "ill-judged" politicizing of the award and his demand that the prize money be spent as he wishes. In reply, Merwin asks, "Is it, after all, dishonoring the present distinction to use it to register once again an abhorrence at being swept along, as we are, and most of the time anonymously, in this evil?"

1972   Declines his election to membership in the National Institute of Arts and Letters, declaring his wish "not to belong to academies and institutes." Father dies in June, and mother dies three months later.

1973   Poetry collection *Writings to an Unfinished Accompaniment* is published by Atheneum, as is book of translations *Asian Figures*, composed of proverbs, short poems, and riddles from several Asian cultures—Korean, Japanese, Chinese, Burmese, Philippine, Malayan, and Laotian.

1974   Receives fellowship from the Academy of American Poets and the Shelley Memorial Award from the Poetry Society of America. Publishes *Osip Mandelstam, Selected Poems*, translations made in collaboration with Princeton professor of comparative literature Clarence Brown (Atheneum).

1975   Collected edition of early volumes, *The First Four Books of Poems*, is published by Atheneum. Merwin makes his first visit to Maui, Hawaii, to study with Zen teacher Robert Aitken. While at the Naropa Institute in Boulder, Colorado, to study Buddhist meditation with the controversial scholar and teacher Chögyam Trungpa Rinpoche, a Halloween party turns violent—Merwin and his companion Dana Naone are forced to strip naked and are brought forcibly before Trungpa. Merwin decides to stay two more days, in order to confront Trungpa privately. He asks, "Did it ever occur to you that you might have made a mistake?" Trungpa tells him, "A tulku [reincarnated lama] never makes a mistake." To which Merwin replies: "You have just told me why you could never have been my teacher."

1976   Spends summer on Maui house-sitting for Robert Aitken, and when Aitken returns in the fall, Merwin accepts offer to live in a small apartment above his garage. Reads about Hawaiian history and comes across, in Aubrey B. Janion's recently published book *The Olowalu Massacre*, the tale "The Leper of Kalala'u," a version of the story that will form the basis of his 1998 book *The Folding Cliffs*.

1977   Publishes poetry collection *The Compass Flower* (Atheneum); *Houses and Travellers* (Atheneum), a series of prose pieces; and translations of *Classical Sanskrit Love Poetry* (with J. Moussaieff Masson, Columbia University Press) and Argentine poet Roberto Juarroz's *Vertical Poetry* (Kayak Books). Accepts membership in National Institute of Arts and Letters, having refused it five years earlier. Buys a run-down cabin and three-and-a-half acres of an old pineapple plantation in Ha'ikū (a Hawaiian word meaning "sharp break"), on the north side of Maui. Gradually, and following his design, a house is built on the property, and he begins an ambitious decades-long project of planting trees, including many endangered species ("I have planted about 850 species of palms, and at least four or five times that many actual trees," he will recall in 2010).

1978   Publishes translation of Euripides' *Iphigeneia at Aulis* (with George E. Dimock, Jr., Oxford University Press) and poetry collection *Feathers from the Hill* (Windhover Press)— sequences of brief poems in which the Hawaiian landscape is first glimpsed in his work. Divorce with Dido is finalized.

1979   Receives Bollingen Prize for poetry, given by the Beinecke
        Library at Yale University (judges are Galway Kinnell, Wil-
        liam Stafford, and Penelope Laurans). Publishes *Selected
        Translations 1968–1978* (Atheneum).

1980   Participates in protests to save sacred ground on the island
        from developers and politicians, and will continue to be
        active in preserving the Hawaiian heritage and the natural
        environment of the islands.

1982   Publishes a book of prose recollections of his childhood,
        Unframed Originals (Atheneum), and poetry collection
        Finding the Islands (North Point Press). Meets Paula Dun-
        away (b. 1936) on a visit to New York.

1983   Publishes *Opening the Hand* (Atheneum). Marries Paula,
        who is mother of two sons by a previous marriage, Matthew
        Carlos Schwartz (b. 1963) and John Burnham Schwartz
        (b. 1965). He and Paula work on their garden by clearing
        the land by hand, with sickles, and with push mowers.

1985   Publishes *Four French Plays* (Atheneum), collecting dra-
        matic translations from the 1950s and early 1960s, and *From
        the Spanish Morning* (Atheneum), which restores to print
        Some Spanish Ballads, Lope de Rueda's *Eufemia*, and *Laz-
        arillo de Tormes.*

1986   Receives the Hawaii Award for Literature, chosen by the
        Hawaii Literary Arts Council. The Merwins expand their
        property to nineteen acres by purchasing two adjoining par-
        cels of land, with the help of a gift from children's publisher
        Margaret McElderry and a legacy from George Kirstein.

1987–89 Publishes new collection *The Rain in the Trees* (Knopf,
        1988), *Selected Poems* (Atheneum, 1988), and, in collabo-
        ration with Sōiku Shigematsu, translation of work by the
        Japanese Zen master and poet Musō Soseki (1275–1351),
        Sun at Midnight: Poems and Sermons (North Point Press,
        1989).

1990   Receives the 1989 Maurice English Poetry Award in Hono-
        lulu. The judge, poet Peter Viereck, writes: "Merwin is a
        poet of overwhelming understatement whose power lies in
        avoiding all facile, flamboyant effects and instead expressing
        his emotions and thoughts with absolute integrity." Dido
        dies; Merwin resumes residencies at the farmhouse in Lacan
        de Loubressac.

1991–93 Publishes *The Lost Upland: Stories of Southwest France* (Knopf, 1992), a prose book that evokes the landscape, history, and people of the Languedoc, and *Travels* (Knopf, 1993); collected edition *The Second Four Books of Poems* is brought out by Copper Canyon Press in 1993.

1994 Receives the first Tanning Prize of $100,000—endowed by painter and poet Dorothea Tanning to honor a living "master" of the art of poetry—by the Academy of American Poets. In the citation, poet James Merrill, who had known him since their undergraduate years, writes: "As a poet W. S. Merwin has charted a course that we, his first, marveling readers, might never have foreseen. From that early work, with its ravishing detours rich in echo and ornament, he has attained—more and more with every collection—a wonderful streamlined diction that unerringly separates and recombines like quicksilver scattered upon a shifting plane, but which remains as faithful to the warms and cools of the human heart as that same mercury in the pan-pipe of a thermometer." Also receives the Lenore Marshall Prize from the Academy of American Poets for *Travels*.

1996 Publishes *The Vixen* (Knopf), a collection largely about his experience living in Lacan de Loubressac and the history of the surrounding region, written in long lines loosely derived from those of classical elegies. Edits *Lament for the Makers: A Memorial Anthology* (Counterpoint), which includes Merwin's long poem of the same title. His translation of poems by Jaime Sabines, *Pieces of Shadow*, published the year before in Mexico, is issued by Marsilio Publishers.

1997 *Flower & Hand: Poems 1977–1983* (Copper Canyon) gathers earlier collections *The Compass Flower*, *Feathers from the Hill*, and *Opening the Hand*.

1998– Publishes book-length poem *The Folding Cliffs: A Narra-*
2002 *tive* (Knopf, 1998) and collections *The River Sound* (Knopf, 1999) and *The Pupil* (Knopf, 2001); translations *East Window: The Asian Translations* (Copper Canyon, 1998), the *Purgatorio* of Dante (Knopf, 2000), and, from Middle English, *Sir Gawain and the Green Knight* (Knopf, 2003); and *The Mays of Ventadorn* (National Geographic Books, 2002), a memoir of time spent in the Languedoc and the work of its twelfth-century bards.

2003   Is the subject of *W. S. Merwin: The Poet's View*, a documentary film by Mel Stuart. Receives in absentia the Gold Medal for Poetry by the American Academy of Arts and Letters. In the response read for him at the ceremony in New York, Merwin writes in part: "Everyone who has directed aspiration, care, and learning to an effort to convey in words the promptings of some inner compulsion has been aware, I imagine, that the more one wants to articulate some feeling—love or grief, shame or indignation or gratitude—the more impossible that seems. I believe this unappeasable urge to utterance is the origin of speech itself, the abiding source of imaginative language and of poetry. I encounter it again whenever the only words for what I want to say are 'thank you' and I am forced to admit how inadequate they are." Contributes to anthology opposing the U.S. invasion of Iraq, *Poets Against the War*, and participates in the reading organized by the anthology's editor, Sam Hamill.

2004   Receives Lifetime Achievement Award by the Lannan Foundation, as well as the Golden Wreath Award of the Struga Poetry Evenings Festival in Macedonia. Publishes essay collection *The Ends of the Earth* (Counterpoint).

2005   Publishes *Migration: New and Selected Poems* (Copper Canyon) and new collection *Present Company* (Copper Canyon), along with a memoir about his life in the 1940s, *Summer Doorways* (Shoemaker & Hoard). *Lazarillo de Tormes* is restored to print in an edition by New York Review Books. In November, *Migration* wins National Book Award, which is accepted for him in New York by stepson John Burnham Schwartz. The judges' citation notes: "The poems in *Migration* speak from a life-long belief in the power of words to awaken our drowzy souls and see the world with compassionate interconnection."

2006   Receives the Rebekah Johnson Bobbitt National Prize for Poetry from the Library of Congress for *Present Company*.

2007   Publishes prose collection *The Book of Fables* (Copper Canyon) and an English edition of *Selected Poems* (Bloodaxe Books).

2008–9   Publishes *The Shadow of Sirius* (Copper Canyon) in 2008, which wins him his second Pulitzer Prize the following year. Receives the *Kenyon Review*'s Award for Literary Achievement in 2009.

2010   Is appointed Poet Laureate of the United States, and serves
        for one year. Announcing the appointment, the Librarian
        of Congress, James H. Billington, says, "William Merwin's
        poems are often profound and, at the same time, accessible
        to a vast audience. He leads us upstream from the flow of
        everyday things in life to half-hidden headwaters of wisdom
        about life itself." The nonprofit Merwin Conservancy is
        founded to ensure the preservation of his property, in co-
        operation with the National Tropical Botanical Garden, as
        a sanctuary for study and research. Is interviewed in PBS
        documentary *The Buddha*.

2013   *Selected Translations* is published by Copper Canyon Press,
        as is Merwin's translation (with Takako Lento) of *Collected
        Haiku of Yosa Buson* and a reissue of his translation of Musō
        Soseki's *Sun at Midnight*. Merwin is the subject of docu-
        mentary *Even Though the Whole World Is Burning*, directed
        by Stefan C. Schaefer.

Note on the Texts

This volume contains six volumes of poetry by W. S. Merwin published from 1996 to 2008, along with sixteen previously uncollected poems.

Describing his process of composition to an interviewer, Merwin remarked, "What I actually do is write very slowly, and change [the poem] a lot as I'm going on. Although very often getting quite close to the final thing right at the beginning, then making minute verbal adjustments until it seems to come out right. But once it reaches a certain point I very seldom go back to it, except maybe either to throw it out or cut hunks out of it, see if I can do with less, see if I've over-written it." Although he has sometimes continued to work on poems after publication in a periodical, Merwin does not revise his poems after they have been included in one of his books.

The present volume prints the texts of the first edition for each of the following books:

The Vixen (New York: Knopf, 1996)
The Folding Cliffs (New York: Knopf, 1998)
The River Sound (New York: Knopf, 1999)
The Pupil (New York: Knopf, 2001)
Present Company (Port Townsend, WA: Copper Canyon, 2005)
The Shadow of Sirius (Port Townsend, WA: Copper Canyon, 2008)

Unlike Merwin's earlier poetry collections, which have been reprinted in editions such as *The First Four Books of Poems* (1975, reprinted 2000) and *The Second Four Books of Poems* (1993), the six volumes included here have not appeared until now in their entirety in a collected edition of Merwin's poetry, although many of their poems were chosen for *Migration: New and Selected Poems* (2005) and the English edition *Selected Poems* (Newcastle upon Tyne: Bloodaxe Books, 2007). Bloodaxe Books also brought out an English edition of *The Shadow of Sirius* in 2009.

The texts of the poems in the "New and Uncollected Poems" section, which were selected by the editor in consultation with Merwin, are printed from the following sources:

The Stone: *The Paris Review*, Fall 1993.
Tide Line Garden: *American Poetry Review*, May–June 1999.
Ogres: *Poets Against the War*, ed. Sam Hamill with Sally Anderson and others (New York: Thunder's Mouth Press/Nation Books, 2003).

The Swallows: *The Yale Review*, January 2006.

Known Sound: *Poetry*, May 2006.

Why Some People Do Not Read Poetry: *The New York Review of Books*, April 30, 2009.

Young Man Picking Flowers: *The New Yorker*, December 7, 2009.

A Message to Po Chu-i: *The New Yorker*, March 8, 2010.

By the Front Door: *The Kenyon Review*, Fall 2010.

Beginners: *American Poetry Review*, November–December 2010.

The Name of the Morning: *American Poetry Review*, November–December 2010.

The Green Fence: *American Poetry Review*, November–December 2010.

Variation on a Theme: *American Poetry Review*, November–December 2010.

Turning: *The New Yorker*, May 16, 2011.

Urticophilia: *The New York Review of Books*, October 13, 2011.

The New Song: *The New Yorker*, December 12, 2011.

On the following pages, a stanza break occurs at the bottom of the page (not including pages in which the break is evident because of the regular stanzaic structure of the poem): 289, 290, 435, 442, 443, 450, 461, 464, 469, 474, 478, 479, 484, 485, 493, 509, 510, 512, 513, 517, 521, 523, 524, 526, 530, 532, 538, 543, 550, 552, 555, 577, 579, 582, 585, 590, 591, 602, 610.

This volume presents the texts of the original printings chosen for inclusion here, but it does not attempt to reproduce nontextual features of their typographic design. The texts are presented without change, except for the correction of typographical errors. Spelling, punctuation, and capitalization are often expressive features and are not altered, even when inconsistent or irregular. The following is a list of typographical errors corrected, cited by page and line number: 73.42, John I; 126.19, 18, Harper's; 171.8, persistance; 197.18, Lauhui; 252.19, 'uluhi; 313.23, bones; 337.15, whom; 338.32, take of; 342.10, whom; 369.27, occurence.

Notes

In the notes below, the reference numbers denote page and line of this volume (the line count includes headings). No note is made for material included in standard desk-reference books. Biblical quotations are keyed to the King James Version. Quotations from Shakespeare are keyed to *The Riverside Shakespeare*, ed. G. Blakemore Evans (Boston: Houghton Mifflin, 1974). For more biographical information than is contained in the Chronology, see W. S. Merwin, *Unframed Originals* (New York: Atheneum, 1982) and *Summer Doorways* (Emeryville, CA: Shoemaker & Hoard, 2005).

THE VIXEN

11.14   Aulis] Port where the Greek fleet embarked for the Trojan War.

11.34   This was the day] November 11, date the Allied powers and Germany signed the armistice in 1918.

17.36   *François de Maynard 1582–1646*] François Maynard, French poet who served as secretary to Margaret of Valois, first wife of French king Henry IV, and as president of the commune of Aurillac in the Auvergne. An acolyte of the poet François de Malherbe (1555–1628), and later a member of the French Academy, he was unsuccessful in winning favor from Cardinal Richelieu, and spent his later years in St. Céré in the Lot, longing to be in Paris again.

17.37–40   When I cannot see . . . black] Based on a passage in one of Maynard's odes, where he laments that he is unable to see his beloved because of a jealous husband.

18.2–12   the syllables . . . demigod] Based on a passage from Maynard's "A Monseigneur le Cardinal de Richelieu."

18.31   I have held a post in Rome] In 1634 Maynard accompanied French ambassador François de Noailles (1584–1645) to Rome and spent two years there.

18.36   gold current of the river Pactolus] A river on the Aegean coast of Turkey. According to legend, King Midas of Phrygia could turn whatever he touched into gold. Seeking to be rid of his power after fatally transforming his daughter into a golden statue, he washed himself in the Pactolus, giving it a golden gleam.

19.1   *Hölderlin at the River*] Friedrich Hölderlin (1770–1843), German poet, who was mentally unstable and cared for from 1807 until his death by a carpenter's family at their home by the Neckar River.

20.2   the red-haired boy] Alain Prévost, a friend of Merwin's at Princeton. See Merwin's *Summer Doorways: A Memoir* (Emeryville, CA: Shoemaker & Hoard, 2005), 54–56.

20.32   Ovid's story of Philomela] See *Metamorphoses*, bk. 6, which tells the story of Procne and Philomela, the daughters of King Pandion of Athens. King Tereus of Thrace was given Procne in marriage but, desiring Philomela, he raped her and cut out her tongue. Philomela told Procne of her violation by weaving a tapestry, and the sisters took revenge by murdering Itys, the son of Tereus and Procne, and serving him to Tereus as a meal. While fleeing from the enraged king, Procne was transformed into a nightingale and Philomela into a swallow. Philomela's suffering has traditionally been associated with the call of the nightingale.

20.33–34   testimonials of Hafiz and Keats] The nightingale appears frequently in the poems of Persian Sufi poet Shams al-Din Hafiz (c. 1325–1390). John Keats (1795–1821) addressed his "Ode to a Nightingale" (1820) to the bird.

20.34–35   Eliot has gone . . . Heart] A reference to "Sweeney Among the Nightingales" (1918) by T. S. Eliot (1888–1965), lines 35–36: "The nightingales are singing near / The Convent of the Sacred Heart." Eliot also makes reference to the story of Philomela in *The Waste Land* (1922).

20.35–36   Ransom has spat . . . numbers] See the closing two stanzas of "Philomela" (1923) by American poet John Crowe Ransom (1888–1974).

23.1   *Battues*] Hunting term from the French word "to beat," referring to the beating of woodland to flush game.

23.19–20   cavalry at Sand Creek] On November 29, 1864, the 3rd Colorado Volunteer Cavalry attacked an encampment of Cheyenne and Arapaho at Sand Creek in southeastern Colorado and killed more than 150 people, mostly women and children.

23.20–21   Jackson's finest . . . Seminoles] During the First Seminole War, 1817–18, in which U.S. Army forces were led by Andrew Jackson (1767–1845).

24.25   Borobudur] Monumental ninth-century Buddhist shrine and pilgrimage site on the island of Java, consisting of a domed temple atop nine stone platforms decorated with reliefs and statues.

28.1   *Peire Vidal*] French troubadour (1175–1205), said to have participated in the Third Crusade.

28.5   where the furs were climbing] Vidal's father was a furrier.

28.30–33   for one woman . . . laughing] According to an apocryphal story in an early commentary about Vidal, the poet clothed himself in the fur of a wolf in an attempt to win the favor of a lady named Loba (she-wolf) of Pueinautier, going so far as to have himself hunted by shepherds. Mauled by their dogs, his half-dead body was brought to Loba, "who began to feel great joy for the madness he had committed and to laugh a great deal, and her husband did the same."

31.32–34   Argentat . . . Murat . . . Courtis] Locations in the department of the Lot, France, and in the Corrèze to the north.

THE FOLDING CLIFFS

45.1   THE FOLDING CLIFFS] For the present edition Merwin has written a new prefatory note.

HOW I CAME TO WRITE *The Folding Cliffs*

When I first came to Hawaii to stay for a while, in the mid-1970s, one of the great magnets of the islands, for me, was the remnant, the continuing echo, of an older, a prior culture, with the remains of an ancient language rooted deeply in the place. I had been drawn to suggestions of any such continuity since my earliest childhood. At that age, of course, I did not realize that my craving for continuity was a longing to see, to reach before and beyond my own culture—the modern urban world inhabited by people who had come, or whose families had come, from somewhere else, and who had no desire to pay further attention to their past. But when I was a small child my mother used to say to me, "This land does not really belong to us. It was stolen from the Indians." I loved books before I could read, and my first favorite was a book of pictures of Indians, people who lived in the woods, as I longed to do in the urban environment of my childhood. Each page, each picture, had a word or two with its picture: "Man," "Indian Man." The words went on telling of the clothes, the dwellings, the surroundings and activities of these people, and I went over and over them and pretended I could read the words, until, in fact, I could. I first learned to read about people who did not read and write. My fascination with those earlier people continued after I went to school and had access to more information about them, and indeed it is still with me. It is common—or it used to be—for boys to go through a phase of wanting to be Indians, usually not for long, or very seriously, and so when grown-ups asked me what I was going to be when I grew up, and I said, "an Indian," they simply raised their eyebrows and figured that I was still at that stage. On the infrequent occasions when I got to play "Cowboys and Indians" I always chose to be an Indian, though that was not the expected choice, and "the Indians," I was reminded, "always lost." (I might add that my mother, in later years, became a child-welfare missionary to the Navajo, and stayed, for short periods, in the Navajo reservation.)

That early directive of mine was the origin of my fascination with the Hawaiian culture, and in my first summer here, housesitting for a professor at the University, I began to read everything I could about the history of Hawaii and of the Hawaiians. In the autumn when the professor came back, Robert Aitken, a Zen teacher whom I had met during the summer, offered me a small apartment up in the trees above the "garage" (his garage, like many Hawaiian garages, was used for almost anything except housing a car), until I could find somewhere of my own. (Housing was scarce in those blessed days before the tidal wave of development.) I went on reading about Maui, and kept exploring the island. I found a just-published (1976) collection of articles about dramatic incidents in "the old Hawaii," compiled and retold by Aubrey P. Janion. The book was called *The Olowalu Massacre*, the subject of the lead article. One of the longest pieces was "The Leper of Kalalau." Janion's editing and recounting were obviously tailored to emphasize violence and sensationalism. Even so, the story remained in my mind and drew me back to re-read it. Janion gave few or no details of his sources, but I traced the Kalalau story and found his (unattributed) source: Frances Frazier's translation of John Sheldon's account, in Hawaiian, of the Kalalau story, as told to Sheldon by Piʻilani herself, and Sheldon's portraits of the central figures. Frances' translation had been published in a learned journal. I made contact with her, and she was a little suspicious of inquiring writers at first, hardly surprising after the way Mr. Janion had simply made use of her work with no acknowledgment, but we got past that during the conversation, and we arranged to meet on Kauai, where we became warm friends. Frances introduced me to Bruce Wichman, scion of an old (by American standards) Kauai family. Bruce knows more about the history and mythology of Kauai— about which he has written a number of books—than anyone alive and he was generous in guiding me to learn about both. And through Bruce I came to know Pat Boland, of the Hawaii Board of Health, who for years had been studying and documenting the leprosy colony at Kalaupapa, on Molokaʻi. Pat introduced me to Agnes Conrad, the Director Emeritus of the Hawaii State Archives. Through my reading at home I would become curious about some subject or other related to the story and wonder whether some documentary evidence related to it existed in the State Archives. I would call Agnes, read her the list, make a date, and meet her at the Archives, and we would go in, and it was like returning to her kingdom with the Fairy Queen. Whatever documents I had listed would be out on a long table. I would examine them, make copies of the important ones, and then we would go out to lunch. Pat Boland and I, in the Archives, went through the death lists from Kalaupapa on microfilm, looking for any mention of Koʻolau's sister. We never found any, but Pat said that was not surprising. Inmates at Kalaupapa sometimes changed their own names there, when they gave up hope of ever returning home, to avoid bringing shame on their families. Or if there was anything suspicious about the way they had been shipped there—as may have been the case with Koʻolau's sister—their names may have been changed by the authorities.

I was well launched on these researches before I had any clear idea of what I wanted them for, beyond satisfying my interest in the story. I was very dubious, for a long time, about exploiting Hawaiian material, when I was not Hawaiian myself. I am not a historian nor a novelist. But in the same years when I was beginning to try to learn more about the Piʻilani-Koʻolau story than was commonly available, I was writing what turned out to be a book of poems set in the past and present, in the place that has been another pole of my life since I first found my way there, in the 1950s, when I was in my twenties. It is a farming community on the uplands of the region known as the Quercy (from the Gaulish tribe the Romans called the Cadurcii) in southwest France. It was a region almost untouched by the postindustrial world and had not been subjected to tourism, when I first saw it. Its past went back to the early troubadours, and the Roman occupation, and prehistory, including one of the first-known Neanderthal burials. The poems that had begun to come to me were evocations of details and moments of that region and my long relation to it, as I returned there after several years' absence. All the poems were in the same form: long lines of alternate lengths, loosely derived and alluding to the classical Greek and Latin elegies. After the series came to its conclusion, it occurred to me one day that if ever I were to try to write about the Pi'ilani-Ko'olau story the only form that I thought possible would be that of a narrative poem, and I realized that the form of the poems I had been writing might be a step toward a long narrative form. Only a poem could present, without altering its own mode, material as diverse as State Department correspondence and Hawaiian chant. I wanted a form that could allude to both its Western origin (since it would be written in English, and I am not a Hawaiian) and to the poetry and traditions of its characters, its setting and situation.

I went on with my amateur research into the story. Frances and I found that we had a small disagreement regarding John Sheldon's invaluable account of the story. Frances accepted his piece without question, as Sheldon expressed it. Sheldon himself was a journalist, as his father had been, and both he and his father were personally involved in Hawaiian family life. He was a fervent monarchist, loyal to the Queen at the time of the takeover of the kingdom by a small group of American businessmen—unscrupulous adventurers whose piracy was conducted under the protection of the guns of the U.S. Navy, on ships anchored in the harbor. Sheldon's sympathy with the Hawaiians' legitimate sovereignty was absolute, and I felt that it colored his portraits of Pi'ilani and Ko'olau and their story. It seemed to me that he had made them exemplars of "good Hawaiians," a shade too piously Christian, rather than portraying them just as they were. Even Sheldon's getting Pi'ilani to pose out on the rocks, holding a rifle, I thought, was meant to evoke admiration and sympathy, and to place her among the frontier heroines of American popular legend at the time. Frances' and my different interpretations did not in the least get in the way of our long friendship.

The form of a long poem began to take shape in my mind. One evening I was sitting thinking about it, and about Hofgaard's store in Waimea, where the locals used to gather and talk story. Hofgaard talked about Pi'ilani in later years, long after she was gone. Some locals were still basically imperialists, and sympathized with Stolz, considered Ko'olau an outlaw and a murderer, and Pi'ilani no better than he was. Hofgaard clearly admired Pi'ilani, and her fearless loyalty to her husband, and spoke of how she had gone back over into Kalalau time and again, after the story there was over, when she heard rumors that Ko'olau's grave had been found and his rifle was up for auction. She had always gone most of the way with someone else, he said, but once at least (I took that to mean the last time) she went entirely alone. As I thought of what he said, I began to imagine her leaving the family's house and the cluster of houses on the coast at Mana, at night, and setting out on the trail up the mountain toward Koke'e, on the cliff above the valley where she had buried him. And as she starts up the mountain she begins the poem.

*

The hardcover (1998) and paperback (2000) editions of *The Folding Cliffs* include the following list of characters and glossary:

CHARACTERS

Archer—Early, unsuccessful farmer at Kekaha, before Knudsen.

Gibson—Walter Murray Gibson, King David Kalākaua's premier and secretary of state during the 1880s.

Hofgaard—Christopher B. Hofgaard. Storekeeper in Waimea, where his emporium was a local gathering place for decades.

Ho'ona—Pi'ilani's father, born on the island of Hawai'i.

Ida—A younger cousin of Pi'ilani's.

Kaleimanu—Son of Ko'olau and Pi'ilani. Named for his grandfather.

Kanaloa—One of the great origin gods of Hawai'i and probably the oldest of them. God of death, of the sea, and of the west.

Kane—Another of the principal gods of Hawai'i. God of origins, the east, life, humankind. High on the summit of Waialeale a huge stone formation comprises the altar of Kane. The number forty was his, representing the forty forms of life. Kane and Kanaloa, in myths, are often in each other's company. Here they are the mountain and the sea.

Kanemahuka—Ko'olau's paternal grandfather.

Kapahu—Pi'ilani's maternal grandfather.

Deborah Kapule—1793–1853—Kauai chief, daughter of ruling chief Kahekili, favorite wife of chief Kaumuali'i. She endured many losses during her lifetime, opposed and survived the Kauai rebellion and massacre, and lived to be one of the most revered and beloved of the Hawaiian elders on the island, and one of the few surviving representatives of the Kauai nobility.

Judge Kauai—A prominent figure in Waimea in the latter part of the nineteenth century. Native Hawaiian, landowner, member of the legislature for several terms.

Kawaluna—Ko'olau's paternal grandfather.

Keiwi—Older friend of Pi'ilani's.

Kekiele—Ko'olau's maternal great-grandfather.

Kepahu—Cowboy friend of Kua's.

Kinoulu—One of Pi'ilani's aunts, a sister of her mother's.

Anne Sinclair Knudsen—1839–1922. Born in Stirling, Scotland, daughter of a distinguished officer in the British Navy. After an interval in New Zealand her family settled in Hawai'i where her mother bought the island of Ni'ihau and land on Kauai near Waimea. Anne married Valdemar Knudsen, Ko'olau's employer.

Valdemar Knudsen—Anne Sinclair's husband, born in Norway, 1819. Rancher and planter on west Kauai. Botanist, ornithologist, archaeologist, linguist, writer in correspondence with many scientists of his time. Married Anne 1867.

Ko'olau—Kaluaiko'olau. Pi'ilani's husband, a cowboy, born in Kekaha in 1862.

Kū—Fourth of the chief Hawaiian gods. The war god.

Kukui—Ko'olau's mother.

Prince Kunuiakea—1851–1903. Known to those sympathetic to him as "The Last Kamehameha," Albert Kukailimoku Kunuiakea was the natural son of King Kamehameha III and a high chief, Jane Lehilani Kaeo. Albert, who was brought up as a Catholic, helped teach Father Damien Hawaiian. He served in the legislature after 1880, and in 1895 was a delegate to the Constitutional Convention. When he died he was accorded a state funeral, partly as a way of mourning the end of a dynasty.

Lono—Another of the principal gods. God of the rain and of the cycle of returning life.

Maka'e—Hawaiian woman, a housekeeper and cook in the Knudsen household.

Me'eawa—Cowboy, employed by Knudsen.

Naea—A neighbor of Pi'ilani's in Kekaha.

Nahola— Pi'ilani's maternal grandfather.

Nakaula—Ko'olau's maternal grandfather.

Kua Papiohuli—Elder friend of Ko'olau's. Cowboy.

Pi'ilani—Hawaiian woman born in Kekaha, 1864.

Pohaku-o-Kauai—Mythological personage, the Rock of Kauai, referred to by Pele as her grandfather.

Puako—A purveyor of Hawaiian lore, west Kauai, mid-century. Cooperative and unreliable.

Reverend Rowell—George Berkeley Rowell, born 1815, Cornish, New Hampshire. Missionary. Sailed to Kauai in 1842. Settled in Waimea. Built a stone church, then a smaller church and a school.

Umi—An ancient chief of Hawai'i.

Father Whitney—The Whitneys were missionaries at Waimea before George Rowell.

GLOSSARY

amakihi—The Amakihis—Latin *Hemignathus*—are a group of small honeycreepers with yellow markings. Some were specific to single islands. A number of them have become extinct in this century.

'awa—Kava; *Piper methysticum*. The root is the source of a narcotic sedative drink.

'elepaio—*Chasiempis sandwichensis*—a small indigenous flycatcher, the Kauai form brownish gray with orange breast.

hala—The "screw pine." Indigenous *Pandanus odoratissimus*, whose long leaves are used for matting and thatch.

haole—Hawaiian word for Caucasians—and by extension for foreign and introduced things. Its overtones pejorative.

hau—*Hibiscus tiliaceous.* A spreading, thicket-forming lowland tree, its bark used for making rope and its light wood for the outriggers of canoes.

Hilinama—On Kauai, the month corresponding to November.

hilu fish—Name for several kinds of Hawaiian reef fish.

Hiva—What the Marquesans called the place they had come from. The main island of the Marquesas, the northernmost of that archipelago, is Nuku Hiva.

Hua—Thirteenth night of the lunar month.

Huna—The name for the eleventh night of the Hawaiian lunar month.

kahuna—A word whose range of meanings refers to mastery of an art, from medicine to divination to black sorcery.

kamani—Alexandrian laurel. A noble tree, to 60' tall. Blunt, magnolia-like leaves, fragrant flowers. The nuts yield medicinal oil that is also used in lamps. Hard, dark wood. Sacred in some parts of Polynesia.

Kao'ea—Star, planet (perhaps Jupiter) or constellation believed to preside over Hanalei on the north coast of Kauai.

kapu—Proscribed. Forbidden. The word that has become familiar in English as "taboo." A system of protocol which sustained the war chiefs. Infractions incurred the death penalty.

koa—The *Acacia koa*; Hawaiian acacia. It is a principal tree of the Hawaiian forests and one of the most beautiful. War canoes were traditionally made from the koa.

kopiko—Any of the *Straussias*, small Hawaiian trees of the coffee and gardenia family, growing as understory plants, generally up to 4500 feet altitude.

kukui—Candlenut tree, *Eleurites moluccana*. A large tree with maple-shaped leaves. The nuts, the size of walnuts, yield an oil used in cooking and for light.

Lantana—The common invasive bush, *Lantana camara*, native to the American tropics, now established in many parts of the warm latitudes.

makua—Father.

makuahine—Mother.

Manahunes—A name with a devious history, at one time designating a people of Tahiti, and later evolving (with the spelling *menehune*) to mean the semi-legendary archaic settlers of Kauai.

milo—A tree, *Thespesia populnea*, found on coasts in the Pacific tropics. It is a shade tree with hibiscus-like flowers and dark, heavy wood used in making bowls and carving. The tree is revered in some places.

mountain apples—*Eugenia malaccensis*. Malay apple—'ohi'a 'ai in Hawaiian. A tropical fruit somewhat resembling certain apples in appearance and taste.

'ohia—*Metrosideros polymorpha* or *M. collinia*. Another of the principal trees of the Hawaiian forest and mythology. A beautiful tree, sacred to the fire goddess Pele and used in her rituals.

olokele—A brilliant scarlet honey-creeper, the Kauai name for the i'iwi, the *Vestiaria coccinea*, with a distinct, ringing call and a gift for mimicry.

Pele—The fire goddess, a central, varying, and extremely important figure in Hawaiian mythology.

Pohaku—The word means rock. Pohaku-o-Kauai, the Rock of Kauai, is both a place and a mythological character in the legend of Pele, who refers to the rock as her grandfather.

poi—Taro root pounded to a smooth paste. A staple of Hawaiian diet.

Palemanō—A point on the coast of Hawaii.

tapa—A cloth, often very fine and durable, made by pounding the paper mulberry or one of several other plants.

taro—*Colocasia esculenta*. An aroid, the staple vegetable of the Hawaiian diet, both root and leaves cooked and eaten. The plant has an important place in Hawaiian mythology, somewhat analogous to that of maize among the indigenous peoples of the Americas.

ti—*Cordyline terminalis*, a plant common in Hawai'i, in lowland forests and gardens, and of great importance in the culture of the Hawaiians. The long, broad shining leaves have been used for ceremonial purposes, for dancers' skirts, for wrapping offerings of food, and for cooking food wrapped in it as tamales are wrapped in corn leaves.

'ulei—Native shrub, *Osteomele anthyllidifolia*, with small white flowers, edible white berries. A member of the Rosaceae related to the hawthorn. Sacred to the goddess Hi'iaka.

uluhe—Any of the so-called false staghorn ferns. Native, creeping, barbed growth in a variety of habitats.

'uwa'u—Or 'ua 'u, or uuau in various texts. The Hawaiian petrel, *Pterodroma phaeopygia*, a bird of the open seas, breeding in burrows on barren mountain slopes, coming and going at night. It is now a rare, endangered, declining species. The Hawaiian name mimics the bird's cry.

50.19   shore of O'omano] Now also called Davidson's Point.

61.22–25   Lahi . . . killed the giant] According to a Hawaiian legend, the boy Lahi would eat only birds, and went with his uncle Kanealohi to Kilohana mountain to eat the 'uwa'u birds (see Glossary) who live there. They killed a giant who attacked them and the birds' nests by luring it into a deep hole.

65.39   Durham Bulls] Shorthorn cattle, originally developed in northern England.

71.15   I'a The Fish The Milky Way] The Hawaiian word "I'a" means both "fish" and "the Milky Way."

79.1   Newe] The Southern Cross.

79.1   Kauana lipo] Literally "the rising of Lipo," a star in the southern sky.

79.2   Haku po kano] "Lord of dark night," the name of an unidentified star.

79.2   Hoku pa'a] The North Star.

79.38   Kaui helani . . . cloud] Kuaihelani is a floating island in Hawaiian mythology.

81.15   Arthur sailing for Iceland] Legendary British king Arthur was said to have conquered Iceland in Geoffrey of Monmouth's twelfth-century chronicle *Historia Regum Brittaniae* (*History of the Kings of Britain*).

81.15   Merlin] The wizard of Arthurian legend.

81.16–17   Brendan . . . ark] According to legend, St. Brendan of Clonfert (c. 484–c. 577), Irish monk, set sail for an edenic land, the Island of the Blessed, that he had seen in a vision.

81.25   Skraelings] Norse term for the indigenous peoples of North America and Greenland.

82.34   Hokuloa and Ka'awela] Venus when seen as the morning star, and the planet Mercury.

90.28   Kapena Kuke] I.e., Captain Cook, British naval officer and explorer James Cook (1728–1779), the first European to visit and map the Hawaiian Islands.

91.5–9   the bay . . . taken from them] At Kealakekua Bay, on the west coast of the island of Hawaii, Cook was killed by Hawaiians during a dispute over a stolen boat.

91.23–24   successor . . . consumption] Cook was succeeded by Captain Charles Clerke (1741–1779), who died of tuberculosis seven months after assuming command.

93.7–9   the English officers . . . Sandwich Islands] Nathaniel Portlock (c. 1748–1817) and George Dixon (1748–1795) were British naval officers during Cook's third expedition to the Hawaiian Islands, and became partners in a fur-trading enterprise.

94.34   Uluka'a] A sacred floating island of the gods in Hawaiian mythology.

94.41–42   Kamehameha . . . war god] Kamehameha I (c. 1758–1819) conquered rival chieftains of all of the Hawaiian Islands but Kauai and in 1810 established the Kingdom of Hawaii.

95.22–23   coming invasion and conquest of Maui] In 1795 Kamehameha's forces conquered the islands of Maui and Moloka'i at the Battle of Kewala.

95.28   at Nu'uanu . . . cliff] At the decisive battle of the conquest of Hawaii, Kamehameha's forces defeated his enemies on Oahu at the Battle of Nu'uanu in May 1795, where more than four hundred men were driven over the cliffs at Nu'uanu Pali to their deaths.

95.33–34   frightened Vancouver . . . Discovery] The HMS *Discovery* explored the west coast of North America and the Hawaiian Islands during its 1791–95 expedition led by George Vancouver (1757–1798).

96.31   The Lonely One] Meaning of the name Kamehameha.

97.4–12   two brothers . . . sandalwood] Kamehameha I offered the American sea captains Nathan Winship, Jonathan Winship Jr., and William Heath Davis a ten-year monopoly on the export of sandalwood and cotton from Hawaii for their role in bringing Kaumuali'i to the negotiations at Oahu in 1810.

102.23   The Dying Christian] Funeral hymn (1781) by English composer Edward Harwood (1707–1787), a musical setting of Alexander Pope's free adaptation (1712) of "Animula vagula blandula," attributed to the dying emperor Hadrian (76–138 C.E.) and translated in this volume by Merwin on p. 570.

119.18   Dr Dole's school] The Dole School (later the Koloa School), mission school at Koloa on Kauai founded by Daniel Dole (1808–1878), American pastor and educator.

121.43   the King and Queen Emma] Kamehameha IV (1834–1863), king of Hawaii, 1855–63, and his queen consort, Emma Na'ea Rooke (1836–1885).

128.23–24   the sickness that was a crime] The Hawaiian Legislature's Act to Prevent the Spread of Leprosy (1865) mandated compulsory isolation and the removal of those deemed "in an advanced state of the disease" to permanent exile in a settlement on the Kalaupapa peninsula on Moloka'i.

128.27–28   judged on Oahu] At the Kahili Hospital and Detention Center outside Honolulu, where it was determined whether patients would be sent to the settlement on Moloka'i.

131.38   the people called Mū] In Hawaiian mythology, a hunting people, wild and hostile, who once lived in the forest.

145.26   a doctor in Norway] Norwegian physician Gerhard Henrik Armauer Hansen (1841–1912).

148.42   priest Damien] Father Damien of Moloka'i, Belgian missionary priest born Joseph de Veuster (1840–1889), canonized as a saint in 2009.

157.2–3   King Kalākaua . . . losing] David Kalākaua (1836–1891), the last reigning king of Hawaii, 1874–91, nicknamed "the Merrie Monarch" because of his indulgent style of life.

157.6–8   not the rightful king . . . throne] The last two reigning kings of Hawaii were determined by popular election after Kamehameha V died without an heir in December 1872. Kalākaua was defeated by William Charles Lunalilo (1835–1874; ruled 1873–74) in 1873 but won a disputed election against dowager queen Emma the following year.

157.13–14   Rice and Isenberg . . . king] The businessmen and politicians William Hyde Rice (1846–1924), his brother-in-law Paul Isenberg (1837–1903), and Sanford Ballard Dole (1844–1926), later first president of the Republic of Hawaii, 1894–98.

157.15–17   The Hawaiian League . . . foreigners] Founded in secret in 1887, the Hawaiian League was an organization of more than four hundred businessmen that aimed to undermine the monarchy. Supported by the Honolulu Rifles, a militia of white volunteers, it threatened an armed uprising and forced upon Kalākaua the 1887 "Bayonet Constitution," which stripped the king of most of his already limited powers.

161.28   a rebellion] The failed insurrection of July 1889 led by Robert Wilcox (1855–1903).

162.20–22   the big Hawaiian Bipikane . . . contempt] During Robert Wilcox's trial on conspiracy charges for his role in the insurrection, Bipikane ("Ox Man" or "Bull Man"), a popular Hawaiian comic actor known for roaring like a bull on the floor of the legislature, was ejected from the courtroom after repeatedly interrupting the prosecutor.

171.20–30   the Reverend Charles McEwen Hyde . . . Stevenson] The letter sent by American Congregationalist missionary Charles McEwen Hyde (1832–1899) to fellow clergyman H. B. Gage containing his contemptuous remarks about Father Damien was first published in San Francisco without his permission in 1889; from Sydney, Australia, Stevenson wrote a scathing rejoinder, "Open Letter to Reverend Doctor Hyde of Honolulu from Robert Louis Stevenson" (1890).

171.35   Vailima] A village south of Apia on Samoa that was the final residence of Robert Louis Stevenson, who had moved to the island in 1890.

173.33   Little Big Horn] Battle, June 25–26, 1876, near the Little Bighorn River in Montana, in which Lakota Sioux, Arapaho, and Cheyenne warriors killed Lieutenant Colonel George Armstrong Custer (1839–1876) and 262 men of the U.S. 7th Cavalry.

173.34   hunt for Geronimo] American forces pursued the war chief Geronimo (1829–1909) and a small band of Chiricahua Apache through Arizona and northern Mexico from May 5, 1886, until their surrender on September 3.

173.36   Ghost Dance] Originating among the Northern Paiutes of Nevada, a late-nineteenth-century pan-Indian religious movement that promised the renewal of the world and a reunification of the living and the dead. Its most important ritual was a ceremonial round dance repeated on successive nights.

173.36–37   Sitting Bull deserved what he got] Fearing a revolt because of the practice of Ghost Dance religious rites among the Lakota Sioux, General Nelson A. Miles (1839–1925) ordered the arrest of Lakota chief and holy man Sitting Bull (c. 1831–1890), who was killed while resisting capture on the Standing Rock Reservation in South Dakota.

173.37   Wounded Knee] Massacre of more than 150 Lakota Sioux by the U.S. 7th Cavalry, at Wounded Knee Creek in South Dakota on December 29, 1890.

175.28–29   the rocks . . . to stone] See Frederick B. Wichman, *Kaua'i: Ancient Place-Names and Their Stories* (Honolulu: University of Hawaii Press, 1998), p. 127: "Na-piliwale, 'clinging ones,' a stone formation on the Manoa ridge, looks like two running figures with their skirts flying up behind them. It was the custom of the four Piliwale sisters to visit a chief's court and remain until all the food in the area had been consumed. Therefore, their appearance heralded a forthcoming famine. They had prodigious appetites and their favorite foods were the freshwater shrimp, the *wi*, freshwater snails, and the fiddlehead of the fern *ho'i'o*. Two of these sisters came to Ha'ena for a visit. Because they were *kupua* and could not tolerate the sun, Lohi'au and his sister Kahua built them a shelter in Maniniholo Cave and another on the ridge where they could enjoy the view. They were fed their favorite foods all through the night and were entertained by every hula dancer of the school at Ke'e. As the night winds grew chill, Kahua ordered the sides of the shed enclosed with mats. The sisters so enjoyed themselves that they forgot the time. Then at dawn Kahua drew aside the wall coverings and the sisters, with cries of dismay, raced down the ridge to the cave. The sun's rays caught them as they ran and they turned to stone. They remain there as a warning to the other two sisters not to visit Kaua'i."

180.40   *Ghosts*] Drama (1882) by Norwegian playwright Henrik Ibsen (1828–1906) about the devastating effects of syphilis on a family.

185.8–9   one of your wife's family Mr Gay] Anne Sinclair Knudsen's nephew, Francis Gay.

185.13   young Mr Rowell] William E. Rowell, a member of the Board of Health.

197.4–11   there is no more Queen . . . Navy] Liliuokalani (1838–1917), queen of Hawaii, 1891–93, proclaimed a new constitution in January 1893 that would restore the monarchy's powers. Backed by the U.S. Navy, the business community responded by deposing the queen and having her placed under house arrest in the royal palace. A Provisional Government was declared on January 17, 1893, led by Sanford B. Dole.

197.24   Lorrin A Thurston born to know better] Native-born Hawaiian businessman and politician Lorrin Andrews Thurston (1858–1931), who drafted the proclamation of the Provisional Government and led a delegation to Washington to negotiate annexation. He helped write the constitution of the Republic of Hawaii, declared in 1894.

211.38   Polihale . . . underworld] Polihale beach is the site of a sacred spring and the ruins of a *heiau* (temple) from where spirits were said to depart for the underworld.

252.39   a'ali'i bushes] Flowering plants in the soapberry family.

269.13–14   my brother . . . Government] John Sheldon (1850–1914), editor-in-chief of the bilingual newspaper the *Hawaii Holomua*, published articles supporting Queen Liliuokalani and opposing the annexationists. He was arrested in 1893 and served two years in prison on charges of "contempt of the government."

272.1   the government's plan . . . language] The speaking or teaching of the Hawaiian language in schools was prohibited by law in 1896.

273.7   Abraham Fornander] Swedish-born journalist and ethnographer (1812–1887) who lived on the island of Hawaii, author of the three-volume *Account of the Polynesian Race* (1878–85).

278.14   Mr Sheldon's book] *Kailuaikoolau!*, published in Hawaiian in 1906; it can be read in English in the translation by Helen N. Frazier, *The True Story of Kaluaikoolau: As Told by His Wife, Piʻilani* (Honolulu: University of Hawaii Press, 2001).

278.22–24   He that dwelleth . . . Almighty] Psalms 91:1.

THE RIVER SOUND

287.1   *Ceremony After an Amputation*] The first joint of Merwin's left index finger was amputated in 1991 in an accident.

288.22   Guarani . . . Morales] From *Leyendas guaraníes* (*Guarani Legends*, Buenos Aires, 1923, new ed. 1946) by the Argentine writer Ernesto Morales (1890–1949).

290.31   designer's name . . . Ours] French landscape architect André Le Nôtre (1613–1700) designed the gardens at Versailles; "le nôtre" means "ours" in French.

293.13   genus . . . Tabernaemontanus] The genus *Tabernaemontana* is named for Jacob Theodor von Bergzabern (c. 1520–1590), German botanist known as Tabernaemontanus.

293.29   kamani] See glossary, *The Folding Cliffs*, p. 652 in this volume.

295.17   Half Moon] Ship in which English explorer Henry Hudson (c. 1565–1611) sailed up the river now named for him in 1609.

297.1   *227 Waverly Place*] From 1969 until 1995, Merwin rented an apartment at 227 Waverly Place in New York's Greenwich Village.

297.31   the hospital] St. Vincent's Hospital.

300.22   Mimir] Giant in Norse mythology, guardian of the well of wisdom.

302.2   *I stop somewhere waiting for you*] Cf. final line of "Song of Myself" (1855) by Walt Whitman (1819–1892).

309.9   *Lament for the Makers*] The title is a reference to "Lament for the Makaris" (1508) by Scottish poet William Dunbar (c. 1460–1520) eulogizing several of the significant writers of his era.

311.31   Oscar Williams' *Treasury*] *A Little Treasury of Modern Poetry, English & American* (1946), edited by the American poet and anthologist Oscar Williams (1900–1964).

312.9–10   Dylan Thomas . . . us] Welsh poet Dylan Thomas (1914–1953) died of alcohol poisoning after a drinking bout at the White Horse Tavern in Greenwich Village.

312.15   the nothing not there] Cf. the final lines of "The Snow Man" (1923) by American poet Wallace Stevens (1879–1955): "For the listener, who listens in the snow, / And, nothing himself, beholds / Nothing that is not there and the nothing that is."

312.16–19 sparrow saying Bethou me . . . Shelley] Cf. Stevens's line from "Notes Toward a Supreme Fiction" (1943): "Be thou me, said sparrow, to the crackled blade"—itself an allusion to "Ode to the West Wind" (1819) by English poet Percy Bysshe Shelley (1792–1822): "Be thou me, impetuous one!"

312.17 his long auroras] A reference to Stevens's collection *The Auroras of Autumn* (1950) and its title poem.

312.20 Arrowsmith] Classical scholar and translator William Arrowsmith (1924–1992), an older fellow student of Merwin's at Princeton.

312.22 Edwin Muir] English poet (1887–1959).

312.28 in the house a few blocks away] American poet Sylvia Plath (1932–1963) committed suicide in London on February 11, 1963.

313.5–7 Ted Roethke . . . night] American poet Theodore Roethke (1908–1963) died on August 1, 1963, after collapsing in a neighbor's swimming pool on Bainbridge Island in Puget Sound.

313.9 MacNeice] Louis MacNeice (1907–1963), Irish poet and playwright.

313.14–15 Jarrell was borne off by a car] American poet Randall Jarrell (1914–1965) was fatally struck by an automobile in Greensboro, North Carolina, on October 14, 1965.

313.18–20 Berryman . . . me] American poet John Berryman (1914–1972), whom Merwin had known as an undergraduate at Princeton, committed suicide by jumping from the Washington Avenue Bridge in Minneapolis on January 7, 1972.

313.21–22 *a jest . . . caravan*] Line 20 of "To Brooklyn Bridge," poem to *The Bridge* (1930) by American poet Hart Crane (1899–1932), describing a man jumping to his death from the Brooklyn Bridge.

313.23 Bones and Henry] Mr. Bones and Berryman's alter ego Henry, characters in Berryman's Dream Song sequence in *77 Dream Songs* (1963) and *His Toy, His Dream, His Rest* (1968).

313.31 who once had helped to set me free] See Chronology, 1946.

314.1 David Jones] English poet and artist (1895–1974).

314.5–8 Lowell . . . *Notebook*] American poet Robert Lowell (1917–1977), who died of a heart attack in a New York taxicab. His collection of poems *Notebook* was published in 1970.

314.13–315.9 Elizabeth Bishop . . . Merrill's] American poets Elizabeth Bishop (1911–1979), James Wright (1927–1980), and Howard Moss (1922–1987); English poet Robert Graves (1895–1985), see also Chronology, 1950–51; American poets Howard Nemerov (1920–1991), William Stafford (1914–1993), and James Merrill (1926–1995).

316.7–8 that story of Nerval's beginning] As recounted in *Les Faux Saulniers: Histoire de l'Abbé du Bucquoy* (*The Salt-Smugglers: The History of the Abbé du Bucquoy*, 1850) by French writer Gérard de Nerval, pen name of Gérard Labrunie (1808–1855). Nerval's fictionalized account, published as a serial in the newspaper *Le National* (October 24–December 22, 1850), tells of his tortuous research into the life of Jean-Albert D'Archambaud, Comte de Bucquoy (c. 1650–1740), by turns a soldier, Trappist monk, and schoolmaster, most famous for his escapes from the prisons at Fort l'Évêque and the Bastille. Much of "Suite in the Key of Forgetting" is made up of Merwin's translations of passages from *The Salt-Smugglers*.

319.9–11   Jean de la France . . . Hope] The bookseller's listing cited by Nerval from the book he saw in Frankfurt: "Jean de la France, Bookseller, rue de la Réforme, à l'Espérance, à Bonnefoy" (Reform Street, in Hope, at Good Faith).

319.13–30   do you remember . . . seed] A paraphrase of the first two stanzas of Nerval's sonnet "Delfica" (1845), addressed to Daphne, nymph who in Greek mythology was transformed into a tree to escape the pursuit of the god Apollo.

319.15   Octavie] An English girl whom Nerval met briefly and fell in love with in the spring of 1835, as told in "Octavie" in his *Les Filles du feu* (*Daughters of Fire*, 1854).

320.27–28   Madame Dunoyer's . . . letters] *Lettres Historiques et Galantes* (7 vols., 1704–17) by Madame Dunoyer, born Anne-Marguerite Petit (1663–1719).

320.32–35   ruinous . . . confirmation] The "Riancey amendment," passed into law in July 1850, levied a one-centime tax per copy of any newspaper featuring a serialized novel in its pages.

321.18–21   the revolt of the Camisards . . . exile] Named for their white shirts, the Camisards were a group of French Calvinists in the mountainous Cévennes region of south-central France who rose up in revolt in 1702. Other Protestants fled France in the decades following Louis XIV's revocation in 1685 of the Edict of Nantes (1598), which had given them political rights and protections.

321.21–23   the league of Lorraine . . . army] A group of salt smugglers in the Lorraine were recruited into the irregular army led by legendary bandit and smuggler Louis Mandrin (d. 1755).

323.36–324.16   was it our poor Gérard . . . Nicolas] See the introductory note to Nerval's poem "El Desdichado" ("The Disinherited"), published by Alexandre Dumas *père* (1802–1870) in his journal *Le Mousquetaire* in 1853.

324.20   the tomb of Rousseau] In *The Salt-Smugglers* Nerval visits the empty tomb of Jean-Jacques Rousseau (1712–1778) at Ermenonville, the philosopher's remains having been removed to the Panthéon in Paris in 1794.

325.28   *Testimony*] Inspired by *Le grand testament* (1462), French poet François Villon (c. 1431–1463). Merwin's poem follows Villon's stanza and rhyme schemes.

329.13–18   Thou . . . thee] Cf. Luke 12:20.

331.11   Rimerton] Village on the Allegheny River in western Pennsylvania, the birthplace of Merwin's father.

340.36   Yatesborough and Rural Valley] Yatesboro and Rural Valley, towns in Armstrong County in western Pennsylvania where Merwin's father led congregations before Merwin was born.

341.3–4   we shall meet . . . shore] From "Sweet By-and-By" (1868), hymn with music by American songwriter Joseph P. Webster (1819–1875) and words by American poet Sanford Fillmore Bennett (1836–1898).

342.10   their child] Hanson Jaynes Merwin, who died soon after birth in 1925. See also "To My Brother," p. 491.

346.7   Therefore will not we fear] Cf. Psalm 46:2.

356.4   Delsol] Fernande Delsol, a neighbor in the Lot.

359.25   Fran's] Frances Kiernan (b. 1944), author and an editor at *The New Yorker*.

362.33   Jannah Arnoux] A neighbor in the Lot, where she lived with her husband Serge (mentioned at 365.4).

363.23   Ricci] The fashion house founded in 1932 in Paris by Italian-born couturier Nina Ricci, born Maria Adélaïde Nielli (1883–1970).

366.27   *Ruhe sanft, mein holdes Leben*] "Gently rest, my dearest love," a soprano aria from Act I of the unfinished opera *Zaide* (1780) by Austrian composer Wolfgang Amadeus Mozart (1756–1791).

367.6   Margaret] Margaret McElderry (1912–2011), children's book publisher.

367.7   John and Aleksandra] Paula Merwin's son, novelist John Burnham Schwartz (b. 1965), and his wife, the screenwriter and food writer Aleksandra Crapanzano (b. 1970).

367.21   Matthew and Karen] Paula Merwin's stepson Matthew Schwartz (b. 1963) and his wife Karen Levesque (b. 1962).

368.16   Little Compton] Town in Rhode Island, where McElderry owned a house.

370.3   Waverly Place] See note 297.1.

371.12   Gruagach] In Scottish folklore, a hobgoblin or sprite.

372.9   Mike Keeley] Edmund Keeley (b. 1928), translator and scholar of modern Greek literature.

372.18   Mary's] Keeley's wife.

372.19   Jacqueline and Clarence Brown] Clarence Brown (b. 1929), professor of comparative literature at Princeton, and his wife. In 1974, Brown and Merwin published a book of translations of Russian poet Osip Mandelstam (1891–1938).

372.33   Galway Kinnell . . . hall] American poet Galway Kinnell (b. 1927) was Merwin's college classmate at Princeton.

373.29   Jay Laughlin] James Laughlin (1914–1997), American publisher and poet.

374.1   James Baker Hall] American poet and novelist (1935–2009).

374.9   Ben Sonnenberg] American writer (1936–2010), publisher of the literary magazine *Grand Street*.

374.17   Richard Howard] American poet and translator (b. 1929).

374.33–34   Grace Schulman] American poet (b. 1935).

375.5   Bill Matthews] William Matthews (1942–1997), American poet.

375.9–10   under my window that Vanguard] The Village Vanguard, Greenwich Village jazz club; the rear of the club was directly below Merwin's apartment at 227 Waverly Place.

375.14   Harry Ford] Merwin's longtime editor (1919–1999), first at Atheneum and later at Knopf.

375.22   Alastair Reid born nomad] Scottish poet, translator, and scholar (b. 1926) who has lived in several countries in continental Europe and Latin America, as well as in the United States.

375.80   Francesco Pellizzi] Italian-born writer, anthropologist, and art collector (b. 1940) who has extensively studied the history and culture of Chiapas.

376.1   Gerald Stern] American poet (b. 1925).

380.31–381.2   St. Augustine . . . palaces of memory] See *Confessions* (397–98), bk. 10, by St. Augustine (354–430): "I come to the fields and vast palaces of memory, where are the treasures of innumerable images, brought into it from things of all sorts perceived by the senses."

383.21   *Moissac*] A town in the Midi-Pyrénées region of southwestern France, famous for its medieval Abbey of Saint-Pierre, with its elaborately carved tympanum.

THE PUPIL

396.17   the hour Marais told us about] In the posthumously published book *The Soul of the Ape* (1969), South African naturalist and poet Eugène Marais (1871–1936) argued that baboons and humans alike show a tendency to "Hesperian depression" at twilight.

396.21–22   returning black ceiling of morphine] From the age of twenty-one Marais was addicted to morphine.

398.9   Rumphius] Georg Eberhard Rumpf, later known as Rumphius (1627–1702), German botanist who lived most of his life in Indonesia cataloguing plant species. In 1670, he was blinded by glaucoma but continued working on his monumental *Herbarium Amboinense*, published posthumously in 1741. See Merwin's "The Blind Seer of Ambon" in the companion volume to this edition, *Collected Poems 1952–1993*.

398.16–17 Vermeij . . . never saw] Geerat J. Vermeij (b. 1946), Dutch-born American evolutionary biologist and paleoecologist, has been blind since the age of three.

398.24 Borges] The sight of Argentine writer Jorge Luis Borges (1899–1986) had deteriorated to the point of blindness by the late 1950s.

398.25 Milton's sonnet] Sonnet beginning "When I consider how my life is spent" (1673), also known as "On His Blindness," by English poet John Milton (1608–1674).

398.26–27 words of Samson] Samson laments his blindness in Milton's *Samson Agonistes* (1671), lines 66–102.

400.1 *The Marfa Lights*] Atmospheric reflections of terrestrial lights in the night skies over Marfa, Texas, which have often been credited as spectral or alien in nature.

412.8 *A Calling*] See 1 Samuel 3.

417.3 returned to the self-portrait] The self-portrait of French painter Jean-Auguste-Dominique Ingres (1780–1867) at age 24 in the collection of the Musée Condé, Chantilly, France, widely accepted by scholars to have been revised by the artist around 1850.

418.7–8 Juniata . . . Marietta] The Juniata River, a tributary of the Susquehanna, and the extinct Marietta River, which flowed through present-day West Virginia and Ohio.

418.8 Fingal's Cave Overture] Symphonic overture also known as the Hebrides Overture (*Die Hebriden*, op. 26), written in 1830 by German composer Felix Mendelssohn (1809–1847).

426.1 *The Black Virgin*] A statue with a shrine in the medieval Chapelle de Notre-Dame at Rocamadour, village built on a cliff overlooking the Alzou River in southwestern France.

426.6 climbed up on its knees to you] Pilgrims to the Black Virgin's shrine would ascend the stone stairway from the village below on their knees.

434.1 *Planh for the Death of Ted Hughes*] *Planh* is an Occitan word for a troubadour's funeral lament. Ted Hughes (1930–1998), English poet, a friend of Merwin's since the mid-1950s.

435.8 *Laelia digbyana*] Brassavola, a species of Honduran orchid first cultivated in England.

435.13 Bruce McGrew] American painter (1937–1999), a close friend of Merwin's.

439.24   *Matthew Shepard*] Shepard (1976–1998), a student at the University of Wyoming, was tortured and murdered by Russell Henderson and Aaron McKinney, who had met Shepard in a bar in Laramie on the night of October 6–7, 1998. After driving to a remote area outside of town, Henderson and McKinney taunted Shepard for being gay, robbed and pistol-whipped him, and left him to die tied to a wire fence. Shepard was found unconscious eighteen hours later and died in a hospital in Fort Collins, Colorado, five days after the attack. Henderson and McKinney were each convicted of murder and sentenced to life terms.

444.8   *Memorandum*] A monologue spoken by Leontes, the king of Sicilia in Shakespeare's *A Winter's Tale* (1611), to Perdita, his daughter by his scorned wife Hermione. The child is banished to the coast of Bohemia, rescued, and raised by shepherds.

446.20   Wyatt was on the way home . . . Dante] Sir Thomas Wyatt (1503–1542), English poet, died of a fever while on a diplomatic mission to greet a delegation representing Holy Roman Emperor Charles V at Falmouth and escort them to the court of Henry VIII. Expelled from his native Florence in 1302, Italian poet Dante Alighieri (1265–1321) died in exile in Ravenna, Italy.

450.4   *Maoli*] A chow dog living with the Merwins, deaf in his old age.

PRESENT COMPANY

461.15–16   the foolish virgins . . . lamps] In the parable of the wise and foolish virgins, Matthew 25:1–13.

468.2   a muse] Clio, muse of history.

471.1   *To Lili's Walk*] Lili (short for Liliko'i, or passion fruit) was a pet chow dog of the Merwins on Maui.

473.8   *Consolations of Philosophy*] Treatise (524) by the Roman philosopher Boethius (c. 480–c. 525) consisting of a dialogue between himself and Lady Philosophy, written while its author was in prison awaiting execution for treason by the Ostrogothic emperor Theodoric.

475.17–18   I see as in a glass darkly] Cf. 1 Corinthians 13:12.

482.26   *To Muku Dreaming*] Muku (in Hawaiian the word refers to "the night of no moon") was a pet chow dog of the Merwins.

484.23   *the Blue Stork*] The logo on a Pennsylvania fuel truck of Merwin's youth.

492.1   *Micky*] One of Merwin's female cousins.

492.25–26   back before Admiral Dewey . . . war] I.e., before the Spanish-American War, 1898. George Dewey (1837–1917) commanded the squadron that defeated the Spanish in Manila Bay on May 1, 1898.

492.26   Ford City bridge] Bridge, 1914–2000, crossing the Allegheny River in Ford City, Armstrong County, Pennsylvania.

493.1   *Doris*] Doris Curran (1933–2000), who for three decades ran a well-known poetry reading series at UCLA.

508.1   *Zbigniew Herbert's*] Zbigniew Herbert (1924–1998), Polish poet and essayist.

521.14   *Tortoiseshell Lyre*] In Greek mythology, Apollo, the god of light and music, acquired from Hermes the first lyre, made from a carved tortoiseshell and cow intestines.

535.3–4   Buffon . . . said] In *Histoire naturelle* (*Natural History*, 44 vols., 1749–1804) by French naturalist Georges Louis Leclerc, Count of Buffon (1707–1788).

537.29   Il Monello] Formerly a restaurant on Second Avenue on Manhattan's Upper East Side. The Merwins ate here, with Fran and Howard Kiernan and two friends, on the night they met.

THE SHADOW OF SIRIUS

545.14   a mote in an eye] Cf. Matthew 7:3.

551.1   Ching and Gypsy] Dogs from Merwin's childhood. Ching was a chow puppy and Gypsy was a stray, both of whom lived briefly in the Merwin household and to whom he was greatly attached. They were both taken away by his parents, and he grieved for them. Ching was the beginning of his lifelong love of chows.

553.8   Czerny] Carl Czerny (1791–1857), Austrian pianist and composer whose exercises for piano became widely used pedagogical scores.

554.3   the Garden of the Gods] A public park near Colorado Springs, Colorado.

561.4   Columba as the story goes] According to legend, St. Columba (521–597), Irish monk who propagated Christianity in Scotland, based his ministry on the island of Iona because it was the first place he landed where he was unable to see Ireland.

561.20   *Cimmerians*] Tribe of ancient nomads about which not much is known; according to Herodotus, they lived near the Black Sea.

563.15–17   Kent said . . . authority] See *King Lear*, I.iv.27–30.

565.2   *Muku, Makana, Koa*] Pet dogs of the Merwins at their residence on Maui.

570.5   *Little Soul*] A translation of the Latin poem "Animula vagula blandula" attributed to the Roman emperor Hadrian. Merwin notes:
    It must have been at some time during my years at the university

that I first encountered this brief, mysterious poem. It is ascribed to the Emperor Hadrian (A.D. 76–138) without any scholarly question that I know of, but it has always seemed surprising to me that a poem so assured in its art, so flawless and so haunting, could have been the only one he ever wrote. Perhaps he wrote poems all his life and this was the only one that was saved, or this one alone was unforgettable.

Certainly, whenever I read it first, I never forgot it, and I examined each of the translations of it into English as I came across them. The one I liked best was by Dudley Fitts. But it was the original that I was happy to return to, as any reader would who could do so.

Ten years or so after I left college I read Marguerite Yourcenar's novel *Hadrian's Memoirs*, in which the poem acquires a resonant imaginary context, memorable in itself, yet it was the original poem that I went on remembering, still ignorant of the circumstances in which it had come to exist. I am not certain whose soul the poem addresses, and as far as I know no one else can be sure of that either, though of course there are rooted assumptions about it.

Although I have tried to translate poetry (in full awareness of the limitations, the utter impossibility of the enterprise) ever since those student days, it never occurred to me to attempt to import this small solitaire. But in the past years poems have come to me arising from events that recalled the familiar Latin phrases, and one day I realized that I knew, suddenly, how I would like to hear the Latin phrases in English—if they could exist in English—and the words of the translation, as they occurred to me, seemed to be as literal as they could possibly be.

579.4   *Ruth Stone*] American poet (1915–2011).

580.12   *Su Tung-p'o*] Pseudonym of Su Shih (1037–1101), Chinese poet, calligrapher, and public official during the Sung Dynasty.

581.1   *Bashō's Child*] See the 1684–85 travel journal, posthumously published as *Nozarashi Kikō* (*Journal of Bleached Bones in a Field*), by the Japanese poet Matsuo Bashō (1644–1694): "I was walking along the Fuji River when I saw an abandoned child, barely two, weeping pitifully. Had his parents been unable to endure this floating world which is as wave-tossed as these rapids, and so left him here to wait out a life brief as dew? He seemed like a bush clover in autumn's wind that might scatter in the evening or wither in the morning. I tossed him some food from my sleeve and said in passing,

> those who listen for the monkeys:
> what of this child
>   in the autumn wind?" (tr. David Landis Barnhill)

590.23   the blackcap that instructed Mendelssohn] See "The Source," p. 423.

591.7   where Hopkins' bones were left] The Jesuit plot at the Prospect Cemetery, Glasnevin, Dublin, which contains the remains of English poet and Jesuit priest Gerard Manley Hopkins (1844–1889).

NEW AND UNCOLLECTED POEMS

616.19   *Po Chu-i*] Po Chu-i (772–846), a Chinese poet and government official during the Tang Dynasty. In 814, his satires of court corruption resulted in his being exiled, but his poems were popular during his lifetime and have remained beloved and influential ever since.

622.12   *Urticophilia*] A Greek-based coinage by Merwin meaning "love of nettles."

Index of Titles and First Lines

THE LIBRARY OF AMERICA SERIES

The Library of America fosters appreciation and pride in America's literary heritage by publishing, and keeping permanently in print, authoritative editions of America's best and most significant writing. An independent nonprofit organization, it was founded in 1979 with seed funding from the National Endowment for the Humanities and the Ford Foundation.

To subscribe to the series or to order individual copies, please visit www.loa.org or call (800) 964.5778.

*This book is set in 10 point ITC Galliard Pro, a
face designed for digital composition by Matthew Carter
and based on the sixteenth-century face Granjon. The paper
is acid-free lightweight opaque and meets the requirements for
permanence of the American National Standards Institute.
The binding material is Brillianta, a woven rayon cloth
made by Van Heek–Scholco Textielfabrieken, Holland.
Composition by David Bullen Design. Printing and
binding by Edwards Brothers Malloy, Ann Arbor.
Designed by Bruce Campbell.*

WITHDRAWN

Gramley Library
Salem Academy and College
Winston-Salem, N.C. 27108